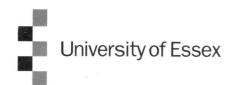 University of Essex

GU00889723

Date Due Back

Stability of Happiness
Theories and Evidence on Whether Happiness Can Change

Stability of Happiness
Theories and Evidence on Whether Happiness Can Change

Kennon M. Sheldon
University of Missouri-Columbia,
Columbia, MO, USA

Richard E. Lucas
Michigan State University,
East Lansing, MI, USA

ELSEVIER

AMSTERDAM • BOSTON • HEIDELBERG • LONDON
NEW YORK • OXFORD • PARIS • SAN DIEGO
SAN FRANCISCO • SINGAPORE • SYDNEY • TOKYO
Academic Press is an imprint of Elsevier

Academic Press is an imprint of Elsevier
32 Jamestown Road, London NW1 7BY, UK
225 Wyman Street, Waltham, MA 02451, USA
525 B Street, Suite 1800, San Diego, CA 92101-4495, USA

British Library Cataloguing-in-Publication Data
A catalogue record for this book is available from the British Library

Library of Congress Cataloging-in-Publication Data
A catalog record for this book is available from the Library of Congress

ISBN: 978-0-12-411478-4

For information on all Academic Press publications
visit our website at elsevierdirect.com

Typeset by MPS Limited, Chennai, India
www.adi-mps.com

14 15 16 17 18   10 9 8 7 6 5 4 3 2 1

**Working together
to grow libraries in
developing countries**

ELSEVIER Book Aid
International

www.elsevier.com • www.bookaid.org

Contents

4.   Is Lasting Change Possible? Lessons from the Hedonic Adaptation Prevention Model

Christina Armenta, Katherine Jacobs Bao, Sonja Lyubomirsky, and Kennon M. Sheldon

5.   Can Happiness Change? Theories and Evidence

Robert A. Cummins

10. Set Point Theory and Public Policy

Richard A. Easterlin and Malgorzata Switek

11. Economic Approaches to Understanding Change in Happiness

Nattavudh Powdthavee and Alois Stutzer

12. Personality Traits as Potential Moderators of Well-Being
Patrick L. Hill, Daniel K. Mroczek, and Robin K. Young

13. Statistical Models for Analyzing Stability and Change in Happiness
Michael Eid and Tanja Kutscher

14. Stable Happiness Dies in Middle-Age: A Guide to Future Research

Ed Diener

List of Contributors

Ivana Anusic Michigan State University, East Lansing, MI, USA

Christina Armenta University of California, Riverside, Riverside, CA, USA

Ragnhild Bang Nes Norwegian Institute of Public Health, Oslo, Norway

Robert A. Cummins Deakin University, Melbourne, VIC, Australia

Cody R. DeHaan University of Rochester, Rochester, NY, USA

Ed Diener University of Illinois, Champaign-Urbana, IL, USA; The Gallup Organization

Richard A. Easterlin University of Southern California, Los Angeles, CA, USA

Michael Eid Freie Universität Berlin, Berlin, Germany

Giovanni A. Fava University of Bologna, Bologna, Italy

Bruce Headey University of Melbourne, Melbourne, VIC, Australia

Patrick L. Hill Carleton University, Ottawa, ON, Canada

Katherine Jacobs Bao University of California, Riverside, Riverside, CA, USA

Tanja Kutscher Freie Universität Berlin, Berlin, Germany

Richard E. Lucas Michigan State University, East Lansing, MI, USA

Sonja Lyubomirsky University of California, Riverside, Riverside, CA, USA

Daniel K. Mroczek Northwestern University, Evanston, IL, USA

Ruud Muffels Tilburg University, Tilburg, the Netherlands

Nattavudh Powdthavee London School of Economics, London, UK

Espen Røysamb University of Oslo, Oslo, Norway

Chiara Ruini University of Bologna, Bologna, Italy

Richard M. Ryan University of Rochester, Rochester, NY, USA

Kennon M. Sheldon University of Missouri-Columbia, Columbia, MO, USA

Alois Stutzer University of Basel, Basel, Switzerland

Malgorzata Switek University of Southern California, Los Angeles, CA, USA

Ruut Veenhoven Erasmus University Rotterdam, Roterdam, The Netherlands; North-West University, Potchefstroom, South Africa

Joar Vittersø University of Tromsø, Tromsø, Norway

Gert G. Wagner German Institute for Economic Research (DIW) and Max Planck Institute, Berlin, Germany

Stevie C.Y. Yap Michigan State University, East Lansing, MI, USA

Robin K. Young Carleton University, Ottawa, ON, Canada

Preface

The right to "pursue happiness" is one of the dominant themes of western culture, and understanding the causes of happiness is one of the primary goals of the positive psychology movement. However, before the causality question can even be considered, a more basic question must be addressed: Can happiness change? Reasons for skepticism include the notion of a "genetic set point" for happiness, i.e., a stable personal baseline of happiness to which individuals will always return, no matter how much their lives change for the better; the life span stability of happiness and happiness-related traits such as neuroticism and extraversion; and the powerful processes of hedonic adaptation, which erode the positive effects of any fortuitous life change. In addition, there are considerable empirical data to suggest that over time, people keep returning to their own baseline levels of happiness. If it is true that happiness can't really change, then the search for the causes of happiness becomes almost moot. A person will either be happy or not, based on factors that are not amenable to control.

This book directly addresses this "elephant in the room," the question that many positive psychologists, well-being researchers, intervention designers, and life coaches would rather avoid: Can a person's well-being be stably altered for the better, such that it remains permanently at a new, higher level than before? After an editorial introduction (Section I), the question is addressed from several theoretical perspectives (Section II; behavioral-genetic, social-cognitive, humanistic, clinical, and social-personality) and several empirical perspectives (Section III; panel studies, longitudinal studies, intervention studies, economic studies, nation-level studies), although of course there is also considerable overlap between the theoretical and empirical sections. Then, Section IV covers thorny issues in doing longitudinal research on the stability of well-being (properly dealing with cohort effects, testing moderator effects, accounting for auto-regressive effects), providing cutting-edge analytical approaches for modeling fluctuating well-being. Finally, the book concludes (in Section V) with a summary evaluation from the Yoda of well-being research, Ed Diener. To cut to the chase, the answer to the question posed above is "Yes." But the route to this conclusion is winding, and the potential diversions many.

This book should be of interest to anybody in the categories listed above: positive psychologists, well-being researchers, intervention designers, and life coaches. However, the book should also be of interest to public policy makers, as they seek to broker new public affordances such as education, health, or retirement assistance; to college and even high school educators and teachers, as they seek to introduce their students to the leading frontier of these vitally important questions; and to intelligent lay-people, who are ready to go "beyond the hype" of the self-help bookshelves to get real scientific information on what they seek. What is it really going to take to boost one's happiness, and then to keep it at the new level?

There are many edited academic books on happiness. However, with very few exceptions, the chapters in those books do not consider our foundational question, of "Can happiness change?" Instead, they simply assume that it can, and proceed to examine various personality, contextual, and cultural correlates of happiness. This book will be the first to bring the "change" question to the fore—the question that we believe must be answered before questions of "how to change happiness" can be taken seriously.

Kennon M. Sheldon
Richard E. Lucas

Chapter 1

Is It Possible to Become a Permanently Happier Person?

An Overview of the Issues and the Book

Kennon M. Sheldon[1] and Richard E. Lucas[2]
[1]*University of Missouri–Columbia, Columbia, MO, USA,* [2]*Michigan State University, East Lansing, MI, USA*

Subjective well-being—a construct that is known more colloquially as "happiness"—is a characteristic that reflects a person's subjective evaluation of his or her life as a whole. Although the construct is based on a person's own perspective, it is thought to reflect something about the actual conditions of people's lives. These conditions include both external conditions such as income and social relationships, as well as internal conditions such as goals, outlook on life, and other psychological resources. Moreover, people who evaluate their lives negatively would likely be motivated to improve the conditions of their lives, and those who evaluate their lives positively would be motivated to maintain or further improve these conditions. Thus, happiness and related constructs are thought to signal how well a person's life is going, which should mean that as a person's life improves, so should the happiness that that person reports.

Over the years, however, at least some researchers became quite skeptical about the possibility for change in happiness. Initial reviews of the literature suggested that few external, objectively measured life circumstances were strongly related to subjective well-being (Diener, 1984; Diener, Suh, Lucas, & Smith, 1999; Wilson, 1967). In addition, some highly cited studies suggested that even individuals who had experienced extremely strong positive and negative life events (such as winning the lottery or becoming disabled) barely differed in their self-reported happiness (e.g., Brickman, Coates, & Janoff-Bulman, 1978; but see Lucas, 2007, for a reinterpretation of this finding). This evidence, when considered in the context of increasing numbers of studies showing strong heritability for reports of happiness and relatively high stability over time, led some to suggest that change was not possible (e.g., Brickman & Campbell, 1971; Lykken & Tellegen, 1996; see also Diener, Lucas, & Scollon, 2006, for a review).

If these perspectives are true, then they present major problems for the field of positive psychology (Seligman & Csikszentmihalyi, 2000). Positive psychology is the scientific study of positive human states, traits, and other characteristics, and positive psychology is premised on the notion that these desirable qualities can all be improved through the application of scientific research (at the population level) and personal effort (at the individual level). Since the very beginning of positive psychology, happiness has been one of the most important topics of study—in part because happiness is so important to most people (hence the thousands of happiness books marketed to laypeople), and in part because the right to "pursue happiness" is a right guaranteed to all U.S. citizens (and citizens of Western democracies more generally). If it turns out that greater happiness cannot be successfully pursued, then it calls into question whether higher levels of other positive personality characteristics (i.e., virtues, strengths, capabilities) are also impossible to achieve. Perhaps positive psychology is ultimately based on an illusion, and perhaps people should learn to be content with who they are and what they have, rather than continually trying to put "legs on a snake," as it were (Gaskins, 1999).

Although there has been increasing research on the question of "sustainable happiness" (i.e., the possibility of achieving a higher level of happiness that is sustainable above one's initial level) in the past decade, there is still little scientific consensus on whether happiness can go up and then stay up (as opposed to falling back to baseline). Some illustrations of the possibilities are given in Figure 1.1 (panels 1a–1c). Notably, Figure 1.1 references only *positive* deviations from initial baselines, but it could just as easily reference *negative* deviations. However, such "sustainable drops" in well-being are not considered in this book, except by Cummins, in Chapter 5.

Panel 1a illustrates a case in which all well-being increases are only temporary, representing mere fluctuations around a constant baseline. Because of autoregressive effects, the person always tends to return to his or her own stable, underlying baseline. This is the assumption of genetic set point theories and theories which propose complete adaptation to all changes. Panel 1b illustrates a case in which the baseline trends upward over time. For a variety of possible reasons, including learning, maturation, or steadily improving life circumstances, well-being is continually improving for this person, although there remain bumps in the road. Panel 1c illustrates a second way that well-being might go up and stay up. The panel illustrates a step function in which the baseline is elevated all at once and remains stable at the new level (the dream of those who buy lottery tickets!). Together, the three panels also illustrate that individual baselines can be located relative to a population baseline, so that we may talk about individual change with respect to population baselines as well as with respect to the person's own prior levels of

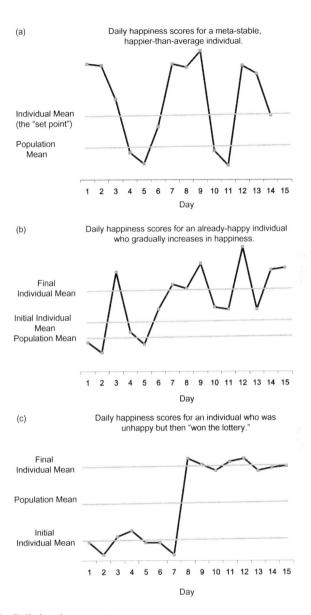

FIGURE 1.1   Daily happiness scores.

well-being. One implication of the autoregressive perspective is that stable patterns of positive change should be rare, the further the person's initial baseline is from the population baseline. An already very happy person should have more difficulty gaining and maintaining new happiness than a person who is only of average happiness initially. In contrast, a person who starts out below the population mean might have an easier time increasing in happiness, to at least a state of moderate contentment.

The goal of this book is to bring together leading scholars with a broad range of perspectives to discuss the question of whether happiness can change. The book is structured in such a way as to highlight three specific sets of issues regarding the extent to which happiness can change. First, in the early parts of the book, we highlight theoretical approaches to understanding change in happiness. In other words, if happiness can or cannot change, it is important to consider why that might be and what theoretical explanations can account for this phenomenon.

For instance, one possibility is that although happiness can change in the short term, long-term levels may be determined primarily by in-born genetic predispositions. In 1996, David Lykken and Auke Tellegen published an article called "Happiness is a stochastic phenomenon," which argued that people's happiness levels are fixed, at least over the long term, by genetic factors that are not changeable. Although people of course fluctuate in the short term in their happiness levels (i.e., they have moods), they will always tend to return to their particular baseline well-being level in the end, "regressing to their own mean," as it were. This mean is commonly referred to as the "happiness set point." In concluding their argument, based on twin study data, Lykken and Tellegen (1996) stated that "trying to become happier is like trying to become taller"—in other words, it will not work.

Although Lykken later backed away somewhat from this position (Lykken, 1999), it remains a widely accepted perspective on the question of whether happiness can change. In this book, Røysamb, Nes, and Vittersø, re-examine this issue, focusing specifically on the theoretical implications of behavioral genetic research on subjective well-being. After providing a very lucid discussion of behavioral genetic approaches, along with a review of behavioral genetic research, they then discuss what the moderate heritability estimates really mean for research on subjective well-being and for individuals who wish to improve their lives. Their discussion points out that the simple tendency to equate "heritable" with "unchangeable" is probably not justified.

Another theoretical reason for pessimism concerning the happiness change question is the phenomenon of hedonic adaptation. Hedonic adaptation, akin to sensory adaptation (Helson, 1964), refers to the tendency to cease noticing particular stimuli over time so that the stimuli no longer have the emotional effects they once had. For instance, we might assume that people who win large sums of money in the lottery will at first be ecstatic but may later adapt as wealth becomes their "new normal." However, hedonic adaptation may also apply to many other life changes besides monetary ones, such as a new car, a new spouse, or a new child. What once provided a thrill becomes a mere part of the background. This phenomenon gives rise to what has been referred to as the "hedonic treadmill" (Brickman & Campbell, 1971); in this view, pursuing happiness is like walking up an escalator going down, so that one's position can never really change. Notably, hedonic adaptation is not necessarily a bad thing: presumably the process is important for helping us to recover from negative events, with the downside that permanent increases due to positive events are unlikely.

Hedonic adaptation theories have become popular partly because of the way they correspond to other well-established processes of adaptation within the human body, including the sensory adaptation processes described previously. However, a close examination of sensory adaptation processes reveals that there are strict limits to the adaptation that can occur. A "room-temperature" building may at first feel quite warm to a person who came in from outside on a very cold day, or it might feel quite cool to someone who came in from outside on a hot summer day. Both people would be expected to adapt to this new temperature, and the room-temperature environment would cease to be noticeable. However, there is actually a very small range of indoor temperatures that people find comfortable and to which they will quickly adapt. Outside this small range, people's experience is lastingly affected. Hedonic adaptation may function in a similar way. People may adapt quickly and easily to new circumstances as they happen, just as we adapt when we come in from the cold to a "room-temperature" location. However, just as few people intentionally keep their homes at a brisk 45 degrees during waking hours (i.e., they never adapt to temperatures this cold), people may never adapt to more extreme circumstances (Lucas, 2007).

An important goal for the section on theoretical perspectives is to put evidence for and against adaptation effects into theoretical context. Armenta, Bao, Lyubomirsky, and Sheldon discuss these issues from the context of intervention studies designed to improve well-being. In their program of research, they address theoretical reasons why some attempts at change may succeed, and they review evidence from intervention studies that address these possibilities. Similarly, DeHaan and Ryan discuss predictions from Self-Determination Theory in regard to the possibility for increased happiness, noting that this is more likely to result from eudaimonic than from hedonic life changes, especially changes that enhance one's overall level of psychological need-satisfaction. In contrast, Cummins discusses the reasons we might expect gains in well-being, or at least certain forms of well-being, to always revert back to baseline levels after a period of adaptation. Cummins also discusses how, in the worst case, baseline levels might become established at a permanent, lower level. Together, the divergent perspectives that these chapters offer should stimulate new competing empirical tests regarding the potential for stable change.

Although the first section of the book addresses theoretical perspectives on the possibility for change (of course, with reference to relevant data regarding these points), the second section focuses more squarely on the empirical evidence that change does or does not occur (regardless of whether those data are especially relevant for a particular theory). Importantly, given the breadth of evidence related to this issue, many of the chapters focus on distinct types of evidence or specific empirical approaches to understanding whether happiness can change. For instance, Headey, Muffels, and Wagner identify a sizeable minority of participants in large panel studies that do report substantial changes in happiness over long periods of time and then identify the factors that may be responsible for that change. They focus on specific life choices that individuals make that may be responsible for these changes. Yap, Anusic, and Lucas also use data from large-scale panel studies, but they focus on identifying how much change occurs and which life events seem to be associated with change. Powdthavee and Stutzer address similar questions with an emphasis on how economists have approached the question of change and the analysis of data that might inform our understanding of these changes.

Other chapters focus on change in subjective well-being in specific contexts. For instance, Ruini and Fava discuss the extent to which happiness can change within the context of therapy, whereas Veenhoven and also Easterlin and Switek discuss whether there are societal factors that lead to long-term changes in national levels of happiness. Although this has been and still is a contentious issue within the literature on subjective well-being, these latter two chapters provide important evidence about the extent to which change does occur at this macro level and whether such changes may be related to government policies.

Finally, the third section discusses some remaining issues in the study of change in subjective well-being. For instance, Eid and Kutscher provide an important overview of methodological and analytical approaches to understanding stability and change, which will be an essential resource for researchers who wish to investigate the many issues raised in the earlier substantive chapters. In addition, Hill, Mroczek, and Young point out that there may be individual differences in the extent to which change can and does occur. Research that takes these individual differences into account may be better able to identify factors that are responsible for stability and change.

The question of whether happiness can change may be the most important question that subjective well-being researchers can tackle. If people's long-term levels of subjective well-being are truly impervious to the effects of changing life circumstances, then attempts at intervention will be doomed to failure, well-being measures will provide little information to guide policy changes, and people's perception that they are pursuing goals to maximize happiness will surely be wrong. Research into the stability of longitudinal well-being remains an area of considerable ambiguity and controversy, and the basic question of whether happiness can change has still not been definitively answered. We hope that by bringing together diverse scholars who approach this question from a wide variety of perspectives, this book will provide an overview of what is known so far and can guide future research on this critical topic.

REFERENCES

Brickman, P., & Campbell, D. (1971). Hedonic relativism and planning the good society. In M. Appley (Ed.), *Adaptation-level theory: A symposium* (pp. 287−305). New York: Academic Press.

Brickman, P., Coates, D., & Janoff-Bulman, R. (1978). Lottery winners and accident victims: Is happiness relative? *Journal of Personality and Social Psychology*, *36*(8), 917−927.

Diener, E. (1984). Subjective well-being. *Psychological Bulletin*, *95*(3), 542−547.

Diener, E., Lucas, R. E., & Scollon, C. N. (2006). Beyond the hedonic treadmill: Revising the adaptation theory of well-being. *American Psychologist*, *61*, 305−314.

Diener, E., Suh, E. M., Lucas, R. E., & Smith, H. L. (1999). Subjective well-being: Three decades of progress. *Psychological Bulletin*, *125*, 276−302.

Gaskins, R. W. (1999). "Adding legs to a snake": A reanalysis of motivation and the pursuit of happiness from a Zen Buddhist perspective. *Journal of Educational Psychology*, *91*, 204−215.

Helson, H. (1964). *Adaptation-level theory: An experimental and systematic approach to behavior*. New York: Harper and Row.

Lucas, R. E. (2007). Long-term disability is associated with lasting changes in subjective well-being: Evidence from two nationally representative longitudinal studies. *Journal of Personality and Social Psychology*, *92*(4), 717−730. Available from http://dx.doi.org/ 10.1037/0022-3514.92.4.717.

Lykken, D. (1999). *Happiness: What studies on twins show us about nature, nurture, and the happiness set-point*. New York, NY: Golden Books.

Lykken, D., & Tellegen, A. (1996). Happiness is a stochastic phenomenon. *Psychological Science*, *7*(3), 186−189.

Seligman, M. E. P., & Csikszentmihalyi, M. (2000). Positive psychology: An introduction. *American Psychologist*, *55*(1), 5−14.

Wilson, W. (1967). Correlates of avowed happiness. *Psychological Bulletin*, *67*(4), 294−306.

Chapter 2

Well-Being: Heritable and Changeable

Espen Røysamb,[1] Ragnhild Bang Nes,[2] and Joar Vittersø[3]

[1]*University of Oslo, Oslo, Norway,* [2]*Norwegian Institute of Public Health, Oslo, Norway,*
[3]*University of Tromsø, Tromsø, Norway*

INTRODUCTION

Research on human happiness and well-being has flourished in recent years, and several subfields within the domain have emerged. One area of research has focused on the *stability and change* of well-being. Longitudinal and intervention-based studies provide evidence of the plasticity of well-being and the potential of increasing happiness (Dyrdal, Røysamb, Nes, & Vittersø, 2011; Lucas, 2007; Lyubomirsky & Layous, 2013; Sheldon & Lyubomirsky, 2012). Another line of research has examined genetic and environmental contributions to individual differences in well-being using quantitative and molecular genetic techniques. The collective findings from these studies indicate both *genetic and environmental* influences on most well-being measures (Bartels & Boomsma, 2009; Lykken & Tellegen, 1996; Nes, Røysamb, Tambs, Harris, & Reichborn-Kjennerud, 2006; Røysamb, Tambs, Reichborn-Kjennerud, Neale, & Harris, 2003).

Are these findings on changeability and heritability mutually contradictory and paradoxical? Does recognition of genetic influences on happiness preclude optimism regarding change potentials? Based on the current evidence, we argue that well-being is both heritable and changeable. Our aim in this chapter is first to review some of the exciting evidence of both changeability and genetic influences. Second, we discuss the concept of heritability along with criticism and caveats of behavior genetic findings. Finally, we present an integrative framework of well-being and change processes, and propose the concept of *positive gene-environment interplay* as a path to increased happiness.

Well-being is a broad term, typically referring to a general idea of goodness in life or what it means to live well (Crisp, 2005). To operationalize well-being for research purposes, researchers have proposed a number of more specific constructs, including subjective well-being (SWB), psychological well-being (PWB), mental well-being (MWB), emotional well-being (EWB), life satisfaction (LS), and emotional happiness (David, Boniwell, & Conley Ayers, 2013; Vittersø & Soholt, 2011). These constructs refer to partly overlapping and partly different phenomena, in the sense that they reflect some common and some unique variance (Chen, Jing, Hayes, & Lee, 2012). Thus, in the present chapter, we sometimes debate these subconstructs specifically, whereas we generally refer to *well-being*, and—in this context—its synonym *happiness*, in a broad sense.

CAN HAPPINESS CHANGE?

The unequivocal answer to this question is positive. Happiness can change, and happiness does change—during a single day and during a lifetime. Nevertheless, several questions pertaining to change are important to consider. How much can happiness change? Are changes in happiness short-term or lasting? Does happiness fluctuate around given set points? How do genetic and environmental factors contribute to stability and change?

There is a wealth of evidence supporting the notion of well-being as changing and changeable (Headey, Muffels, & Wagner, 2010; Lucas, 2007; Lyubomirsky, Sheldon, & Schkade, 2005). This volume contains reports from key researchers in the field, providing various types of compelling evidence for the dynamic nature of well-being. Thus, we primarily refer to other parts of this book for theories and studies of the changeability of happiness. Here, we briefly summarize overall findings from partly separate fields of inquiry, including longitudinal studies, intervention studies, natural quasi-experiments, national comparison studies, and clinical psychology/psychotherapy research.

Longitudinal studies of well-being typically report *moderate stability* (Dyrdal et al., 2011; Eid & Diener, 2004; Lucas & Diener, 2008; Lucas & Donnellan, 2007; Nes et al., 2006). Although cross-time correlations for well-being vary depending on the given measure, sample and timespan, they rarely exceed 0.6 and rarely drop below 0.3 (Diener, Inglehart, & Tay, 2013). A time1−time2 correlation of around 0.5 suggests that at any given time point, 50% of the variance is accounted for by a stability factor with the remaining 50% representing change or time-specific variation. Longer timespans typically yield lower stability than shorter timespans, and long-term change is therefore substantial. Knowing a person's well-being level today thus provides some, yet only some, basis for predicting the same person's well-being in 10 years' time.

Happiness intervention studies have been crucial in testifying to human change potentials and in identifying effective factors for generating increased well-being (Lyubomirsky & Layous, 2013; Seligman, Steen, Park, & Peterson, 2005; Sheldon & Lyubomirsky, 2012), as also evidenced by recent meta-analyses (Bolier et al., 2013; Sin & Lyubomirsky, 2009). Interventions such as gratitude exercises, cultivation of optimism, and use of character strengths represent novel strategies that have been shown to affect the happiness level of participants—and also contribute to more than temporary change. Although it is rarely feasible to adhere fully to the experimental ideal of double-blind randomized controlled trials (RCTs) in this field, the evidence converges on a substantial benefit of several intervention strategies. Of note, interventions appear to differ in their effectiveness (Seligman et al., 2005), indicating that the changes recorded do not mainly reflect a general training effect. With some interventions found particularly effective, and others not, more credibility is established for specific intervention strategies, and further understanding of their potent change mechanisms is likely to result from such studies.

Natural quasi-experiments represent another set of relevant studies for examining stability and change in well-being over time. Both positive (e.g., lottery winning, marriage) and negative life events (e.g., accidents, divorce, unemployment) are associated with temporary, and, to some extent lasting, changes in well-being (Diener, Lucas, & Scollon, 2006; Lucas, 2007; Luhmann, Hofmann, Eid, & Lucas, 2012). Because exposures to life events are not random in the population (Kendler & Karkowski-Shuman, 1997), evidence of causality is not entirely conclusive. Yet, recent studies have shown a nuanced picture of short- and long-term changes following various life events. One promising design for this research field can be found in co-twin control studies. By studying well-being in identical (monozygotic) twins discordant for a certain exposure (e.g., life event), one is able to approach a randomized matched-pair design and generate evidence of causal effects. For example, in a co-twin control study of SWB and longevity, Sadler and colleagues found environmental exposures, rather than genes, to account for the increased longevity associated with high well-being (Sadler, Miller, McGue, & Christensen, 2009).

National differences in well-being also provide evidence for the changeability of well-being. There is substantial variation in mean level well-being across different countries (Diener, Tay, & Oishi, 2013; Veenhoven, 2009), even between neighboring countries with similar populations. This suggests a change potential in most countries. Because national and individual differences might be explained by partly different factors, research into the predictors of national differences is crucial to understand the role of governance, economy, health care, and culture in generating well-being. Although national differences typically are smaller than individual differences within nations (Diener, Helliwell, & Kahneman, 2010; Vittersø, Røysamb, & Diener, 2002), the notion of lifting an entire nation by only a fraction of a standard deviation implies a huge total gain.

Clinical psychology and therapy research has not played a central role in the well-being field. Nevertheless, important lessons may be learned from this area. The lifetime prevalence of any mental disorder is roughly 50% (Kessler et al., 2005; Kessler, Petukhova, Sampson, Zaslavsky, & Wittchen, 2012), yet many of those who experience such problems return to flourishing lives. Mental health problems such as depression, anxiety, substance dependence, and eating disorders are negatively correlated with various well-being measures, yet ill-being and well-being are typically not seen as polar opposites (Keyes, 2013; Nes et al., 2013). Recent genetically informative studies confirm that genetic vulnerability for depression and internalizing disorders is inversely related to the genetic disposition for well-being, but also that there are unique genetic and environmental components of ill-being and well-being (Kendler, Myers, Maes, & Keyes, 2011; Nes et al., 2013). Studies on the development and treatment of mental disorders and subclinical psychological problems testify to a general human plasticity and a potential to change. Following trauma, conflicts, stressors, and major negative life events, onset of anxiety or depression may occur in previously healthy individuals. Furthermore, psychotherapy comprises an array of interventions aiming to generate a shift from ill-being to well-being and well-functioning, and numerous studies provide evidence of their effectiveness (Nieuwsma et al., 2012; Weisz, Weiss, Han, Granger, & Morton, 1995). Thus, our knowledge about the onset and treatment of ill-being also represents an important basis for understanding the changeability of well-being. In summary, several different strands of research provide evidence of both stability and change in well-being and suggest a relatively dynamic nature of human happiness.

HERITABILITY

Before reviewing empirical findings from twin and family studies on well-being and happiness, we briefly outline some of the key concepts, methods, and logic of genetically informative studies (i.e., twin and family studies).

Twin Research and Biometric Modeling

Family resemblance can be attributable to both nature and nurture. Basic genetically informative designs use the known genetic relationship between family members—usually monozygotic (MZ) and dizygotic (DZ) twins—to estimate the contribution of unknown genes and environmental factors to the observed variation in a given characteristic—or *phenotype*—such as well-being. Some studies have included data also from other types of relatives such as non-twin siblings (Bartels & Boomsma, 2009; Stubbe, Posthuma, Boomsma, & De Geus, 2005) and parents and offspring (Nes, Czajkowski, & Tambs, 2010). Other studies include both twins reared together and twins reared apart (Tellegen et al., 1988).

Because well-being constitutes a multifactorial and polygenetic characteristic (i.e., many different genes are involved), statistical methods can be employed to estimate the relative proportions of variation attributable to genetic and environmental factors. The resulting estimates are calculated without specifying any DNA sequences or any specific environmental influences. Rather, their contributions are inferred and modeled as latent variables.

The most basic design explores *whether* and *to what extent* genes are involved (i.e., estimates heritability), whereas the more advanced designs allow for further exploration of *how* genes and environmental influences are involved (e.g., whether the genetic and environmental influences are specific to a given characteristic or shared with other traits, or contingent on specific circumstances).

Two types of genetic influences (additive and nonadditive) and *two* types of environmental influences (shared and nonshared) can be estimated in standard twin studies. *Additive genetic influences* comprise effects from an unknown number of individual genetic loci whose effects combine additively. By contrast, *nonadditive genetic influences* reflect interaction among alleles (gene variants) at the same locus (dominance) or across loci (epistasis). The overall genetic effect is termed *heritability* and reflects the part of the total variation attributable to genetic factors. *Broad-sense* heritability (H^2) refers to effects from both additive and nonadditive genetic influences, and *narrow-sense* heritability (h^2) refers only to the additive ones.

The *shared*, or *common, environment* includes environmental influences that contribute to similarity in reared-together family members and constitutes a measure of environmental effects rather than the environment as such. Whereas objective environments refer to environmental circumstances as they might be observed, effective environments are defined by the outcomes they produce. Standard twin studies estimate only the effective environment, not the objective environment. When objectively shared family factors (e.g., conflict) affect siblings in a family differently (e.g., increasing risk of anxiety in one sibling and not the other), they are classified as nonshared. This latter effect, the *nonshared environment*, reflects all the nongenetic sources of differences among family members as well as measurement error and stochastic chance effects.

The two environmental and two genetic components are usually derived by specifying a mathematical model according to the differential degree to which pairs of MZ and DZ co-twins are correlated for genetic and environmental effects. Because MZ co-twins have identical DNA, both types of genetic effects are perfectly correlated in these pairs. By contrast, DZ co-twins (and siblings) share on average 50% of their segregating genes, giving a genetic correlation of 0.5 for additivity and 0.00−0.25 for nonadditivity. The shared environment includes all environmental influences causing twin resemblance regardless of zygosity and is correlated 1.0 in all zygosity groups, whereas the nonshared environment is, by definition, uncorrelated.

The difference in observed similarity between MZ and DZ twins is central to estimates of heritability, and a crude estimate of narrow heritability is given by the following formula: $h^2 = 2 \times (r_{MZ} - r_{DZ})$, that is, two times the difference between MZ and DZ correlations.

Multivariate analyses extend the basic univariate model by decomposing the variance *and* the covariance between different indicators or different time points into genetic and environmental components. This enables investigation of whether the same factors contribute to several correlated characteristics (e.g., well-being and optimism) or a given characteristic over time (e.g., in childhood and adolescence). These multivariate models are more statistically powerful than univariate models and consequently provide more precise estimates of the latent effects.

Findings: Univariate Studies

In recent years we have witnessed an increasing number of genetically informative studies on well-being (Archontaki, Lewis, & Bates, 2013; Bartels & Boomsma, 2009; Caprara et al., 2009; De Neve, Christakis, Fowler, & Frey, 2012; Franz et al., 2012; Gigantesco et al., 2011; Keyes, Myers, & Kendler, 2010; Mosing et al., 2012; Nes et al., 2006; Røysamb et al., 2003; Schnittker, 2008), including twin studies, adoption studies, family studies, and molecular genetic studies. We will shortly review the main findings, yet for a start, it seems fair to summarize the cross-sectional findings as typically revealing *heritabilities* in the range of 0.25—0.55. This implies a substantial genetic contribution to human well-being. Importantly, however, the findings also represent robust evidence of strong environmental influences.

Table 2.1 displays an overview of some key studies that have examined genetic and environmental influences on well-being. Collectively, these studies are based on samples of more than 80,000 twins and family members, from several different countries, and covering the life span from early adolescence through senior years. A number of different well-being constructs have been studied, including subjective well-being, psychological well-being, mental well-being, and life satisfaction. Despite some potentially interesting differences across measures and samples, the findings converge on a moderate heritability of well-being. Of note, the magnitude of the genetic influences corresponds to that typically found for common mental disorders such as anxiety and depression, and is lower than those reported for schizophrenia, bipolar disorder, and general intelligence (Bouchard, 2004; Plomin, DeFries, Craig, & McGuffin, 2003).

In Table 2.1, the upper part shows studies examining momentary states of well-being or positive affect. The middle section ("time-specific"), comprising the bulk of studies, reports findings based on general measures (e.g., SWLS) at single time points. Finally, the lower section comprises longitudinal studies investigating the genetic contribution to the stable component of

TABLE 2.1 Key Studies of Genetic and Environmental Factors in Well-Being, with Heritability Estimates

Happiness Type	Reference & Year	N	Age	Sample Type	Phenotype	Instrument	H^2/h^2	c^2	e^2
Momentary									
	Riemann et al., 1998	600	18–70	Twins reared together	Positive mood	Mood scale	.00–.21	.07–.16	.71–.84
	Eid et al., 2003	278	18–70	Twins reared together	PA	PA scale	.36	–	.64
	Menne-Lothmann et al., 2012	520	M = 27	Female twins reared together	Momentary PA, reward	Four items	–	.00–.34	.66–1.0
Time-specific									
	Tellegen et al., 1988	804		Twins reared together/apart	WB	MPQWB	.40–.48	.13–.22	.38–.40
	Røysamb et al., 2002	5,140	18–25	Twins reared together	SWB	SWB index	.46–.54	–	.46–.54
	Røysamb et al., 2003	6,576	18–31	Twins reared together	SWB	SWB index	.44	–	.56
	Stubbe et al., 2005	5,668	14–88	Twins and siblings	LS	SWLS	.38	–	.62
	Steger et al., 2007	336	M = 49	Twins reared together	Character strengths	VIA	.12–.58	–	.42–.88
	Nes et al., 2008	8,045	18–31	Twins reared together	LS	LS	.17–.35	.00–.11	.66–.71
	Schnittker, 2008	2,330	25–74	Twins and siblings	Happiness (PA)	PA scale	.36	.06	.57
	Caprara et al., 2009	856	23–24	Twins reared together	SWB	SWLS	.59	–	.41
	Bartels & Boomsma, 2009	5,024	13–28	Twins and siblings	SWB, subhappiness, QoL	SWLS, SHS, Cantril	.36–.47	–	.53–.64
	Nes et al., 2010	60,000	18–80	Twins, siblings, parents	SWB	SWB index	.33–.36	.00–.12	.64–.67

(Continued)

TABLE 2.1 (Continued)

Happiness Type	Reference & Year	N	Age	Sample Type	Phenotype	Instrument	H^2/h^2	c^2	e^2
	Gigantesco et al., 2011	742	23–24	Twins reared together	PWB dimensions	PWB	.37–.64		.36–.63
	De Neve, Christakis, Fowler, & Frey, 2012	1,098		Twins reared together	LS	LS	.33	–	.67
	Archontaki et al., 2013	1,674	M = 45	Twins reared together	PWB	PWB	.30–.52	–	.48–.70
	Franz et al., 2012	1,226	51–55	Male twins reared together	PWB, LS, WB	PWB, MPQWB, LS	.19–.50	.01–.02	.49–.79
	Mosing et al., 2012	2,937	61–66	Twins reared together	Flow proneness	SFPQ	.41	–	.59
Stable									
	McGue et al., 1993	254	17–37	Twins reared together/ apart	Dispositional WB	MPQWB	.95	–	.05
	Lykken & Tellegen, 1996	254	17–37	Twins reared together/ apart	Dispositional WB	MPQWB	.80	–	.20
	Nes et al., 2006	8,045	18–31	Twins reared together	Dispositional SWB	SWB index	.80	–	.20
	Nes et al., 2013	8,045	18–36	Twins reared together	Dispositional LS	LS	.72	–	.28

Notes: SWLS = Satisfaction With Life Scale (Diener et al., 1985); MPQ = Multidimensional Personality Questionnaire (Tellegen, 1982); SHS = Subjective Happiness Scale (Lyubomirsky & Lepper, 1999); Cantril = Cantril's ladder (Cantril, 1965); SWB index = Subjective Well-Being index (Moum et al., 1990); PWB = Ryff Psychological Well-Being Scale (Ryff & Keyes, 1995); SWB Questionnaire = Subjective Well-Being Questionnaire (King & Landau, 2003); AP Scale = The Aggregated Positive Affect Scale (Riemann, Angleitner, Borkenau, & Eid, 1998); VIA = Values in Action (Peterson & Seligman, 2003); BABS = Bradburn Affect Balance Scale (Bradburn, 1969); LS = Life Satisfaction single item; PAS = Positive Affect Scale (MIDUS, Mroczek & Kolarz, 1998); QoL = Quality of Life; SFPQ = Swedish Flow Proneness Questionnaire (Ullén et al., 2012); PE = Positive Emotionality; PA = Positive Affect.

Momentary: current/in-situation measures; Time-specific: general measure at single time point (e.g., SWLS); Stable: longitudinal data with two or more measurements. H^2/h^2 = heritability; c^2 = common environment variance; e^2 = nonshared environment variance.

well-being. As can be seen, genetic factors appear to play a limited role only in momentary states, a moderate role in cross-sectional general experiences, and a substantial role in long-term well-being.

In addition to genetically informative research focusing explicitly on the well-being measures mentioned previously, several studies have reported genetic effects for related constructs. For example, substantial heritabilities have been reported for optimism (Caprara et al., 2009; Mosing, Zietsch, Shekar, Wright, & Martin 2009; Plomin et al., 1992), positive emotionality (e.g., Johnson, McGue, & Krueger, 2005; Krueger, South, Johnson, & Iacono, 2008; Tellegen et al., 1988), and resilience (Waaktaar & Torgersen, 2012).

Another noteworthy finding from genetically informed studies of well-being is the general absence of common environmental effects (Nes, 2010). That is, family resemblance in well-being seems to be mainly due to shared genes. Environmental factors are evidently important but seem to be non-shared (i.e., unique to the individual), implicating that the environment tends to influence family members differently. Shared family factors such as parenting and family events may still be relevant to well-being, but do not usually contribute to resemblance within families or twin pairs (i.e., do not have general effects). A certain factor may thus be shared in terms of exposure, but not in terms of effects. For example, two twins may be exposed to the same parenting style yet react differently and not become similar because of this parenting.

Findings: Bi- and Multivariate Studies

Whereas the initial twin studies primarily focused on disentangling the genetic and environmental contributions to single well-being measures at single time points, the field has moved forward in several important directions. One set of studies explored the genetic and environmental contributions to associations between *well-being* and *various health-related constructs*. Twin data enable estimation of the extent to which genes and environments explain the observed correlations between two or more phenotypes. For example, given a negative correlation between well-being and depression, it would be pertinent to examine the sources of this association. Are there partly overlapping genetic factors, implying that genes that contribute to well-being also act as protective factors against depression? Or do certain environmental factors simultaneously contribute to well-being and protect against depression? Genetic factors have been found to play an important role in the associations between well-being and sleep problems (Nes, Røysamb, Reichborn-Kjennerud, Tambs, & Harris, 2005), perceived health (Røysamb et al., 2003), depression (Franz et al., 2012; Nes et al., 2013), internalizing and externalizing disorders (Bartels, Cacioppo, van Beijsterveldt, & Boomsma, 2013; Kendler, Myers, & Keyes, 2011; Kendler et al., 2011) as well as subclinical levels of anxiety and depressive symptoms

(Nes, Czajkowski, Røysamb, Reichborn-Kjennerud, & Tambs 2008). Typically, environmental factors also contribute to the examined associations, but often to a lesser degree. Moreover, both genes and environmental factors represent unique influences that contribute to the specific variance in well-being.

Another group of recent studies has applied multivariate modeling to disentangle the genetic and environmental structure *underlying a set of different well-being constructs*. One study modeled the factors underlying psychological well-being, trait well-being, life satisfaction, self-esteem, and depression (Franz et al., 2012) and found two general factors with substantial genetic variance and a set of mostly environmental factors explaining the unique variance of each specific phenotype. In a similar vein, the underlying structure of quality of life in general, satisfaction with life, quality of life at present, and subjective happiness was found to be accounted for by additive and nonadditive genetic, as well as nonshared environmental, factors (Bartels & Boomsma, 2009). Correlations among the indicators were largely attributable to shared genes, however, suggesting that these four indicators do not differ at the genetic level. Another study reported high heritability (72%) for a latent factor of mental well-being, which accounted for the covariance among emotional, social, and psychological well-being (Keyes et al., 2010). Finally, high genetic correlations were found for the six subcomponents of psychological well-being, with the environmental effects being mostly trait specific (Archontaki et al., 2013).

Findings: Stability and Change

The multivariate twin model has also been successfully applied to examine genetic and environmental contributions to stability and change in well-being (Kendler et al., 2011; Lykken & Tellegen, 1996; McGue, Bacon, & Lykken, 1993; Nes et al., 2013; Nes et al., 2006). Whereas environmental influences are commonly assumed to be related to both stability and change, genetic factors are often implicitly assumed to represent static influences throughout the life span. However, genetic influences imply neither immutability nor stability (Pedersen & Reynolds, 1998), and new genetic effects may emerge at different developmental stages throughout the life span. Genes contributing to well-being among adolescents are not necessarily the same as those contributing to well-being later in life. Even moderately stable traits might be influenced by differing sets of genes at different life stages (Plomin, 1986). In theory, both genetic and environmental factors might therefore represent sources of both change and continuity.

Yet the studies published to date collectively indicate that genes primarily generate stability, whereas environmental influences generate both stability and change, although mainly the latter (Johnson, McGue, & Krueger, 2005; Lykken & Tellegen, 1996; McGue, 1993; Nes et al., 2006). Stability in well-being commonly accounts for 50% of the cross-sectional variation (Lucas & Donnellan, 2007; Schimmack, Krause, Wagner, & Schupp, 2010), and two longitudinal studies on subjective well-being have indicated that as much as 80% of this stable level is attributable to genes (Lykken & Tellegen, 1996; Nes et al., 2006) (see Table 2.1). Likewise, stability in positive emotionality as measured by the Multidimensional Personality Questionnaire (Johnson et al., 2005) and dispositional life satisfaction (Nes et al., 2013) appear to be largely attributable to genes. Conjointly, the findings are in line with a theory that posits a general well-being set point or set range (see more below), or a general readiness to perceive and interpret the world more or less positively, which is fairly stable across time and strongly influenced by genes. By contrast, environmental influences seem to be as important for change as genetic factors are to stability. Around 80% of the change variance appears to be accounted for by environmental factors.

Of note, however, environmental influences might also generate stability over time. Johnson and colleagues (2005) have, for example, reported that when accounting for measurement error, 40% of the variation in personality, including the higher-order factor positive emotionality, was attributable to stable environmental factors. Also, Nes and colleagues (2006) reported 20%−25% of the phenotypic cross-time correlations for subjective well-being to be due to environmental sources. Whether these stable environmental influences reflect long-term effects from past or persistent events or consistently occurring factors in the environment was not explored.

Lastly, there is also evidence for some new genetic variance emerging over time. Cross-time correlations between genetic factors for well-being have been estimated to 0.78−0.85 in a sample of young adult Norwegian twins (Nes et al., 2006). Although new genetic variance may reflect changes at the molecular level, it may also reflect alterations in psychosocial circumstances of sufficient magnitude to elicit new genetic influences for SWB. The genetic effects on change thus suggest that despite the DNA not undergoing change, different life situations, circumstances, or developmental stages are likely to make different genetic factors for well-being salient.

Gene-Environment Interplay

In addition to operating as sources of main effects, genes and environment may interact and correlate in several ways. Four specific types of gene environments interplay, all of which may be highly relevant for well-being, have been outlined in the field, including (i) heritability-environment interaction, (ii) gene-environment correlation (rGE), (iii) gene-environment interaction (GxE), and (iv) epigenetics (Caspi & Moffitt, 2006; Moffitt, Caspi, & Rutter, 2006).

Heritability-environment interaction refers to variation in the magnitude of the genetic and environmental influences across population strata. Several studies have explored heritability-environment interaction for well-being related phenomena and shown that family factors such as marital status, socioeconomic factors, and parenting may moderate genetic and environmental influences on well-being. The heritability of subjective well-being has, for example, been reported to vary across marital status, with lower heritability estimates for individuals with a marital or equivalent partner (Nes, Røysamb, Harris, Czajkowski, & Tambs, 2010). Another study examining the impact of financial standing found environmental influences on life satisfaction to decrease with increasing income, whereas the proportion of the variation due to genetic factors increased with increasing income (Johnson & Krueger, 2006). Heritability and both shared and nonshared environmental factors for positive emotionality have also been shown to vary as a function of adolescents' perceived relationship with their parents (Krueger et al., 2008).

Gene-environment correlation (rGE) implicates that the probability of exposure to environmental influences is not random, but partly dependent on an individual's genotype (i.e., the nature of nurture). rGE is commonly classified as *passive, active,* or *evocative* (McGue, 2010; Rutter, Moffitt, & Caspi, 2006; Scarr & Weinberg, 1983). Passive rGE refers to situations in which an individual inherits both genes and environmental circumstances that mutually reinforce each other. A relevant example to well-being research would be when children of happy parents inherit genes associated with happiness as well as experience emotionally stable, happy, and supportive parents (i.e., double advantage). Individuals are also active agents in selecting their environments (active rGE) and, in turn, trigger responses (evocative rGE) that commonly boost and strengthen their genetic propensities. Children with temperaments high in positivity and sociability tend to actively seek out circumstances matching their (partly genetic) disposition (active rGE) and may elicit more positive and supportive responses in parents and others (evocative rGE). For example, in the study by Krueger and colleagues (2008), adolescents with a genetic propensity to positive emotionality were reported to elicit more positive regard in their parents.

Gene-environment interaction (GxE) occurs when the effect of exposure to a given environmental factor is conditional on the individual's specific genotype or, conversely, when the genotype's effect is moderated by the environment. There has been high interest in this type of interplay over the past decade, and in fact, GxE has been suggested to constitute the norm in relating genetic polymorphisms to specific behavior (Canli, 2004; Canli & Lesch, 2007). Numerous studies have shown variants of specific genes (e.g., MAO-A, SLC6A4, COMT, 5HTTLPR) to be associated with specific behavioral expressions (e.g., antisocial behavior, depression, psychotic symptoms) if exposed to given life circumstances such as maltreatment, adverse life stressors, and drugs (Caspi et al., 2002; Caspi et al., 2005; Caspi et al., 2003). The GxE approach is likely to be productive, but so far few have explored the GxE interaction for well-being.

Relevant for GxE interaction is also the notion of *vantage sensitivity* (Pluess & Belsky, 2013). Whereas the traditional diathesis-stress framework focuses on the combination of vulnerabilities and stressors in generating mental disorders, the concept of vantage sensitivity focuses on variation in responses to positive experiences as a function of endogenous characteristics. Some individuals—with a given genetic disposition—might have a heightened sensitivity to positive exposures, resulting in an added benefit from specific experiences.

Epigenetic mechanisms reflect long-lasting alterations in gene expression that are not associated with changes in the DNA sequence (Tsankova, Renthal, Kumar, & Nestler, 2007) and thus constitute biological processes in which environmental effects are mediated through gene expression or through altered chromosomal structure. Epigenetic modification is likely to be important for our understanding of the molecular basis of complex and multifactorial characteristics such as happiness and well-being and may account for some of the variation that has previously been attributed to heritability and environmental factors (Petronis, 2010). In fact, the epigenetic perspective has been suggested as a unifying principle in the etiology of complex traits. However, the epigenetic pathways that link specific genes to behavioral expressions are likely to be utterly complex and are to date mainly unexplored.

What Heritability Is (Not) About

Heritability is a population statistic that refers to the proportion of total variance in a given characteristic (i.e., phenotype) accounted for by genetic variance (Plomin et al., 2003; Turkheimer, 2000). As such, it is parallel to any other effect represented as R^2—for example, the variance in well-being accounted for by marital status, negative life events, or happiness interventions. Thus, heritability is merely a sample-based estimate of a source of variance in a given population. Note also that the estimate will depend on the relative amount of environmental variance. Therefore, heritability may vary across different populations, age groups, genders, nations, and cohorts. Body height may serve as an illustrating example. In the industrialized world, studies have shown heritabilities of around 80%—90% for body height (Bergin et al., 2012; Dubois et al., 2012). Two hundred years ago the heritability was assumedly substantially lower—not because of changes in the genetic variance but because of higher variability in nutrition during childhood. Thus, with better nutrition for all, there are fewer environmental differences left to explain the total variation. Similarly, in countries with greater environmental variation (e.g., socioeconomic differences), the heritability of well-being may be lower than the heritability estimated in countries with fewer social inequalities.

In its basic form, heritability can be defined by the formula

$$Heritability = \frac{V_g}{V_g + V_e} \qquad (2.1)$$

where V_g equals genetic variance and V_e equals environmental variance. V_g and V_e contribute to the observed phenotypic variance, V_{ph}, thus:

$$V_{ph} = V_g + V_e \qquad (2.2)$$

Note that in this simple formulation, additive and nonadditive genetic factors are combined into a total genetic effect. Likewise, common and nonshared environments are combined into total environmental variance. One key reminder is that of heritability as relative to the environmental variance. That is, increased environmental variance by necessity implies reduced heritability.

Another key point is that the estimated V_e typically includes naturally occurring environmental factors only, as in life-as-usual, and does not capture the effects of potential interventions. That is, in population-based twin studies, the environmental variance includes factors such as life events and social influences, but unless a substantial proportion of the sample has been exposed to an intervention, we are unlikely to detect any such effects. Adding a new intervention variance (V_i) to the existing V_e could, in theory, reduce heritability and also increase well-being. For example, laser surgery for vision correction represents an intervention that counteracts the partly genetic disposition to near- or farsightedness. The first introduction of laser operations in a population would represent an added environmental variance that could result in a reduced proportion of genetic variance in the total phenotypic variance.

To grasp the nature of the heritability construct, ponder the following question: What is the heritability of number of fingers on people's hands in the adult population? Actually, although the fetal development of fingers obviously is genetically driven, the heritability is probably very low. First, there is very little genetic variance. With the exception of some mutations, we all have 10-finger genes. Second, most of the (little) phenotypic variance (i.e., people having anything but 10 fingers) is due to accidents and other environmental exposures. Thus, the observed variance, if any, is mostly accounted by environmental factors, which implies negligible heritability.

The notion of heritability as a population statistic also implies that it is not meaningful to index the heritability for a single individual. If well-being is found to have a heritability of 40%, this does not mean that 40% of a person's well-being is inherited. To use body height again as an example, despite a heritability of around 85%, it would not make sense to claim that a person who is 170 cm tall has received 145 cm (170 × 0.85) from her or his genes and another 25 cm from the environment.

If heritability is not a relevant construct at the individual level, how can we represent the *happiness range* and *change potential* of individuals given a certain genetic disposition? We propose a way of translating heritability

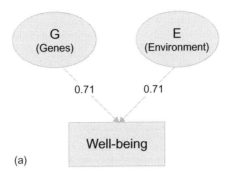

FIGURE 2.1A   Basic model of the influence of genes (G) and environment (E) on the observed phenotype of well-being. In this example, G and E have equal effects (0.71), implying a heritability of 50% (0.71 squared).

estimates into a conception of individual change potentials. Figure 2.1a illustrates Equation 2.1 (shown previously) and also represents part of the univariate latent factor model typically used in analyses of twin data. In this example, the genetic and environmental factors have equally strong effects on well-being, implying a heritability of 50% (i.e., 0.71 squared). Both latent factors, G and E, and the phenotype, well-being, are standardized.

In Figure 2.1b, the phenotypic variance is shown by the upper curve, with SD = 1. The lower curve represents the environmental variance in phenotypic well-being and has a standard deviation of 0.71 (hence variance of 0.5). For both curves, the vertical dotted lines designate the area under the curve containing 95% of the distribution.

Consider a thought experiment. Imagine a person who has not only one co-twin, but 99 "co-twins," all together 100 genetically identical individuals. Imagine also that these 100 people have an average genetic propensity for well-being (a potential set point), thus having a zero score on the latent G-factor in Figure 2.1a. All differences among the 100 "twins" will be due to environmental differences. Disregarding the 5% extreme scorers, 95% of the "twins" will have a well-being range within +/−1.39 SD (1.96 × 0.71). Thus, the range between the dotted lines of the lower curve (labeled "environmental variance" in Figure 2.1b) can be seen as the *natural well-being range* for any individual with a given genetic disposition. With a lower or higher genetic disposition, the curve would move left or right, respectively. Yet the happiness potential of most individuals is substantial.

We move next to empirical data to further illustrate the point of individual happiness ranges. The data are based on the Norwegian Twin Registry (Harris, Magnus, & Tambs, 2006; Nilsen et al., 2013). A total of 7,947 twins responded to a questionnaire including an index of SWB. Several papers have been published on these data, showing a heritability of 0.44 (Nes et al., 2005; Røysamb et al., 2003). Figure 2.2a shows the distribution of

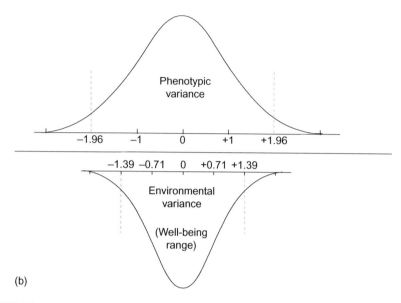

(b)

FIGURE 2.1B The upper curve represents the theoretical normal distribution of phenotypic variance in well-being. The lower curve represents the distribution of the environmental contribution to phenotypic variance (SD = 0.71, variance = 0.5). The lower curve thereby also reflects the hypothetical range of well-being scores among genetically identical individuals (see text for the example of 100 "twins"). Vertical dotted lines demarcate area under curves comprising 95% of the sample (i.e., +/−1.96 for the upper curve and +/−1.39 [0.71 × 1.96] for the lower curve). Shown values at the lower curve are standardized scores of the upper curve.

well-being scores for the whole sample transformed into a 0−10 scale (mean = 7.11, SD = 1.59).

Focusing now on the MZ twins (n = 2,554), we calculated the difference score within each pair of twins. Figure 2.2b shows the distribution of difference scores. Roughly half the sample (51.4%) had a difference score of at least +/−1.00, and the remaining half of pairs had an absolute difference of less than 1 point on the 0−10 scale. The mean absolute difference was 1.28 (median = 1.00). Thus, in this sample of twins, with a fairly typical mean level and distribution of well-being, and a substantial heritability, the intra-pair differences among identical twins were still substantial. The difference distribution is normal, with most pairs showing moderate differences. Nevertheless, the level of variability within pairs points to substantial influences from environmental factors and a considerable range of change.

Thus far, our examples have focused on cross-sectional measures, where moderate heritability estimates are found. However, as reviewed, longitudinal twin studies indicate that around 80% of the stable variance in well-being is accounted for by genetic factors (Nes et al., 2006). Does this imply that environmental factors, such as happiness interventions, cannot

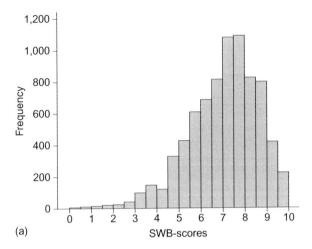

FIGURE 2.2A   Distribution of well-being scores (0–10) in a sample of twins (N = 7,947).

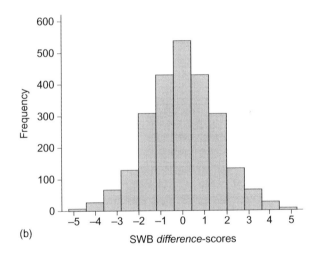

FIGURE 2.2B   Distribution of observed difference scores (twin1 − twin2) among identical (MZ) twins (N = 2,554).

have lasting effects? We believe the answer is no—for several reasons. First, again the extant estimates are based on equations that do not include potential interventions, only the naturally occurring life events and activities. Second, even without specific interventions, there are important within-pair differences across time. To illustrate this, we used our longitudinal data including well-being measures at two time points with 6 years apart (N = 1,577 MZ twins). Sample mean scores were 7.24 (T1) and 7.28 (T2). We selected twins who were lastingly very happy (n = 194), that is, who scored high (above 8.5) at both Time1 and Time2. The mean scores of this subsample were 9.25 and 9.22 at the two time points, respectively. If these stable high scores were due to a genetic disposition solely, we would expect their identical co-twins to show the same level of well-being. However, the co-twins of the very happy twins scored 8.4 (T1) and 8.34 (T2). Thus, the lastingly very happy twins have co-twins with higher than average scores as well, in accordance with the heritability estimates. Nevertheless, despite the same genetic make-up, at some point the two twins in each pair have split into somewhat different well-being paths. Because the twins are genetically similar, the differences are generally due to environmental factors. It remains to explore whether these include activities, life choices, life events, or other factors, but certain (unknown) factors lead some twins into lastingly more well-being than their co-twins. As such, these data support the notion of environmental effects as not only temporary, but possibly also long term.

Caveats and Criticism

Critics of twin studies and behavior genetic findings often refer to violations of the *Equal Environment Assumption* (EEA) as causing inflated heritability estimates (Richardson & Norgate, 2005). The EEA is a basic premise of the twin model and involves the assumption that MZ and DZ co-twins are exposed to the same amount of common environment. If MZ twins are treated more similarly—for example, more often being dressed alike—than DZ twins, this treatment or environmental exposure could lead to higher MZ similarity and thus artificially inflated heritability estimates.

However, there are some requirements for EEA violations to represent a problem. First, there has to be evidence of more similar treatment of MZ than DZ twins. Second, the treatment must causally affect the phenotype in focus—for example, well-being. If MZ twins are indeed dressed more alike than DZ twins, but variation in dressing is unrelated to happiness, then the EEA holds. To our knowledge, there is no empirical evidence of EEA violations that have caused inflated heritabilities in the well-being literature. Support for the robustness of findings is also implied by the convergence of results from classic twin studies and studies of twins reared apart. Although the majority of studies have used samples of twins reared together, evidence from twin- and sibling-adoption studies in general support findings from the former (Lykken & Tellegen, 1996; Matteson, McGue, & Iacono, 2013; Tellegen et al., 1988).

Noteworthy is also the notion of *evocative gene-environment correlation* (McGue, 2010; Rutter et al., 2006). Genetic dispositions may activate certain responses from the environment. Friendly and smiling people activate different responses than do hostile and criticizing people. If MZ twins, with identical genetic dispositions, tend to activate similar social responses, then the similarity in environmental exposure is genetic in its origin. Thus, MZ twins may be treated similarly because of their genetic similarity evoking similar responses in others. The mechanisms involved in gene-environment correlations are important for our understanding of the etiological processes of well-being but should not be seen as a violation of the EEA.

Sibling interaction effects are related to, yet different from, the equal environment assumption. Given that our happiness in general partly depends on the happiness of close family members, and that MZ twins tend to have a particularly close relationship with their co-twins, there might be stronger mutual influences (sibling interaction) among MZ than DZ twins. The notion of happiness as contagious (Fowler & Christakis, 2008) refers primarily to an environmental influence. If happiness is more contagious among MZ than DZ twins, this could contribute to higher MZ than DZ correlations. However, a recent study found adopted adolescents to resemble their biological family, but not their social family, on happiness (Matteson et al., 2013), thus indicating limited happiness contagion between family members.

The basic twin model is also based on the assumption of *random mating*. Nonrandom mating implies that people tend to fall in love with, and have children with, partners who resemble themselves. There is evidence of nonrandom, or assortative, mating for physical traits such as height and weight, health behaviors, and psychological characteristics such as personality traits, intelligence, and mental health (Ask, Idstad, Engdahl, & Tambs, 2013; Ask, Rognmo, Torvik, Røysamb, & Tambs, 2012; Dufort, Kovess, & Boivin, 1994; Merikangas, 1982). If parents of twins have somewhat similar genetic dispositions for well-being, this could have implications for the parameters estimated. MZ twins share 100% of their genes, regardless of parental resemblance. In contrast, DZ twins share 50% of their segregating genes under the random mating model, but could share a higher proportion of genes if their parents have more than randomly shared genes. This would imply an increased DZ correlation, compared to that of the random model, which in effect would lead to artificially *decreased heritability estimates* (given $h^2 = 2 \times (r_{MZ} - r_{DZ})$) and increased estimates of common environmental effects. Nonrandom mating may partly be controlled for in extended study designs using data from both twins and parents, and there is no evidence to date that nonrandom mating substantially influences behavior genetic findings on well-being.

TOWARD AN INTEGRATED MODEL OF GENES, ENVIRONMENT, AND CHANGE

There is overwhelming evidence of substantial genetic influences on human happiness (Bartels & Boomsma, 2009; Nes, 2010). We believe the well-being field can benefit strongly from not disregarding or dismissing this evidence. Rather, by incorporating current knowledge about the role of genetic and environmental factors, the field is set to move forward to a deeper understanding of processes generating both stability and change in happiness. Recognizing the influence of genetic factors in well-being does not imply a pessimistic outlook on the prospect of change. On the contrary, genes provide us with a potential for change, and by taking into account the role of genes, we may be able to obtain an integrated understanding of change and thereby also develop more effective interventions.

Genes, Set Points, and Change

The finding of genetic factors accounting for a high proportion of the stable variance in well-being (Lykken & Tellegen, 1996; Nes et al., 2006) accords with the theoretical notion of a genetically based set point or set range (Fujita & Diener, 2005; Lucas, 2007; Lykken, 1999). Set point theory has been disputed (Diener et al., 2006; Headey, 2013), and there is a growing need for a more nuanced understanding of set points and change processes. Given that we accept the set point notion as a theoretical construct, several important questions may be raised.

First, how much time do we (have to) spend at the set point? As human lives unfold, happiness naturally fluctuates—depending on external events and our own making of activities, social relations, and life choices. Recall that the twin data (see earlier) indicated that roughly half the sample of identical twins reported well-being scores of more than $+/-1$ point apart from their co-twin (0−10 scale). Additionally, the theoretical example of 100 identical "twins" showed a substantial phenotypic variation around a genetic mean. Thus, we are probably rarely at our exact set point. On average, people would spend roughly half of the time below and half of the time above their set points. However, if there was a fixed set point, theoretically there is no reason why we should be unable to increase the time spent above this point. Happiness interventions (see, e.g., Armenta, Bao, Lyubomirsky, & Sheldon, Chapter 4 in this volume) are partly about nurturing the factors that contribute to moving up and remaining above a theoretical set point, and growing evidence testifies to their effectiveness (Bolier et al., 2013; Sin & Lyubomirsky, 2009). Of note, if set points are simply operationalized as the mean value of lifetime well-being (Headey, 2013), we will necessarily spend roughly half of the time above or below this point. However, if set points are conceived as an intrinsic tendency (analogous to a disposition to body weight, cholesterol level, or musical talent), there is certainly potential for moving to and remaining on the desired side of this point.

Yet the issue of set points might be more complex. A second important question concerns how set is the set point? Although our genes remain the same throughout life, gene expression may be turned on or off, and different genes may contribute to happiness under different circumstances, activities, and life phases (Nes et al., 2010; Nes et al., 2006; Røysamb, Harris, Magnus, Vittersø, & Tambs, 2002). The genetic dispositions that contribute to the well-being of a 20-year-old college student might be partly different from those contributing to the same person's well-being at age 50. As well-being flows from a continuous interplay between genes and environment, theoretically it would be possible to alter the genetically based set point, not by altering the genes, but by altering activities and circumstances to allow for flourishing of genetically based potentials. For example, a person with a highly creative disposition (or musical talent, sports talent, intelligence, sociability) might alter her set point by creating a life conducive to the expression of this potential. In this sense, we have not one but several possible set points—depending on the life situations and activities we choose, create, or are exposed to. This way of conceptualizing set points accords with recent findings suggesting that life changes such as unemployment or marriage may alter individual set points (Lucas, 2007; Lucas, Clark, Georgellis, & Diener, 2004). The notion of various possible set points also accords with findings of national differences in well-being. Nations or states with high well-being scores may be seen as doing well at creating environments that allow for optimal set points. If governments build dance floors, people will be happy to do the dancing.

Positive Gene-Environment Interplay

We have reviewed some of the ways genes and environments can operate, interact, and correlate. Here, we argue that these mechanisms may be used actively to generate trajectories of increased well-being. We suggest *positive gene-environment interplay* as a general concept that includes collaboration and matchmaking between genes and environments. Theoretically, well-being may be enhanced through seeking and creation of environments—including activities, exposures, and relationships—that promote expression and flourishing of genetic potentials (and possibly protect against vulnerabilities).

Although the term *positive gene-environment interplay* is new, we believe that the processes involved are implicitly present in several extant happiness-enhancing strategies. For example, the intervention activity "using signature strengths in a new way" (Seligman et al., 2005) includes identification of individual top character strengths and exploration of new ways to use these strengths. Given that character strengths are partly heritable (Steger, Hicks, Kashdan, Krueger, & Bouchard, 2007), this activity may be seen as creating environments that allow for increased use of genetic potentials and thereby building of positive experiences and competencies.

At a more general level, *person-activity fit* (Lyubomirsky & Layous, 2013; Sheldon & Lyubomirsky, 2007) has been proposed as a key moderator of the effects of positive activities. Because there is individual heterogeneity in the types of activities that are optimal for enhancing well-being, identification of activities that fit an individual's personality is seen as crucial. The notion of person-activity fit is congruent with a model of positive gene-environment interplay—or cooperation between genetic dispositions and choice of activities. Optimal matchmaking could include both amplifying and compensatory processes. By amplifying, we mean active creation of positive gene-environment correlations in which activities provide opportunities to express talents and potentials. Compensatory processes might include identification and acceptance of vulnerabilities (e.g., anxieties, addictions, lack of impulse control) followed by activities for building experiences and competencies that either balance these vulnerabilities or lead them into functional pathways. Generally, our key point is that gene-environment interplay occurs naturally, that some variants of such interplay are highly beneficial for well-being, and that happiness intervention studies could benefit from explicitly addressing the notion of genetic and environmental matchmaking.

CONCLUSIONS

Our aim has been to review some recent findings from genetically informative studies and discuss their implications for the prospect of change in well-being. Based on the current knowledge, we believe it is fair to conclude the following:

- Well-being is both heritable and changeable.
- Behavior genetic findings also imply robust evidence of environmental causes of well-being.
- Genetic factors contribute primarily to stability in well-being; environmental factors predominantly contribute to short- and long-term change.
- Heritability estimates depend on environmental variation.
- Genetic factors appear to contribute to individual set points or set ranges. Yet, because genetic influences are conditional on the environment, set points might be changed by altering activities, exposures, life choices, and relations.
- Happiness results from a continuous interplay between genes and environments. Change theories and interventions might benefit from the notion of positive gene-environment interplay. Gene-environment matchmaking implies creating environments and activities that allow for flourishing of genetic potentials—and buffer against vulnerabilities.

Finally, modern well-being research has grown into a large scientific field including several subfields and specialties. Exciting progress is continuously reported. Whereas focus on the core issues within each subfield is necessary to continued progress, we also believe in the importance of building integrative frameworks. Our aim has been to try to show that findings of change-ability and heritability are not incongruent. On the contrary, models of change and models of heritability might jointly contribute to a new understanding of how happiness operates and evolves and to the development of optimal strategies for enhanced and sustained human well-being.

REFERENCES

Archontaki, D., Lewis, G. J., & Bates, T. C. (2013). Genetic influences on psychological well-being: a nationally representative twin study. *Journal of Personality, 81*(2), 221−230.

Ask, H., Idstad, M., Engdahl, B., & Tambs, K. (2013). Non-random mating and convergence over time for mental health, life satisfaction, and personality: The Nord-Trondelag health study. *Behavior Genetics, 43*(2), 108−119.

Ask, H., Rognmo, K., Torvik, F. A., Røysamb, E., & Tambs, K. (2012). Non-random mating and convergence over time for alcohol consumption, smoking, and exercise: The Nord-Trondelag Health Study. *Behavior Genetics, 42*(3), 354−365.

Bartels, M., & Boomsma, D. I. (2009). Born to be happy? The etiology of subjective well-being. *Behavior Genetics, 39*(6), 605−615.

Bartels, M., Cacioppo, J. T., van Beijsterveldt, T. C. E. M., & Boomsma, D. I. (2013). Exploring the association between well-being and psychopathology in adolescents. *Behavior Genetics, 43*(3), 177−190.

Bergin, J. E., Neale, M. C., Eaves, L. J., Martin, N. G., Heath, A. C., & Maes, H. H. (2012). Genetic and environmental transmission of body mass index fluctuation. *Behavior Genetics, 42*(6), 867−874.

Bolier, L., Haverman, M., Westerhof, G. J., Riper, H., Smit, F., & Bohlmeijer, E. (2013). Positive psychology interventions: A meta-analysis of randomized controlled studies. *BMC Public Health, 13*, 119.

Bouchard, T. J. (2004). Genetic influence on human psychological traits—A survey. *Current Directions in Psychological Science, 13*(4), 148−151.

Bradburn, N. M. (1969). *The structure of psychological well-being.* New York: Plenum.

Canli, T. (2004). Functional brain mapping of extraversion and neuroticism: Learning from individual differences in emotion processing. *Journal of Personality, 72*(6), 1105−1132.

Canli, T., & Lesch, K. P. (2007). Long story short: The serotonin transporter in emotion regulation and social cognition. *Nature Neuroscience, 10*(9), 1103−1109.

Cantril, H. (1965). *The pattern of human concerns* (4th ed.). Cambridge: Cambridge University Press.

Caprara, G. V., Fagnani, C., Alessandri, G., Steca, P., Gigantesco, A., Sforza, L. L. C., et al. (2009). Human optimal functioning: The genetics of positive orientation towards self, life, and the future. *Behavior Genetics, 39*(3), 277−284.

Caspi, A., McClay, J., Moffitt, T. E., Mill, J., Martin, J., Craig, I. W., et al. (2002). Role of genotype in the cycle of violence in maltreated children. *Science, 297*(5582), 851−854.

Caspi, A., & Moffitt, T. E. (2006). Gene-environment interactions in psychiatry: Joining forces with neuroscience. *Nature Reviews Neuroscience, 7*(7), 583−590.

Caspi, A., Moffitt, T. E., Cannon, M., McClay, J., Murray, R., Harrington, H., et al. (2005). Moderation of the effect of adolescent-onset cannabis use on adult psychosis by a functional polymorphism in the catechol-O-methyltransferase gene: Longitudinal evidence of a gene X environment interaction. *Biological Psychiatry, 57*(10), 1117−1127.

Caspi, A., Sugden, K., Moffitt, T. E., Taylor, A., Craig, I. W., Harrington, H., et al. (2003). Influence of life stress on depression: Moderation by a polymorphism in the 5−HTT gene. *Science, 301*(5631), 386−389.

Chen, F. F., Jing, Y., Hayes, A., & Lee, J. M. (2012). Two concepts or two approaches? A bifactor analysis of psychological and subjective well-being. *Journal of Happiness Studies, 14*(3), 1033−1068.

Crisp, R. (2005). Well-being. In E. N. Zalta (Ed.), *The Stanford encyclopedia of philosophy.* Available from http://plato.stanford.edu/archives/win2005/entries/well-being/.

David, S. A., Boniwell, I., & Conley Ayers, A. (2013). *The Oxford handbook of happiness.* New York, NY: Oxford University Press.

De Neve, J. E., Christakis, N. A., Fowler, J. H., & Frey, B. S. (2012). Genes, economics, and happiness. *Journal of Neuroscience, Psychology, and Economics, 5*, 4.

Diener, E., Emmons, R. A., Larsen, R. J., & Griffin, S. (1985). The Satisfaction with life scale. *Journal of Personality Assessment, 49*(1), 71–75.

Diener, E., Helliwell, J. F., & Kahneman, D. (2010). *International differences in well-being.* New York, NY: Oxford University Press.

Diener, E., Inglehart, R., & Tay, L. (2013). Theory and validity of life satisfaction scales. *Social Indicators Research, 112*(3), 497–527.

Diener, E., Lucas, R. E., & Scollon, C. N. (2006). Beyond the hedonic treadmill: Revising the adaptation theory of well-being. *American Psychologist, 61*(4), 305–314.

Diener, E., Tay, L., & Oishi, S. (2013). Rising income and the subjective well-being of nations. *Journal of Personality and Social Psychology, 104*(2), 267–276.

Dubois, L., Kyvik, K. O., Girard, M., Tatone-Tokuda, F., Perusse, D., Hjelmborg, J., et al. (2012). Genetic and environmental contributions to weight, height, and BMI from birth to 19 years of age: An international study of over 12,000 twin pairs. *Plos One, 7*(2), e30153.

Dufort, G. G., Kovess, V., & Boivin, J. F. (1994). Spouse similarity for psychological distress and well-being—a population study. *Psychological Medicine, 24*(2), 431–447.

Dyrdal, G. M., Røysamb, E., Nes, R. B., & Vittersø, J. (2011). Can a happy relationship predict a happy life? A population-based study of maternal well-being during the life transition of pregnancy, infancy, and toddlerhood. *Journal of Happiness Studies, 12*(6), 947–962.

Eid, M., & Diener, E. (2004). Global judgments of subjective well-being: Situational variability and long-term stability. *Social Indicators Research, 65*(3), 245–277.

Eid, M., Riemann, R., Angleitner, A., & Borkenau, P. (2003). Sociability and positive emotionality: Genetic and environmental contributions to the covariation between different facets of extraversion. *Journal of Personality, 71*(3), 319–346.

Fowler, J. H., & Christakis, N. A. (2008). Dynamic spread of happiness in a large social network: Longitudinal analysis over 20 years in the Framingham heart study. *British Medical Journal, 337*, a2338.

Franz, C. E., Panizzon, M. S., Eaves, L. J., Thompson, W., Lyons, M. J., Jacobson, K. C., et al. (2012). Genetic and environmental multidimensionality of well- and ill-being in middle aged twin men. *Behavior Genetics, 42*(4), 579–591.

Fujita, F., & Diener, E. (2005). Life satisfaction set point: Stability and change. *Journal of Personality and Social Psychology, 88*(1), 158–164.

Gigantesco, A., Stazi, M. A., Alessandri, G., Medda, E., Tarolla, E., & Fagnani, C. (2011). Psychological well-being (PWB): A natural life outlook? An Italian twin study on heritability of PWB in young adults. *Psychological Medicine, 41*(12), 2637–2649.

Harris, J. R., Magnus, P., & Tambs, K. (2006). The Norwegian Institute of Public Health twin program of research: An update. *Twin Research and Human Genetics, 9*(6), 858–864.

Headey, B. (2013). Set-point theory may now need replacing: Death of a paradigm? In D. Boniwell, & C. Ayers (Eds.), *The Oxford handbook of happiness* (pp. 887–900). New York, NY: Oxford University Press.

Headey, B., Muffels, R., & Wagner, G. G. (2010). Long-running German panel survey shows that personal and economic choices, not just genes, matter for happiness. *Proceedings of the National Academy of Sciences of the United States of America, 107*(42), 17922–17926.

Johnson, W., & Krueger, R. F. (2006). How money buys happiness: Genetic and environmental processes linking finances and life satisfaction. *Journal of Personality and Social Psychology, 90*(4), 680–691.

Johnson, W., McGue, M., & Krueger, R. F. (2005). Personality stability in late adulthood: A behavioral genetic analysis. *Journal of Personality, 73*(2), 523–552.

Kendler, K. S., & Karkowski-Shuman, L. (1997). Stressful life events and genetic liability to major depression: Genetic control of exposure to the environment. *Psychological Medicine, 27*(3), 539–547.

Kendler, K. S., Myers, J. M., & Keyes, C. L. M. (2011). The relationship between the genetic and environmental influences on common externalizing psychopathology and mental wellbeing. *Twin Research and Human Genetics, 14*(6), 516–523.

Kendler, K. S., Myers, J. M., Maes, H. H., & Keyes, C. L. M. (2011). The relationship between the genetic and environmental influences on common internalizing psychiatric disorders and mental well-being. *Behavior Genetics, 41*(5), 641–650.

Kessler, R. C., Berglund, P., Demler, O., Jin, R., Merikangas, K. R., & Walters, E. E. (2005). Lifetime prevalence and age-of-onset distributions of DSM-IV disorders in the national comorbidity survey replication. *Archives of General Psychiatry, 62*(6), 593–602.

Kessler, R. C., Petukhova, M., Sampson, N. A., Zaslavsky, A. M., & Wittchen, H. -U. (2012). Twelve-month and lifetime prevalence and lifetime morbid risk of anxiety and mood disorders in the United States. *International Journal of Methods in Psychiatric Research, 21*(3), 169–184.

Keyes, C. L. M. (2013). Promotion and protection of positive mental health: Towards complete mental health in human development. In D. Boniwell, & C. Ayers (Eds.), *The Oxford handbook of happiness* (pp. 915–925). New York, NY: Oxford University Press.

Keyes, C. L. M., Myers, J. M., & Kendler, K. S. (2010). The structure of the genetic and environmental influences on mental well-being. *American Journal of Public Health, 100*(12), 2379–2384.

King, J. E., & Landau, V. I. (2003). Can chimpanzee (*Pan troglodytes*) happiness be estimated by human raters? *Journal of Research in Personality, 37*(1), 1–15.

Krueger, R. F., South, S., Johnson, W., & Iacono, W. (2008). The heritability of personality is not always 50%: Gene-environment interactions and correlations between personality and parenting. *Journal of Personality, 76*(6), 1485–1522.

Lucas, R. E. (2007). Adaptation and the set-point model of subjective well-being: Does happiness change after major life events? *Current Directions in Psychological Science, 16*(2), 75–79.

Lucas, R. E., Clark, A. E., Georgellis, Y., & Diener, E. (2004). Unemployment alters the set point for life satisfaction. *Psychological Science, 15*(1), 8–13.

Lucas, R. E., & Diener, E. (2008). Personality and subjective well-being. In O. P. John, R. W. Robins, & L. A. Pervin (Eds.), *Handbook of personality: Theory and research* (3rd ed., pp. 795–814). New York, NY: Guilford Press.

Lucas, R. E., & Donnellan, M. B. (2007). How stable is happiness? Using the STARTS model to estimate the stability of life satisfaction. *Journal of Research in Personality, 41*(5), 1091–1098.

Luhmann, M., Hofmann, W., Eid, M., & Lucas, R. E. (2012). Subjective well-being and adaptation to life events: A meta-analysis. *Journal of Personality and Social Psychology, 102*(3), 592–615.

Lykken, D. (1999). *Happiness: What studies on twins show us about nature, nurture, and the happiness set-point.* New York, NY: Golden Books.

Lykken, D., & Tellegen, A. (1996). Happiness is a stochastic phenomenon. *Psychological Science, 7*(3), 186–189.

Lyubomirsky, S., & Layous, K. (2013). How do simple positive activities increase well-being? *Current Directions in Psychological Science, 22*(1), 57−62.

Lyubomirsky, S., & Lepper, H. S. (1999). A measure of subjective happiness: Preliminary reliability and construct validation. *Social Indicators Research, 46*(2), 137−155.

Lyubomirsky, S., Sheldon, K. M., & Schkade, D. (2005). Pursuing happiness: The architecture of sustainable change. *Review of General Psychology, 9*(2), 111−131.

Matteson, L. K., McGue, M. K., & Iacono, W. (2013). Is dispositional happiness contagious? The impact of the well-being of family members on individual well-being. *Journal of Individual Differences, 34*(2), 90−96.

McGue, M. (1993). From proteins to cognitions: The behavioral genetics of alcoholism. In R. Plomin, & G. E. McClearn (Eds.), *Nature, nurture & psychology* (pp. 245−268). Washington, DC: American Psychological Association.

McGue, M. (2010). The end of behavioral genetics? *Behavior Genetics, 40*(3), 284−296.

McGue, M., Bacon, S., & Lykken, D. T. (1993). Personality stability and change in early adulthood: A behavioral genetic analysis. *Developmental Psychology, 29*(1), 96−109.

Menne-Lothmann, C., Jacobs, N., Derom, C., Thiery, E., van Os, J., & Wichers, M. (2012). Genetic and environmental causes of individual differences in daily life positive affect and reward experience and its overlap with stress-sensitivity. *Behavior Genetics, 42*(5) 778−786.

Merikangas, K. R. (1982). Assortative mating for psychiatric disorders and psychological traits. *Archives of General Psychiatry, 39*(10), 1173−1180.

Moffitt, T. E., Caspi, A., & Rutter, M. (2006). Measured gene-environment interactions in psychopathology. Concepts, research strategies, and implications for research, intervention, and public understanding of genetics. *Perspectives on Psychological Science, 1*(1), 5−27.

Mosing, M. A., Pedersen, N. L., Cesarini, D., Johannesson, M., Magnusson, P. K. E., Nakamura, J., et al. (2012). Genetic and environmental influences on the relationship between flow proneness, locus of control and behavioral inhibition. *Plos One, 7*(11), e47958.

Mosing, M. A., Zietsch, B. P., Shekar, S. N., Wright, M. J., & Martin, N. G. (2009). Genetic and environmental influences on optimism and its relationship to mental and self-rated health: A study of aging twins. *Behavior Genetics, 39*(6), 597−604.

Moum, T., Naess, S., Sorensen, T., Tambs, K., & Holmen, J. (1990). Hypertension labeling, life events and psychological well-being. *Psychological Medicine, 20*(3), 635−646.

Mroczek, D. K., & Kolarz, C. M. (1998). The effect of age on positive and negative affect: A developmental perspective on happiness. *Journal of Personality and Social Psychology, 75*(5), 1333−1349.

Nes, R., Czajkowski, N., Røysamb, E., Reichborn-Kjennerud, T., & Tambs, K. (2008). Well-being and ill-being: Shared environments, shared genes? *Journal of Positive Psychology, 3* (4), 253−265.

Nes, R. B. (2010). Happiness in behaviour genetics: Findings and implications. *Journal of Happiness Studies, 11*(3), 369−381.

Nes, R. B., Czajkowski, N., & Tambs, K. (2010). Family matters: Happiness in nuclear families and twins. *Behavior Genetics, 40*(5), 577−590.

Nes, R. B., Czajkowski, N. O., Røysamb, E., Orstavik, R. E., Tambs, K., & Reichborn-Kjennerud, T. (2013). Major depression and life satisfaction: A population-based twin study. *Journal of Affective Disorders, 144*(1−2), 51−58.

Nes, R. B., Røysamb, E., Harris, J. R., Czajkowski, N., & Tambs, K. (2010). Mates and marriage matter: Genetic and environmental influences on subjective well-being across marital status. *Twin Research and Human Genetics, 13*(4), 312−321.

Nes, R. B., Røysamb, E., Reichborn-Kjennerud, T., Tambs, K., & Harris, J. R. (2005). Subjective wellbeing and sleep problems: A bivariate twin study. *Twin Research and Human Genetics*, *8*(5), 440−449.

Nes, R. B., Røysamb, E., Tambs, K., Harris, J. R., & Reichborn-Kjennerud, T. (2006). Subjective well-being: Genetic and environmental contributions to stability and change. *Psychological Medicine*, *36*(7), 1033−1042.

Nieuwsma, J. A., Trivedi, R. B., McDuffie, J., Kronish, I., Benjamin, D., & Williams, J. W. (2012). Brief psychotherapy for depression: A systematic review and meta-analysis. *International Journal of Psychiatry in Medicine*, *43*(2), 129−151.

Nilsen, T. S., Knudsen, G. P., Gervin, K., Brandt, I., Røysamb, E., Tambs, K., et al. (2013). The Norwegian Twin Registry from a public health perspective: A research update. *Twin Research and Human Genetics*, *16*(1), 285−295.

Pedersen, N. L., & Reynolds, C. A. (1998). Stability and change in adult personality: Genetic and environmental components. *European Journal of Personality*, *12*(5), 365−386.

Peterson, C., & Seligman, M. E. P. (2003). Character strengths before and after September 11. *Psychological Science*, *14*(4), 381−384.

Petronis, A. (2010). Epigenetics as a unifying principle in the aetiology of complex traits and diseases. *Nature*, *465*(7299), 721−727.

Plomin, R. (1986). *Development, genetics, and psychology*. Hillsdale, NJ: Lawrence Erlbaum Associates, Inc.

Plomin, R., DeFries, J. C., Craig, I. W., & McGuffin, P. (2003). *Behavioral genetics in the post-genomic era*. Washington, DC: American Psychological Association.

Plomin, R., Scheier, M. F., Bergeman, C., Pedersen, N. L., Nesselroade, J., & McClearn, G. (1992). Optimism, pessimism and mental health: A twin/adoption analysis. *Personality and Individual Differences*, *13*(8), 921−930.

Pluess, M., & Belsky, J. (2013). Vantage sensitivity: Individual differences in response to positive experiences. *Psychological Bulletin*, *139*(4), 901−916.

Richardson, K., & Norgate, S. (2005). The equal environments assumption of classical twin studies may not hold. *British Journal of Educational Psychology*, *75*, 339−350.

Riemann, R., Angleitner, A., Borkenau, P., & Eid, M. (1998). Genetic and environmental sources of consistency and variability in positive and negative mood. *European Journal of Personality*, *12*(5), 345−364.

Røysamb, E., Harris, J. R., Magnus, P., Vittersø, J., & Tambs, K. (2002). Subjective well-being: Sex-specific effects of genetic and environmental factors. *Personality and Individual Differences*, *32*(2), 211−223.

Røysamb, E., Tambs, K., Reichborn-Kjennerud, T., Neale, M. C., & Harris, J. R. (2003). Happiness and health: Environmental and genetic contributions to the relationship between subjective well-being, perceived health, and somatic illness. *Journal of Personality and Social Psychology*, *85*(6), 1136−1146.

Rutter, M., Moffitt, T. E., & Caspi, A. (2006). Gene-environment interplay and psychopathology: Multiple varieties but real effects. *Journal of Child Psychology and Psychiatry*, *47* (3−4), 226−261.

Ryff, C. D., & Keyes, C. L. M. (1995). The structure of psychological well-being revisited. *Journal of Personality and Social Psychology*, *69*(4), 719−727.

Sadler, M., Miller, C., McGue, M., & Christensen, K. (2009). Longevity and subjective well-being: A cotwin control study. *Behavior Genetics*, *39*(6), 678.

Scarr, S., & Weinberg, R. A. (1983). The Minnesota adoption studies: Genetic differences and malleability. *Child Development*, *54*(2), 260−267.

Schimmack, U., Krause, P., Wagner, G. G., & Schupp, J. (2010). Stability and change of well being: An experimentally enhanced latent state-trait-error analysis. *Social Indicators Research*, 95(1), 19–31.

Schnittker, J. (2008). Happiness and success: Genes, families, and the psychological effects of socioeconomic position and social support. *American Journal of Sociology*, 114, S233–S259.

Seligman, M. E. P., Steen, T. A., Park, N., & Peterson, C. (2005). Positive psychology progress: Empirical validation of interventions. *American Psychologist*, 60(5), 410–421.

Sheldon, K. M., & Lyubomirsky, S. (2007). Is it possible to become happier? (And if so, how?). *Social and Personality Psychology Compass*, 1(1), 129–145.

Sheldon, K. M., & Lyubomirsky, S. (2012). The challenge of staying happier: Testing the hedonic adaptation prevention model. *Personality and Social Psychology Bulletin*, 38(5), 670–680.

Sin, N. L., & Lyubomirsky, S. (2009). Enhancing well-being and alleviating depressive symptoms with positive psychology interventions: A practice-friendly meta-analysis. *Journal of Clinical Psychology*, 65(5), 467–487.

Steger, M. F., Hicks, B. M., Kashdan, T. B., Krueger, R. F., & Bouchard, T. J., Jr. (2007). Genetic and environmental influences on the positive traits of the values in action classification, and biometric covariance with normal personality. *Journal of Research in Personality*, 41(3), 524–539.

Stubbe, J. H., Posthuma, D., Boomsma, D. I., & De Geus, E. J. C. (2005). Heritability of life satisfaction in adults: A twin-family study. *Psychological Medicine*, 35(11), 1581–1588.

Tellegen, A. (1982). *Brief manual for the multidimensional personality questionnaire*. Minneapolis: University of Minnesota.

Tellegen, A., Lykken, D. T., Bouchard, T. J., Wilcox, K. J., Rich, S., & Segal, N. L. (1988). Personality similarity in twins reared apart and together. *Journal of Personality and Social Psychology*, 54(6), 1031–1039.

Tsankova, N., Renthal, W., Kumar, A., & Nestler, E. J. (2007). Epigenetic regulation in psychiatric disorders. *Nature Reviews Neuroscience*, 8(5), 355–367.

Turkheimer, E. (2000). Three laws of behavior genetics and what they mean. *Current Directions in Psychological Science*, 9(5), 160–164.

Ullen, F., de Manzano, O., Almeida, R., Magnusson, P. K. E., Pedersen, N. L., Nakamura, J., & Madison, G. (2012). Proneness for psychological flow in everyday life: Associations with personality and intelligence. *Personality and Individual Differences*, 52(2), 167–172.

Veenhoven, R. (2009). Well-being in nations and well-being of nations: Is there a conflict between individual and society? *Social Indicators Research*, 91(1), 5–21.

Vittersø, J., Røysamb, E., & Diener, E. (2002). The concept of life satisfaction across cultures: Exploring its diverse meaning and relation to economic wealth. In E. Gullone, & R. Cummins (Eds.), *Social indicators research book series: The universality of quality of life constructs*. Dordrecht: Kluwer Academic Publishers, pp. 81–103.

Vittersø, J., & Soholt, Y. (2011). Life satisfaction goes with pleasure and personal growth goes with interest: Further arguments for separating hedonic and eudaimonic well-being. *Journal of Positive Psychology*, 6(4), 326–335.

Waaktaar, T., & Torgersen, S. (2012). Genetic and environmental causes of variation in trait resilience in young people. *Behavior Genetics*, 42(3), 366–377.

Weisz, J. R., Weiss, B., Han, S. S., Granger, D. A., & Morton, T. (1995). Effects of psychotherapy with children and adolescents revisited: A meta-analysis of treatment outcome studies. *Psychological Bulletin*, 117(3), 450–468.

Chapter 3

Symptoms of Wellness: Happiness and Eudaimonia from a Self-Determination Perspective

Cody R. DeHaan and Richard M. Ryan

University of Rochester, Rochester, NY, USA

The rise of positive psychology has reawakened some age-old questions about happiness and well-being: What is happiness? How can we attain it? How can we maintain it once we have it? Religion, philosophy, psychology, economics, and many other fields have all grappled with these questions about the nature and causes of happiness. Yet solutions to attaining and maintaining happiness remain matters of active scholarly debate.

One reason there is such active inquiry and research in happiness is the fact that many researchers and theorists have increased the status of happiness. Some have equated happiness with psychological wellness (e.g., Kahneman, 1999); in fact, for some theorists happiness is viewed as "the people's choice" of a wellness variable, both because it is part of the common parlance and understanding, and additionally because it supplies an atheoretical route to discovering what constitutes "the good life" (see Kashdan, Biswas-Diener, & King, 2008). Others have suggested that happiness and positive emotions are central catalysts of human learning and growth (e.g., Fredrickson, 2004). With such importance placed on happiness, it is no wonder that the concept has become both more studied and more scrutinized.

THE STABILITY OF HAPPINESS

If the questions of happiness's functional importance aren't weighty enough, there are additional wrinkles in the conundrum of happiness. One such wrinkle is evidence that people have characteristic set points (Sheldon & Lyubomirsky, 2004) and characteristic styles of appraising happiness and distress (e.g., Weinstein, Brown, & Ryan, 2009). Considerable research indicates that happiness, when assessed in a global way, is relatively stable across the life span. Evidence also suggests substantial heritability of happiness and subjective well-being (e.g., Bartels et al., 2010; Rietveld et al., 2013), although different aspects of happiness and well-being may be differently heritable. For example, Franz et al. (2012) reported that psychological well-being is more heritable than life satisfaction. Nonetheless, the very consistency in how people answer questions about, or experience, general happiness, whether due to genes or stable response sets, raises concerns.

Researchers investigating set points and the stability of happiness have applied varied conceptualizations to the problem, including the concepts of *hedonic adaptation* (Frederick & Loewenstein, 1999) and *hedonic treadmill* (Brickman & Campbell, 1971; Diener, Lucas, & Scollon, 2006). Hedonic adaptation describes adaptation to affectively relevant stimuli—the attenuation of the felt emotions around a change in consequences. Hedonic adaptation allows us to reduce the impact of steady or continuous affective inputs, as well as to be more sensitive of changes around these baselines (Frederick & Loewenstein, 1999). In other words, these ideas propose that humans eventually return to a normative level of happiness after any event moves them away (in either direction) from that level. For example, an increase may bring some immediate additional happiness, but these effects will quickly fade as expectations adjust, bringing happiness back to a baseline. These depictions of happiness have implicit in them assumptions leading to the treadmill metaphor, including that happiness has long-term stability, that this stability is in part genetically influenced, and that life changes that bring about increased happiness do so only briefly, as individuals will quickly habituate to change. Yet, this set of rather widely accepted ideas paints a troubling portrait for anyone who hopes to enhance happiness, with many processes serving to dampen or minimize the perceived impact of potentially positive influences.

Attempting to more clearly define factors that contribute to a person's level of happiness, Sheldon and Lyubomirsky (2004) specified three main factors. The first component is a genetically determined *set point* that determines how happy someone will be when other factors are neutral. The second component is the *circumstances of the individual's life*, or the relatively static or stable (though not necessarily entirely unchangeable) elements of life including factors such as demographics, sex, age, race, and physical location. The third and final component is made up of *intentional activities* that one engages with, including engaging in certain activities or approaching life situations with a given outlook. In a set of three studies, Sheldon and Lyubomirsky (2006) followed college participants over a semester, and assessed changes in both circumstances (e.g., a change in living situation) as well as in activities (e.g., joining a new club). In these studies, increases in happiness at the midpoint of the semester were associated with both positive changes in circumstances and activities, whereas at the end of the semester, only increases due to changes in activities remained. Sheldon and Lyubomirsky suggest that, while relatively stable and slow-to-change forces (e.g., set points and life circumstances) play an important role in happiness, individuals also exert leverage through their intentional activities and pursuits: To some extent, people can seize responsibility for their own happiness.

Variability Amidst Stability

In summarizing this recent research on happiness, we note that it highlights the stability, and slow-to-change nature, of overall happiness. Yet most of us probably have a different experience of happiness. What is most accessible and phenomenally salient to most individuals is not the stability of our happiness, but rather the variability and fluctuations in happiness that we experience. In certain types of contexts, we feel happy, and in other types of contexts, we feel unhappy or perhaps even perturbed. Supporting this view is a large body of experience-sampling and diary-based methods, which attest not only to a high degree of variability in happiness within persons, but also the fact that this within-person variability is predictable (Brown & Ryan, 2003; Brown, Ryan, & Creswell, 2007). Because of this predictable variation in happiness, any understanding of happiness must account for both of these aspects, that is, for both the overall stability of individual differences in happiness, as well as the considerable variability of moment-to-moment assessments.

The Significance of Happiness

In sum, questions of happiness predominate today's positive psychology, in part because happiness has been implicated in (and by some equated with) growth and wellness; because happiness appears to have both genetic and experience-dependent determinants; because happiness so saliently varies from moment to moment within this overall stability; and because there is debate about what type of happiness-related actions, if any, foster wellness.

In this chapter we discuss these questions about happiness through the lens of *Self-Determination Theory* (SDT; Deci & Ryan, 2000; Ryan & Deci, 2000). SDT is an empirically driven, contemporary theory that directly speaks to all these issues, seeing happiness (i.e., positive affect) as an organismic signal that fluctuates strongly with need-supportive and need-thwarting contexts. Yet given its signal function, SDT does not view happiness as an end in itself, but rather as an informational input to fuller functioning. That is, SDT does not posit happiness as an organismic ideal—rather the ideal within SDT is a fully functioning, mentally well individual. Wellness in SDT's view is about being authentically in touch with one's surroundings and inward states, experiencing congruency rather than merely positive affect, and being able to use emotional inputs to volitionally regulate reactions and subsequent behavior. At the same time, SDT predicts that certain activities and lifestyles, particularly those associated with eudaimonic living, supply the most reliable paths to happiness and positive affect, and further suggests that not all culturally rewarded or valued endeavors can accomplish that aim. In what follows we detail these formulations and their relevance to happiness.

SELF-DETERMINATION THEORY

SDT is a broad theory of human growth, integrity, and wellness that views humans as inherently oriented toward mastering their environment and integrating new experiences into the self (Ryan & Deci, 2000). Yet these integrative and growth-oriented processes do not occur in all situations; these processes are either fostered or undermined by specifiable conditions. The social world can either support growth and integration leading to positive outcomes and wellness, or it can fail to support (or even actively thwart) them, and instead cause defense, suffering, and ill-being (Vansteenkiste & Ryan, 2013). The characteristics of social contexts upon which outcomes hinge have, accordingly, been shown to be those that support three *basic psychological needs* (see Deci & Ryan, 2000).

Within SDT, basic psychological needs are not defined as merely subjective preferences, but rather as nutriments essential to psychological growth, wellness, and integrity (Ryan, 1995). Given this constrained definition, SDT has identified only three such needs. The first, the need for *autonomy*, refers to the need to experience behavior as self-endorsed and volitional. Autonomy is afforded when people feel choice and voice in behaving, and is diminished when they experience behavior as driven by pressures, external rewards, or coercion. Relatedness is the need to feel connected and significant to others. Relatedness is enhanced when one cares for or is cared for by others, and is diminished by social exclusion or disconnection. *Competence* refers to capability and effectiveness with the important activities one engages in life. The need for competence concerns feeling confident and effective in one's actions, and this need is supported by well-structured contexts that afford positive feedback and mastery experiences. Each of these three needs has been shown to be necessary for psychological wellness in people regardless of culture, age, gender, or other socioeconomic factors. Whenever these needs are fulfilled, people flourish; when they are frustrated, wellness wanes. As an example, Chirkov, Ryan, Kim, and Kaplan (2003) showed that basic need satisfaction was critical in predicting wellness across countries as varied as South Korea, Russia, Turkey, and the United States. Similarly, using measures of psychological needs reflective of SDT's basic needs, Diener, Ng, Harter, and Arora (2010) showed that basic psychological need satisfactions were among the strongest predictors of positive affect across the globe.

The Self-Determination Theory Approach to Happiness and Wellness

SDT's approach to wellness grows out of its roots in organismic theorizing, in which wellness is defined in terms of full and integrated functioning (Deci & Ryan, 1985; Ryan, 1995). Full functioning would be defined in terms of persons being able to volitionally regulate and fully experience their activities, and pursue what is intrinsically valuable to them. Thus, wellness is not a content of living, but rather defined by a process of open awareness and integrative self-regulation (Ryan, Deci, Gronick, & La Guardia, 2006).

Within SDT, happiness is considered a variable of importance in its own right. Clearly, people value happy states, and states of positive affect are associated with high-quality motivation and functioning, including the state of intrinsic motivation (Deci & Ryan, 2000; Huta & Ryan, 2010). At the same time, within SDT, a strong distinction is made between happiness, understood as the presence of positive affect and absence of negative affect (Kahneman, 1999), and wellness, understood as full, integrative functioning (Ryan, Huta, & Deci, 2008).

As we have pointed out in numerous places, when a person is psychologically well, there is coherence and congruence to his or her functioning, and this congruence is associated with deep satisfactions of basic psychological needs. Integration in action is thus often associated with high levels of happiness because full, healthy functioning is adaptive and inherently satisfying. Happiness so defined is, in this respect, an excellent *symptom* of wellness (Niemiec & Ryan, 2013; Ryan & Huta, 2009), as generally happiness is an important indicator of healthy functioning. Yet importantly, autonomous or congruent actions are not always positively toned. Within the SDT conceptualization of wellness, in the face of certain events, such as the death of a loved one, one would be considered more fully functioning and well if he or she could experience negative feelings (such as grief, loss, and sadness) instead of ignoring them or reframing the event as "positive" (Ryan & Deci, 2001). Similarly, being aware of stressors and perturbation is an important element in informed choices and self-regulation. Indeed, within SDT, full functioning involves an open receptivity to emotions, even when one chooses not to act on them.

In addition, there are some pursuits and mental states in which positive affect and wellness are disconnected. For example, in certain phases of bipolar disorders, pervasive positive affect can be a symptom of illness rather than wellness. In other contexts, positive affect is associated with gratifications that can be harmful, as in drug and gambling addictions, or certain narcissistic disorders. Finally, small boosts in positive affect may support behaviors such as consumerism, compulsions, or materialism that do not have a long-term wellness yield, as we discuss. In these and other ways, one should not make the mistake of identifying happiness and wellness, even while appreciating their typically robust association within any given sample.

SDT and the Eudaimonic Tradition

SDT's focus on full functioning has linked it with eudaimonic thinking, a tradition that also distinguishes mere happiness from living well. The concept of eudaimonia has its roots in Aristotelian philosophy (Ryan & Deci, 2001; Waterman, 2012), and deals with the content and process of a life well lived (Ryan, Curren, & Deci, 2012). Specifically, the eudaimonic perspective on well-being does not focus on a particular outcome in the way that the hedonic perspective focuses on happiness, but instead concerns the prescriptions for living a complete human life that will achieve valued human potentials (Ryan, Huta, & Deci, 2008). Within this perspective, happiness is not interchangeable with wellness, nor is happiness the focus or aim of living well. Yet happiness is expected as a probable outcome when one lives a eudaimonic lifestyle. Conversely, in SDT's view, shallow or inauthentic pursuits (e.g., those that don't reflect intrinsic values) may bring about temporary pleasure or happiness but do not sustain wellness. At the same time, SDT recognizes happiness as a symptom of wellness because the presence of happiness is often indicative of need-satisfying, authentic, eudaimonic living.

Emotions and Wellness in SDT

SDT has a specific view on the function of emotions, including those associated with happiness within healthy self-regulation. Theoretically, emotions serve an *informational function* (Ryan et al., 2006), providing information about whether one is "on track," so to speak, in regards to the satisfaction of the basic psychological needs. That is, when people satisfy needs for autonomy, competence, and relatedness, they typically show a rise in positive emotions and a decrease in negative ones. Interestingly, such effects are apparent in both moment-to-moment experience sampling research (e.g., Ryan, Bernstein, & Brown, 2010) and in general survey findings (e.g., Chirkov et al., 2003). However, such emotions are not infallible indicators because they can be triggered and influenced in many ways, sometimes in activities that are not related to basic need satisfactions (Vansteenkiste & Ryan, 2013).

Indeed, considerable research within SDT has shown the relations between basic psychological need satisfaction and multiple indicators of well-being, including positive affect, at both between-person and within-person levels of analysis. In one early study, Sheldon, Ryan, and Reis (1996) demonstrated the role of both stable trait levels of autonomy and competence, as well as the fluctuating daily levels of those same traits, in predicting positive affect, lack of negative affect, vitality, and lack of physical symptoms. On days that participants experienced greater satisfaction of needs for autonomy and competence, they showed enhanced outcomes. Yet, independent of these daily affects, people who had more need satisfaction also displayed greater well-being on average. Reis, Sheldon, Gable, Roscoe, and Ryan (2000), in later work, measured all three needs, and results showed that satisfactions for autonomy, competence, and relatedness, both on average and daily levels, were all important for outcomes, including indicators of happiness.

Ryan, Bernstein, and Brown (2010) extended this research to adult workers. This work focused on the "weekend effect," or the uplifting effects that weekends seem to have. This idea of the weekends having a positive effect was supported by the data—on weekends, people experienced more positive affect, less negative affect, greater vitality, and fewer physical symptoms. In addition, these effects were found across gender, as well as across varying trait levels of well-being. These effects were also found when contrasting work-related and non-work-related activities: People experienced more positive mood and increased vitality with non-work-related activities. In both of these models, the role of the basic psychological needs as mediators for the relations of weekday/weekend and work-related/non-work-related activities on outcomes was tested. The boost provided by weekends was largely mediated by autonomy and relatedness; for most workers, both of these need satisfactions were lower on weekdays, leading to less positive outcomes. When work-related and non-work-related activities were compared, autonomy, relatedness, and competence fully mediated the relations between activities and outcomes. This study thus provides compelling evidence for the role of social contexts, in this case experiences at work, in supporting the satisfaction of basic psychological needs, and highlighting how need satisfaction predicts both within-person as well as between-person indicators of happiness and well-being.

Recent work by Howell and colleagues has highlighted the strong link between even momentary need satisfaction and well-being (Howell, Chenot, Hill, & Howell, 2011). They reported two studies: one in which participants completed hourly diaries of basic psychological need satisfaction and well-being (assessed with measures of happiness, enjoyment, and lack of stress), and another in which participants recalled their hourly need satisfaction and well-being for the preceding 18 hours. On average, hourly increases in autonomy and relatedness were associated with increased happiness and enjoyment and decreased stress. In addition, daily need satisfaction showed a similar pattern of results, with increased autonomy and relatedness being associated with greater happiness and enjoyment and decreased stress. Importantly, daily satisfaction of all three needs was positively associated with overall life satisfaction. A further analysis showed that life satisfaction moderated the relation between momentary autonomy and relatedness and momentary happiness, with those showing greater life satisfaction at the trait level having a stronger link between need satisfaction and happiness. This work provides support for the association between need satisfaction and well-being outcomes, but highlights the importance of eudaimonic factors.

Need frustration. Beyond considerations of basic psychological *need satisfaction*, recent research has been seeking greater understanding of the role of basic psychological *need frustration.* Previously it was implicitly assumed that the experience of satisfaction of needs being actively thwarted was one endpoint of a single continuum, with the other endpoint being need satisfaction, and lack of need satisfaction being somewhere in between. Yet, recent research highlights that need frustration could be measured uniquely. In a series of studies on athletes, the unique associations among need satisfaction, need frustration, and various outcomes were assessed, including positive and negative affect during sports activities (Bartholomew, Ntoumanis, Ryan, Bosch, & Thøgersen-Ntoumani, 2011). Autonomy support received from coaches led to increased need satisfaction, which in turn was strongly related to greater vitality and positive affect. Controlling coaches, on the other hand, led to increased need frustration, which in turn was strongly related to more negative affect, and in some samples more depression and more disordered eating. In a second study, autonomy support from coaches was again related to greater need satisfaction, but in this case greater need satisfaction was related to greater positive affect, decreased negative affect, and lower burnout; greater need frustration was associated only with more negative affect and more burnout. A third study replicated these results longitudinally, again showing that coaches' autonomy support was most predictive of athletes' need satisfaction, which in turn was most predictive of positive affect, whereas coaches' control was most predictive of athletes' need frustration, which in turn was most predictive of negative affect and physical symptoms. This set of studies seems to suggest that autonomy support leads most strongly to need satisfaction, which in turn is most highly related to positive outcomes, whereas controlling environments lead most strongly to need frustration, which in turn yields negative outcomes.

MOTIVATIONAL CONSIDERATIONS

SDT suggests that all motivated behaviors can be classified along a continuum from motivations or behavioral regulations that are more *autonomous* and integrated to the self, to those that are more *controlled* or experienced as external to the self. There are five points along the continuum of motivated behaviors, the first four of which are extrinsically motivated. *External regulation* is the least autonomous of these, and indicates behaviors that are enacted purely to gain externally controlled rewards or avoid punishments. *Introjected regulation* represents an external regulation that's been partially internalized, meaning that the external contingencies are no longer present, but taking their place is a framework of contingent self-worth and shame- or guilt-avoidance that is present within the individual. A major form of introjected regulation is represented by *ego involvement* (Ryan, 1982), in which a person's behavior is driven by self-esteem-related concerns. *Identified regulation* is yet more autonomous, characterizing actions that are engaged because they are consciously valued and endorsed, but not necessarily integrated with the larger ecosystem of values and beliefs within an individual. The final type of extrinsic regulation is *integrated regulation*, which describes behaviors that are brought into cohesion, or reciprocally assimilated, with the individual's other values and beliefs. Integrated regulation is still extrinsically motivated, in that the intent is to attain outcomes independent of the satisfactions inherent in acting, but it is nonetheless highly volitional and autonomous, being whole-heartedly endorsed by the individual. The fifth type of motivation, *intrinsic motivation*, entails behaving because of the activity's inherent enjoyment and satisfactions. It is this criterion that separates intrinsically motivated behaviors from those that are extrinsically motivated.

Because SDT is focused on the content of life leading to wellness, it thus follows that engaging in behaviors, identities, vocations, and avocations autonomously, rather than heteronomously, is expected to lead to greater basic psychological need satisfaction, and thus consequent well-being and happiness. Indeed, autonomous motivation has been linked to many positive outcomes. For example, motivation at work has been identified as an important predictor of outcomes. Ilardi, Leone, Kasser, and Ryan (1993) examined the role of motivation in the workplace on employees' satisfaction with work and general well-being. To the extent that employees were autonomously motivated, they evidenced greater need satisfaction, greater satisfaction with work, and higher well-being, findings that have since been widely replicated (Gagné, Deci, & Ryan, 2013; Van den Broeck, Lens, De Witte, & Coillie, 2013).

In line with a eudaimonic perspective, when people direct their autonomous activities toward meaningful and valued endeavors, they especially derive basic need satisfactions. For example, in a set of studies, Weinstein and Ryan (2010) examined the role of helpers' autonomous motivation in fostering both their own and recipients' well-being and positive experience. An initial diary method assessed individuals' engagement in prosocial behavior. On average, helping others was related to small increases in subjective well-being, vitality, and self-esteem. However, when proscocial behavior was autonomously motivated, these outcomes were significantly enhanced. In addition, the three basic psychological needs were shown to mediate between autonomous helping and these enhanced well-being outcomes. Another study provided an experimental analogue, showing that participants given a choice to donate to others experienced more positive affect and vitality than those instructed to do so. Once again, the three basic psychological needs mediated the relation between autonomous helping and changes in well-being. Additional experiments in this series showed further that only when helping was enacted autonomously did recipients of help show well-being benefits. That is, when recipients felt they were being willingly helped, both their wellness and that of the helper were enhanced. It seems clear that in the realm of prosocial behavior, motivation and need satisfaction are critical predictors in the happiness and well-being experienced during these activities.

AWARENESS AND AUTONOMOUS REGULATION: THE ROLE OF MINDFULNESS

Mindfulness is defined as an open and receptive awareness and attention, or a quality of consciousness, characterized by a clear awareness of the present moment (Brown & Ryan, 2003). When engaging with life in a mindful way, one is fully attending to and aware of what is going on for himself or herself at any given moment, but is not overwhelmed by or subjected to those experiences or immediately judging of or reactive to them. Although mindfulness has its roots in Buddhism and other related traditions, it has been increasing in popularity within psychological research.

In developing a scale to measure mindfulness, Brown and Ryan (2003) used a theoretically grounded and empirically based factor analytic approach to create the *Mindful Attention Awareness Scale* (MAAS). This scale measures mindfulness in everyday life, independent of attitude, motivational intent, and common outcomes, leaving items such as "I could be experiencing some emotion and not be conscious of it until some time later," and "I rush through activities without being really attentive to them" (reverse scored). In varied samples, mindfulness was positively related to openness to experience and awareness of internal states, and negatively related to social anxiety and rumination, among other relevant constructs. Data also revealed positive associations between mindfulness and positive affect, life satisfaction, and vitality, whereas it was negatively correlated with negative affect, symptoms of depression and anxiety, and the presence of physical symptoms.

Importantly, and in addition to these relations with positive outcomes on the whole, mindfulness was also associated with greater satisfaction of the three basic psychological needs for autonomy, competence, and relatedness. Several studies in this series supported the important role of mindfulness in processes that support more aware, autonomous self-regulation, resulting in greater well-being. In one such study, mindfulness was shown to moderate the relationship between implicit and explicit measures of self-awareness of affect, supporting the role of mindfulness in facilitating awareness of implicit emotions and potentially facilitating well-being (Brown & Ryan, 2003). In another, trait mindfulness predicted more autonomous activity day to day, and as such, lower levels of negative affect. Independent effects for state mindfulness were found, with mindfulness on a given day predicting greater autonomous activity, decreased negative affect, and increased positive affect on a given day.

In similar research, Weinstein, Brown, and Ryan (2009) explored the role of mindfulness in coping with stress. Across four studies, mindfulness was associated with lower appraisals of stress in demanding situations and more adaptive coping strategies in the face of stress. Mindfulness also predicted greater well-being, measured by greater positive affect, less negative affect, and greater vitality. Mediation analyses demonstrated that the relations between mindfulness (both state and trait) and well-being were mediated by both appraising situations as less stressful and using more adaptive strategies in coping with stress.

This research, taken together, points to the important role that autonomous motivation plays in a life well lived, producing well-being, and as a result, happiness. In addition, mindful attention and awareness facilitate autonomous engagement with life, as well as more adaptive engagement with stressful situations, paving the way for eudaimonic well-being as conceptualized within SDT.

GOALS AND ASPIRATIONS

The behaviors, identities, vocations, and avocations that we engage in our lives are often organized around goals or aspirations toward which we are striving. When one examines these goals, it is clear that goals can vary on many dimensions. Kasser and Ryan (1993, 1996) examined goals in a series of studies, suggesting that there are two different categories of aspirations. *Intrinsic aspirations* refer to goals that produce relatively direct satisfaction of the basic psychological needs, whereas extrinsic aspirations refer to those that are less likely to produce (or do not at all produce) satisfaction of the needs. Examples of intrinsic aspirations include personal growth, community involvement, and affiliation, whereas extrinsic aspirations are exemplified by seeking wealth, fame, and image. Importantly, it's not the simple fact of holding extrinsic aspirations that is negative; instead, it's the relative balance of intrinsic and extrinsic aspirations that together determine the movement toward wellness or ill-being that one's life takes.

In their early research, Kasser and Ryan (1996) explored the relations of aspirations and well-being. In multiple studies, they found that placing higher value-intrinsic values such as personal growth, intimate relationships, and community contributions was positively related to happiness, self-actualization, and vitality, whereas an emphasis on extrinsic values such as financial success or image was associated with more negative affect and symptoms of depression and anxiety. This general set of findings established that placing greater value on intrinsic aspirations (relative to extrinsic aspirations) was associated with well-being outcomes; placing greater value on extrinsic aspirations relative to intrinsic showed the opposite, a result that has since been widely replicated (Kasser, 2002; Kasser et al., in press).

Some have argued that perhaps the relations between aspirations and outcomes could vary by vocation—in essence, a matching hypothesis. For example, Sagiv and Schwartz (2000) suggested that a focus on materialism should lead to positive outcomes in environments that strongly value materialism. To address this concern, Vansteenkiste, Duriez, Simons, and Soenens (2006) assessed the aspirations of two groups of students: those in business and those in teaching. As is expected, business students valued extrinsic aspirations more highly than teaching students and intrinsic aspirations less than teaching students. Yet the relations between intrinsic aspirations and greater well-being, as well as extrinsic aspirations and lower well-being, were equivalent for both groups. That is to say, no evidence for a matching hypothesis was found; placing greater value on intrinsic aspirations was a path to well-being, whereas focusing on extrinsic aspirations was not, regardless of context.

SOCIAL AND ENVIRONMENTAL FACTORS

The factors that we mention in the preceding sections that are associated with both eudaimonia and happiness—namely, autonomous motives, mindful awareness, and a focus on intrinsic goals—are all variables that are centered on individuals. Yet in addressing the factors that promote and thwart human flourishing and the happiness that attends it, SDT strongly emphasizes the impact of social and environmental inputs (Ryan & Deci, 2000). Indeed, as Sheldon and Lyubomirsky (2004) point out, it is the circumstances of one's life that also contribute to levels of happiness.

Within SDT, these life circumstances specifically affect happiness through their effects on basic psychological need satisfactions and frustrations. Social contexts that are consistently thwarting of our needs can greatly limit our ability to be fully functioning and well and thus expectably are also associated with less positive and more negative affect. Conversely, need supportive contexts enhance wellness and the happiness associated with it. Because the SDT literature is replete with empirical demonstrations of this point, we highlight just a few representative findings.

Legate, Ryan, and Weinstein (2012) examined the effect of autonomy supportive versus more controlling social contexts on the well-being of lesbian, gay, and bisexual (LGB) individuals. In their research, they identified significant variation in how "out" individuals were in various contexts, such as with friends, family, and coworkers—that is, there were contexts in which individuals felt freer to disclose aspects of their sexual identity, and others in which they felt they could not, or did not desire to, disclose. Overall, greater disclosure was associated with greater well-being, as indicated by fewer depressive symptoms, less anger, and greater self-esteem. In daily life contexts in which their autonomy was supported, LGB persons tended to be both more likely to be open about their sexual identity and to show increases in well-being. Notably, however, disclosing in controlling contexts was not associated with greater well-being. This research indicates that autonomy support is critical for authentic functioning and disclosure of sexual identity, as well as the fact the individuals experience varying support for autonomy, with corresponding variations in wellness and positive feelings.

Many adults around the world spend a significant amount of time at work, suggesting that this would be a critical context for need support or thwarting to occur. Workplace autonomy support has been identified as an important factor in employee outcomes, including well-being. In a study of state-owned companies in Bulgaria, Deci and colleagues examined the role of an autonomy-supportive work climate in need satisfaction, engagement, and well-being of employees (Deci et al., 2001). To the extent that the workplace was supportive of employees' need for autonomy, workers reported greater need satisfaction, and need satisfaction in turn predicted positive outcomes, including greater engagement at the workplace, as well as less anxiety and greater self-esteem. In addition, the study compared this model to a sample of American workers at a private company and found equivalent relationships, supporting the role of the social context (here, workplaces) in their relation to need satisfaction and wellness. Baard, Deci, and Ryan (2004) similarly showed that perceptions of autonomy support from managers were a significant predictor of need satisfaction, which was in turn related to lower depression and anxiety. Further, work previously reviewed by Ryan et al. (2010) revealed lower need satisfaction during work, as opposed to nonwork moments, and this lower satisfaction was associated with increases in negative affect, physical symptoms, and decreases in positive affect and vitality. Such studies highlight the important role that need support in work environments has on well-being and affect.

Parenting is another critical domain in which need support can significantly impact well-being and children's happiness. Considerable research has shown that controlling parents undermine and autonomy-supportive parents facilitate children's wellness (Ryan et al., 2006). Yet control can take many forms. For example, Assor, Roth, and Deci (2004) examined the effect of *parental conditional regard* on internalization and well-being. Parental conditional regard is a strategy whereby the parents control their children by conveying that they are unlovable if they do not live up to parental standards. Assor et al. demonstrated that mothers' conditional regard was associated with children having greater introjected (as opposed to autonomous) regulation. In turn, this introjected regulation was related to ill-being outcomes. In addition, those subjected to conditional regard reported more short-lived satisfaction after successes, meaning that happiness from success was more fleeting. They also evidenced greater guilt and shame and less stable self-esteem. Sadly, parents who had been subject to conditional regard as children were later more likely to report using conditional regard with their own children. Thus, not only does conditional regard have negative consequences, but those subjected to it are more likely to use it themselves, propagating its negative effects.

Other studies by Weinstein et al. have examined the role of parental autonomy support in homophobia and, in one study, contingent self-esteem (Weinstein, et al., 2012). When participants in the studies reported their parents as controlling when they were growing up, there was a discrepancy between two measures of sexuality: explicit sexuality as measured by a traditional Likert scale from "gay" to "straight," and implicit sexuality as assessed by a reaction time task measuring speed of associations between "me," "others," "gay," and "straight" words. This discrepancy in itself was thought to be an indicator of poor integration of sexual identity. Accordingly, important consequences were found when this discrepancy was present, including greater homophobia and more contingent self-esteem. Contingent self-esteem is the extent that one must act in certain ways to feel good about oneself, or to have self-esteem, and is seen as an indicator of ill-being within SDT (Deci & Ryan, 1995). In sum, it's clear that parental control has a wide range of negative consequences, and that parental autonomy support provides the basis for integration and well-being.

We have provided just a few examples, but the extensive body of work exploring the role of social and environmental factors within SDT research produces a convincing picture. The affordances social contexts provide for basic need satisfaction affect the motivations through which individuals engage in their daily activities and the goals toward which they strive, strongly impacting well-being and the happiness that tends to covary with it. The psychological need supportive versus thwarting character of social contexts, from classrooms to boardrooms to bedrooms, thus matters for wellness and happiness.

This principle of how environments impact wellness extends beyond proximal environments (such as family, peer, classroom, or work situations) to the distal or pervasive environments, such as people's cultures, economic systems, and governmental styles. All of these distal factors have an influence on both happiness and people's functioning. SDT specifically suggests that many of the positive effects of distal factors such as democracy, national wealth, economic distribution and justice, and other matters work in large part through their direct and indirect effects on psychological needs. For example, economic opportunity and fairness affect experiences of autonomy, competence, and relatedness powerfully, with resultant effects on wellness. This idea that the effect of distal factors on wellness works through need satisfaction also helps explain why wealth excess and certain types of advantages fail to enhance wellness beyond certain levels (e.g., Kasser et al., in press). In short, features of environments, both distal and proximal and "positive" or "negative," work their impact ultimately through the basic psychological needs of the individual persons embedded within them.

CONCLUSIONS

The SDT conceptualization of happiness is one that is based on a core principle: living in a way that satisfies the three basic psychological needs for autonomy, competence, and relatedness is a reliable route to well-being and the happiness that is typically associated with it (Ryan, Curren, & Deci, 2012; Ryan, Huta, & Deci, 2008). This expected relationship between need satisfaction and happiness applies to people's daily activities, the identities they hold, the goals they strive for, and the interpersonal relationships in which they are engaged. Thus, assessments of general need satisfaction predict overall happiness ratings, domain need satisfactions predict domain happiness, and situational need satisfaction predict momentary happiness (e.g., Vallerand, 1997).

There is without a doubt overall stability in happiness. Sheldon and Lyubomirski (2006) defined three main determinants of happiness levels: namely, a genetically influenced set point, the circumstances of one's life, and intentional activities. SDT research speaks particularly to the latter two issues: the circumstances and social contexts of one's life (both proximal and distal) and one's motivated, intentional activities. Clearly, behaviors, identities, aspirations, and contexts that fulfill the basic psychological needs bring about well-being and happiness, as does being in contexts that support those needs.

Moreover, consideration of the nature of happiness as both a relatively stable individual difference yet as a highly variable and sensitive variable at a within-person level of analysis reveals that its most important functions are largely as an informational input, important to self-regulation. Informational use of happiness can enhance intentional engagement in activities that will ultimately enhance wellness, and healthy self-regulation depends on the detection of variability around this set point. To this end, within-person variation around a normalized range is a positive thing for the organism, because it provides the basis for evaluating what is ultimately satisfying of the basic psychological needs and what is ultimately thwarting.

Yet in this regard, happiness is an organismic guide and input, rather than an ideal for wellness or some kind of ultimate aim for personality. Instead, SDT suggests that full functioning and self-realization are more appropriate aims. Nonetheless, there could be worse aims than happiness, because insofar as both SDT and more general eudaimonic thinking are correct, then the happiest individuals and societies will be those in which an emphasis is more on supports for basic need satisfactions rather than on extrinsic outcomes per se.

In fact, theorizing and research from SDT suggest several reliable routes to full functioning and well-being and resultant happiness, all of which function because they are satisfying the three basic psychological needs for autonomy, competence, and relatedness. There is clear evidence that pursuing intrinsic goals and aspirations such as giving to one's community, engaging in personal growth, and working toward close relationships fosters greater happiness. In contrast, living life with happiness as the ultimate goal is likely to lead people to shallower pursuits and activities that aren't fulfilling of the basic psychological needs, thus failing to bring about stable and lasting happiness. Additionally, engaging in activities for which one is autonomous will bring about greater need satisfaction and, ultimately, wellness and the happiness associated with it.

Finally, being in social contexts that support basic psychological needs, not to mention creating such environments, will also lead to greater need satisfaction and thus wellness. Because our "environments," both proximal and distal, are not just external elements that befall us, but are also, in part, our own social constructions and investments, they are something that can and should be critiqued. SDT provides a strong set of criteria for this critique, asking: Do social practices and policies facilitate or undermine basic need satisfactions? Applying such an evidence-focused critique and testing interventions based on it can provide yet another route to fostering both individual and societal wellness and happiness.

REFERENCES

Assor, A., Roth, G., & Deci, E. L. (2004). The emotional costs of parents' conditional regard: A self-determination theory analysis. *Journal of Personality*, *72*(1), 47−88.

Baard, P. P., Deci, E. L., & Ryan, R. M. (2004). Intrinsic need satisfaction: A motivational basis of performance and well-being in two work settings. *Journal of Applied Social Psychology*, *34*(10), 2045−2068.

Bartels, M., Saviouk, V., de Moor, M. H. M., Willemsen, G., van Beijsterveldt, T. C. E. M., Hottenga, J.-J., et al. (2010). Heritability and genome-wide linkage scan of subjective happiness. *Twin Research and Human Genetics*, *13*(2), 135−142.

Bartholomew, K. J., Ntoumanis, N., Ryan, R. M., Bosch, J. A., & Thøgersen-Ntoumani, C. (2011). Self-Determination Theory and diminished functioning: The role of interpersonal control and psychological need thwarting. *Personality and Social Psychology Bulletin*, *37*(11), 1459−1473.

Brickman, P., & Campbell, D. T. (1971). Hedonic relativism and planning the good society. In M. H. Apley (Ed.), *Adaptation-level theory: A symposium* (pp. 287−302). New York: Academic Press.

Brown, K. W., & Ryan, R. M. (2003). The benefits of being present: Mindfulness and its role in psychological well-being. *Journal of Personality and Social Psychology*, *84*(4), 822−848.

Brown, K. W., Ryan, R. M., & Creswell, J. D. (2007). Mindfulness: Theoretical foundations and evidence for its salutary effects. *Psychological Inquiry*, *18*(4), 211−237.

Chirkov, V., Ryan, R. M., Kim, Y., & Kaplan, U. (2003). Differentiating autonomy from individualism and independence: A self-determination theory perspective on internalization of cultural orientations and well-being. *Journal of Personality and Social Psychology*, *84*(1), 97.

Deci, E. L., & Ryan, R. M. (1985). *Intrinsic motivation and self-determination in human behavior*. New York: Plenum.

Deci, E. L., & Ryan, R. M. (1995). Human autonomy: The basis for true self-esteem. In M. Kernis (Ed.), *Agency, efficacy, and self-esteem* (pp. 31−49). New York: Plenum.

Deci, E. L., & Ryan, R. M. (2000). The "what" and "why" of goal pursuits: Human needs and the self-determination of behavior. *Psychological Inquiry*, *11*(4), 227−268.

Deci, E. L., Ryan, R. M., Gagné, M., Leone, D. R., Usunov, J., & Kornazheva, B. P. (2001). Need satisfaction, motivation, and well-being in the work organizations of a former eastern bloc country: A cross-cultural study of self-determination. *Personality and Social Psychology Bulletin*, *27*(8), 930−942.

Diener, E., Lucas, R. E., & Scollon, C. N. (2006). Beyond the hedonic treadmill: Revising the adaptation theory of well-being. *American Psychologist*, *61*(4), 305−314.

Diener, E., Ng, W., Harter, J., & Arora, R. (2010). Wealth and happiness across the world: Material prosperity predicts life evaluation, whereas psychosocial prosperity predicts positive feeling. *Journal of Personality and Social Psychology*, *99*, 52−61.

Franz, C. E., Panizzon, M. S., Eaves, L. J., Thompson, W., Lyons, M. J., Jacobson, K. C., et al. (2012). Genetic and environmental multidimensionality of well- and ill-being in middle aged twin men. *Behavioral Genetics, 42*, 579–591.

Frederick, S., & Loewenstein, G. (1999). Hedonic adaptation. In D. Kahneman, E. Diener, & N. Schwartz (Eds.), *Well-being: The foundations of hedonic psychology* (pp. 302–329). New York: Russell Sage Foundation.

Fredrickson, B. L. (2004). Gratitude, like other positive emotions, broadens and builds. In R. A. Emmons, & M. E. McCullough (Eds.), *The psychology of gratitude* (pp. 145–166). New York: Oxford University Press.

Gagné, M., Deci, E. L., & Ryan, R. M. (2013). Self-determination theory. In E. H. Kessler (Ed.), *Encyclopedia of management theory* (pp. 687–691). Thousand Oaks, CA: Sage.

Howell, R. T., Chenot, D., Hill, G., & Howell, C. J. (2011). Momentary happiness: The role of psychological need satisfaction. *Journal of Happiness Studies, 12*(1), 1–15.

Huta, V., & Ryan, R. M. (2010). Pursuing pleasure or virtue: The differential and overlapping well-being benefits of hedonic and eudaimonic motives. *Journal of Happiness Studies, 11*, 735–762.

Ilardi, B. C., Leone, D., Kasser, T., & Ryan, R. M. (1993). Employee and supervisor ratings of motivation: Main effects and discrepancies associated with job satisfaction and adjustment in a factory setting. *Journal of Applied Social Psychology, 23*(21), 1789–1805.

Kahneman, D. (1999). Objective happiness. In D. Kahneman, E. Diener, & N. Schwartz (Eds.), *Well-being: Foundations of hedonic psychology* (pp. 3–25). New York: Russell Sage Foundation.

Kashdan, T. B., Biswas-Diener, R., & King, L. A. (2008). Reconsidering happiness: The costs of distinguishing between hedonics and eudaimonia. *Journal of Positive Psychology, 3*(4), 219–233.

Kasser, T. (2002). *The high price of materialism.* Cambridge, MA: The MIT Press.

Kasser, T., Rosenblum, K. L., Sameroff, A. J., Deci, E. L., Niemiec, C. P., Ryan, R. M., et al. (in press). Changes in materialism, changes in psychological well-being: Evidence from three longitudinal studies and an intervention experiment. *Motivation and Emotion.*

Kasser, T., & Ryan, R. M. (1993). A dark side of the American dream: Correlates of financial success as a central life aspiration. *Journal of Personality and Social Psychology, 65*(2), 410–422.

Kasser, T., & Ryan, R. M. (1996). Further examining the American dream: Differential correlates of intrinsic and extrinsic goals. *Personality and Social Psychology Bulletin, 22*(3), 280–287.

Legate, N., Ryan, R. M., & Weinstein, N. (2012). Is coming out always a "good thing"? Exploring the relations of autonomy support, outness, and wellness for lesbian, gay, and bisexual individuals. *Social Psychological and Personality Science, 3*(2), 145–152.

Niemiec, C. P., & Ryan, R. M. (2013). What makes for a life well lived? Autonomy and its relation to full functioning and organismic wellness. In S. David, I. Boniwell, & A. Conley Ayers (Eds.), *Oxford handbook of happiness* (pp. 214–226). Oxford: Oxford University Press.

Reis, H. T., Sheldon, K. M., Gable, S. L., Roscoe, J., & Ryan, R. M. (2000). Daily well-being: The role of autonomy, competence, and relatedness. *Personality and Social Psychology Bulletin, 26*(4), 419–435.

Rietveld, C. A., Cesarini, D., Benjamin, D. J., Koellinger, P. D., De Neve, J.-E., Tiemeier, H., et al. (2013). Molecular genetics and subjective well-being. *Proceedings of the National Academy of Sciences of the United States of America, 110*(24), 9692–9697.

Ryan, R. M. (1982). Control and information in the intrapersonal sphere: An extension of cognitive evaluation theory. *Journal of Personality and Social Psychology, 43*, 450–461.

Ryan, R. M. (1995). Psychological needs and the facilitation of integrative processes. *Journal of Personality*, *63*, 397–427.

Ryan, R. M., Bernstein, J. H., & Brown, K. W. (2010). Weekends, work, and well-being: Psychological need satisfactions and day of the week effects on mood, vitality, and physical symptoms. *Journal of Social and Clinical Psychology*, *29*(1), 95–122.

Ryan, R. M., Curren, R., & Deci, E. L. (2012). What humans need: Flourishing in aristotelian philosophy and self-determination theory. In A. Waterman (Ed.), *The best within us: Positive psychology perspectives on eudaimonia* (pp. 57–76). Washington, DC: American Psychological Association.

Ryan, R. M., & Deci, E. L. (2000). Self-determination theory and the facilitation of intrinsic motivation, social development, and well-being. *American Psychologist*, *55*(1), 68.

Ryan, R. M., & Deci, E. L. (2001). On happiness and human potentials: A review of research on hedonic and eudaimonic well-being. *Annual Review of Psychology*, *52*(1), 141–166.

Ryan, R. M., Deci, E. L., Grolnick, W. S., & La Guardia, J. G. (2006). The significance of autonomy and autonomy support in psychological development and psychopathology. In D. Cicchetti, & D. J. Cohen (Eds.), *Developmental psychopathology, Vol. 1: Theory and method* (pp. 795–849). Hoboken, NJ: John Wiley & Sons.

Ryan, R. M., & Huta, V. (2009). Wellness as healthy functioning or wellness as happiness: The importance of eudaimonic thinking (response to the Kashdan et al. and Waterman discussion). *The Journal of Positive Psychology*, *4*, 202–204.

Ryan, R. M., Huta, V., & Deci, E. L. (2008). Living well: A Self-Determination Theory perspective on eudaimonia. *Journal of Happiness Studies*, *9*(1), 139–170.

Sagiv, L., & Schwartz, S. H. (2000). Value priorities and subjective well-being: Direct relations and congruity effects. *European Journal of Social Psychology*, *30*(2), 177–198.

Sheldon, K. M., & Lyubomirsky, S. (2004). Achieving sustainable new happiness: Prospects, practices, and prescriptions. In P. A. Linley, & S. Joseph (Eds.), *Positive psychology in practice* (pp. 127–145). Hoboken, NJ: Wiley.

Sheldon, K. M., & Lyubomirsky, S. (2006). Achieving sustainable gains in happiness: Change your actions, not your circumstances. *Journal of Happiness Studies*, *7*(1), 55–86.

Sheldon, K. M., Ryan, R., & Reis, H. T. (1996). What makes for a good day? Competence and autonomy in the day and in the person. *Personality and Social Psychology Bulletin*, *22*, 1270–1279.

Vallerand, R. J. (1997). Toward a hierarchical model of intrinsic and extrinsic motivation. In M. P. Zanna (Ed.), *Advances in experimental social psychology* (Vol. 29, pp. 271–360). San Diego: Academic Press.

Van den Broeck, A., Lens, W., De Witte, H., & Van Coillie, H. (2013). Unraveling the quantity and quality of workers' motivation for well-being: A person centered perspective. *Journal of Vocational Behavior*, *82*, 69–78.

Vansteenkiste, M., Duriez, B., Simons, J., & Soenens, B. (2006). Materialistic values and well-being among business students: Further evidence of their detrimental effect. *Journal of Applied Social Psychology*, *36*(12), 2892–2908.

Vansteenkiste, M., & Ryan, R. M. (2013). On psychological growth and vulnerability: Basic psychological need satisfaction and need frustration as a unifying principle. *Journal of Psychotherapy Integration*, *23*(3), 263–280.

Waterman, A. S. (2012). Introduction. Considering the nature of a life well lived. In A. S. Waterman (Ed.), *The Best within us: Positive psychology perspectives on eudaimonia* (pp. 3–18). Washington, DC: American Psychological Association.

Weinstein, N., Brown, K. W., & Ryan, R. M. (2009). A multi-method examination of the effects of mindfulness on stress attribution, coping, and emotional well-being. *Journal of Research in Personality*, *43*, 374–385.

Weinstein, N., & Ryan, R. M. (2010). When helping helps: Autonomous motivation for prosocial behavior and its influence on well-being for the helper and recipient. *Journal of Personality and Social Psychology*, *98*(2), 222.

Weinstein, N., Ryan, W. S., DeHaan, C. R., Przybylski, A. K., Legate, N., & Ryan, R. M. (2012). Parental autonomy support and discrepancies between implicit and explicit sexual identities: Dynamics of self-acceptance and defense. *Journal of Personality and Social Psychology*, *102*(4), 815–832.

Chapter 4

Is Lasting Change Possible? Lessons from the Hedonic Adaptation Prevention Model

Christina Armenta,[1] Katherine Jacobs Bao,[1] Sonja Lyubomirsky,[1] and Kennon M. Sheldon[2]

[1]*University of California, Riverside, Riverside, CA, USA,* [2]*University of Missouri-Columbia, Columbia, MO, USA*

Happiness is highly valued both in Western society and in cultures all around the world (Diener, 2000). Many individuals spend their lifetimes searching for ways to achieve happiness and are confronted with a dizzying array of information to achieve their goal—from self-help books and motivational seminars to commercial advertising promoting cars, drinks, and technology as sources of well-being. Unfortunately, both anecdotal and scientific evidence yields mixed evidence with respect to the question of whether it is even possible to change one's level of happiness. A principal reason for pessimism is that people possess a surprising ability to become accustomed to positive life changes—via a process called hedonic adaptation—possibly because they have genetically influenced happiness set points to which they return even after major ups and downs (Lyubomirsky, Sheldon, & Schkade, 2005). In this chapter, we discuss the implications of hedonic adaptation for sustainable happiness, and the ways that one might achieve lasting happiness change by thwarting adaptation.

HEDONIC ADAPTATION

What Is Hedonic Adaptation?

Hedonic adaptation is the process by which people "get used to" events or stimuli that elicit emotional responses. After the experience of a positive or negative stimulus or event, one generally experiences a gain or loss in well-being (Frederick & Loewenstein, 1999). For example, a newlywed may experience a boost in well-being due to the positive events and emotions associated with the new marriage. These events might include moving into a new house together, throwing dinner parties as a couple, or even the simple act of being able to call one's new spouse "husband" or "wife." However, this change in well-being is ultimately followed by a gradual return to base-line. As the newlyweds become accustomed to the changes in their lives associated with marriage, the happiness they initially experienced begins to decline and eventually returns to baseline.

Hedonic adaptation occurs to both positive and negative events, and some amount of adaptation—even in the positive domain—may be benefi-cial. Frederick and Loewenstein (1999) have argued that hedonic adaptation is evolutionarily adaptive. When individuals experience high levels of posi-tive or negative affect, they cannot help but focus on those intense feelings. This acute attention on their affect can make it difficult to function, because people need to concentrate on their basic needs in order to survive and thrive. Thus, people hedonically adapt as a means of reducing high arousal, allowing them to redirect their attention to more important needs, as well as to novel opportunities and threats. Also, high arousal may be physiologically harmful if experienced chronically, so reducing it may help people avoid physical ailments such as stress-related illness.

What Is *Not* Hedonic Adaptation?

Hedonic adaptation is similar to, yet distinct from, several other related processes. Because hedonic adaptation involves becoming accustomed to a stimulus, it is often confused with a similar concept, desensitization. Both hedonic adaptation and desensitization reduce the emotional intensity of an event. However, hedonic adaptation diminishes that intensity by shifting the perceptions of the positivity or negativity of a stimulus, such that what was initially observed as positive or negative becomes neutral (Frederick & Loewenstein, 1999). Consequently, people become more sensitive to differ-ences in a stimulus. For example, a person moving into a 400-square-foot apartment may not initially observe much of a difference between his apart-ment and the 450-square-foot apartment next door. However, after he adapts to his current apartment, the apartment next door begins to appear much larger and more favorable in comparison. He may even become motivated to try to switch apartments. Desensitization, by contrast, reduces the affective intensity of an event more generally. It is characterized by reduced sensitiv-ity toward differences in a stimulus. People who are desensitized would not notice the difference between their current 400-square-foot apartment and the 450-square-foot apartment next door, nor would they be motivated to attempt to substitute their apartment for the larger one. Thus, although desen-sitization and hedonic adaptation share certain characteristics, hedonic adaptation cannot be explained as merely desensitization to a stimulus.

The literature on hedonic adaptation involves several methodological issues. One concern is whether people truly adapt to life changes, or if the evident decline in well-being is a result of scale norming (Frederick & Loewenstein, 1999). Researchers generally measure happiness by asking participants to indicate their overall level of happiness on a scale from low to high (e.g., 1 to 7). Given the subjectivity of this approach, people may interpret the scale differently. For example, one person may interpret a 7 as being the absolute highest level of happiness a person could possibly achieve, whereas another may interpret a 7 as manifesting a high level of happiness in comparison to the average person. One alternative explanation for why people who have undergone a major life change (e.g., amputation) are not as unhappy as we might expect is that they might normalize the scale. In other words, they might subconsciously rate themselves relative to other amputees rather than to the average healthy person. Frequency measures of affect avoid some of the issues of scale norming. These measures gauge the amount of time a person experiences positive affect versus negative affect. The valence of an event (i.e., positive versus negative) is also less subject to scale norming (Diener, Larsen, Levine, & Emmons, 1985). Thus, these methodological issues are not insurmountable.

Finally, social desirability may play a role in adaptation to life events (Frederick & Loewenstein, 1999). People may exaggerate their level of happiness after a positive event, such as marriage, because they believe it is expected of them. By the same token, people may minimize the amount of adaptation they have experienced to a negative event, such as the death of a spouse or a messy divorce, which they are expected to grieve. Findings regarding the length of time it takes to adapt to events may therefore be biased. However, this problem may be minimized—although not eliminated—by asking questions in such a way as to not draw attention to the purpose of the study. For example, large-scale longitudinal panel studies contain many questions, so participants are unlikely to observe a connection between measures of well-being and questions about their life status (e.g., marriage, job loss), and thus are somewhat less likely to be influenced by social desirability.

EVIDENCE SUPPORTING HEDONIC ADAPTATION

Adaptation to Negative Events

Negative events—both large and small—are a normal part of daily life. Even minor negative events can impact a person's mood and can sometimes feel overwhelming (Kanner, Coyne, Schaefer, & Lazarus, 1981). Major events, on the other hand, can be traumatic. Nevertheless, people show a remarkable capacity to adapt even to major negative events.

Disability. Disability is a negative life event that can impact almost every aspect of an individual's life. Most people imagine that it must be extremely difficult, if not impossible, to adapt to disability. However, research suggests that people who experience a new disability do recover somewhat, although not completely, from the event (Lucas, 2007). In a 19-year panel study, participants' well-being was measured for several years before and after a disability was incurred. As such, researchers were able to observe whether the change in well-being was due to pre-event levels of happiness or the disability itself. Disabled people showed a significant decline in happiness in the first year of the disability, but, over time, their levels of well-being gradually approached their baseline. However, this adaptation was not complete, and individuals did not return to their initial happiness levels, even when controlling for changes in employment status and income. Furthermore, not surprisingly, participants with severe disabilities experienced a larger drop in well-being—and developed a lower baseline for happiness—compared to those with mild disabilities. This pattern is likely due to the number and magnitude of negative events associated with severe disabilities, such as the need for caretaking.

Divorce. In the United States, nearly half of all first marriages end within 20 years (Copen, Daniels, Vespa, & Mosher, 2012). As such, it is important to understand the lasting hedonic impact of divorce. An 18-year panel study (Lucas, 2005) found that people began to decline in well-being in the years before a divorce. Following the divorce, they gradually began to return toward their baseline levels of happiness, with changes in well-being leveling off approximately 5 years later. However, participants in this study did not return to their initial levels of happiness, suggesting that, on average, they only partially adapted to divorce. Another investigation, however, found that individuals adapted to divorce both rapidly and completely (Clark, Diener, Georgellis, & Lucas, 2008).

The circumstances surrounding a divorce may influence a person's rate or degree of adaptation (Lucas, Clark, Georgellis, & Diener, 2003). For example, one investigation found that those who did not remarry during the course of the study showed longer-lasting declines in well-being than those who remarried (Lucas, 2007). These individual differences may help explain why some people return to their baseline level of happiness following a divorce, whereas others never fully adapt.

Widowhood. Widowhood can be a traumatic life event. Research shows that after the death of a spouse, people experience a significant decline in well-being (Lucas & Clark, 2006). This impact on well-being begins to dissipate approximately 2 years after the loss. As time passes, widows and widowers gradually approach their initial level of happiness but do not completely return to it, even 8 years after losing their spouse (however, see Clark et al., 2008, for evidence of complete adaptation). Researchers found that people's reactions to widowhood impacted their degree of adaptation, such that a more positive immediate reaction was associated with greater adaptation (Lucas et al., 2003).

Other individual differences undoubtedly play a role in the extent to which people adapt to widowhood. One study found that individuals whose spouses were seriously ill prior to death were more likely to be depressed, to rate their spouses negatively, and to show improvement after the death of their spouses (Bonanno et al., 2002). Individuals in this situation would most likely show complete adaptation to widowhood. By contrast, those who were dependent on their spouses for both emotional and financial resources would likely never fully adapt.

Unemployment. In today's economy, unemployment has become a common occurrence. Research has shown that after people become unemployed, they experience a decline in happiness, followed by an approach to baseline (Clark & Georgellis, 2013; Lucas, Clark, Georgellis, & Diener, 2004). Interestingly, however, such individuals never fully reach their baseline levels of happiness, providing evidence for partial adaptation. Furthermore, the effect of unemployment on well-being may last much longer than the unemployment itself: people do not fully adapt to becoming unemployed even after being re-employed (Lucas et al., 2004).

People's initial reactions to the unemployment may impact the process of adaptation, such that the more negatively individuals react to unemployment, the less they eventually adapt to it (Lucas et al., 2004).

Adaptation to Positive Events

Negative life events undoubtedly play a major role in happiness and its pursuit, as people try to protect their well-being by anticipating them, avoiding them, and trying to adapt or cope with them. Positive life events play a distinct role in the pursuit of happiness because many believe that the secret to happiness is simply to experience more positive events and achieve their goals, like getting married, having kids, and striking it rich (Lyubomirsky, 2013). In other words, people tend to focus on trying to change their life circumstances in order to achieve greater happiness. Although the attainment of major life goals is indeed associated with increased well-being (Brunstein, 1993; Sheldon & Elliot, 1998, 1999; Sheldon & Kasser, 1998), unfortunately people can become accustomed to positive life changes in much the same way that they become accustomed to negative ones.

Marriage. Approximately 90% of people eventually get married (Myers, 2000). A meta-analysis revealed that marriage is associated with relatively higher well-being (Haring-Hidore, Stock, Okun, & Witter, 1985). According to Clark and Georgellis (2012), people generally experience a boost in happiness prior to marriage as they become engaged, anticipate their wedding, and eventually get married. Over time, however, people eventually return to their initial level of happiness. In fact, on average, individuals were found to fully adapt to marriage within 2 years (Clark & Georgellis, 2013; Clark et al., 2008).

Despite findings of adaptation to marriage, individual differences are likely to be present. One 15-year longitudinal study explored individual differences in rates of adaptation to marriage (Lucas et al., 2003). Researchers found that adaptation depended on participants' initial reactions to marriage. Newlyweds who showed a strong positive reaction to marriage were better able to maintain their boost in well-being than those who reacted less strongly or negatively. Interestingly, participants who reported higher well-being at baseline were relatively less likely to react very positively to marriage. One possible reason is the boost in social support that new marriage delivers. Research has found happier people to have stronger support networks (Myers, 2000). Unhappy people may, therefore, react more positively to the social support that their spouses provide because they are not getting that support elsewhere.

New job. Beginning a new job can be a very exciting time in a person's life, particularly in the current economy. One study, however, found evidence for complete adaptation to making a job change (Boswell, Boudreau, & Tichy, 2005). In this study, a job change was defined as either a promotion in the same organization or voluntarily leaving one's job for a position elsewhere. In the year prior to changing jobs, managers reported relatively low job satisfaction, possibly due to increasing dissatisfaction with their current job, which may have ultimately motivated them to look for a change (Griffeth, Hom, & Gaertner, 2000). Boswell and his colleagues found, as expected, that managers experienced a surge in job satisfaction immediately after starting their new position. However, within the following year, their well-being fell back to their initial levels.

Interestingly, this same study found that individuals who changed jobs multiple times followed the same pattern with each subsequent job change. That is, each job change was associated with a boost in well-being followed by a return to baseline. One reason for this pattern is that each career move led to meeting new people and facing new job opportunities and challenges—exciting at first but associated with diminished positive emotions over time. Furthermore, managers may have declined in well-being due to escalating aspirations. During the interview process, employers tend to focus on the positive attributes of the job (e.g., 24-hour gym, child care; Ilgen, 1971) and new employees may quickly take these attributes for granted and soon desire even more.

Birth of a child. The birth of a child is a long-awaited and joyous event for many couples. In one investigation, women reported higher well-being up to 3 years before the birth of a child, perhaps as they anticipated the joys of motherhood (Clark & Georgellis, 2013). However, they rapidly reverted to their baseline levels of happiness shortly after the birth of the child. By contrast, men did not experience a significant boost in happiness. Other research has found evidence that although women experienced a greater surge in happiness, men and women showed comparable patterns of anticipation and adaptation (Clark et al., 2008). Similarly, in a 22-year panel study, both parents experienced a boost in well-being immediately following the birth of a child, but returned to their baseline levels of well-being within 2 years, suggesting that parents react similarly to parenthood (Dyrdal & Lucas, 2013). However, this study also found individual differences in rates of adaptation. For example, parents with high initial levels of well-being experienced a smaller boost in happiness after becoming a parent and decreased more in happiness after their child's birth, compared to those with lower baseline levels of well-being. In addition, new parents who reacted more positively to the birth of the child maintained their happiness boost much longer than those who reacted less strongly.

A meta-analysis of this literature found divergent effects of childbirth on well-being depending on the component of well-being—cognitive (e.g., life satisfaction) versus affective (e.g., positive emotions)—that was measured (Luhmann, Hofmann, Eid, & Lucas, 2012). On average, parents reported receiving a boost in life satisfaction after the birth of the child, followed by a rapid decrease back toward baseline. At the same time, parents reported experiencing fewer positive emotions immediately following the birth of their child, but the number of positive emotions increased over time. These findings suggest that although parents quickly return to their initial levels of life satisfaction, they also experience an increasing number of positive emotions associated with parenthood.

Cosmetic surgery. Nearly 6.5 million aesthetic surgeries are performed worldwide every year (International Society of Aesthetic Plastic Surgery, 2011). This statistic indicates that a large number of people seek to improve some aspect of themselves through surgery. One study found that participants who received cosmetic surgery experienced more positive outcomes than those who did not undergo surgery but were similarly dissatisfied with a particular physical feature (Margraf, Meyer, & Lavallee, 2013). Furthermore, surgery patients reported maintaining their boost in well-being up to a year later. The investigators found that participants reported an increase in self-esteem after the surgery, and this increased self-esteem may have pushed them to seek out experiences and friendships they were previously hesitant to pursue. Although this study did not find evidence of adaptation, it is possible that participants would begin to decline in well-being several years after receiving the cosmetic surgery, as the events and emotions associated with the surgery may take more time to become accustomed to. For example, after cosmetic surgery, a man may receive many compliments, which gives him the confidence to meet new people, become active in new activities, and seek out more challenging career opportunities. Cosmetic surgery may, therefore, lead to a series of new positive events and emotions, thus slowing adaptation.

HEDONIC ADAPTATION PREVENTION MODEL

In an ideal world, people would fully adapt to negative life changes and experience sustained well-being from positive life changes. Although individuals do adapt to adverse events, this adaptation is often incomplete. Furthermore, people appear to adapt much more quickly and completely to positive events—a phenomenon that functions as an obstacle to achieving lasting happiness. As a result, research has begun to focus on ways to thwart hedonic adaptation to positive events.

The rate of adaptation varies for both positive and negative events. Some people appear to adapt quickly to changes in their lives, whereas others adapt much more slowly. These differences may be due to variation in the activities that individuals engage in following a circumstantial change. The Hedonic Adaptation Prevention (HAP) model and its variants (Lyubomirsky, 2011; Sheldon & Lyubomirsky, 2012) (this model used to be called the Hedonic Adaptation to Positive and Negative Events model, but now we refer to it as the Hedonic Adaptation Prevention model) explain how and why people adapt to both positive and negative changes in their lives and identify ways in which they can incorporate different activities into those changes in order to influence the rate of adaptation (see Figure 4.1 for the model's depiction of positive adaptation). In this chapter, we primarily focus on adaptation to positive events, proposing how people may be able to gain the maximum level of happiness from the good things in their lives.

In short, the HAP model posits that adaptation proceeds via two separate paths, such that initial happiness gains keyed to a positive life change (e.g., a

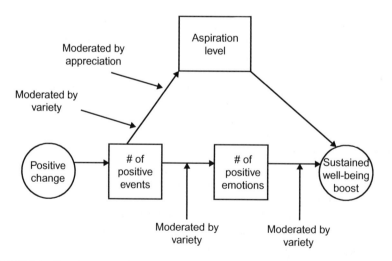

FIGURE 4.1   **Hedonic Adaptation Prevention model.** *Adapted from "The challenge of staying happier: Testing the Hedonic Adaptation Prevention (HAP) model" by K. M. Sheldon and S. Lyubomirsky (2012),* Personality and Social Psychology Bulletin, 38, 670–680.

new romance or job) are eroded over time. The first path specifies that the stream of positive emotions and events resulting from the positive life change may lessen over time, sending people's happiness levels back to their baseline. The second, more counterintuitive, path specifies that the stream of positive events resulting from the change may increase people's aspirations about the positivity of their lives, such that circumstances that used to produce happiness are now taken for granted; the person wants more. Furthermore, the HAP model suggests two important moderators of the hedonic adaptation process. First, the more variable (and perhaps surprising) one's positive events, the more likely they'll produce frequent positive emotions and sustained well-being and the less likely they'll raise one's aspiration level. Second, the model specifies that continued appreciation of the positive change can forestall rising aspirations and thus thwart adaptation.

Sheldon and Lyubomirsky (2012) have found evidence to support the complete HAP model. Participants were initially asked to fill out baseline measures of well-being. Six weeks later, they were instructed to reflect on a positive life change that had recently occurred. Participants reported a boost in happiness after the positive life change. However, the researchers also found differences in the rates of adaptation to positive life changes, suggesting variations in the behaviors of participants who adapted quickly versus slowly. Accordingly, the HAP model explains how a positive life change that occurred at the beginning of the study can have lasting effects on one's happiness 6 weeks later.

Mediators of the Hedonic Adaptation Process

A positive change in one's life is associated with a stream of positive events and emotions (Lyubomirsky, 2011). As people adapt to this life change, they form expectations that eventually alter the experience of the associated positive events.

Positive emotions and events. As mentioned previously, one pathway by which people adapt to positive changes is through declining positive emotions and events (see Figure 4.1, bottom path; Sheldon & Lyubomirsky, 2012; Lyubomirsky, 2011). When individuals experience a positive change, they also experience an increase in positive emotions and events connected to this change. For example, after marriage, people encounter a lot of new and exciting events. They may go on a honeymoon to a romantic location they have never visited before or create a home together. They may also receive a lot of attention and positive reactions from family and friends. These positive events give rise to more positive emotions, such as excitement, joy, and love. As time passes, however, the positive events and emotions become less common and less novel. Furthermore, people may begin to take these events and emotions for granted, and they become the new standard or "new normal" (Sheldon & Lyubomirsky, 2012). Although people still encounter positive events associated with the initial change (the marriage), those events may decline in positivity over time (Lyubomirsky, 2011). As such, the initial boost begins to wear off, and the newlyweds begin to adapt. Sheldon and Lyubomirsky (2012), in the study described earlier, found that participants who continued to experience positive events and emotions associated with their initial life change reported higher well-being at the end of the study than those who did not. This finding suggests that positive events should be optimized to slow down adaptation.

Aspirations. Increasing aspirations are another way in which people adapt to positive changes (see Figure 4.1, top path; Sheldon & Lyubomirsky, 2012). As people become accustomed to the events associated with their positive change, they begin to require more to sustain the same level of happiness. For example, a woman whose husband washes the dishes every day would come to expect it. She may then begin to want him to do more work around the house, such as vacuuming the living room or cleaning the bathrooms, to get the same delight and satisfaction she felt when her husband first began helping with the housework. People may also show increasing desires for more following a job promotion. After the employee adapts to the positive events surrounding a promotion, he may begin to aspire for an ever higher income or more authority over his subordinates. In many cases, these aspirations can no longer be fulfilled and the person's well-being declines. Thus, aspirations can be a barrier to sustainable happiness.

In the Sheldon and Lyubomirsky study (2012), as hypothesized by the HAP model, rising aspirations predicted lower well-being at the 6-week follow-up. Accordingly, this route should be minimized to impede adaptation to positive life changes. However, one set of studies found no relationship between well-being and height of aspirations (Jacobs Bao, Layous, & Lyubomirsky, 2013). A more important factor seemed to be whether or not participants were able to fulfill their aspirations. In this study, higher aspirations were found to be harmful when they could no longer be fulfilled. At some point, the aspirations may become too high, and people are eventually unable to fulfill them.

Moderators of the Hedonic Adaptation Process

Variety. People adapt most easily to constant stimuli, rather than to changing, unpredictable stimuli (Lyubomirsky, 2011). Constant stimuli lack novelty, allowing them to fall out of one's awareness. Over time, the positive events that arise as a result of making a life change become predictable and expected, and as such, they no longer contribute to one's well-being. Supporting the HAP model (see top left, Figure 4.1), Sheldon and Lyubomirsky (2012) found that greater variety in one's positive events tempered aspirations. Accordingly, greater variety allowed people to remain satisfied with their life change. For example, if a new homeowner experiences many varied events, such as neighborhood strolls and block parties, she will not feel the need to move to an even better location. Indeed, the effect of emotions on well-being was found to be greater when the events experienced after a life change were characterized by a high level of variety, suggesting that variety moderates the relationship between positive life changes and well-being.

More evidence for the importance of variety in impeding adaptation comes from a 6-week-long intervention in which participants were randomly assigned to make a dynamic and variable life change versus a static, one-time change. Participants who reported that their change added variety to their lives experienced the greatest increase in well-being (Sheldon & Lyubomirsky, 2009). Greater variety in events associated with a life change also allows people to maintain their boost in happiness. For example, participants who reported greater variety in a recent life change maintained the boost in well-being more than those who reported less variety (Sheldon, Boehm, & Lyubomirsky, 2012). Finally, another investigation by the same authors found that participants who were randomly assigned to vary acts of kindness that they performed for people in their lives maintained their boost in happiness better than those who did not vary them. These studies support the moderating role of variety in the adaptation process (see Figure 4.1, bottom).

Variety increases the complexity of a situation, thereby making it more interesting (Berlyne & Boudewijns, 1971) and allowing individuals to maintain their curiosity and awareness. Increased interest and curiosity may help explain why research has found that experiencing more variety in the events surrounding a positive life change diminishes the likelihood of rising aspirations (Sheldon & Lyubomirsky, 2012). Individuals will not covet even more desirable life changes if their current life change is still able to maintain their attention.

Experiences characterized by more variety are associated with higher happiness levels than those characterized by less variety (cf. Van Boven, 2005; Van Boven & Gilovich, 2003). For example, during a sightseeing vacation, people may be more likely to partake in activities that they do not normally choose and encounter many unexpected events. In contrast, material purchases, such as a new couch, are not generally dynamic or surprising. After the person becomes accustomed to her new couch, there is nothing new and exciting about it, and the object no longer produces boosts in happiness. One reason that vacations are associated with greater happiness boosts than material purchases may be that the former offer more variety.

Surprise. As a close cousin of variety, surprise is also important in thwarting adaptation, perhaps because surprising events are not easily understood (Wilson & Gilbert, 2008). For example, a new bride whose husband plans surprise trips or occasionally brings flowers "just because" will not show adaptation to her marriage as quickly. She will not have a ready answer for why her husband is planning these events, and he will keep her guessing about what might come next. Indeed, the initial surprise of a marriage proposal and the sheer number of new and varied events that occur during the engagement period may be one reason that couples' well-being soars prior to marriage. A surprising event is often hard to explain away. In one study, researchers randomly approached people at a library and gave them a dollar coin with an attached card (Wilson, Centerbar, Kermer, & Gilbert, 2005). In the "uncertain" condition, the card explained that the researcher was from a society that committed random acts of kindness. This vague information prevented participants from easily explaining why they received the money. The "certain" condition involved a card that explained to participants why they were given a dollar. The researchers found that those who could not be certain of why they received the money experienced a greater increase in positive mood. Surprise keeps things exciting and fresh, allowing the person to remain content with what she has.

Another study found that participants who received surprising personal feedback (e.g., "Your biggest strength is humor") continued to increase in well-being even after the study was over, whereas those who were not surprised by the feedback did not show this boost (Jacobs Bao, Boehm, & Lyubomirsky, 2013). Incorporating variety and surprise into the events surrounding the positive change can thus help thwart adaptation (Sheldon & Lyubomirsky, 2012).

Appreciation. People who experience higher levels of appreciation toward a positive life change adapt more slowly (Sheldon & Lyubomirsky, 2012). Appreciating a fortunate life turn forces people to attend to it and notice all of the nuances associated with it. As such, they are also less likely to aspire for something even better. The more people appreciate an event, the more reasons they may find to feel happy as a result of it. A person who appreciates his wife and new marriage is less likely to take the things she does for granted. Instead, he may feel lucky that he has her in his life. As such, he would experience the higher levels of well-being associated with newly married life for longer. Failure to appreciate a positive change is a sign that the individual no longer notices or pays heed to that change, which signals complete adaptation. In support of this idea, Sheldon and Lyubomirsky (2012) found that people who reported higher levels of appreciation for their life change also showed lower aspirations and higher well-being (see appreciation depicted as a moderator in Figure 4.1). Thus, appreciation can help thwart adaptation.

According to Kahneman and Thaler (2006), life circumstances (e.g., a new car or job) continue to influence a person's well-being for as long as they draw his attention. As he adapts to the car or job, however, the novelty wears off and they fade into the background of his awareness. One study found that those who continued to be aware of their positive life changes adapted less quickly to them (Sheldon & Lyubomirsky, 2009). Therefore, maintaining one's attention on a life change—whether by appreciating it or simply focusing on it—is another way to forestall adaptation.

Hedonic Adaptation to Negative Life Changes

Although much of our discussion has focused on adaptation to positive life changes, the HAP model can also explain adaptation to the negative (see Lyubomirsky, 2011, for a detailed discussion). A critical difference is that after experiencing a negative life change, people are usually interested in speeding up the adaptation, not slowing it down.

People become accustomed to negative life changes in much the same way they do to positive ones (Lyubomirsky, 2011). Over time, the negative events associated with a negative life change—e.g., downsizing to a smaller house or leaving one's spouse—become less unexpected. Accordingly, these events trigger fewer and less intense negative emotions. At the same time, people tend to lower positive aspirations about their lives. Adaptation to negative life changes is therefore characterized by experiencing fewer negative emotions and decreasing aspirations.

If an individual's goal is to return to his baseline level of happiness after experiencing a negative event, he must apply what is known about thwarting hedonic adaptation in a different way (Lyubomirsky, 2011). For example, experiencing more variable and unexpected events can help thwart adaptation to both positive and negative life changes. Therefore, minimizing the variety and surprise associated with a negative life change should accelerate adaptation. Furthermore, events continue to impact well-being for as long as they capture people's attention. Although maintaining awareness and attention to positive events has been found to be beneficial, this attention—if it involves systematic analysis—may also lead people to understand these events, thus allowing them to adapt (Lyubomirsky, Sousa, & Dickerhoof, 2006). As such, this phenomenon may be beneficial in accelerating adaptation to negative events by helping people understand, explain, and come to terms with a negative event. People can also accelerate adaptation by laboring to reduce their aspirations. For example, after a breakup, a woman can work at accepting the loss of her former significant other and focus on the benefits of being single. In sum, by bringing the HAP model to bear on both good and bad turns of events, people can learn to thwart adaptation to positive changes in their lives and accelerate adaptation to negative ones.

FUTURE DIRECTIONS AND QUESTIONS

Our research team has been investigating the sustainability of positive changes in well-being for more than a decade. The HAP model, described here, represents the current culmination of this thinking. As described previously, Sheldon and Lyubomirsky (2012) provided the best evidence to date for the HAP model, via a sophisticated longitudinal test of the model in the context of naturally occurring data. However, much more research—especially experimental research—remains to be done. Any of the factors identified in the HAP model might be manipulated experimentally, including manipulations of initial positive life changes (e.g., by inducing participants to commence a rewarding new activity), manipulations of the number and quality of positive events resulting from these changes, manipulations of the variety or surprisingness of those events, manipulations of appreciation for the initial changes, and manipulations that prompt increasing (or decreasing) aspirations for more of the events (e.g., via provision of social comparison information). As we more fully develop and test the HAP model, we are striving to move beyond self-reports of happiness, to ensure that the processes the model describes are observable to others and are not accounted for by self-report biases.

We are also interested in a variety of broader questions that emerge from our approach. One concerns "optimal negativity." Are there some conditions under which momentary negative experiences should be focused on—and their well-being consequences suffered—in service of greater well-being in the future? Feeling genuine chagrin for one's mistakes (such as speaking harshly to a child), and feeling the guilt and remorse that accompany those mistakes, may guide better decision making in the future. Perhaps one should not adapt to such chagrin or remorse too quickly. More generally, is there an ideal ratio of positive to negative experience that promotes maximal long-term well-being, besides "all positive" and "no negative"? Fredrickson and Losada (2005) argued that there may be such a ratio, but more recent work has called their proposed ratio into question (Brown, Sokal, & Friedman, 2013). To date, little evidence indicates that negative experiences have positive functions, but intuition suggests otherwise.

Another theoretical issue concerns the half-life of positive events. In essence, the HAP model describes how to "milk" a positive life change to maximize the duration of its effect on happiness. For some positive changes, this process may be essentially never-ending (i.e., one can continue to derive hedonic benefits from one's long-term partner throughout one's life), but other life changes have a statute of limitations, as it were. Perhaps a person can appreciate the new painting or the new job for only so long before its potential to affect him is exhausted and he needs to go out and procure another painting or another job. We certainly do not advocate that people stick it out rigidly in formerly rewarding situations or relationships after "the thrill is gone;" instead, we advocate exploring whether the thrill can be rekindled, using the recommendations of our model, before deciding to move on.

In a related vein, we do not advocate that people never "aspire for more" than their current situation or set of skills or occupations. Obviously, future aspirations are a large part of what drives sustained effort, goal attainment, and personal growth (Sheldon & Elliot, 1999). Although a Buddhist perspective may eschew such aspirations, we do not. Instead, we caution against allowing one's aspirations to creep up before one has experienced the full potential enjoyment of what one already has. Rising aspirations (as in rising materialism or rising consumption) should not be a mindless coping strategy to manage internal restlessness; instead, rising aspirations should occur only after the statute of limitations has expired on one's current status quo. Determining the when, how, and why of such inflection points remains a major challenge for future research.

CONCLUSION

People have a remarkable capacity to adapt to changes in their lives—a capacity that compels them to return to their prior emotional baselines. This process, however, appears to be asymmetric across positive and negative domains. Although individuals show some adaptation to negative life changes, they often never completely return to their initial level of happiness following traumatic events. This evidence suggests that, in answer to this book's titular question, "well-being *can* change"—but, unfortunately, not in the direction most would prefer! Furthermore, people appear to adapt much more quickly and completely to positive life changes than negative ones. This evidence demonstrates that the average person does not obtain sustainable pleasure from her positive life changes—no matter how wonderful they may be initially—thwarting her goal to become lastingly happier. Taken together, evidence concerning greater adaptation to positive than to negative life changes breeds pessimism about whether sustainable positive change in well-being is even possible.

Fortunately, the HAP model suggests ways for individuals to obtain longer-lasting boosts in well-being from the positive changes in their lives. Increasing the variety and surprisingness of the positive events deriving from any pleasant life change helps maintain an inflow of momentary positive experiences and helps prevent rising aspirations for more and more. Furthermore, truly appreciating a life change helps people be content with what they have and prevents them from prematurely increasing their desires for something better. Thus, research supporting the HAP model suggests that, at least up to some as yet undetermined limit, sustainable positive change in well-being is indeed possible, if the person lives her life in the right way. However, it is not necessarily easy to accomplish this. Effort and some degree of mindfulness are both essential. Fortunately, the "work" of positive living is likely to be inherently engaging and reinforcing, once the right habits are acquired.

REFERENCES

Berlyne, D. E., & Boudewijns, W. J. (1971). Hedonic effects of uniformity in variety. *Canadian Journal of Psychology/Revue Canadienne de Psychologie, 25*(3), 195–206.

Bonanno, G. A., Wortman, C. B., Lehman, D. R., Tweed, R. G., Haring, M., Sonnega, J., et al. (2002). Resilience to loss and chronic grief: A prospective study from preloss to 18-months postloss. *Journal of Personality and Social Psychology, 83*(5), 1150–1164.

Boswell, W. R., Boudreau, J. W., & Tichy, J. (2005). The relationship between employee job change and job satisfaction: The honeymoon-hangover effect. *Journal of Applied Psychology, 90*(5), 882–892.

Brown, N. J., Sokal, A. D., & Friedman, H. L. (2013). The complex dynamics of wishful thinking: The critical positivity ratio. *American Psychologist, 68*(9), 801–813.

Brunstein, J. (1993). Personal goals and subjective well-being: A longitudinal study. *Journal of Personality and Social Psychology, 65,* 1061–1070.

Clark, A. E., Diener, E., Georgellis, Y., & Lucas, R. E. (2008). Lags and leads in life satisfaction: A test of the baseline hypothesis. *Economic Journal, 118*(529), F222–F243.

Clark, A. E., & Georgellis, Y. (2013). Back to baseline in Britain: Adaptation in the British Household Panel Survey. *Economica, 80*(319), 496–512.

Copen, C. E., Daniels, K., Vespa, J., & Mosher, W. D. (2012). *First marriages in the United States: Data from the 2006–2010 national survey of family growth. (NHSP Publication No. 49).* Hyattsville, MD: National Center for Health Statistics. Retrieved from: <http://www .cdc.gov/nchs/products/nhsr.htm>.

Diener, E. (2000). Subjective well-being: The science of happiness and a proposal for a national index. *American Psychologist, 55*(1), 34–43.

Diener, E., Larsen, R. J., Levine, S., & Emmons, R. A. (1985). Intensity and frequency: Dimensions underlying positive and negative affect. *Journal of Personality and Social Psychology, 48*(5), 1253–1265.

Dyrdal, G. M., & Lucas, R. E. (2013). Reaction and adaptation to the birth of a child: A couple-level analysis. *Developmental Psychology, 49*(4), 749–761.

Frederick, S., & Loewenstein, G. (1999). Hedonic adaptation. In D. Kahneman, E. Diener, & N. Schwarz (Eds.), *Well-being: The foundations of hedonic psychology* (pp. 302–329). New York: Russell Sage Foundation.

Fredrickson, B., & Losada, M. (2005). Positive affect and the complex dynamics of human flourishing. *American Psychologist, 60*(7), 678–686.

Griffeth, R. W., Hom, P. W., & Gaertner, S. (2000). A meta-analysis of antecedents and correlates of employee turnover: Update, moderator tests, and research implications for the next millennium. *Journal of Management, 26*(3), 463–488.

Haring-Hidore, M., Stock, W. A., Okun, M. A., & Witter, R. A. (1985). Marital status and subjective well-being: A research synthesis. *Journal of Marriage and the Family,* 947–953.

Ilgen, D. R. (1971). Satisfaction with performance as a function of the initial level of expected performance and the deviation from expectations. *Organizational Behavior and Human Performance, 6*(3), 345–361.

International Society of Aesthetic Plastic Surgery. (2011). *ISAPS International Survey on Aesthetic/Cosmetic Procedures Performed in 2011.* Retrieved from <http://www.isaps.org/ isaps-global-statistics-2011.html>.

Jacobs Bao, K., Boehm, J. K., & Lyubomirsky, S. (2013). Using surprise to stay happier: Thwarting hedonic adaptation to positive events. Unpublished manuscript.

Jacobs Bao, K., Layous, K., & Lyubomirsky, S. (2013). *Aspirations and well-BEING: A study of high school students.* New Orleans, LA: Poster presented at the Annual Meeting of the Society of Personality and Social Psychology.

Kahneman, D., & Thaler, R. H. (2006). Anomalies: Utility maximization and experienced utility. *Journal of Economic Perspectives, 20*(1), 221–234.

Kanner, A. D., Coyne, J. C., Schaefer, C., & Lazarus, R. S. (1981). Comparison of two modes of stress measurement: Daily hassles and uplifts versus major life events. *Journal of Behavioral Medicine, 4*, 1–39.

Lucas, R. E. (2005). Time does not heal all wounds: A longitudinal study of reaction and adaptation to divorce. *Psychological Science, 16*(12), 945–950.

Lucas, R. E. (2007). Long-term disability is associated with lasting changes in subjective well-being: Evidence from two nationally representative longitudinal studies. *Journal of Personality and Social Psychology, 92*(4), 717–730.

Lucas, R. E., & Clark, A. E. (2006). Do people really adapt to marriage? *Journal of Happiness Studies, 7*(4), 405–426.

Lucas, R. E., Clark, A. E., Georgellis, Y., & Diener, E. (2003). Reexamining adaptation and the set point model of happiness: Reactions to changes in marital status. *Journal of Personality and Social Psychology, 84*(3), 527–539.

Lucas, R. E., Clark, A. E., Georgellis, Y., & Diener, E. (2004). Unemployment alters the set point for life satisfaction. *Psychological Science, 15*(1), 8–13.

Luhmann, M., Hofmann, W., Eid, M., & Lucas, R. E. (2012). Subjective well-being and adaptation to life events: A meta-analysis. *Journal of Personality and Social Psychology, 102*(3), 592–615.

Lyubomirsky, S. (2011). Hedonic adaptation to positive and negative experiences. In S. Folkman (Ed.), *Oxford handbook of stress, health, and coping* (pp. 200–224). New York: Oxford University Press.

Lyubomirsky, S. (2013). *The myths of happiness: What should make you happy, but doesn't, what shouldn't make you happy, but does.* New York: Penguin Press.

Lyubomirsky, S., Sheldon, K. M., & Schkade, D. (2005). Pursuing happiness: The architecture of sustainable change. *Review of General Psychology, 9*(2), 111–131.

Lyubomirsky, S., Sousa, L., & Dickerhoof, R. (2006). The costs and benefits of writing, talking, and thinking about life's triumphs and defeats. *Journal of Personality and Social Psychology, 90*, 692–708.

Margraf, J., Meyer, A. H., & Lavallee, K. L. (2013). Well-being from the knife? Psychological effects of aesthetic surgery. *Clinical Psychological Science, 1*(3), 239–252.

Myers, D. G. (2000). The funds, friends, and faith of happy people. *American Psychologist, 55*(1), 56–67.

Sheldon, K. M., Boehm, J. K., & Lyubomirsky, S. (2012). Variety is the spice of happiness: The hedonic adaptation prevention (HAP) model. In I. Boniwell, & S. David (Eds.), *Oxford handbook of happiness* (pp. 901–914). Oxford: Oxford University Press.

Sheldon, K. M., & Elliot, A. J. (1998). Not all personal goals are personal: Comparing autonomous and controlled reasons as predictors of effort and attainment. *Personality and Social Psychology Bulletin, 24*, 546–557.

Sheldon, K. M., & Elliot, A. J. (1999). Goal striving, need satisfaction, and longitudinal well-being: The self-concordance model. *Journal of Personality and Social Psychology, 76*, 482–497.

Sheldon, K. M., & Kasser, T. (1998). Pursuing personal goals: Skills enable progress, but not all progress is beneficial. *Personality and Social Psychology Bulletin, 24*, 1319–1331.

Sheldon, K. M., & Lyubomirsky, S. (2009). Change your actions, not your circumstances: An experimental test of the sustainable happiness model. In A. K. Dutt, & B. Radcliff (Eds.), *Happiness, economics, and politics: Toward a multidisciplinary approach* (pp. 324–342). Cheltenham: Edward Elgar.

Sheldon, K. M., & Lyubomirsky, S. (2012). The challenge of staying happier: Testing the hedonic adaptation model. *Personality and Social Psychology Bulletin, 38*(5), 670−680.

Van Boven, L. (2005). Experientialism, materialism, and the pursuit of happiness. *Review of General Psychology, 9,* 132−142.

Van Boven, L., & Gilovich, T. (2003). To do or to have? That is the question. *Journal of Personality and Social Psychology, 85,* 1193−1202.

Wilson, T. D., Centerbar, D. B., Kermer, D. A., & Gilbert, D. T. (2005). The pleasures of uncertainty: Prolonging positive moods in ways people do not anticipate. *Journal of Personality and Social Psychology, 88*(1), 5−21.

Wilson, T. D., & Gilbert, D. T. (2008). Explaining away: A model of affective adaptation. *Perspectives on Psychological Science, 3*(5), 370−386.

Chapter 5

Can Happiness Change?
Theories and Evidence

Robert A. Cummins

Deakin University, Melbourne, VIC, Australia

INTRODUCTION

To a subjective well-being (SWB) novitiate, this book title must seem strange. Of course happiness changes! Every day we experience substantial fluctuations in happiness. When we experience praise, our happiness rises; and when we are scolded, it falls. But this is not the topic under discussion. The form of happiness change implied by the title is a long-term change in happiness. Can people be induced to experience more or less mood happiness on average, over the course of a week, month, or year? This confusion over the meaning of *happiness* raises the crucial issue of nomenclature.

PROBLEMS OF NOMENCLATURE

As every non-native speaker knows, English is a wretched language. It is full of inconsistencies and irregularities, but perhaps its most confusing aspect is that almost every word seems to have more than one meaning. Happiness is no exception (see Diener, 2006, for a nomenclature review; and Diener, Scollon, & Lucas, 2004, for a historical review).

To illustrate this diversity, Veenhoven (2010a, 2010b) uses the word *happiness* in its most inclusive form, to mean all positive feelings about the self. Narrowing the field somewhat are Chang and Nayga (2010), who use happiness as a synonym for SWB. Rather more specifically, this word has been used to exclude cognition, as average levels of positive and negative affect (Seidlitz & Diener, 1993). Finally, and most specifically, happiness refers to a single affect within the classification system described by the circumplex model of affect (Russell, 2003).

Happiness is also used to imply different temporal durations. In common usage, it refers to a short-lived emotional reaction to a positive experience

75

(Frijda, 1999). There is also, however, a very different form of happiness, which is a long-duration, positive mood trait (Seidlitz & Diener, 1993). This mood happiness is not tied to a specific percept and is experienced as a diffuse affective feeling (Morris, 1999; Ruckmick, 1936).

These meanings are all so different from one another that simply assembling literature on *happiness change* would be uninformative. Within this chapter, the term *happiness* is used to refer to the following meaning:

1. It describes a single affect within the circumplex model of affect (see, e.g., Yik, Russell, & Feldman Barrett, 1999).
2. It refers to mood happiness in the form of a genetically based, long-term, dispositional affect that is an important component of both SWB and homeostatically protected mood (HPMood; see later). It is also an important component of personality.

THE PERSONALITY CONNECTION

One of the most durable findings in relation to mood happiness and SWB is their temporal stability (Headey & Wearing, 1992). As a contemporary example, the Australian Unity Wellbeing Index (AUWI) has monitored the SWB of the Australian population on a cross-sectional basis since 2001 using the Personal Well-being Index (International Well-being Group, 2013). Twenty-nine surveys were conducted from 2001 to 2013, each involving a new sample of 2,000 people (Cummins et al., 2013b). All results are standardized to a 0−100 scale and, using the survey mean scores as data, the average of these surveys is 75 points with a standard deviation of 0.8 points. So, how is such stability between surveys achieved? Personality seems an obvious candidate.

From the 1980s, it has been generally agreed that personality is stable in adulthood (Costa, McCrae, & Zonderman, 1987; McCrae & Costa, 1990), that it has a dominantly genetic basis (McGue, Bacon, & Lykken, 1993), and that it correlates strongly with SWB (Diener, Suh, Lucas, & Smith, 1999; Sheldon, 2004; Sheldon, Cheng, & Hilpert, 2011). This correlation is most evident with the dimensions of extraversion and neuroticism (Diener & Lucas, 1999). Thus, several eminent researchers came to the conclusion that personality is responsible for SWB stability (e.g., DeNeve & Cooper, 1998; Emmons & Diener, 1985; Headey & Wearing, 1992; Vitterso & Nilsen, 2002), with Diener et al. (1999) suggesting that the link is the result of "inborn individual differences in the nervous system." Thus, the presumed causal pathway was from genetically guided neurological wiring, yielding an idiosyncratic mix of extraversion/neuroticism, which controlled the average level of SWB.

Within this belief system, it is envisaged that the connection between SWB and personality is through "gene-environment correlations" (Lykken, Bouchard, McGue, & Tellegen, 1992; Scarr & McCartney, 1983). That is, genetically distinct individuals have a particular personality that tends to elicit idiosyncratic forms of experience (Headey & Wearing, 1989). Thus, the stability of SWB is derived from the predictable and stable set of resulting experiences for each person (Caspi, Elder, & Bern, 1987; Diener et al., 1999; Millon, 1981).

However, complicating this story is the fact that SWB exhibits both state and trait properties (Diener et al., 1999). That is, although SWB is generally stable, it can also change under the influence of some life events, generally returning to origin (Headey & Wearing, 1989). While state changes in SWB are easily accounted for through daily events and experiences, it is more difficult to explain the return of SWB to baseline after chronic displacement.

The dominant explanation, as reinforced by major reviews (e.g., Diener et al., 1999), is the Headey and Wearing (1989, 1992) proposition that personality restores equilibrium by predisposing particular kinds of life events. That is, people with strong extraversion, who experience reduced SWB, will gradually return their SWB to origin through the repeated experience of positive life events. However, this does not explain how someone high on neuroticism recovers from low SWB.

To account for the return of SWB to origin from both enhanced and diminished levels, researchers have proposed a variety of other processes. They include habituation, adaptation, coping strategies, and changing goals (Diener et al., 1999). However, the integration of these processes with the personality-SWB connection has not been articulated.

Also notable is that evidence for the SWB-personality connection is purely correlational. Thus, theoretically, the affective content of SWB could be driving personality, with high positive affect (PA) yielding high extraversion and high negative affect (NA) yielding high neuroticism. This possibility looks more like a probability when considering the developmental sequence. For example, Goldsmith and Campos (1986) proposed, from their studies of infants, that a characteristic emotional style emerges early in life under the influence of genetic direction. This emotional style, they suggest, is somewhat stable across time and could provide the building blocks for adult personality. Indeed, the similarity of early temperamental dimensions and adult personality traits has been noted by many authors (e.g., Digman & Shmelyov, 1996; Rothbatt & Ahadi, 1994).

The clear implication of this early childhood research is that genetic factors cause differences in the reactivity of the emotional centers of the brain. These factors predispose infants to experience greater or lesser degrees of pleasant and unpleasant moods and emotions. It seems likely, therefore, that these differences in affect not only influence the development of personality but also, and perhaps independently, represent a biological predisposition to experience higher or lower levels of SWB in adulthood.

The first researcher to suggest this reverse causal pathway was Davern (2004). She examined mood and personality in terms of their relative capacity to capture SWB variance. From a pool of 31 affects, representing the octants of the circumplex, she found only 6 made a significant, unique contribution to general life satisfaction (GLS). These comprised *contented, happy, energized, satisfied, stressed,* and *pleased.* Collectively, these six affects (described as *Core Affect,* a term adopted from Russell, 2003) accounted for 64% of the variance in GLS and, given their relative contributions to this variance, Davern concluded that SWB judgments mainly comprise pleasant affect.

In a subsequent study, Davern, Cummins, and Stokes (2007) used these six affects together with the seven cognitive discrepancies of Multiple Discrepancies Theory (MDT; Michalos, 1985), and Extraversion and Neuroticism (Costa & McCrae, 1980), in a hierarchical regression to predict SWB measured by the Personal Well-being Index (International Well-being Group, 2013). This study found that Core Affect accounted for 66% of the variance, MDT contributed a further 2%, while personality failed to make a significant contribution. A subsequent revision of this model identified a more parsimonious measure of Core Affect, which reduced the number of affects from six to three (happy, contented, and excited). Structural equation modeling found that 90% of the variance in SWB was contributed by these three affects, with a small contribution from MDT (Michalos, 1985) and none from personality.

This was the first demonstration that affect, not personality, may be the main determinant of adult life satisfaction and SWB. These findings have essentially been replicated by Blore, Stokes, Mellor, Firth, and Cummins (2011) and by Tomyn and Cummins (2011). These three core affects of happy, contented, and excited/alert have been further characterized by Cummins (2010) as a set point for mood happiness.

SET POINTS FOR MOOD HAPPINESS

The first reported use of the term *set point* in the context of SWB was by McGue et al. (1993). They stated that, after perturbation/displacement, SWB returns to its pre-event level (i.e., "… to a stable set point that we hypothesize is predominantly influenced by genetic factors," p. 105). They also adhered to the common view—that genetic factors are responsible for stable personality, which, in turn, produces stable levels of SWB. They did not comment on the proposed genetic link between a set point and personality.

Subsequent authors have maintained the lead role of personality in SWB set points by suggesting that genetically driven differences in personality cause ("at least in part": Diener, Lucas, & Scollon, 2006) individual differences in "biological set points of emotional experience" (Diener & Lucas, 1999; Diener et al., 1999) or "positive emotional set points" (Diener et al., 2006). Thus, they conclude, "personality factors may predispose individuals to experience different levels of well-being" (Diener et al., 2006, p. 307). These set points, so conceived, are seen as comprising some balance between PA and NA (Diener & Lucas, 1999), such that this affective balance then perfuses SWB to create a stable, idiosyncratic level for each person. However, as argued in the previous section, it now appears more likely that this order of causation is reversed. That is, the affective set point is genetically predisposed and the resulting affect drives both personality and SWB.

Such a characterization of set points, comprising affect in the form of homeostatically protected Mood (HPMood; Cummins, 2010), was inspired by Russell's (2003) view of core affect. Russell conceived Core Affect as a neuro-physiologically generated affect comprising the simplest, constant, non-reflective feeling. It was envisaged as a genetically determined individual difference, not modifiable by conscious experience (Lyubomirsky, Sheldon, & Schkade, 2005), and yet being a ubiquitous component of conscious experience. These properties are also attributed to HPMood (Cummins, 2010) with the additional specification that the affective content of this mood can be characterized as a fixed combination of content, happy, and alert.

This story has been taken to a new level by a recent publication (Cummins, Li, Wooden, & Stokes, 2014) claiming to demonstrate the existence of such set points. The data used to make this determination were derived from 7,356 respondents who provided GLS data each year for 10 consecutive years. Data analysis involved the progressive elimination of unreliable data for each individual based on confidence limits, with the data remaining considered an approximation of each person's set point. The discovered set points have a normal population distribution within 70 to 90 points, with an average of 80, referenced to a 0−100 point scale.

It is proposed that each set point for HPMood has two purposes. First, it provides a standard against which the strength of positive emotion is judged. The maintenance of this standard level is managed by homeostatic control, to be discussed in the next section. Second, it provides a gentle background level of activated-positive affect which perfuses thoughts about the self, but most strongly perfuses abstract feelings about the self, such as elicited through the GLS question "How satisfied are you with your life as a whole?" This high HPMood content causes people to naturally feel positive when evaluating themselves in general terms.

In addition to perfusing GLS, HPMood also strongly perfuses other self-report constructs with high personal-abstract content, such as self-esteem, optimism, and perceived control (see Lai & Cummins, 2012). Some examples of item wording will serve to demonstrate this personal-affective content. Included in the Rosenberg self-esteem scale (Rosenberg, 1979) is "On the whole, I am satisfied with myself." Within the Life Orientation Test (Carver & Scheier, 2003) is "In uncertain times, I usually expect the best." And within the Perceived Control Scale (Chambers, Hollway, Parsons, & Wallage, 2003) is "When something bad happens to me—I look for different ways to improve the situation." Due to such personal-abstract items, the

HPMood content is high, with the result that levels of these constructs are generally held close to set point and therefore close to one another.

A further consequence of this common affective content is that the preceding scales predictably and strongly intercorrelate with one another and with SWB. This is due to HPMood being an individual difference. That is, people with a high set point respond very positively to all of these scales due to their common perfusion with high HPMood, whereas people with a low set point respond rather lower. The influence of HPMood as an individual difference may also be responsible for shared variance causing the General Factor of Personality (Rushton & Erdle, 2010). Thus, due to the normal distribution of set points within general population samples (Cummins et al., 2014), the HPMood content within these scales is represented as shared variance, hence causing the correlations. If this variance of HPMood is removed using covariance (Lai & Cummins, 2012), the correlations between these measures are dramatically reduced.

This description of HPMood as providing a constant, gentle, background level of activated-positive affect is consistent with its proposed adaptive value as a persistent mood enhancer. However, the description so far provided in relation to set points is incomplete in several respects. One of these is that, in order for HPMood to provide a standard level of background affect for each person, some processes must operate to bring experienced affect back to set point after a perturbation caused by an emotional experience. Previous discussion has discounted personality as responsible for this return. Homeostasis is an alternative.

SUBJECTIVE WELL-BEING HOMEOSTASIS

Subjective Well-being (SWB) Homeostasis Theory asserts that each individual's set point for HPMood is defended. This defense is provided by processes that are instrumental in returning resting levels of affect back to set point after an emotional event. One line of evidence supporting the operation of such processes comes from studying SWB as measured by either GLS or the Personal Well-being Index. Because such measures are highly saturated with HPMood, as has been described, measured SWB is a reasonable proxy for HPMood under benign living conditions. Measured SWB is not, however, proxy for HPMood under conditions of strong positive or negative emotion.

The remarkable stability of average SWB in Australia has been mentioned. However, the personal experience of affect from moment to moment is not stable. Because HPMood is merely a background affect, the conscious experience of affect is often dominated by the momentary experience of emotions. These emotions, generated in response to relevant percepts, are likely to be stronger sources of affect than HPMood. Thus, when they occur, experienced affect will be different from set point.

Such discrepancies, we propose, activate homeostatic processes with the aim of returning experienced affect to its set point. Because of this repeated cycle of emotion-induced variation in affect and homeostatic defense, actual affective experience normally oscillates around its set point. However, these oscillations are generally of a minor extent because established life routines serve to generally protect against strong emotional challenges. As a consequence, provided that homeostasis remains in control, the oscillations in affective experience remain within the individual's set point range. This accounts for the appearance of SWB stability when averaged across a population sample.

The preceding description of homeostasis is somewhat similar to that suggested by Carver (1998), who proposed that the term *resilience* be used to denote homeostatic return to a prior condition. However, his explanation of recovery is limited to adaptation and conceives a return to a baseline, as do also Headey and Wearing (1989). The current account is different in proposing a return to set point due to the integrated action of stabilizing homeostatic forces, which include automatic emotion correction, behavior, habituation, adaptation, and a system of both external and internal cognitive buffers. It is proposed that it is the combined power of these processes that accounts for the return of SWB to set point after a major emotional event has taken experienced affect beyond the set point range.

Returning Overly High SWB to Set Point

Immediately after SWB is threatened by a positive emotional event, a variety of unconscious devices are activated. They include at least an enhanced probability of approach behavior, habituation, and adaptation.

This enhanced probability of approach behavior is a homeostatic hazard. Because the experience is pleasurable, people feel motivated to extend their period of engagement, with the aim of maintaining the level of positive affect above the level of HPMood. However, this is not generally adaptive because it alters cognitive processing in ways that may not be normally beneficial. For example, high positive affect causes less careful processing of available information useful for decision making (Forgas, 2008). In practice, however, strong positive experience cannot be naturally maintained for long due to habituation and adaptation.

The process of *habituation* is a general term meaning decreasing responsiveness to a repeated stimulus (Thompson, 2009). It is not due to sensory adaptation or motor fatigue, but rather is an adaptive behavior involving a form of primitive learning. Its purpose is to conserve resources by reducing the response to stimuli that are predictable. So, for example, the tick of the bedside clock quickly becomes unnoticed as habituation takes control. Equally, habituation explains why the 10th lick of an ice cream tastes less intense than the first, as habituation erodes its initial impact. Eating out in fine restaurants every day also loses its initial charm, but here the active process is adaptation.

The process of adaptation is best understood through Adaptation Level Theory (Helson, 1964). The general principle is that, under regular circumstances of living, people naturally adapt to a point of affective neutrality. This is their adaptation level (AL), and it has two important characteristics. First, it is the benchmark against which people judge the strength of current positive or negative experience. Second, AL can be raised or lowered by past experience (Eiser & Stroebe, 1972), and so AL moderates the impact of current experience. Consider, for example, an extremely positive event, such as winning a million dollars. While this obviously causes intensely positive feelings because the experience is so much more positive than AL, it also causes AL to shift upward. This has dampening consequences for future levels of pleasure. That is, because momentary pleasurable experiences are referenced to AL, and because AL has become more positive, such experiences are felt as less intense. Importantly, however, the same process works in reverse to assist recovery from misfortune. If someone suffers a sudden loss of functioning, such as through adventitious paraplegia, then that person's reduced level of pleasure causes AL to drop. This has the effect of causing the person to gain pleasure from minor sources of positive input that would not previously have been noticed (Brickman & Campbell, 1971).

The combined forces of habituation and adaptation are powerful reasons to expect that above set point levels of SWB are hard, if not impossible, to maintain. These same processes also explain why the techniques of positive psychology have such weak long-term effectiveness to raise SWB in normally functioning people (Cummins, 2013b).

Returning Low SWB to Set Point

Avoidance of negative experiences through anticipatory behavior is the most effective way to defend against low SWB. Such behaviors constitute a complementary process to homeostasis, originally referred to as *predictive homeostasis* (Moore-Ede, 1986) and now called *allostasis* (Sterling & Eyer, 1988). This term describes planning to deal effectively with future challenges by appropriate behaviors and resource acquisition. However, allostatic strategies will not prevent negative challenges occurring from time to time. Such challenges have the potential to dominate conscious affect, and so cause the experienced level of SWB to move below set point. When this occurs, the processes of returning low SWB back to set point are complex.

The most immediate response to a negative homeostatic threat is to make positive emotions highly accessible (DeWall, Deckman, Pond, & Bonser, 2011). Following or contemporaneous with this, again, behavior plays a central role. If they can, people disengage from unpleasant situations. However, when disengagement is not possible, other kinds of solutions must be found. One of these is to call on resources that have been nurtured in anticipation of such homeostatic challenge. Building such resources is part of the allostatic process, and three key resources for this purpose are relationships, money, and meaningful occupation.

These "external buffers" protect HPMood by facilitating adaptive behaviors (Ensel & Lin, 1991). Almost universally, the research literature attests to the power of good relationships to moderate the influence of potential stressors on SWB (Sarason, Sarason, & Pierce, 1990). Money is also a powerful external buffer that protects HPMood through its potential to purchase defensive resources. For example, wealthy people pay others to perform homeostatically challenging tasks they do not wish to do themselves. Finally, having a personally meaningful occupation provides many defensive benefits. Paid employment, in particular, provides a sense of purpose and structure to life, facilitates connection to similarly oriented people, and likely benefits household resilience through income and/or support. The combined use of such resources to deal with specific challenges has been referred to by Schulz and Heckhausen (1996) as *selective primary control*.

When allostatic preparation is insufficient to deal effectively with a challenge, and SWB homeostasis continues to be threatened, internal cognitive resources are activated. These "positive cognitive buffers" employ cognition as a homeostatic defense against negative experience. Three such buffers have been identified, and they correspond with the same three constructs used by Taylor and Brown (1988) as evidence of positive distortion in self-evaluation. They are self-esteem (i.e., feelings of self-worth; Cummins & Nistico, 2002), perceived control (i.e., perception that one can achieve desired outcomes through one's own actions; Folkman & Moskowitz, 2000; Thompson, Armstrong, & Thoman, 1998), and optimism (i.e., the belief that one's future is positive; Peterson, 2000).

All three of these positive buffers are in intimate, conscious interaction with momentary experience. They are all strongly perfused with HPMood, which is delivered at the level of each set point. Their mechanism of defense is to psychologically reconstruct bad events in a way to minimize the negativity and maximize the advantage to the self. Thus, for example, a failure of primary control (Rothbaum, Weisz, & Snyder, 1982) causing SWB to fall may be counteracted by thinking that the failure experience will be of future benefit (Affleck & Tennen, 1996). An assault on optimism may be countered by the thought that "tomorrow will be better than today," while diminished self-esteem may give rise to understanding that the person responsible for the personal affront is unworthy of friendship (Wills, 1981).

In summary, homeostasis theory proposes these three constructs as the primary cognitive buffers in protecting the positive-activated affect generated as HPMood. Empirical evidence comes from the use of multiple regression. For example, Cummins et al. (2013b) provide tables showing the contribution of individual domains to GLS using combined survey data from the

Australian Unity Wellbeing Index (Appendix Table A 2.17.1, N = 57,580). The seven PWI domains together account for 51.2% of the variance in GLS, which is apportioned as 36.5% shared and 14.7% unique variance. Of this unique variance, 13.3%, or 89.3% of the unique variance accounted for, comes from the three domains of standard of living, relationships, and achieving in life. These three domains may be figuratively considered to represent the corners of a Golden Triangle of Happiness. The reason for their preeminence is that each domain encompasses a double benefit; they provide both resources to avoid homeostatic defeat and resources to recover when things go wrong. Relationships do this through social support (protective) and intimate sharing (recovery). Money does it through the purchase of both protective and recovery resources. Meaningful activity does it through providing a sense of purpose and structure to life (protective) while also facilitating connection to similarly oriented people and, if the activity is a paid job, then it also provides income (recovery).

While the preceding account has some merit as an internally consistent account of homeostatic defense and recovery, it rests on the proposition of set points. The existence of these hypothetical constructs has received much attention. Some of the evidence against set point theory will now be examined.

CHALLENGES TO SET POINT THEORY

One Set Point or Many?

Diener et al. (2006) claimed that each person has "... multiple happiness set points" (p. 305). They reached this conclusion through the following logical trail: (a) A happiness set point "... implies that well-being is a single entity with a single baseline." (b) They state that Lucas, Diener, and Suh (1996) showed that "... the global category of happiness is composed of separable well-being variables" (Diener et al., 2006, p. 307). (c) Because these well-being variables sometimes move in different directions, the idea of a unitary set point is not tenable.

The following problems with this conclusion can be noted:

1. The nomenclature problem is evident, with *happiness* used as a synonym of *well-being*. Their argument is not relevant to a set point for HPMood.
2. If variables can move either in the same or different directions, they are independent of one another. Such independence cannot be used to inform the existence of set points. The affects *aroused* and *pleased* are commonly used to depict orthogonality on the circumplex (e.g., Yik, Russell, & Steiger, 2011). This does not infer a set point for *aroused*.
3. It is well established that response format is one of the critical factors that influences the apparent bipolarity or independence of affect scales (Schimmack, 2005; Schimmack, Böckenholt, & Reisenzein, 2002; Segura & González-Romá, 2003). Importantly, therefore, the presented results cannot be reliably used to determine the existence of multiple set points.

4. In support of their claim, the authors present results on positive affect (PA) and negative affect (NA) from the Victoria Quality of Life Panel Study (Headey & Wearing, 1989, 1992). Notably, however, the measures of PA and NA were made using the Bradburn Affect Balance Scale (Bradburn, 1969). Despite its name, this scale is far from a pure measure of affect. For example, it asks people to reflect over the past few weeks whether they have felt "proud because someone complimented you on something you had done" (PA) and "so restless you couldn't sit long in a chair" (NA). Restricting the experience of *pride* to a compliment places an unnecessary caveat on the affect, while *restlessness* does not necessarily imply negative affect. Restlessness may signal an imminent positive event, such as the return of a lover.

In summary, the notion of multiple set points does not survive scrutiny. Perhaps the idea that set points change will do better.

Joy, Misery, and Myth of Changing Set Points

Various authors (Diener et al., 2006; Headey, Muffels, & Wagner, 2012; Veenhoven, 1994) have claimed that idiosyncratic and unchanging set points for SWB cannot exist because SWB varies within individuals over time. In fact, an understanding of HPMood explains why set points and changing SWB can co-exist.

Central to this understanding is recognizing the status of set points as hypothetical constructs and that any measurement attributed to them can only be made using self-report data. It then follows logically that, because humans have a single flow of conscious experience, a self-report involving affect will be dominated by the strongest source. Either the momentary affect of joy or the chronic misery of depression will dominate the self-report. This does not necessarily imply a changed HPMood set point.

As previously discussed, HPMood is proposed as a weak, constant, positive-activated mood, which backgrounds the affective experience and causes positive bias in cognitions concerning the self (Cummins & Nistico, 2002). This background role allows the set point level of HPMood to be adaptive, which it would not be if it normally dominated awareness (see Schwarz & Clore, 1983, 1996). As noted by Morris (1999), background mood becomes irrelevant when there is a mismatch between such mood and an emotion-inducing percept. Such a discrepancy is apparent when an emotion is generated to match the percept. Thus, experiences providing joy and misery will generate far stronger affects, as emotion, than is provided by the HPMood of set points. The experience of these emotions will then infiltrate the experience of SWB and so cause measured SWB to reflect the emotion far more than the set point.

This explanation is analogous to changes in body temperature. Prolonged exposure to a sufficiently hot or cold thermal challenge will cause core body temperature to rise or fall beyond its normal range of operation. This does not represent a change in set point for core body temperature (37°C). Such changes represent defeat of homeostasis and, after the source of thermal challenge is removed, body temperature will revert to its set point. Thus, consistent with this analogy, changes in measured SWB due to emotions such as joy or misery are not evidence for a changing set point.

Individual Differences in Adaptation

The third challenge to set point homeostasis is offered by Diener et al. (2006), who stated

An implicit assumption of the hedonic treadmill theory (Brickman & Campbell, 1971), is that adaptation to circumstances occurs in similar ways for all individuals. If adaptation results from automatic and inevitable homeostatic processes, then all individuals should return to neutrality or at least to their own unique baseline. But we have found individual differences in the rate and extent of adaptation that occurs even to the same event. (p. 30)

The key misunderstanding in this quotation is that homeostatic processes, including adaptation, will "inevitably" return SWB to their "own unique baseline." On the contrary, while homeostatic processes are, indeed, common to all individuals, their capacity to return SWB to its set point is variable. The speed of return depends on the relative power of the challenge versus the power of the homeostatic resources. The body temperature analogy is again apposite in discussing the "inevitability" of return to set point. In this case, persistent homeostatic failure results in death through hypo- or hyperthermia, with no return to set point.

This misinterpretation based on inevitability goes back to McGue et al. (1993), who reported a study on SWB stability. After concluding that more than 80% of the stable variance in personality is due to genetic factors, they also noted evidence from other studies showing that strong life experiences cause reported SWB to change. In commenting on such changes, they concluded: "In every case, however, the effect associated with each of these events eventually wanes; typically within 1 year, sense of well being has returned to its pre-event level (i.e., to a stable set point that we hypothesize is predominantly influenced by genetic factors)" (p. 105). As evidence, they cited the results of Brickman, Coates, and Janoff-Bulman (1978); Okun, Olding, and Cohn (1990); Murrell and Himmelfarb (1989); and Wortman and Silver (1982).

In fact, not one of the references cited by McGue et al. (1993) supports an inevitable recovery of SWB to pre-event levels. Brickman et al. (1978) did not report the pre-event levels of their measures; Murrell and

Himmelfarb (1989) measured depression, not SWB; and Wortman and Silver (1982) referred to an unpublished conference paper. Only the meta-analysis of Okun et al. (1990) partially supported the proposition of inevitable return. Their analysis involved 30 intervention studies attempting to increase the SWB of people who were elderly. Their finding that SWB returned to baseline was, thus, confined to studies reporting attempts to raise SWB above baseline. Homeostasis theory explicitly describes why such return is almost inevitable for people operating close to their set point at baseline (see Cummins et al., 2013b). Such inevitability does not apply, however, to people who are well below their set point at baseline.

Homeostasis theory also accounts for individual differences in the rate of adaptation to negative percepts. As has been argued, the power of homeostasis to return SWB after a perturbation depends on the balance between the power of the challenge and the strength of available resources. Because of this, individual differences in the rate and extent of adaptation are inevitable.

In summary, not one of these critiques of set point theory withstands close scrutiny. So now it is time to examine some of the commonly cited evidence for changes in happiness.

CAN LEVELS OF HAPPINESS CHANGE?

In his major work on "Authentic Happiness," Seligman (2002) subscribed to the idea that we "each have a personal set range for our level of positive (and negative) emotion, and this range may represent the inherited aspect of overall happiness" (p. 48). He saw the mission of positive psychology as teaching people to change their life circumstances "in order to live in the uppermost part of your range" (p. 60). Among the major techniques proposed for achieving this are two experiential enhancing techniques (savoring and mindfulness) and one technique to deny the force of habituation (to temporally spread the events that produce pleasure far enough to generate a craving).

There are aspects of this view that accord with the preceding text. Although set points have now been demonstrated (Cummins et al., 2014), they are for the positive-activated HPMood, not for emotions and not for negative affect. Whether and to what extent people can experience a chronic level of positive mood that is at a level above their set point remains moot. Certainly the theory, as outlined in this chapter, proposes that the forces of homeostatic return are likely to increase with the distance between the experienced level of affect and set point. So it may well be possible to have the persistent experience of a small increment of happiness that remains within the set point range. The essential questions then concern the circumstances under which such change may occur, the magnitude of change, and for how long change can be maintained.

The answer to all three of these questions depends on two critical circumstances. The first is whether the level of happiness at baseline is above or below its set point. The second is the strength, character, and duration of the agent causing change.

Return to Set Point After a Strong Positive Event Is Inevitable

If the rise in happiness was caused by an unchanging stimulus, such as vanilla ice cream, then the strength of the happiness rise will be variable, depending on personal and situational variables. However, the unchanging nature of the stimulus ensures that universally, habituation and adaptation will rapidly reduce the power of the stimulus. Consequently, despite the continued presence of ice cream, the level of induced happiness will return to set point within a short time.

The power of the stimulus to raise happiness could be enhanced in two ways. First, habituation could be delayed by introducing variation, such as providing more than one flavor of ice cream. However, the habituation processes will likely recognize this as only a slight variation on the basic stimulus, and so the return to set point will be only marginally delayed.

Second, as suggested by Seligman (2002), habituation could be delayed by increasing the interval between repeated exposure to the stimulus. However, such a strategy has two interesting outcomes in relation to SWB. First, intermittent experiences will cause bursts of positive emotion, certainly not continued elevation of happiness above its set point. Second, success in delaying habituation means an increased probability of raising adaptation level, even when the inducing stimuli are variable.

As the inducing stimuli become more complex, such as the pleasures purchased by a large windfall of money, the happiness rises will be more prolonged, at least initially, due to the multiple and variable stimuli involved. The combined experiences of the new car, fine dining, and theater will certainly delay habituation. However, all stimuli, including drugs, will eventually become familiar, predictable, and so become habituated. Moreover, as has been said, persistent elevations in levels of happiness will cause an upward shift in adaptation level, thereby negating the experience of elevated mood. The only uncertainty is how long the return process will take.

This understanding of necessary recovery to set point is consistent with the notion of the "hedonic-treadmill" (Brickman & Campbell, 1971), recognized also by Seligman (2002) who suggested that, as people accumulate more material possessions and accomplishments, their "expectations" also rise. This implies, he stated, that in order to boost their level of happiness "... into the upper reaches of its set range" (p. 49), people must be forever chasing new sources of stimulation. While this is theoretically feasible given infinite resources, in practice, the forces of habituation and adaptation will prevail, and all attempts to chronically raise happiness above its set point through this means will fail.

Finally, consideration must be given to the determined efforts to raise happiness levels through the application of programs of training, often under the auspices of positive psychology. There are two crucial perspectives in relation to such studies. The first is that all such programs of training are subject to the same processes of habituation and adaptation as have been described. It is therefore not surprising that reviews of gratitude training (Cummins, 2013b) and forgiveness training (Cummins, 2013a) find the effi-cacy of such procedures to be minimal. These reviews also find claims of efficacy to have been seriously overstated within the relevant literature. Moreover, although positive psychology techniques may raise the well-being of people in homeostatic defeat, at least on a short-term basis, a wide variety of other interventions are probably just as effective. The crucial demonstra-tion, that positive psychology techniques are superior to standard interven-tions, has yet to be reported.

The conclusion in relation to increased happiness now seems clear. The hedonic system is designed to allow pleasure through a brief elevation of happiness above its set point, but not to allow prolonged positive change in mood that is different from the set point programming. Assuming that each set point represents the most adaptive level of HPMood for that person, the processes that have been described make good sense. They are designed to support the genetic determination of the set point as an idiosyncratic, optimal chronic level of HPMood.

Return to Set Point Following a Strong Negative Event Is not Inevitable

Whereas set point recovery from a positive event is certain, recovery from a negative event is not. At the simplest level, even minor negative percepts are unreliably managed by habituation. The ticking clock may re-enter con-sciousness during a period of insomnia. Adaptation to negative challenge is more reliable, such as adjusting to reduced physical capacity with age, but this also is easily defeated by the co-occurrence of joint pain.

The power of the higher-level processes of homeostatic recovery that have been previously described (accessibility of positive emotions, the defen-sive resources of the "Golden Triangle," and cognitive buffers), to return SWB to set point after a downward perturbation, is far from guaranteed. Indeed, there is a good adaptive reason for making recovery from negative events less certain.

Whereas positive percepts serve to motivate approach behavior, which is generally only adaptive in the short term, negative percepts serve to motivate avoidant behavior. Here, survival may well depend on continued attention to harmful stimuli. The sound of a twig breaking at night may signal the approach of a predator. Rapid habituation and adaptation to such signals would be maladaptive. Pain is another example. Here, the percept signals damaged tissue that requires constant protection to allow repair.

In terms of negative emotions, Seligman (2002) also recognized limits to recovery. He cited, as examples, the death of one's child or spouse in a car crash (p. 49). A more common cause is an ongoing and dominantly negative life situation. Examples are the chronic existential fatigue commonly experienced by informal caregivers (Carers Australia, 2013; Cummins, Hammond, & Campbell, 2012), the negative social interactions experienced by people with schizophrenia (Yanos, Rosenfield, & Horwitz, 2001), or the worthlessness experienced by people who are long-term unemployed (Hattie, 1992). The critical cause of homeostatic failure in all of these situations, where the level of SWB is chronically reduced below the set point range, is the dominance of the challenge over available resources. Under such conditions, the homeostatic system cannot supply adequate defense, so it chronically forfeits control to the challenging agent, and this results in a level of SWB consistently below its set point range. Such a maintained low level of SWB is a harbinger of pathology, most particularly depression (Cummins, 2010).

Any Demonstration of SWB Change Is Baseline-Dependent

Perhaps the most profound understanding to emerge from this analysis is that the measured outcomes of attempts to raise happiness depend critically on levels at baseline. The baseline levels are probably more important than the nature of the intervention itself. Two studies are cited here to demonstrate the power of this insight. The *sine qua non* is knowledge about the normative range for the dependent variable in question.

In Australia, this range has been calculated from data supplied by two projects as the Household, Income and Labour Dynamics in Australia (HILDA) survey (Cummins et al., 2014) and the Australian Unity Wellbeing Index (AUWI) survey (Cummins et al., 2013b). The former citation is to an empirical demonstration that set points for general life satisfaction (GLS) appear to have been demonstrated between the levels of 71 and 90 points on a standard 0−100 point scale, from no satisfaction to complete satisfaction. It is also estimated that each set point has a normal operating range (set point range) of around 18−20 points. From this information, the following deductions can be made regarding normative ranges for individual SWB scores: (a) any value <50 points is likely to represent a case of homeostatic failure. The reason is that 50 points is two standard deviations ($2 \times 20 = 40$) below the highest set point ($90 - 40 = 50$). It is, therefore, the lowest value that could be considered part of a set point range. (b) Any value above 70 points is likely to represent a case of homeostatic integrity, where the SWB value lies at or above set point. The reason is that all set points exist above 70. (c) SWB values in the range 50−70 lie in the zone of homeostatic compromise, where all values lie below their set point but not so far below as to necessarily represent homeostatic defeat.

The second determination of SWB norms comes from the 29 consecutive surveys of the AUWI. Each survey provides scores from 2,000 respondents. If the scores from the available 57,648 individual respondents are used as data (Cummins et al., 2013b, Appendix 2, Table A 2.20), the mean is 75.27 points and the standard deviation is 12.45. Thus, two SDs below the mean is 50.37 points, with scores below this indicative of homeostatic failure. This is a remarkable degree of correspondence with the preceding calculation from set points—points made from a different data set.

These 29 survey mean scores can also be used as data (Cummins et al., 2013b, Appendix 2, Table A 2.21). The derived mean is 75.26 points with a standard deviation of 0.73. This provides a normal range for population mean scores (mean $\pm 2 \times 0.73$) of 73.80 to 76.72 points. Thus, group mean scores that lie outside this range evidence a higher than normal incidence of respondents in homeostatic failure.

These estimates of normal ranges can be used to make predictions as to the likelihood that an intervention designed to raise SWB will succeed. If the baseline level of SWB is at or above either the average set point or the normal range, then the probability of an intervention causing SWB to remain persistently higher is extremely low. If, however, the baseline measure of SWB is below 70 points, then this signals a higher than normal proportion of respondents in homeostatic distress. In this circumstance, an intervention can potentially increase SWB on a chronic basis up to the level required for respondents to regain contact with their set point.

Two examples of data supporting these predictions will be provided. The first was conducted between 2010 and 2012 as a pilot study to determine the effectiveness of the Carers Australia counseling intervention (Cummins et al., 2012). This intervention is offered to informal carers, defined as persons who provide unpaid support to family members or friends who have a disability or are aged and frail (Carers Australia, 2013). Each intervention involves a 1 hour per week counseling session over 6 consecutive weeks. Given that the counseling profession is unregulated in Australia, the content of the counseling sessions is highly variable. The dependent variable was the Personal Well-being Index, and 85 people were measured prior to the first session and 3 months after the last.

The results showed that prior to the counseling, the group mean was 58.13 points, which is extremely low, being some 21 standard deviations below the normative range for group mean scores. At the second measure, SWB had risen 7.51 points to an average 65.64 points, representing an 11.44% increase on initial values. Thus, due to the low initial level, this mild and highly variable form of intervention caused a substantial rise in SWB.

The second study offers a more refined look at the predictions (Tomyn, Weinberg, & Cummins, 2014). This involves a sample of 4,243 adolescents, judged to be "at risk" due to school or family difficulties or direct contact with the law. They participated in a remedial government program providing individualized, case-managed supportive services. The PWI was used to measure the SWB of each participant before the program and again after 5 months. The sample was divided into three subgroups using baseline values of 0–50, 51–69, and 70 + points. The level of increase in mean PWI for these three groups was 23.75, 12.08, and 1.48 points, respectively. These results are perfectly consistent with prediction from homeostasis theory.

CONCLUSIONS

It is interesting to consider this chapter in the context of a quote from the authors who coined the expression "hedonic treadmill" more than 40 years ago. After noting the inevitability of adaptation to heightened positive affect, they tried to give hope by stating ". . . we should not ignore the possibility of a purely physical or physiological and nonrelativistic solution to the problem of happiness. There may be a new drug, a method of brain stimulation, or a happiness pill that will move people to any level of good feeling they choose whenever they choose. Short of this, however, there may be no way to permanently increase the total of one's pleasure except by getting off the hedonic treadmill entirely" (Brickman & Campbell, 1971, p. 300).

This statement has given rise to much anguish in the literature, with authors decrying the notion that "happiness cannot be increased." But the intervening years have witnessed much new understanding concerning this topic, some of which is melded within homeostasis theory. So, now it is time to move on from the treadmill as some absolute statement of fact. Within the new theoretical perspective, the treadmill survives for people already operating at a level of SWB consistent with their set point. The forces of habituation and adaptation ensure this. However, for people who have a level of happiness below their set point, the treadmill does not apply. For these people an increase in happiness can be achieved, up to the level of their set point, through the provision of additional resources. Attempting to ensure that each citizen experiences happiness within his or her set point range would seem a worthy policy goal for governments.

ACKNOWLEDGMENTS

I thank Ann-Marie James for her assistance in the production of this manuscript and Shelley McGillivray for her comments on an earlier draft.

REFERENCES

Affleck, G., & Tennen, H. (1996). Construing benefits from adversity: Adaptational significance and dispositional underpinnings. *Journal of Personality, 64*(4), 899–922.

Blore, J. D., Stokes, M. A., Mellor, D., Firth, L., & Cummins, R. A. (2011). Comparing multiple discrepancies theory to affective models of subjective wellbeing. *Social Indicators Research*, *100*(1), 1–16. Available from http://dx.doi.org/10.1007/s11205-010-9599-2.

Bradburn, N. M. (1969). *The structure of psychological well-being*. Chicago: Aldine.

Brickman, P., & Campbell, D. T. (1971). Hedonic relativism and planning the good society. In M. H. Appley (Ed.), *Adaptation-level theory: A symposium* (pp. 287–302). New York: Academic Press.

Brickman, P., Coates, D., & Janoff-Bulman, R. (1978). Lottery winners and accident victims: Is happiness relative? *Journal of Personality and Social Psychology*, *36*(8), 917–927.

Carers Australia. (2013). Statistics. Retrieved September 4, 2013, from <http://www.carersaustralia.com.au/aboutcarers/statistics>.

Carver, C. S. (1998). Resilience and thriving: Issues, models, and linkages. *Journal of Social Issues*, *54*, 245–266.

Carver, C. S., & Scheier, M. (2003). Optimism. In S. J. Lopez, & C. R. Sydner (Eds.), *Positive psychological assessment: Handbook of models and measures*. Washington, DC: American Psychological Association.

Caspi, A., Elder, G. H., & Bern, D. J. (1987). Moving against the world: Life-course patterns of explosive children. *Developmental Psychology*, *23*, 308–313.

Chambers, S., Hollway, J., Parsons, E. R., & Wallage, C. (2003). *Perceived control and wellbeing*. Melbourne, Australia: Paper presented at the 5th Australian Conference on Quality of Life.

Chang, H. H., & Nayga, R. M. (2010). Childhood obesity and unhappiness: The influence of soft drinks and fast food consumption. *Journal of Happiness Studies*, *11*(3), 261–276.

Costa, P. T., & McCrae, R. (1980). Influence of extraversion and neuroticism on subjective well-being: Happy and unhappy people. *Journal of Personality and Social Psychology*, *38*, 668–678.

Costa, P. T., McCrae, R. R., Jr., & Zonderman, A. B. (1987). Environmental and dispositional influences on well-being: Longitudinal follow-up of an American national sample. *British Journal of Psychology*, *78*, 299–306.

Cummins, R. A. (2010). Subjective wellbeing, homeostatically protected mood and depression: A synthesis. *Journal of Happiness Studies*, *11*, 1–17. Available from http://dx.doi.org/10.1007/s10902-009-9167-0.

Cummins, R. A. (2013a). Limitations to positive psychology predicted by subjective well-being homeostasis. In M. L. Wehmeyer (Ed.), *Oxford handbook of positive psychology and disability* (pp. 509–526). New York: Oxford University Press.

Cummins, R. A. (2013b). Positive psychology and subjective wellbeing homeostasis: A critical examination of congruence. In D. Moraitou, & A. Efklides (Eds.), *Quality of life: A positive psychology perspective* (pp. 67–86). New York: Springer.

Cummins, R. A., Hammond, T., & Campbell, P. (2012). *Carers counselling intervention study* (Vol. 2). Melbourne: Australian Centre on Quality of Life, School of Psychology, Deakin University.

Cummins, R. A., Li, L., Wooden, M., & Stokes, M. (2014). A demonstration of set-points for subjective wellbeing. *Journal of Happiness Studies*, *15*, 183–206. Available from http://dx.doi.org/10.1007/s10902-013-9444-9.

Cummins, R. A., & Nistico, H. (2002). Maintaining life satisfaction: The role of positive cognitive bias. *Journal of Happiness Studies*, *3*(1), 37–69.

Cummins, R. A., Woerner, J., Weinberg, M., Collard, J., Hartley-Clark, L., Perera, C., et al. (2013b). Australian Unity Wellbeing Index: Report 29.0, *The wellbeing of Australians. Two extra hours, mothers and mothers-in-law*. Retrieved September 4, 2013, Melbourne: Australian Centre on Quality of Life, School of Psychology, Deakin University. From <http://www.deakin.edu.au/research/acqol/index_wellbeing/index.htm>.

Davern, M. (2004). Subjective wellbeing as an affective construct. Unpublished doctoral thesis. Deakin University, Melbourne. Retrieved from <http://www.deakin.edu.au/research/acqol/theses/index.htm>.

Davern, M., Cummins, R. A., & Stokes, M. (2007). Subjective wellbeing as an affective/cognitive construct. *Journal of Happiness Studies*, *8*(4), 429−449. Available from http://dx.doi.org/10.1007/s10902-007-9066-1.

DeNeve, K. M., & Cooper, H. (1998). The happy personality: A meta-analysis of 137 personality traits and subjective well-being. *Psychological Bulletin*, *124*, 197−229.

DeWall, C. N., Deckman, T., Pond, R. S., & Bonser, I. (2011). Belongingness as a core personality trait: How social exclusion influences social functioning and personality expression. *Journal of Personality*, *79*, 1281−1314.

Diener, E. (2006). Guidelines for national indicators of subjective well-being and ill-being. *Journal of Happiness Studies*, *7*(4), 397−404.

Diener, E., & Lucas, R. E. (1999). Personality and subjective wellbeing. In D. Kahneman, E. Diener, & N. Schwarz (Eds.), *Well-being, the foundations of hedonic psychology* (pp. 213−229). New York: Russell Sage Foundation.

Diener, E., Lucas, R. E., & Scollon, C. N. (2006). Beyond the hedonic treadmill: Revising the adaptation theory of well-being. *American Psychologist*, *61*(4), 305−314. Available from http://dx.doi.org/10.1037/0003-066X.61.4.305.

Diener, E., Scollon, C. N., & Lucas, R. E. (2004). The evolving concept of subjective well-being. The multifaceted nature of happiness. In P. T. Costa, & I. C. Siegler (Eds.), *Recent advances in psychology and aging* (pp. 188−219). Amsterdam, The Netherlands: Elsevier Science BV.

Diener, E., Suh, E. M., Lucas, R. E., & Smith, H. L. (1999). Subjective well-being: Three decades of progress. *Psychological Bulletin*, *125*(2), 276−302.

Digman, J. M., & Shmelyov, A. G. (1996). The structure of temperament and personality in Russian children. *Journal of Personality and Social Psychology*, *71*, 341−351.

Eiser, J. R., & Stroebe, W. (1972). *Categorization and social judgement*. London: Academic Press.

Emmons, R. A., & Diener, E. (1985). Personality correlates of subjective well-being. *Personality and Social Psychology Bulletin*, *11*, 89−97.

Ensel, W. M., & Lin, N. (1991). The life stress paradigm and psychological distress. *Journal of Health and Social Behavior*, *32*(4), 321−341.

Folkman, S., & Moskowitz, J. T. (2000). Positive affect and the other side of coping. *American Psychologist*, *55*(6), 647−654.

Forgas, J. P. (2008). The strange cognitive benefits of mild dysphoria: On the evolutionary advantages of not being too happy. In J. P. Forgas, M. G. Haselton, & W. von Hippel (Eds.), *Evolutionary psychology and social cognition* (pp. 107−121). New York: Psychology Press.

Frijda, N. H. (1999). Emotions and hedonic experience. In D. Kahneman, E. Diener, & N. Schwarz (Eds.), *Well-being: The foundations of hedonic psychology* (pp. 190−210). New York: Russell Sage Foundation.

Goldsmith, H. H., & Campos, J. J. (1986). Fundamental issues in the study of early temperament: The Denver twin temperament study. In M. E. Lamb, A. L. Brown, & B. Rogoff (Eds.), Advances in Developmental Psychology (pp. 231−283). Hillsdale, NJ: Erlbaum.

Hattie, J. (1992). *Self-concept*. Hillsdale, NJ: Lawrence Erlbaum Associates Publishers.

Headey, B., Muffels, R., & Wagner, G. G. (2012). Choices which change life satisfaction: Similar results for Australia, Britain and Germany. *Social Indicators Research*. Available from http://dx.doi.org/10.1007/s11205-012-0079-8.

Headey, B., & Wearing, A. (1989). Personality, life events, and subjective well-being: Toward a dynamic equilibrium model. *Journal of Personality and Social Psychology, 57*, 731–739. Available from http://dx.doi.org/10.1037/0022-3514.57.4.731.

Headey, B., & Wearing, A. (1992). *Understanding happiness: A theory of subjective well-being.* Melbourne: Longman Cheshire.

Helson, H. (1964). *Adaptation-level theory: An experimental and systematic approach to behavior.* New York: Harper and Row.

International Wellbeing Group. (2013). *Personal Wellbeing Index Manual*, 5th ed. <http://www.deakin.edu.au/research/acqol/instruments/wellbeing-index/pwi-a-english.pdf>.

Lai, L. C. H., & Cummins, R. A. (2012). The contribution of job and partner satisfaction to the homeostatic defense of subjective wellbeing. *Social Indicators Research.* Available from http://dx.doi.org/10.1007/s11205-011-9991-6.

Lucas, R. E., Diener, E., & Suh, E. (1996). Discriminant validity of well-being measures. *Journal of Personality and Social Psychology, 71*(3), 616–628.

Lykken, D. T., Bouchard, T. J., Jr., McGue, M., & Tellegen, A. (1992). Emergenesis: Genetic traits that may not run in families. *American Psychologist, 47*, 1565–1577.

Lyubomirsky, S., Sheldon, K. M., & Schkade, D. (2005). Pursuing happiness: The architecture of sustainable change. *Review of General Psychology, 9*, 111–131.

McCrae, R. R., & Costa, P. T., Jr. (1990). *Personality in adulthood.* New York: Guilford Press.

McGue, M., Bacon, S., & Lykken, D. T. (1993). Personality stability and change in early adulthood: A behavioral genetic analysis. *Developmental Psychology, 29*, 96–109. Available from http://dx.doi.org/10.1037/0012-1649.29.1.96.

Michalos, A. C. (1985). Multiple discrepancies theory (MDT). *Social Indicators Research, 16*, 347–413.

Millon, T. (1981). *Disorders of personality: DSMIII: Axis II.* New York: Wiley.

Moore-Ede, M. C. (1986). Physiology of the circadian timing system: Predictive versus reactive homeostasis. *American Journal of Physiology, Regulatory, Integrative and Comparative Physiology, 250*, R737–R752.

Morris, W. N. (1999). The mood system. In D. Kahneman, E. Diener, & N. Schwarz (Eds.), *Well-being: The foundations of hedonic psychology* (pp. 169–189). New York: Russell Sage Foundation.

Murrell, S. A., & Himmelfarb, S. (1989). Effects of attachment bereavement and pre-event conditions on subsequent depressive symptoms in older adults. *Psychology and Aging, 4*, 166–172.

Okun, M. A., Olding, R. W., & Cohn, C. M. (1990). A meta-analysis of subjective well-being interventions among elders. *Psychological Bulletin, 108*, 257–266.

Peterson, C. (2000). The future of optimism. *American Psychologist, 55*, 44–56.

Rosenberg, M. (1979). *Conceiving the self.* New York: Basic Books.

Rothbatt, M. K., & Ahadi, S. A. (1994). Temperament and the development of personality. *Journal of Abnormal Psychology (Special Issue: Personality and Psychopathology), 103*, 55–66.

Rothbaum, F., Weisz, J. R., & Snyder, S. S. (1982). Changing the world and changing the self: A two-process model of perceived control. *Journal of Personality and Social Psychology, 42*(1), 5–37.

Ruckmick, C. A. (1936). *The psychology of feeling and emotion.* New York: McGraw-Hill.

Rushton, J. P., & Erdle, S. (2010). No evidence that social desirability response set explains the general factor of personality and its affective correlates. *Twin Research and Human Genetics, 13*(2), 131–134.

Russell, J. A. (2003). Core affect and the psychological construction of emotion. *Psychological Review, 110*(1), 145−172.

Sarason, I. G., Sarason, B. R., & Pierce, G. R. (1990). Social support: The search for theory. *Journal of Social and Clinical Psychology, 9*(1), 133−147.

Scarr, S., & McCartney, K. (1983). How people make their own environments: A theory of genotype-environment effects. *Child Development, 54*, 424−435.

Schimmack, U. (2005). Response latencies of pleasure and displeasure ratings: Further evidence for mixed feelings. *Cognition and Emotion, 19*, 671−691.

Schimmack, U., Böckenholt, U., & Reisenzein, R. (2002). Response styles in affect ratings: Making a mountain out of a molehill. *Journal of Personality Assessment, 78*, 461−483.

Schulz, R., & Heckhausen, J. (1996). A life span model of successful aging. *American Psychologist, 51*(7), 702−714.

Schwarz, N., & Clore, G. L. (1983). Mood, misattribution, and judgements of well-being: Informative and directive functions of affective states. *Journal of Personality and Social Psychology, 45*(3), 513−523.

Schwarz, N., & Clore, G. L. (1996). Feelings and phenomenal experience. In E. T. Higgins, & A. W. Kruglandski (Eds.), *Social psychology: Handbook of basic principles* (pp. 433−465). New York: Guilford Press.

Segura, S. L., & González-Romá, V. (2003). How do respondents construe ambiguous response formats of affect items? *Journal of Personality and Social Psychology, 85*, 956−968.

Seidlitz, L., & Diener, E. (1993). Memory for positive versus negative life events: Theories for the differences between happy and unhappy persons. *Journal of Personality and Social Psychology, 64*, 654−664.

Seligman, M. E. P. (2002). *Authentic happiness: Using the new positive psychology to realize your potential for lasting fulfillment*. New York: The Free Press.

Sheldon, K. M. (2004). *Optimal human being: An integrated multilevel perspective*. Mahwah, NJ: Erlbaum.

Sheldon, K. M., Cheng, C., & Hilpert, J. (2011). Understanding well-being and optimal functioning: Applying the multilevel personality in context (MPIC) model. *Psychological Inquiry, 22*(1), 1−16.

Sterling, P., & Eyer, J. (1988). Allostasis: A new paradigm to explain arousal pathology. Handbook of life stress. In S. Fisher, & J. Reason (Eds.), *Cognition and Health* (pp. 629−649). New York: John Wiley & Sons.

Taylor, S. E., & Brown, J. D. (1988). Illusion and well-being: A social psychological perspective on mental health. *Psychological Bulletin, 103*, 193−210.

Thompson, R. F. (2009). Habituation: A history. *Neurobiology of Learning and Memory, 92*, 127−134.

Thompson, S. C., Armstrong, W., & Thoman, C. (1998). Illusions of control, underestimations, and accuracy: A control heuristic explanation. *Psychological Bulletin, 123*, 143−161.

Tomyn, A. J., & Cummins, R. A. (2011). Subjective wellbeing and homeostatically protected mood: Theory validation with adolescents. *Journal of Happiness Studies, 12*(5), 897−914. Available from http://dx.doi.org/10.1007/s10902-010-9235-5.

Tomyn, A. J., Weinberg, M. K., & Cummins, R. A. (accepted April 5, 2014). Intervention efficacy among "at risk" adolescents: A test of Subjective Wellbeing Homeostasis Theory. *Social Indicators Research*, 10.1007/s11205-014-0619-5.

Veenhoven, R. (1994). Is happiness a trait? *Social Indicators Research, 32*, 101−160.

Veenhoven, R. (2010a). Greater happiness for a greater number. Is that possible and desirable? *Journal of Happiness Studies, 11*(5), 605−629.

Veenhoven, R. (2010b). World database of happiness. <http://worlddatabaseofhappiness .eur.nl>.

Vitterso, J., & Nilsen, F. (2002). The conceptual and relational structure of subjective well-being, neuroticism, and extraversion: Once again, neuroticism is the important predictor of happiness. *Social Indicators Research, 57*(1), 89.

Wills, T. A. (1981). Downward comparison principles in social psychology. *Psychological Bulletin, 90*, 245–271.

Wortman, C., & Silver, R. (1982). *Coping with undesirable life events.* Washington, DC: Paper presented at the 90th Annual Convention of the American Psychological Association.

Yanos, P. T., Rosenfield, S., & Horwitz, A. V. (2001). Negative and supportive social interactions and quality of life among persons diagnosed with severe mental illness. *Community Mental Health Journal, 37*, 405–421.

Yik, M., Russell, J. A., & Steiger, J. H. (2011). A 12-point circumplex structure of core affect. *Emotion, 11*(4), 705–731.

Yik, M. S. M., Russell, J. A., & Feldman Barrett, L. F. (1999). Structure of self-reported current affect: Integration and beyond. *Journal of Personality and Social Psychology, 77*, 600–619.

Chapter 6

National Panel Studies Show Substantial Minorities Recording Long-Term Change in Life Satisfaction: Implications for Set Point Theory

Bruce Headey,[1] Ruud Muffels,[2] and Gert G. Wagner[3]

[1]*University of Melbourne, Melbourne, VIC, Australia,* [2]*Tilburg University, Tilburg, the Netherlands,* [3]*German Institute for Economic Research (DIW) and Max Planck Institute, Berlin, Germany*

The central proposition of set point theory is that adult life satisfaction is stable in the medium and long term. Proponents of set point theory accept that major life events can produce temporary fluctuations, but they hold that satisfaction usually reverts to set point within a year or two (Brickman & Campbell, 1971; Clark, Diener, Georgellis, & Lucas, 2004; 2008). A recent, thorough reassessment concluded that the only fairly common life event that has lasting effects in lowering life satisfaction is repeated or long-term unemployment (Clark et al., 2008). The sudden death of one's child and the onset of disability or chronic illness in later years also have long-term negative effects (Lucas, 2007; Mehnert, Kraus, Nadler, & Boyd, 1990; Wortman & Silver, 1987). No discrete event has definitely been shown to improve satisfaction, although cosmetic surgery is a candidate (Frederick & Loewenstein, 1999; Wengle, 1986).

The aim of this chapter is to show that substantial minorities, but not majorities, of respondents in long-running German, British, and Australian household panel surveys have recorded large (not just statistically significant) long-term changes in life satisfaction. These three panels—the German Socio-Economic Panel Study (GSOEP), the British Household Panel Study (BHPS), and the Household Income and Labor Dynamics Australia Survey (HILDA)—are clearly among the best available datasets worldwide, because

99

they permit *direct tests* of the stability of adult life satisfaction. So the results seriously undermine set point theory as usually understood.

It is important to realize that set point theory can be directly tested only with long-term panel data. Only by directly observing the life satisfaction of adults over a long period of time can researchers ascertain whether satisfaction really is stable. Until the GSOEP, BHPS, and HILDA became available, all the evidence for and against set point theory was *indirect* and *inferential*. Stability was inferred from links between life satisfaction and the stable, partly genetic personality traits of neuroticism and extroversion (Costa & McCrae, 1980). It has also been shown that stability is partly due to the influence of parental upbringing on the life satisfaction of children, including children who have long since left the parental home and partnered themselves (Aguche & Trommsdorff, 2010; Headey, Muffels, & Wagner, 2013).[1] Stability has been inferred from evidence about adaptation to major life events (Brickman & Campbell, 1971; Headey & Wearing, 1989). In the special case of income gains, Easterlin (1974, 2005) suggested that adaptation was facilitated by social comparisons with the neighboring Joneses whose incomes were also going up. Finally, and apparently conclusively, stability was inferred from twin studies that estimated the genetic component of happiness at 40%–50%, based on comparisons of cross-sectional and over-time correlations in the happiness of monozygotic and dizygotic twins (Lykken, 1999; Lykken & Tellegen, 1996). However, as Huppert (2005) pointed out, Lykken and Tellegen's twin studies could be interpreted as showing that even monozygotic twins have only moderately stable levels of happiness (correlation of 0.55 over a 9-year period).

A second aim of this chapter is to provide some preliminary explanations of change. The finding that most discrete life events do not produce lasting change has been taken as lending support to the view that set points are more or less fixed. We offer limited evidence to challenge this finding later. But even if it were accepted, it would still be a mistake—a non sequitur—to jump to the conclusion that because discrete life events do not produce change, then change does not happen. In this chapter, again using evidence mainly from the three national panels, we direct attention to variables other than life events, namely, life priorities and behavioral choices, that can change satisfaction. Relevant life priorities include a commitment to pro-social/altruistic values and family values rather than material values. Relevant behavioral choices include choice of partner (particularly the personality of one's partner), active social and community participation, volunteering, a preferred work–leisure balance, regular exercise, and churchgoing.

---

1. Parental influence on children's long-term life satisfaction is not just due to genetic/inherited personality traits. There appear to be additional effects due to parental upbringing and modeling (see Aguche & Trommsdorff, 2010; Headey, Muffels, & Wagner, 2013).

A CRUCIAL DEFINITIONAL ISSUE: HOW TO DEFINE THE SET POINT?

Many subjective well-being (SWB) researchers have referred to a life satisfaction set point (or baseline) and asserted that it is stable, without actually providing an operational definition of the set point. What do we mean by the set point, and how can we assess whether an individual has deviated from his/her set point or remains at or close to it? A useful introspective exercise—or thought experiment—for SWB researchers is to ask themselves what their own set point is, responding on a 0−10 scale (because that is what survey respondents usually have to do). Having answered the initial question, they might then ask themselves why they think their set point is at the level it is. Finally, what evidence, if it turned up, would show that they did not really have a set point, or that it was at a different level from where they thought it was, that it had changed over the years, or that their explanation (or theory) about their own set point was incorrect?

The answers given by the SWB researchers might run like this:

I'm usually about 7 or 8 on a 0−10 Life Satisfaction scale. If you ask me on a normal day in a normal mood for year after consecutive year, 7 or 8 is what I would usually answer. I think the results would be pretty stable. Why do I think I score 7 or 8? It is mainly due to personality. How do I rate on the NEO personality inventory?[2] I rate about average on the neuroticism trait, fairly high on extroversion, high on openness to experience, and about average on agreeableness and conscientiousness. Because neuroticism is negatively related to life satisfaction, while extroversion, agreeableness, and conscientiousness are positively related, and openness is unrelated, that gives me an overall rating on life satisfaction that is about average, or a bit above average.

This account suggests that operational measures of the set point could be based on *either* taking an average (or perhaps a weighted average) of each individual's life satisfaction scores over a period of several consecutive years, *or* based on predictions of life satisfaction (e.g., regression predictions) made from ratings on personality traits.

These leads will be followed up in the next section. For now, let us continue the thought experiment and ask, "What evidence could confirm or falsify my theory about my own set point?"

One possibility is that repeated measures of my satisfaction would show large fluctuations, which did not appear to be around any stable mean. In that case, I would not really have a set point.[3] Another possibility is that my results would be stable in most

---

2. The NEO is a widely used personality inventory. The five measured traits are those referred to in the text (Costa & McCrae, 1991).

3. This logical possibility is not followed up in the chapter. It is not clear how exactly one could confirm that an individual's life satisfaction followed no discernible pattern at all over a period of years.

years but would occasionally fluctuate perhaps due to major life events. This would be in line with set point theory. A further possibility is that my results would be stable for several consecutive years, but then would change by a substantial amount (either upward or downward on the scale) and remain stable at their new level in subsequent years. From this evidence, we would conclude that my set point had changed. Still another possibility, regardless of whether my satisfaction ratings were stable or not, is that my personality theory would turn out to be false or weak. That is, my satisfaction ratings might be only weakly correlated with personality traits. This last inference would, of course, have to be based on interpersonal evidence, not just evidence about one person.

OPERATIONAL DEFINITIONS

Plainly, debates about whether individual set points are stable or subject to change in the medium or long term cannot be resolved without precise working definitions. Before we suggest some reasonable definitions, it may be useful to mention one unsatisfactory definition that has been used or, more often, just implied in previous research. Researchers assessing the impact of life events have sometimes treated a single measure of life satisfaction as the "set point" prior to an event. Clearly, this is unsatisfactory because a single measure cannot possibly provide evidence about whether life satisfaction is stable, about whether it is, in any sense, "set." In the context of assessing the effects of life events, a single measure is further confounded by the possibility that some events are anticipated by the individuals to whom they happen, with the result that life satisfaction changes prior to the event and not just afterward. Clark, Georgellis, Lucas, and Diener (2004) showed that anticipatory changes occur in relation to both marital separation and unemployment.

Two working definitions or measures of the life satisfaction set point are now suggested, together with criteria for assessing set point change:

1. *Multiyear (e.g., 5-year) averages of life satisfaction.* A multiyear average (mean) of individual life satisfaction ratings has the advantage of ironing out temporary fluctuations, which could be due to transient factors, including mood at time of interview. This approach to defining the set point has been used by previous SWB researchers (Fujita & Diener, 2005) and is similar to the approach taken by economists when they want a measure of "permanent" income. Ideally, one would wish to take medium-term (e.g., 5-year) averages, and this is what we do in analyzing data from the GSOEP survey, which has run for more than 25 years. In analyzing the BHPS and HILDA surveys, which have not been running for as long, we use 3-year averages.

2. How to assess whether a person's set point has changed? One possibility would be to regard any statistically significant change (e.g., at the 0.001 level) between one 5-year period and a later period as indicative of set

point change. Alternatively, as is done here, one might adopt a more stringent criterion, requiring individual changes of more than 25, 33.3, or 50 percentiles within the life satisfaction distribution in order to infer that a set point change had occurred.

3. *Set point predicted by personality traits.* An alternative idea is that set points are a function of personality, so one would expect a person's life satisfaction scores to fluctuate around the level predicted by his or her personality traits. Following this approach, initial or baseline set points can be estimated as the satisfaction scores that respondents are predicted to get in a baseline period on the basis of their scores on the NEO-AC personality traits. Possible changes in individual set points can then be viewed as the difference between predicted scores in the baseline period and actual scores in later 5-year periods.

THE GERMAN (GSOEP), BRITISH (BHPS), AND AUSTRALIAN (HILDA) HOUSEHOLD PANEL SURVEYS

The German (GSOEP) panel is the longest running of these national household panels. It began in 1984 in West Germany with a sample of 12,541 respondents (Wagner, Frick, & Schupp, 2007). Interviews have been conducted annually ever since. Everyone in sample households aged 16 and over is interviewed. The cross-sectional representativeness of the panel is maintained by interviewing "split-offs" and their new families. So when a young person leaves home ("splits off") to marry and set up a new family, the entire new family becomes part of the panel. The sample was extended to East Germany in 1990, shortly after the Berlin Wall came down, and since then has also been boosted by the addition of new immigrant samples, a special sample of the rich, and recruitment of new respondents partly to increase numbers in "policy groups." There are now more than 60,000 respondents on file, including some grandchildren as well as children of the original respondents. The main topics covered in the annual questionnaire are family, income, and labor force dynamics. A question on life satisfaction has been included every year.

The British (BHPS) panel was launched in 1991 with about 10,300 individuals in 5,500 households (Lynn, 2006). However, a question about life satisfaction was not included until 1996, so in this chapter, only 1996–2010 data are used. As in Germany, all individuals in the household aged 16 and over are interviewed. Again, sample representativeness is maintained by including split-offs and their new households. The British panel has been augmented by booster samples for Scotland and Wales in 1991 and a new Northern Ireland sample in 2001. A major change occurred in 2010 when the panel was merged into the new United Kingdom Household Longitudinal Study ("Understanding Society"), which has a much larger sample and many additional questions, especially in the health area. Only data provided by the original panel members are analyzed here.

The Australian (HILDA) panel began in 2001 with a sample of 13,969 individuals in about 7,700 households (Watson & Wooden, 2004). Interviews were achieved in 61% of in-scope households. In the Australian panel, all household members aged 15 and over are interviewed. Following rules similar to the Germans and British, individuals who split off from their original households continue in the panel, and members of their new households join it. In 2009 (the latest year of data used), interviews were conducted with 13,301 individuals in 7,234 households.

For this chapter, the sample in each country is restricted to prime age adults, defined as those aged 25 to 69. The aim is to restrict analysis to mature-age individuals who, according to set point theory, should have stable levels of life satisfaction. The lower age limit excludes younger individuals whose personalities may still be changing. The top limit excludes senior citizens whose life satisfaction, in some cases, will be declining due to declining health (Gerstorf et al., 2010).

MEASURES

The research teams that run the three panels have developed slightly differing measures for most concepts used in this chapter. However, despite differences of language, question wording, and response scales, nearly all results replicate across the three countries.

We first describe how the dependent variable, life satisfaction, is measured in the three panels. Then we describe explanatory variables used here to account for medium- and long-term change in life satisfaction.

The Dependent/Outcome Variable: Life Satisfaction

In the German and Australian panels, life satisfaction is measured on a 0–10 scale (German mean = 7.0, standard deviation = 1.8; Australian mean = 7.8, SD = 1.5). A response of 0 means "totally dissatisfied," and 10 means "totally satisfied." In Britain, a 1–7 scale is used (mean = 5.2, SD = 1.2).

Single-item measures of life satisfaction are plainly not as reliable or valid as multi-item measures, but are widely used in international surveys and have been reviewed as acceptably reliable and valid (Diener, Suh, Lucas, & Smith, 1999; Lucas & Donnellan, 2007).

Explanatory Variables

The explanatory variables included in the analyses that follow are life priorities, self and partner personality traits, social participation, the balance between work and leisure (work-life balance), physical exercise, and churchgoing.

Personality Traits of Self and Partner

In 2005, the research teams running the three panels all included a full set of personality measures for the first time. The chosen instrument in each country was a short version of the NEO (Costa & McCrae, 1991). The British and German panels included very short versions of the five scales—just three items/questions to measure each trait—which are reported to be satisfactorily reliable and to correlate highly with longer versions of the NEO preferred by psychologists (Gerlitz & Schupp, 2005).[4] The Australian panel included seven items per trait (Saucier, 1994).

Psychologists usually take the view that personality is about 40%–50% hereditary and quite stable, at least from the age of about 25 or 30 onward (Roberts, Walton, & Viechtbauer, 2006). It should be stressed that, by including personality traits measured in 2005 on the right side of equations to account for life satisfaction in earlier as well as later years, we are, in effect, assuming that personality is completely stable. If it were completely stable, then, of course, it would not matter when it was measured. However, the assumption may not be entirely correct. It has been suggested that ratings on personality traits may be changed to a moderate degree by life experiences such as having a stable marriage or an absorbing job (Roberts et al., 2006; Scollon & Diener, 2006).

LIFE PRIORITIES, GOALS, OR VALUES

SWB researchers are understandably keen to measure what are variously termed *life priorities* or *goals* or *values*. However, it has proved difficult to obtain valid measures. In a very thorough investigation, two pioneers of SWB research, Andrews and Withey (1976), reported that measures of the priority attached to goals, asked on scales running from "very important" to "not at all important," appeared to suffer from social desirability bias, with respondents all giving high ratings to family goals. Importance scores also had low test–retest reliability. A further possible problem was that importance scores and satisfaction scores in most life domains turned out to be moderately correlated. This might mean that people were quite good at getting what they wanted from life—a result in line with economists' utility maximization assumption—or might suggest some reverse causation, with respondents tending to attribute importance to domains they were already well satisfied with, perhaps as a psychological mechanism to boost their overall life satisfaction (Andrews & Withey, 1976). In general, respondents whose life satisfaction was high tended to rate most domains as very important, whereas unhappy or depressed respondents tended (presumably as a

---

4. Even the short version of the scale released by Psychological Assessment Resources has 60 items, 12 items per trait (Costa & McCrae, 1991).

consequence of unhappiness) to rate most domains as relatively unimportant. An underlying problem, which may partly account for measurement difficulties, is that most people are not of a philosophical bent and do not regularly think about their life priorities.

The German panel group decided to tackle these issues afresh and appears to have made considerable improvements in life priorities/goals/values measurement. Their approach is based on a classification initially developed by Kluckhohn and Strodtbeck (1961). Kluckhohn and Strodtbeck set out to measure three sets of life priorities:

- Material priorities and career success
- Family priorities: marriage, children, and the home
- Pro-social or altruistic priorities: friendship, helping others, social and political activism

Using this framework, the German research group developed survey items that have a stable factor structure and adequate test—retest reliability (Headey, 2008; Wagner et al., 2007). Life priorities have been measured intermittently (rather than annually) in GSOEP, starting in 1990. The specific questions asked in different waves of the survey have varied somewhat; here, we use data from the 1990, 1992, 1995, 2004, and 2008 surveys in which the questions were nearly identical. In these surveys 9 or 10 items were included,[5] all asked on a 1—4 scale running from "very important" to "not at all important." In each wave, the items formed three distinct, replicating factors: a *material priorities* factor, a *family priorities* factor, and a *pro-social or altruistic priorities* factor (Headey, 2008).

A *material priorities* index was constructed that gave equal weight to "being able to buy things" and "success in your job." Similarly a *family priorities* index gave equal weight to items relating to the importance of marriage and children. Finally, the *pro-social/altruistic priorities* index gave equal weight to "being involved in social and political activities" and "helping other people."

The Australian panel has included questions on life priorities only once (2001), and the British panel only twice (1998, 2003). Rather than follow the German panel approach of measuring priorities according to an *a priori* classification, these two research teams reverted to the earlier approach of presenting respondents with a rather miscellaneous list, which nevertheless overlapped substantially with the German list. Here, we analyze only priorities included in all three surveys, because a subsidiary aim of this chapter is to assess the extent to which degrees of change in life satisfaction and in the factors causing life satisfaction replicate cross-nationally.

---

5. Ten items were included in 1990, 1992, and 1995 and then nine in 2004 and 2008. The item dropped in 2004 and 2008 related to the importance of having a wide circle of friends, which loaded on the pro-social factor.

In the British panel, questions were asked on a 1−10 scale ("not at all important" to "very important"). Respondents rated the importance of "money" (material priority), "a good partnership" and "having children" (family priorities), and "good friends" (friendship priority, but without a community participation aspect). In the Australian survey, questions were included about the various priorities on a 0−10 scale ("not at all important" to "very important"). Key items related to the importance of "your family" (family priority) and "involvement in your local community" (community priority but without a friendship aspect). The question intended to tap material priorities was somewhat ambiguous. Respondents rated the importance of "your financial situation." This item could have assessed the extent to which respondents were concerned or worried about their financial situation, rather than, or as well as, the priority they attached to material success.

We have not attempted to assess the effects of changes in life priorities in this chapter. Because the questions have been asked only once in Australia, twice in Britain, and intermittently in Germany, the data are not really suited to analysis of change. Instead, we have averaged respondents' scores on priorities for the waves in which they participated.

BEHAVIORAL CHOICES: PARTNER PERSONALITY TRAITS, SOCIAL PARTICIPATION, THE WORK−LEISURE TRADE-OFF, REGULAR EXERCISE, AND CHURCHGOING

Choice of Partner—Especially His/Her Personality Traits

It comes as no surprise that a person's choice of partner can have an effect on his or her own life satisfaction. In all three panels, both partners in sample households are interviewed. In this chapter, we hypothesize that one partner's personality traits can influence the other partner's satisfaction, over and above the influence of his or her own traits. Because neuroticism is the NEO-AC trait most strongly (negatively) related to life satisfaction, we hypothesize that partner neuroticism will affect one's own satisfaction.

Active Social and Community Participation

The three panel surveys differ somewhat in how they measure participation in social activities. In the Australian panel, respondents are asked a single question about how frequently they meet with "friends and relatives." The response scale runs from 1 (every day) to 7 (less than every 3 months).[6] In the British panel, there are two separate items, one relating to frequency of "meeting with friends and relatives" and one to frequency of "talking with

---

6. For each country, response scales relating to social participation have been reversed so that a high score reflects high participation.

neighbors." These questions are asked on a response scale running from "on many days" (code 1) to "never" (code 5). For present purposes, these highly correlated items have been combined into a social participation index. In the German panel, the social participation index used here combines two correlated items about frequency of "meeting with friends, relatives or neighbors" and "helping out friends, relatives or neighbors."[7] The response scale has just three points: "every week," "every month," and "seldom or never."[8]

An advantage is that the social participation questions have been asked every year in all three panels, so it is possible to analyze the effects on life satisfaction of changes in participation levels.

The Work–Leisure Trade-off: Preferred and Actual Working Hours

The trade-off between paid work and leisure is central to welfare economics. Welfare economists assume that leisure is pleasurable, whereas work is less pleasurable but necessary to pay for consumption (Little, 2002). It is further assumed that the balance that individuals (and households) choose between work and leisure reflects the priority they attach to consumption versus leisure. The validity of this last assumption has rarely been directly tested, but the panel datasets make a rough test possible.

Respondents in the Australian and German panels are asked both how many hours per week they actually work (in all jobs combined, if they have more than one job) and how many they would prefer to work. The gap between these two figures can be treated as a rough measure of the degree to which they are achieving their preferred trade-off/choice between work and leisure. Here, we classify individuals whose actual working time is within 3 hours of their preferred time as having their preferences met. We treat those who work over 3 hours more than they want as "overworked," and those who work over 3 hours less than they want as "underworked." Other hours "gaps" were tested, but the 3-hour variables showed the highest correlation with life satisfaction.

In the British panel, respondents are asked how many hours they work (in all jobs combined), and whether they would prefer to work more hours than they do now, fewer, or the same. They are not asked precisely how many hours they would prefer to work, so designating them as "overworked," "underworked," or having their preferences met is a somewhat cruder exercise than in the Australian and German panels.

---

7. The correlations have varied from year to year but are usually around 0.3.
8. "Seldom" and "never" have been included as separate categories in more recent waves of GSOEP.

Because questions about preferred working hours are asked every year in all three panels, we can assess the extent to which changes in work−leisure balance are associated with changes in life satisfaction.

Regular Exercise

In all three panels, a single question has been asked repeatedly (but not in the British survey annually) about participation in sports and/or exercise. Again, questions differ slightly. In the Australian panel, respondents are asked about how frequently they take moderate or intensive physical activity lasting for at least 30 minutes. The response scale runs from 0 ("not at all") to 5 ("every day"). In the British panel, a question is asked every 2 years about how often respondents walk, swim, or play sports. The 5-point response scale runs from "at least once a week" to "never/almost never." Finally, in the German dataset, there is an annual question about participation in active sports or exercise. The 1−4 response scale runs from "almost never" to "at least once a week."

Churchgoing

Many previous research papers have noted the positive cross-sectional association between churchgoing and/or religious belief and life satisfaction (for a recent review, see Myers, 2013). Using the German data, we can go further and estimate whether changes in churchgoing are associated with medium-term gains and losses of life satisfaction. (In the other two panels, questions on churchgoing have been asked only intermittently, so analysis of change is less feasible.)

Analysis of Change Based on Moving 5-Year or 3-Year Averages of Life Satisfaction

In this chapter, one of our aims is to offer some preliminary explanations of medium- and long-term change in life satisfaction. For reasons already explained, it makes no sense for this purpose to use single-year measures of satisfaction. For Germany, we used *5-year moving averages of life satisfaction* (1984−1988, 1985−1989, 1986−1990, and so on).[9] For the shorter Australian and British panels, which are available only for 9 and 12 years, respectively, it was infeasible to use 5-year blocks, so we settled for *3-year moving averages.*[10]

In summary, all analyses in the paper that are concerned with explaining change are based on 5- or 3-year moving averages of life satisfaction ratings.

---

9. The 5-year measures have a mean of 7.0 and a standard deviation (SD) of 1.4.
10. BHPS: mean = 5.2, SD = 1.0. HILDA: mean = 7.8, SD = 1.2.

We then use annual measures of independent (explanatory) variables in trying to account for medium-term change in life satisfaction.

It should be noted that values for some variables that were not included in every wave of the panel surveys have been imputed. Oddly, the life satisfaction question was omitted from the British survey in 2001 and 2009. We simply averaged results for the years immediately before and after the missing years to obtain imputations. More importantly, the NEO-AC has been asked only once in each panel (in 2005), so we needed to assume that personality is stable and impute it for all other years. Not to have done so would have voided all longitudinal analyses.

In any panel survey, what are called "panel conditioning effects" are a possible source of bias. That is, panel members might tend to change their answers over time—and answer differently from the way nonpanel members would answer—as a consequence just of being panel members. In all three panels, there is some evidence that panel members, in their first few years of responding, tend to report higher life satisfaction scores than when they have been in the panel for a good many years (Frijters, Haisken-DeNew, & Shields, 2004). This could be due to "social desirability bias"—a desire to look good and appear to be a happy person, which is stronger in the first few years of responding than in later years. Or it could be due to a "learning effect"—learning to use the middle points of the 0−10 or 1−7 scale rather than the extremes and particularly the top end.

To compensate for these possible sources of bias, we included in all equations a variable that measured the number of years in which each panel member had already responded to survey questions.

RESULTS

Set Point Theory: Is Life Satisfaction Really Stable?

We now use evidence from the three national panel studies to assess whether life satisfaction really is stable in the medium and long term. Tables 6.1, 6.2, and 6.3 give results for "balanced panels" of adults aged 25 to 69 in, respectively, Germany, Britain, and Australia. The "balanced panels" comprise respondents who reported their life satisfaction in every year of the survey to date. It should be noted that use of balanced panels, although essential for the analysis here, greatly reduces sample sizes. The German balanced panel comprises 1,110 respondents and is restricted to those who were living in West Germany in the 1980s when the survey began. The British and Australian balanced panels number 2,102 and 5,536, respectively. Longitudinal weights, provided by the survey managers, are used in an attempt to correct for this panel size reduction, but the representativeness of the remaining panel must be in some doubt (further discussion later).

TABLE 6.1 Germany (GSOEP)
Long-term Change in the Life Satisfaction (LS) Set Points of Adults Aged 25–69: Alternative Measures[a]

Life Satisfaction Scale (0–10)	Measure 1 5-Year Means: Change in LS between 1984–1988 and 2004–2008, % of Sample	Measure 2 Personality: Difference between Personality Prediction of LS 2004–2008 and Actual LS 1984–1988, % of Sample
Change of 25 percentiles or more		
upward	*18.7*	*25.7*
downward	*19.7*	*24.2*
total	*38.4*	*49.9*
Change of 33.3 percentiles or more		
upward	*11.8*	*19.1*
downward	*13.5*	*18.6*
total	*25.3*	*37.7*
Change of 50 percentiles or more		
upward	*4.7*	*9.0*
downward	*7.4*	*10.0*
total	*12.1*	*19.0*

[a]*Source: GSOEP 1984–2008: A balanced panel of respondents aged 25–69 who reported life satisfaction each year in 1984–2008 (N = 1,110). Results are weighted, using a 1984–2008 longitudinal weight.*

The first column in each table reports results for the first of our alternative measures of the set point, namely, multiyear means of life satisfaction. The second column gives results for set points defined as predictions, or really postdictions, based on the NEO personality traits. The reason for using postdictions, rather than predictions, is that in each of the national questionnaires the NEO was included only toward the end of the survey periods covered here. It therefore makes sense to make our initial regression predictions for the periods in which the personality inventory was actually included and then postdict (rather than predict) life satisfaction for earlier periods. For example, in the German case, we "predicted" each person's life satisfaction for 2004–2008 on the basis of NEO measures taken in 2005, and then compared these results with actual life satisfaction scores for the 1984–1988 period.

TABLE 6.2 *Britain (BHPS) Long-Term Change in the Life Satisfaction (LS) Set Points of Adults 25–69: Alternative Measures[a]*

Life Satisfaction Scale (1–7)	Measure 1 3-Year Means: Change in LS Between 1996–1998 and 2008–2010, % of Sample	Measure 2 Personality: Difference Between Personality Prediction of LS 2008–2010 and Actual LS 1996–1998, % of Sample
Change of 25 percentiles or more		
upward	*16.1*	*24.1*
downward	*16.7*	*21.4*
total	*32.8*	*45.5*
Change of 33.3 percentiles or more		
upward	*10.3*	*17.3*
downward	*10.4*	*15.0*
total	*20.7*	*32.3*
Change of 50 percentiles or more		
upward	*3.2*	*8.3*
downward	*5.5*	*7.7*
total	*8.7*	*16.0*

[a]*Source: BHPS 1996–2010: A balanced panel of respondents aged 25–69 who reported life satisfaction each year in 1996–2010 (N = 2,102). Results are weighted, using a 1996–2010 longitudinal weight.*

Because our aim is to estimate long-term change, Tables 6.1 to 6.3 deal with changes in life satisfaction for the longest available period in each country. For example, for Germany, the table reports changes occurring between 1984 and 1988 (the first 5-year period) and between 2004 and 2008, the latest 5-year period for which data are available.

It is clear that, whichever operational measure of the set point is used, substantial minorities—but not majorities—in all three countries must be assessed as having recorded large (and not merely statistically significant) changes in their life satisfaction set points. In Germany, the country for which we have the longest period of evidence, the multiyear mean measure (measure 1 in Table 6.1), indicates that 38.4% of the panel recorded changes that moved them 25 percentiles or more up or down the life satisfaction distribution between the baseline period of 1984–1988 and 2004–2008. Just over a quarter, 25.3%, recorded changes that moved them up or down by

TABLE 6.3 Australia (HILDA)
Long-Term Change in the Life Satisfaction (LS) Set Points of Adults 25–69: Alternative Measures[a]

Life Satisfaction Scale (0–10)	Measure 1 3-Year Means: Change in LS between 2001–2003 and 2007–2009, % of Sample	Measure 2 Personality: Difference between Personality Prediction of LS 2007–2009 and Actual LS 2001–2003, % of Sample
Change of 25 percentiles or more		
upward	13.4	21.5
downward	13.0	19.8
total	*26.4*	*41.3*
Change of 33.3 percentiles or more		
upward	8.5	15.5
downward	7.5	13.8
total	*16.0*	*29.3*
Change of 50 percentiles or more		
upward	3.3	7.6
downward	3.3	6.5
total	*6.6*	*14.1*

[a]*Source: HILDA 2001–2009: A balanced panel of respondents who reported life satisfaction each year in 2001–2009 (N = 5,536). Results are weighted, using a 2001–2009 longitudinal weight.*

33.3 percentiles or more, and 12.1% moved by 50 percentiles or more (e.g., from above the 75th percentile to the 25th percentile or below).

The percentages of respondents reporting substantial degrees of change in life satisfaction in Britain and Australia appear lower at first reading, but the reason is only that shorter time periods are involved: 12 years for Britain and 9 for Australia, compared with 25 for Germany. Table A6.1 in Appendix 6.1 provides more detailed evidence for Germany, showing percentages reporting substantial change in each successive 5-year period after the baseline period of 1984–1988. A comparison of results in this table with the British and Australian results in Tables 6.2 and 6.3 makes it clear that the degrees of change in all three countries are about the same for any given time period.

Personality postdictions of life satisfaction are quite weak for all three countries. The NEO personality measures included in these surveys account for only a moderate amount of variance in satisfaction: 13.4% in Germany,

16.4% in Britain, and 11.9% in Australia. If we were to rely on this approach to measuring the set point, then we would have to conclude that very large minorities change their set points in each country. We would have to say that in Germany 49.9% changed by 25 percentiles or more, 37.7% changed by 33.3 percentiles, and 19.0% changed by 50 percentiles or more.

It seems reasonable to infer that personality postdictions of life satisfaction provide less satisfactory measures of the set point than multiyear means. Psychologists would rightly point out that, if longer and more valid versions of the NEO scales had been used, the variance accounted for would have been somewhat greater. However, reviews of the evidence have generally concluded that, even when personality traits are measured with long and well-validated questionnaires, they account for only moderate amounts of variance in life satisfaction (Lucas, 2008). It seems certain that stable personality traits help to stabilize satisfaction ratings over time, but they do not account for a great deal of inter-person variance.

In all three countries, the longer the time period that elapses, the more respondents report levels of life satisfaction that are substantially changed from their baseline measure. This is best appreciated with correlational data. In Germany, the correlation between Life Satisfaction 1984—1988 and Life Satisfaction 1989—1993 was 0.70. Later, 5-year correlations with the 1984—1988 baseline result were 0.54 (for 1994—1998), 0.47 (for 1999—2003), and 0.45 (for 2004—2008). These declining correlations show a pattern of change typical of any longitudinal, attitudinal dataset. However, they run counter to set point theory as usually understood.

Possible Concerns and Sensitivity Analysis

It could be argued that the balanced panels used in these tables may be unrepresentative of the three national populations. This is certainly a possibility. Respondents who remain in panels for a long time may well be different in some respects from people who drop out. However, experienced survey researchers know that the hardest people to retain in any survey are the young, those who move from house to house a lot, and those whose lives undergo major changes (e.g., marital separation, unemployment, and extended job search). People whose lives are less subject to change are more likely to remain in panels. This makes it likely that, if there is any selection bias in our balanced panels, it is toward people whose lives have been relatively stable and who may therefore be less (not more) likely than others to record large changes in life satisfaction.

Using the longer-running German panel, we performed a number of sensitivity analyses to see if serious variations in results were found, compared with what is reported in Table 6.1. Instead of taking the mean of each 5-year period to measure changes in life satisfaction, we took the median. This made virtually no difference. Nor did analysis based on removing apparent outlying scores (one or two outliers) in each 5-year period.

Finally, and at the cost of further reducing the size of the balanced panel, we removed all respondents to whom major life events happened in either or both of 1984–1988 and 2004–2008. We then reanalyzed changes in life satisfaction for this 25-year period. The reason for doing this was that it could be argued that one cannot get a valid reading of a person's set point in a period just before, during, or just after a major life event. The life events that led to removals from the panel were as follows: got married/partnered, child born, separated or divorced, partner died, became unemployed, own business failed, real disposable income changed by more than 20% in the past year, became seriously disabled, and went to the doctor 25 times or more in the past year. Of course, this is by no means a full list of major life events, but it reflects what is available in the GSOEP. Again, the reanalyzed results showed degrees of change little different from what is reported in Table 6.1 (for more detail, see Headey, 2010).

EXPLAINING MEDIUM- AND LONG-TERM CHANGE IN LIFE SATISFACTION: LIFE PRIORITIES AND BEHAVIORAL CHOICES

As previously mentioned, one persistent finding that has bolstered set point theory is that most life events appear not to cause medium- or long-term changes in life satisfaction. SWB researchers have tended to draw the conclusion that, if even major events have no lasting impact, then medium- and long-term life satisfaction "must" be stable. In the next few sections, we summarize relatively new lines of research that show that choices about life priorities (values, goals) can change medium-term life satisfaction, as can behavioral choices relating to one's partner, work–leisure balance, social participation, physical exercise, and church-going. Recall that by *medium-term life satisfaction*, we mean 3- or 5-year moving averages.

Life Priorities, Values, or Goals

Several papers have reported that giving top priority to material goals/values is inimical to happiness (Diener & Fujita, 1995; Diener & Seligman, 2004; Kasser & Kanner, 2004; Nickerson, Schwarz, Diener, & Kahneman, 2003). Experimental and survey evidence indicates that people who spend more money on others and relatively less on themselves have higher life satisfaction (Dunn, Aknin, & Norton, 2008). Headey, Muffels, and Wagner (2011), analyzing data from the three national panel studies, reported that individuals who give relatively high priority to pro-social, altruistic goals and also family goals and lower priority to material and career goals have higher life satisfaction and that these differences persist over time (see also Emmons, 1986). The results held, controlling for the effects of personality traits. Several studies have indicated that volunteering, engaging in altruistic community activities, and repeatedly carrying out "good deeds" are associated with higher subjective well-being (Harlow & Cantor, 1996; Lyubomirsky, 2008; Thoits & Hewitt, 2001).

In trying to explain why people who give priority to pro-social/altruistic and family goals appear more satisfied than those who prioritize material and career goals, Headey (2008) suggested that a key distinction may lie between zero sum and nonzero sum goals.[11] Generally speaking, material and career goals (also status goals) are zero sum. They can be pursued only at the expense of someone else: "my gain is your loss." It follows that there are bound to be many losers and that almost all those who win in round 1 will lose in round 2 or later rounds. So, on average and for most people, prioritizing zero sum goals may turn out to be a recipe for disappointment rather than life satisfaction. By contrast, family goals and pro-social goals are generally (although not necessarily) nonzero sum. If family relationships improve, or pro-social goals are achieved, everyone can be better off; there do not have to be any losers.

BEHAVIORAL CHOICES

A diverse set of behavioral choices, which also appear to have nonzero sum implications, are associated with higher levels of life satisfaction.

Choice of Partner

One key choice, unsurprisingly, is choice of partner. Again using data from the three national panels, Headey et al. (2011) showed that individuals who choose (or are chosen by) partners who rate high on the personality trait of neuroticism have lower life satisfaction than those whose partners are more emotionally stable. This finding held net of (controlling for) a person's own personality traits. Furthermore, differences in life satisfaction due to partner neuroticism persisted even after more than 20 years of marriage, indicating the very long-term effects of choice of partner (Headey, Muffels, & Wagner, 2010). Partner neuroticism has long been known to have damaging effects on marital satisfaction (Robins, Caspi, & Moffitt, 2000), so it is plausible that life satisfaction is affected as well. It is also clear that the marital satisfaction and life satisfaction of partners are quite highly correlated,

---

11. See also Hirsch (1976) and Frank (1985) who make a similar distinction between positional and nonpositional goods.

although their satisfaction levels do not become more similar over time (Schimmack & Lucas, 2010).

The evidence that partner neuroticism matters to one's own life satisfaction should probably lead to a reinterpretation of the finding that getting married/partnered is one of those life events that produces only a temporary change (usually a gain) in life satisfaction, but that the long-term effect is zero (Campbell, Converse, & Rodgers, 1976; Clark et al., 2008; Lucas, Clark, Georgellis, & Diener 2003). The evidence is that individuals who marry/partner someone who is more neurotic than average will record a long-term loss of life satisfaction, whereas those who marry someone who is more emotionally stable than average will record a long-term gain. Because about 50% of people are likely to fall into both camps, the finding that, on average, getting married makes no long-term difference to life satisfaction makes arithmetic sense but is seriously misleading.[12]

Work–Leisure Balance

Headey et al. (2010, 2011) attempted to test the validity of the welfare economist's assumption that a key trade-off affecting utility lies between work (benefit: more consumption) and leisure (benefit: more pleasure). Until quite recently, most economists denied the validity of interpersonal measures and, hence, comparisons of utility, but some are now accepting that standard life satisfaction scales are adequately reliable and valid (Frey & Stutzer, 2002).

Headey et al. (2010, 2011) reported that people who are able to arrange their lives so that they work within plus or minus 3 hours of their preferred working time have higher life satisfaction than those who work longer than they want or less than they want. The relationship between "work–leisure balance" and life satisfaction held in Germany, Britain, and Australia, net of controls for personality traits, life priorities, and standard socioeconomic variables. Further, panel regression fixed effects analyses showed that *changes* over time in "work-life balance" were associated with *changes* in life satisfaction.[13]

Active Social Participation and Volunteering

A matter of individual choice, which has nonzero sum implications, is the extent to which one spends leisure time participating in social and

---

12. It seems possible that the same misleading results may be found in relation to other life events that may benefit some people's life satisfaction but hurt others'—e.g., retirement.

13. Psychologists may be more accustomed to thinking of fixed effects regressions as "within-person" regressions. Because only change over time "within persons" is analyzed, the effects of omitted (usually unmeasured) factors that are constant (fixed) over time are automatically controlled.

community activities. There is abundant evidence that individuals with richer social networks or more social capital enjoy greater life satisfaction (Argyle, 2001; Bradburn, 1969; Harlow & Cantor, 1996; Putnam, 2000). The three national panel datasets go beyond measuring static social networks and provide annual measures of frequency of social interaction with friends, relatives, and neighbors. In all three national panels, it was found that respondents who reported high levels of interaction were more satisfied with life than those who were less sociable (Headey et al., 2011). Again, fixed effects analysis indicated that changes over time in social activity were associated with changing levels of life satisfaction. These findings held good, net of the effects of personality traits and life priorities/values.

Somewhat related to active social and community participation is volunteering. This is also usually found to be associated with higher levels of life satisfaction (Thoits & Hewitt, 2001). The result holds using fixed effects models of the German and British but not the Australian national panel data (Headey et al., 2011).

Regular Exercise

The health domain is also nonzero sum; plainly, gains to one's health are unlikely to be associated with consequent losses to anybody else's health. Further, adopting a healthy lifestyle is, for most Western people, a matter of relatively free choice. A great deal of previous research has been concerned with the impact of exercise, body-mass index, and other lifestyle variables on health rather than life satisfaction. Reviews of the evidence relating to life satisfaction have generally suggested positive relationships, but with an important "reverse causation" caveat, namely, that people who are happier in the first place may choose more exercise and a healthier diet (Argyle, 2001; Diener & Biswas-Diener, 2008).

The only "healthy lifestyle" measure that has been included annually in the three national panels relates to frequency of taking exercise or participating in sports. In all three countries, frequent exercise is associated with higher life satisfaction, and changes in frequency are associated with changes in satisfaction (Headey et al., 2011). These relationships hold net of personality traits and life priorities/values. The panel analysis fixed effects approach does not rule out the possibility of some reverse causation, but a more plausible interpretation (it is suggested) is that personality traits are causally antecedent and affect both choice of lifestyle and life satisfaction.

Churchgoing

As previously mentioned, many researchers have reported a positive cross-sectional relationship between life satisfaction and churchgoing. However, as with many cross-sectional relationships, doubts have been expressed about whether the relationship is causal. In the German panel, churchgoing has been measured at regular intervals, so we can take one more step toward establishing causation by seeing whether changes in frequency of church attendance are associated with changes in life satisfaction. It turns out that they are. Headey, Schupp, Tucci, and Wagner (2010) found that individuals who increased their church attendance also recorded increases in satisfaction, whereas those whose attendance declined recorded declines in satisfaction. Results held net of the effects of personality traits and standard socioeconomic variables.[14] It should also be mentioned that regular churchgoers have several other characteristics that contribute to life satisfaction. They give relatively high priority to altruistic and family values, and lower priority to material values, than infrequent or nonchurch-goers. They also spend more time on volunteering and charitable activities than nonchurchgoers.

Do Some People's Personality Traits Predispose Them to Gains or Losses of Life Satisfaction?

This section has been mostly about choices that can change life satisfaction. Clearly, one's own personality traits are scarcely a matter of personal choice, and it might be thought that, because adult personality is more or less stable, it could not be associated with change in life satisfaction. There is, however, some evidence that extroverted people may be predisposed toward gains in life satisfaction, while relatively neurotic people may be predisposed toward losses. It is known that extroverts are more likely than average to experience positive life events (e.g., job promotion), whereas neurotic people are more likely than average to experience adverse events (e.g., job loss) (Headey & Wearing, 1989; Magnus, Diener, Fujita, & Pavot, 1993). Further, it has been shown that when positive events happen to extroverts, they extract more satisfaction than others (Larsen & Ketelaar, 1991; Lucas & Baird, 2004). Similarly, relatively neurotic individuals experience more negative affect than average in the face of adverse events (Larsen, 1992). Could it be that, by repeatedly extracting more satisfaction than average from positive events, some extroverts register lasting gains in life satisfaction? Similarly, is it possible that some neurotic individuals register lasting losses of life

---

14. The issue of whether religious belief or church attendance is the prime cause of life satisfaction is often raised (Myers, 2013). Because strength of religious belief has only been measured occasionally in the panels, we were unable to assess its relationship to *changes* in life satisfaction. The issue may be moot, however, because the cross-sectional correlation between religious belief and church attendance is over 0.6.

satisfaction as a result of repeatedly experiencing worse than average reactions to adverse events (Huppert, 2005)? Headey (2010) found some panel evidence to support both of these conjectures. It does appear that extroverts are somewhat more likely than others to record long-term gains in life satisfaction and that neurotic people are likely to record long-term losses (see also Scollon & Diener, 2006). There is no direct evidence, however, about which specific life events or sequences of events trigger these gains and losses of life satisfaction.

In short, it does seem possible that some people's personality traits predispose them to changes in life satisfaction. This inference is tentative, however, not only because the specific events that may bring about change are unclear, but also because the evidence implies a logical consequence that is perhaps implausible. The logical consequence is that some extroverts must be repeatedly increasing their life satisfaction, and some neurotic individuals must be in repeated decline. This is not impossible but seems somewhat implausible.

CONCLUSIONS

The best, most direct way to test set point theory is to measure degrees of change in adult life satisfaction (subjective well-being) in national representative panel surveys. The three most readily available panels are the GSOEP, BHPS, and HILDA. In these panels, large minorities, although not majorities, have recorded substantial and apparently lasting changes in life satisfaction. Germany, Britain, and Australia are fairly affluent, stable Western countries. It is quite likely that more change will be found (if and) when evidence becomes available from poorer countries that have experienced wars in recent times or more serious social, economic, and political crises.

Until long-term panel data became available, it was reasonable to claim that the balance of evidence was in favor of set point theory. It was also the case that, until fairly recently, there was little convincing evidence about causes of change in life satisfaction. Most major life events appeared to produce only temporary fluctuations, with reversion to set point being the norm. However, in the past decade or so, evidence has slowly accumulated that indicates that changes in life satisfaction can be partly explained by differing life priorities (values, goals) and behavioral choices. Evidence from fixed effects panel regressions is, perhaps, particularly convincing in showing that when individuals change their choices, then changes also occur in life satisfaction. Recall that, in this type of regression, the effects of all factors that are constant over time (e. g., family background, personality traits), whether measured or unmeasured, are automatically removed. Fixed effects results show that choices relating to active social participation, volunteering, work—leisure balance, regular exercise, and churchgoing can change life satisfaction. Choice of partner also appears to have long-term effects.

Attributing life satisfaction or other personal outcomes to *choice* is sometimes regarded as problematic in the social sciences, although not in economics. Obviously, many choices are more or less constrained. However, it seems reasonable to suggest that choices relating to social participation, volunteering, exercise, and churchgoing are not seriously constrained. Nor, perhaps, are choices relating to life priorities/values. Choices about working hours and work—leisure balance are, in many cases, constrained by financial pressures and lack of flexibility on the part of employers. Choices relating to partner personality traits may be relatively unconstrained, but the relevant evidence may not be transparent!

In claiming that conscious choices can improve or worsen life satisfaction, we are not denying the prevalence or importance of adaptation in response to life changes. It is clear that most people fully adapt to most life events. They probably *partially adapt* to changes resulting from personal choices. For example, the effects on life satisfaction of starting a program of regular exercise or striking a more preferred work—leisure balance may be greater in the short run than the long run. Nevertheless, the evidence in this chapter, which relates to 3- and 5-year time periods (medium-term change), suggests that full adaptation does not occur.

On the basis of current evidence, it might be possible to salvage a "weak" version of set point theory. This weak version would say that a majority of adults in Western countries appear to have stable levels of life satisfaction, due to stabilizing factors including personality traits and parental influence. However, the purpose of a scientific theory or paradigm is not just to summarize and account for existing evidence, but also to direct attention to promising lines of future research. Set point theory directed the attention of SWB researchers to factors that stabilize well-being. The main future challenge is to develop a revised theory that focuses more on variables, particularly personal and public policy choices, that can bring about changes and, potentially, improvements in well-being.

APPENDIX 6.1

TABLE A6.1 Germany (GSOEP)
Long-Term Change in the Life Satisfaction (LS) Set Points of Adults Aged 25-69: 5-Year Mean Change from 1984–1988 to 2004–2008[a]

Life Satisfaction Scale (0–10)	Change in LS Between 1984–1988 and 1989–1993, % of Sample	Change in LS Between 1984–1988 and 1994–1998, % of Sample	Change in LS Between 1984–1988 and 1999–2003, % of Sample	Change in LS Between 1984–1988 and 2004–2008, % of Sample
Change of 25 percentiles or more				
upward	11.5	15.7	18.2	18.7
downward	11.1	16.5	19.5	19.7
total	*22.6*	*32.2*	*37.7*	*38.4*
Change of 33.3 percentiles or more				
upward	6.4	10.9	12.4	11.8
downward	6.6	11.5	13.7	13.5
total	*13.0*	*22.4*	*26.1*	*25.3*
Change of 50 percentiles or more				
upward	2.4	4.4	5.5	4.7
downward	2.3	4.8	6.1	7.4
total	*4.7*	*9.2*	*11.6*	*12.1*

[a]*Source: GSOEP 1984–2008: A balanced panel of respondents aged 25–69 who reported life satisfaction each year in 1984–2008 (N = 1,110). Results are weighted, using a 1984–2008 longitudinal weight.*

CORRELATIONS OF LIFE SATISFACTION$_{1984-1988}$ WITH LIFE SATISFACTION IN LATER 5-YEAR PERIODS

The 5-year Pearson correlations of Life Satisfaction$_{1984-1988}$ with each successive 5-year period become progressively weaker. The correlation with Life Satisfaction$_{1989-1993}$ is 0.70; with Life Satisfacton$_{1994-1998}$, it is 0.54; with Life Satisfaction$_{1999-2003}$, it is 0.47; and with Life Satisfaction$_{2004-2008}$, it is 0.45. This is the pattern of change to be expected in almost any longitudinal attitudinal dataset. However, it runs counter to set point theory, as usually understood.

REFERENCES

Aguche, A., & Trommsdorff, G. (2010) Transmission of well-being between mothers, fathers and adolescent children: The role of parenting and personality factors, *9th International German Socio-Economic Panel Users Conference*, Berlin, June 30–July 1.

Andrews, F. M., & Withey, S. B. (1976). *Social indicators of well-being*. New York: Plenum.

Argyle, M. (2001). *The psychology of happiness* (2nd ed.). London: Taylor and Francis.

Bradburn, N. M. (1969). *The structure of psychological well-being*. Chicago: Aldine.

Brickman, P. D., & Campbell, D. T. (1971). Hedonic relativism and planning the good society. In M. H. Appley (Ed.), *Adaptation level theory* (pp. 287–302). New York: Academic Press.

Campbell, A., Converse, P. E., & Rodgers, W. R. (1976). *The quality of American life*. New York: Sage.

Clark, A. E., Diener, E., Georgellis, Y., & Lucas, R. E. (2008). Lags and leads in life satisfaction: A test of the baseline hypothesis. *Economic Journal, 118*, 222–243.

Clark, A. E., Georgellis, Y., Lucas, R. E., & Diener, E. (2004). Unemployment alters the set point for life satisfaction. *Psychological Science, 15*, 8–13.

Costa, P. T., & McCrae, R. R. (1980). Influences of extraversion and neuroticism on subjective well-being. *Journal of Personality and Social Psychology, 38*, 668–678.

Costa, P. T., & McCrae, R. R. (1991). *The NEO PI-R*. Odessa, FL: Psychological Assessment Resources.

Diener, E., & Biswas-Diener, R. (2008). *Happiness: Unlocking the mysteries of psychological wealth*. Oxford: Blackwell.

Diener, E., & Fujita, F. (1995). Resources, personal strivings and subjective well-being: A nomothetic and ideographic approach. *Journal of Personality and Social Psychology, 68*, 926–935.

Diener, E., & Seligman, M. E. P. (2004). Beyond money: Toward an economy of well-being. *Psychological Science in the Public Interest, 5*, 1–31.

Diener, E., Suh, E. M., Lucas, R. E., & Smith, H. L. (1999). Subjective well-being: Three decades of progress. *Psychological Bulletin, 25*, 276–302.

Dunn, E. W., Aknin, L. B., & Norton, M. I. (2008). Spending money on others promotes happiness. *Science, 319*, 1687–1688.

Easterlin, R. A. (1974). Does economic growth improve the human lot? Some empirical evidence. In P. A. David, & M. W. Reder (Eds.), *Nations and households in economic growth* (pp. 89–125). New York: Academic Press.

Easterlin, R. A. (2005). Building a better theory of well-being. In L. Bruni, & P. Porta (Eds.), *Economics and happiness: Framing the analysis*. Oxford: Oxford University Press.

Emmons, R. A. (1986). Personal strivings: An approach to personality and subjective well-being. *Journal of Personality and Social Psychology, 51*, 1058–1068.

Frank, R. H. (1985). The demand for unobservable and other nonpositional goods. *American Economic Review, 75*, 279–301.

Frederick, S., & Loewenstein, G. (1999). Hedonic adaptation. In D. Kahneman, E. Diener, & N. Schwarz (Eds.), *Well-being: The foundations of hedonic psychology* (pp. 302–329). New York: Russell Sage.

Frey, B. S., & Stutzer, A. (2002). What can economists learn from happiness research? *Journal of Economic Literature, 40*, 402–435.

Frijters, P., Haisken-Denew, J. P., & Shields, M. A. (2004). Money does matter! Evidence from increasing real incomes and life satisfaction in East Germany following reunification. *American Economic Review, 94*, 730–741.

Fujita, F., & Diener, E. (2005). Life satisfaction set-point: Stability and change. *Journal of Personality and Social Psychology, 88*, 158–164.

Gerlitz, J.-Y., & Schupp, J. (2005) *Zur Erhebung der Big-Five-basierten Persoenlichkeitsmerkmale im SOEP.* <www.diw.de/deutsche/produkte/publikationen/researchnotes/docs/papers/rn4.pdf>.

Gerstorf, D., Ram, N., Hidajat, M., Mayraz, G., Lindenberger, U., Schupp, J., et al. (2010). Late-life decline in well-being across adulthood in Germany, the UK, and the US: Something is seriously wrong at the end of life. *Psychology and Aging, 25*, 477–485.

Harlow, R. E., & Cantor, N. (1996). Still participating after all these years: A study of life task participation in later life. *Journal of Personality and Social Psychology, 71*, 1235–1249.

Headey, B. W. (2006). Subjective well-being: Revisions to dynamic equilibrium theory using national panel data and panel regression methods. *Social Indicators Research, 79*, 369–403.

Headey, B. W. (2008). Life goals matter to happiness: A revision of set-point theory. *Social Indicators Research, 86*, 213–231.

Headey, B. W. (2010). The set-point theory of well-being has serious flaws: On the eve of scientific revolution? *Social Indicators Research, 97*, 7–21.

Headey, B. W., Muffels, R. J. A., & Wagner, G. G. (2010). Long-running German panel survey shows that personal and economic choices, not just genes, matter for happiness. *Proceedings of the National Academy of Sciences, 107*(42), 17922–17926.

Headey, B. W., Muffels, R. J. A., & Wagner, G. G. (2011). Choices which change life satisfaction: Similar results for Australia, Britain and Germany. *Social Indicators Research, 102*(4), 1–31.

Headey, B. W., Muffels, R. J. A., & Wagner, G. G. (2013). Parents transmit happiness along with associated values and behaviors to their children: A lifelong happiness dividend? *Social Indicators Research, 116*, 903–933.

Headey, B. W., Schupp, J., Tucci, I., & Wagner, G. G. (2010). Authentic happiness theory supported by impact of religion on life satisfaction: A longitudinal analysis with data for Germany. *Journal of Positive Psychology, 5*, 73–82.

Headey, B. W., & Wearing, A. J. (1989). Personality, life events and subjective well-being: Towards a dynamic equilibrium model. *Journal of Personality and Social Psychology, 57*, 731–739.

Hirsch, F. (1976). *Social limits to growth.* Cambridge, MA: Harvard University Press.

Huppert, F. (2005). Positive mental health in individuals and populations. In F. Huppert, N. Baylis, & B. Keverne (Eds.), *The science of well-being* (pp. 307–340). Oxford: Oxford University Press.

Kasser, T., & Kanner, A. D. (Eds.), (2004). *Psychology and consumer culture: The struggle for the good life in a materialistic world.* Washington, DC: American Psychological Association.

Kluckhohn, F. R., & Strodtbeck, F. L. (1961). *Variations in value orientations.* Evanston, IL: Row, Peterson.

Larsen, R. J. (1992). Neuroticism and selective encoding and recall of symptoms: Evidence from a combined concurrent-retrospective study. *Journal of Personality and Social Psychology, 62*, 489–498.

Larsen, R. J., & Ketelaar, T. (1991). Personality and susceptibility to positive and negative emotional states. *Journal of Personality and Social Psychology, 61*, 132–140.

Little, I. M. D. (2002). *A critique of welfare economics.* Oxford: Oxford University Press.

Lucas, R. E. (2007). Long-term disability is associated with lasting changes in subjective well-being: Evidence from two nationally representative longitudinal studies. *Journal of Personality and Social Psychology, 92,* 717−730.

Lucas, R. E. (2008). Personality and subjective well-being. In M. Eid, & R. J. Larsen (Eds.), *The science of subjective well-being* (pp. 171−194). New York: Guilford Press.

Lucas, R. E., & Baird, B. M. (2004). Extraversion and emotional reactivity. *Journal of Personality and Social Psychology, 86,* 473−485.

Lucas, R. E., Clark, A. E., Georgellis, Y., & Diener, E. (2003). Reexamining adaptation and the set point model of happiness: Reactions to change in marital status. *Journal of Personality and Social Psychology, 84,* 527−539.

Lucas, R. E., & Donnellan, M. B. (2007). How stable is happiness? Using the STARTS model to estimate the stability of life satisfaction. *Journal of Research in Personality, 41,* 1091−1098.

Lykken, D. (1999). *Happiness: What studies on twins show us about nature, nurture and the happiness set-point.* New York: Golden Books.

Lykken, D., & Tellegen, A. (1996). Happiness is a stochastic phenomenon. *Psychological Science, 7,* 186−189.

Lynn, P. (2006). *Quality profile: BHPS version 2.0: Waves 1 to 13.* University of Essex: Institute for Social Research. 1991−2003.

Lyubomirsky, S. (2008). *The how of happiness: A scientific approach to getting the life you want.* New York: Penguin.

Magnus, K., Diener, E., Fujita, F., & Pavot, W. (1993). Extraversion and neuroticism as predictors of objective life events: A longitudinal analysis. *Journal of Personality and Social Psychology, 65,* 1046−1053.

Mehnert, T., Kraus, H. H., Nadler, R., & Boyd, M. (1990). Correlates of life satisfaction in those with a disabling condition. *Rehabilitation Psychology, 35,* 3−17.

Myers, D. G. (2013). Religious engagement and well-being. In S. A. David, I. Boniwell, & A. Conley Ayers (Eds.), *The Oxford book of happiness* (pp. 88−100). Oxford: Oxford University Press.

Nickerson, C., Schwarz, N., Diener, E., & Kahneman, D. (2003). Zeroing in on the dark side of the American dream: A closer look at the negative consequences of the goal for financial success. *Psychological Science, 14,* 531−536.

Putnam, R. D. (2000). *Bowling alone: The collapse and revival of American community.* New York: Simon & Schuster.

Roberts, B. W., Walton, K., & Viechtbauer, W. (2006). Patterns of mean-level change in personality traits across the life course: A meta-analysis of longitudinal studies. *Psychological Bulletin, 132,* 3−27.

Robins, R. W., Caspi, A., & Moffitt, T. E. (2000). Two personalities, one relationship: Both partners' personality traits shape the quality of their relationship. *Journal of Personality and Social Psychology, 79,* 251−259.

Saucier, G. (1994). Mini-markers: A brief version of Goldberg's big five markers. *Journal of Personality Assessment, 63,* 506−516.

Schimmack, U., & Lucas, R. E. (2010). Environmental influences on subjective well-being: A dyadic latent panel analysis of spousal similarity. *Social Indicators Research, 98,* 1−21.

Scollon, C. N., & Diener, E. (2006). Love, work and changes in extraversion and neuroticism over time. *Journal of Personality and Social Psychology, 91,* 1152−1165.

Thoits, P. A., & Hewitt, L. N. (2001). Volunteer work and well-being. *Journal of Health and Social Behavior, 42,* 115−131.

Wagner, G. G., Frick, J. R., & Schupp, J. (2007). Enhancing the power of the German Socio-Economic Panel Study (SOEP)—evolution, scope and enhancements. *Schmoeller's Jahrbuch, 127,* 139–169.

Watson, N., & Wooden, M. (2004) Assessing the Quality of the HILDA Survey Wave 2 Data, HILDA Technical Paper, 5/04.

Wengle, H. (1986). The psychology of cosmetic surgery: A critical overview of the literature 1960–1982. *Annals of Plastic Surgery, 16,* 435–443.

Wortman, C. B., & Silver, R. C. (1987). Coping with irrevocable loss. In G. R. Vanderbos, & B. K. Bryant (Eds.), *Cataclysms, crises, catastrophes: Psychology in action* (pp. 189–235). Washington, DC: American Psychological Association.

Chapter 7

Does Happiness Change? Evidence from Longitudinal Studies

Stevie C. Y. Yap, Ivana Anusic, and Richard E. Lucas
Michigan State University, East Lansing, MI, USA

Subjective well-being (SWB) reflects a person's subjective evaluation of the quality of his or her life as a whole. This construct is typically measured using global questions that ask respondents how they feel in general, or through intensive assessments of how a person feels on a moment-to-moment basis. SWB is important partly because laypeople value it; in general, people prefer to be happy with their lives rather than unhappy. In addition, an increasing amount of research suggests that SWB is actually good for people. It can lead to additional positive outcomes in people's lives such as better health or increased productivity (Lyubomirsky, King, & Diener, 2005).

If SWB is something that people value, either for intrinsic reasons or as a means to obtain other outcomes, then an important goal for research is to understand how SWB can be improved. The applied value of well-being research would be dramatically reduced if there was ultimately nothing that could be done to improve it. In addition, some have suggested that it might be useful to track well-being for policy purposes (Diener, Lucas, Schimmack, & Helliwell, 2009), but such programs would provide little value if well-being was unaffected by policies or features of daily life that these policies directly affect. Therefore, one of the most fundamental questions that well-being researchers must tackle is whether SWB can change.

Historically, there has been some amount of skepticism regarding the possibility of change in SWB. This skepticism was due, in part, to early research that emphasized the relatively strong role that personality traits played as predictors of subjective well-being, at least in comparison to the role that situational and environmental factors played (Diener & Lucas, 1999).

For instance, early work often compared the size of demographic predictors such as age, gender, income, and education to personality predictors such as extraversion and neuroticism. Typically, this research found that demographic predictors and factors other than personality traits were only weakly correlated with SWB (Diener, Suh, Lucas, & Smith, 1999), whereas the associations with personality were much stronger (Steel, Schmidt, & Shultz, 2008). Similarly, robust and widely replicated research from behavioral geneticists showed that heritabilities for well-being variables tend to be moderate in size, whereas the effects of shared environments tend to be small or nonexistent (e.g., Tellegen et al., 1988). These results seemed to confirm the idea that personality, but not environments, mattered for well-being.

In addition to this indirect evidence regarding the possibility for change, a number of studies appeared to show strong stability of well-being measures over time or—even more dramatically—an apparent imperviousness to change in spite of the most extreme events imaginable. Most famously, Brickman, Coates, and Janoff-Bulman (1978) suggested that neither winning the lottery nor suffering a severe spinal-cord injury will lead to lasting changes in happiness. As a result of this evidence, researchers posited that numerous factors worked to prevent lasting changes in subjective well-being (Diener, Lucas, & Scollon, 2009). For instance, the emotional reactions to the world that might form a basis of subjective well-being judgments might be strongly and directly influenced by stable personality traits so that our perception of the world around us may be more important in driving well-being than the actual events that happen. Alternatively, Headey and Wearing (1991) suggested that personality characteristics influence the events that happen to us, and in general, these processes serve to maintain an equilibrium in well-being (even if the traits themselves do not directly cause the emotional reactions).

Still another possibility was that the weak effects of situational factors result not from an overwhelming influence of personality traits but from adaptation processes that are actually functional (Frederick & Loewenstein, 1999). There are numerous reasons to expect that it might be advantageous to attend to change in one's environment rather than characteristics that remain stable. Therefore, evolution may prepare organisms to adapt to constant stimuli both in terms of their physical reactions (in the case of temperature, smells, visual stimuli in the environment, or brightness of light) and in their emotional reactions. If so, then *adaptation* (in the sense of getting used to constant stimuli) might be *adaptive* (in the sense of helping the organism that has this capability). So not only did the evidence appear to support the idea that life circumstances played a small role in subjective well-being, but there were (and still are) compelling theoretical reasons to expect such effects.

Yet despite this skepticism, there are reasons to remain hopeful about the possibility of change in well-being. Many of the chapters in this book discuss specific theoretical reasons that change might be attainable or specific routes to change. Our chapter addresses a more basic question of whether the evidence from longitudinal studies suggests that change does, in fact, occur. Specifically, we review recent longitudinal findings on the rank-order stability of well-being, along with studies that examine mean-level change following major life events. These studies, which improve on those mentioned previously in many ways, show that considerable change does occur, which provides initial evidence that interventions to improve well-being may be possible.

UNDERSTANDING CHANGE THROUGH STABILITY COEFFICIENTS

A common approach to studying whether life satisfaction can change is to study stability of individual differences in life satisfaction. This approach can inform us about the extent to which rank-ordering between individuals is preserved over time. For example, if Samantha was happier than Jonathan when they were kids, will she still be happier in adulthood? Traditionally, questions such as this one are studied by examining test–retest correlations of life satisfaction over time. Higher retest correlations would indicate that rank-order was preserved to a greater degree than lower correlations. In turn, these high retest correlations would suggest that happiness does not change much, at least over the time period being studied.

Early studies on stability of individual differences in life satisfaction were almost exclusively based on two-wave designs. Moreover, they generally examined correlations over relatively short retest intervals—weeks, months, at best up to a few years (e.g., Pavot & Diener, 1993). Information from these studies can tell us about the extent to which individual differences are preserved over such time periods. However, they do not allow for broad conclusions about stability over time because two-wave retest correlations obscure influences of different factors on life satisfaction, some of which lead to stability and some of which lead to change (Conley, 1984; Fraley & Roberts, 2005). This leads to difficulties in interpreting two-wave retest correlations in the context of stability.

For example, what does a 1-month retest correlation of .7 tell us about stability of life satisfaction? Can we say that life satisfaction has changed, or should we say that life satisfaction is stable? We would likely make different conclusions if the 10-year retest correlation was also .7 than if this 10-year stability coefficient was .1. In the former case, we may conclude that although life satisfaction may not be perfectly stable in the short term, individual differences are quite well preserved over very long time periods. In the latter case, we might conclude that there is much change in life satisfaction because it is difficult to predict rank-ordering over longer periods of time from people's initial standing.

The problems involved in this example are not just due to the short time frame of the 1-month retest correlation. They are also due to the limitations of two-wave designs. For instance, even if we found that the 1-year stability of life satisfaction was .7, it is impossible to predict from this value whether the 5-year stability will be equally high or whether it will be zero. As we discuss in more detail later, some underlying models—such as a purely autoregressive model—would mean that a 1-year stability of .70 would translate into a 5-year stability of just .17 (the formula to get this value involves taking the stability for one interval—a year in this case—to the power of the number of intervals: $.7^5 = .17$). Other, equally plausible models, however, might suggest that the .70 stability over a 1-year interval would be maintained even over periods that are many years longer. In short, it is simply not possible to distinguish between short-term change and long-term stability from a two-wave retest correlation.

ALTERNATIVES TO TWO-WAVE DESIGNS

Although it is difficult to draw conclusions about stability from any single retest correlation, a pattern of retest correlations obtained over different retest intervals provides more information about the extent of stability and change over time as well as different processes that may influence life satisfaction over time (Conley, 1984; Fraley & Roberts, 2005). In general, correlations are highest over shortest retest intervals, lower over longer retest intervals, but asymptotic at a value higher than zero. This pattern is seen across different psychological constructs (e.g., intelligence, personality) and suggests multiple influences on constructs over time. For example, Fraley and Roberts (2005) suggested that influences of developmental constants (e.g., genotype) are reflected in the asymptote because they lead to stability over time. In contrast, they suggested the cumulative effects of occasion-specific influences were responsible for the decay of retest correlations over time and that person-environment interactions resulted in increasing stability over the life span. To understand whether happiness can change, we need to understand the extent to which these stable and changing influences affect life satisfaction.

With multiwave longitudinal designs, it is possible to use trait-state analytic models that can separate influences of more stable factors from less stable factors (Cole, Martin, & Steiger, 2005; Eid & Diener, 2004; Kenny & Zautra, 1995, 2001; Steyer, Schmitt, & Eid, 1999). Although these models vary in details, they generally assume three types of influences on a construct. First, there are stable influences that do not change even over very long periods of time, such as developmental constants suggested by Fraley and Roberts (2005). These may include biological factors such as one's genetic make-up, but also reflect very stable features of the environment or the effects of early environment that have had a lasting impact. Because these types of factors do not change over time, they allow us to perfectly predict a person's future standing on a construct. Stable influences are the reason that retest correlations do not reach zero even at very long retest intervals.

On the other end of the trait-state continuum, there are influences that produce changes even over very short time periods. These may reflect influences of random measurement error, transient influences that may not be related to the construct at hand (e.g., effect of mood on judgments of overall life satisfaction), or relevant influences whose effect is limited to the length of the retest interval. Because these factors differ from one measurement occasion to another, they make it impossible to predict future life satisfaction from today's life satisfaction.

In between these two extremes, there are factors that produce longer-lasting changes in rank-ordering. They include random events that affect life satisfaction and whose influences gradually accumulate over time, as well as person-environment interactions that lead to steadily diverging life satisfaction trajectories as people select environments that continually make them more (or less) happy. Because of the cumulative effect of these influences, they make it more difficult to predict future life satisfaction over longer time intervals than over shorter time intervals. Isolating these different influences on life satisfaction over time can tell us more about causes of stability and change than two-wave retest correlations.

Although state-trait models can provide valuable information about stability and change over time, their use in research has been somewhat limited. One difficulty in applying these models is that they require longitudinal studies with at least four but preferably many more testing occasions (Cole et al., 2005; although simpler models that allow for the separation of some components can be tested with just three waves; see Anusic, Lucas, & Donnellan, 2012). Moreover, for one to be able to identify all three sources of influence, these studies need to span long periods of time (i.e., many years). Fortunately, several large longitudinal studies exist that fit these criteria. These studies survey nationally representative samples of residents of Germany (German Socio-Economic Panel—GSOEP), Great Britain (British Household Panel Study—BHPS), Australia (Household, Income, and Labour Dynamics in Australia—HILDA), and Switzerland (Swiss Household Panel—SHP), and have been asking participants about their life satisfaction every year for many years (e.g., the German panel has been ongoing since 1984).

One particular trait-state model, Kenny and Zautra's (2001) Stable Trait Autoregressive Trait State (STARTS) model, has been used to study life satisfaction over time. The STARTS model partitions observed variance in a construct into three components. The stable trait (ST) variance reflects stable influences. The autoregressive trait (ART) variance reflects influences that produce slow changes over time (e.g., life events, person-environment interactions). The state (S) variance reflects occasion-specific influences that produce changes even over short periods of time (e.g., measurement error, transient influences). Multivariate versions of this model can isolate separate state variance into measurement error and true, occasion-specific variance (Lucas & Donnellan, 2012).

Lucas and Donnellan (2007) used the STARTS model to study life satisfaction over time in the GSOEP and the BHPS. In this study, 8,632 German participants provided 21 waves of life satisfaction data, and 9,437 British participants provided 8 waves of data. The authors found that stable influences (ST) accounted for 34% and 38% of observed variance in life satisfaction in the GSOEP and the BHPS, respectively. Slowly changing influences (ART) accounted for 34% of observed variance in the German sample and 29% of variance in the British sample. In both samples, 33% of variance was occasion-specific (i.e., due to state factors).

These results were replicated in another study in which the authors used more waves and larger samples from the GSOEP and the BHPS (Lucas & Donnellan, 2012). In addition, the authors fit the STARTS model to data obtained from the HILDA and the SHP. The results were similar to those obtained from other samples: stable trait accounted for 31% and 26% of observed variance in the HILDA and the SHP, respectively; autoregressive trait comprised 32% and 36% of variance in the two datasets; whereas 37% and 38% of variance was due to occasion-specific factors. Thus, there is substantial agreement across large datasets from four countries that about a third of variance in life satisfaction is stable even over very long time periods, another third changes slowly over time, and the remaining third is occasion-specific.

Separating different influences on life satisfaction can allow researchers to investigate further processes that underlie these influences. For example, Lucas and Donnellan (2007) found that the proportion of life satisfaction variance that is accounted for by the stable trait was incrementally higher for older age groups than young adults. A possible reason for this finding is that people's life circumstances become increasingly stable over time, leading to increasing stability in life satisfaction. Luhmann, Schimmack, and Eid (2011) applied the STARTS model to life satisfaction and income and found that most of the association between the two variables occurred at the trait level. This finding suggests that same processes may lead to stability in life satisfaction and income. In a longitudinal study of spouses, Schimmack and Lucas (2010) found that similar factors lead to stability and slow changes in life satisfaction in spouses, but that occasion-specific factors likely differ. Researchers have also used the STARTS model to further examine sources of occasion-specific influences. For example, Lucas and Donnellan (2012) found that on average 26% of the occasion-specific variance in life satisfaction was shared with satisfaction with specific life domains (e.g., health, housing), whereas the remaining 74% was likely due to other, less reliable influences.

Complex models like the STARTS are challenging to estimate and thus are not always ideal. However, the logic behind these models can be used even when the models themselves are not tested specifically. Researchers have also used other approaches to study life satisfaction over long periods of time, and these studies generally reach similar conclusions to those that use more complex models (although they have less quantitative precision). For example, to study whether there was a set point of life satisfaction, Fujita and Diener (2005) used the GSOEP to compare average life satisfaction in the first 5 years of study with the 5-year average 12 years later (also see Headey, Muffels, & Wagner, 2010). They found that baselines of almost a quarter of the participants changed significantly over this time period. They also found that it was the least satisfied people who were more likely to change in the future.

In sum, empirical evidence suggests that there are processes that lead to both stability and change in well-being. About a third of observed variance in life satisfaction is influenced by factors that promote stability, and another third is influenced by factors that lead to slow changes over time. The remaining variance is specific to the year of measurement and includes measurement error. Separating these influences is the key to understanding processes that promote stability and change over time. Longitudinal studies using newer modeling techniques are useful for accomplishing this goal.

LINKING CHANGE TO THE EXPERIENCE OF LIFE EVENTS

The research described in the preceding section is important for the question of whether happiness can change because it describes, on average, how stable happiness measures are. When we look at rank-order stability, it is possible to determine whether, in a typical population, those people who are happy at one point in time are still happier than others many years later. If stability is low, then this provides evidence that happiness can and does change, even if the studies themselves do not provide evidence about what is causing that change. On the other hand, if stability is extremely high, then it suggests that the broad range of events that tend to happen to people over time do not lead to major changes in the rank-order of happiness in a population. Thus, research that examines rank-order stability provides important information that can be used to guide subsequent theories about how much change we should expect to find and what sorts of factors should promote that change. Notably, the research described previously suggests that long-term stability coefficients bottom out at around .25 to .30, which means that over long periods of time, considerable change in well-being measures does occur.

Unfortunately, studies that focus solely on test–retest correlations do very little to provide evidence about the factors that actually do lead to change. Thus, researchers have turned to alternative methods to determine

responses, and such biases may have colored participants' responses in much of the initial research in this area.

To address these limitations, recent work has begun to use more sophisticated designs to evaluate the association between major life events and SWB. For instance, recent research that has evaluated the association between various major life events and SWB has examined these questions using very large nationally representative panel studies. This line of research has several advantages over the initial research described previously, and although it is not without limitations of its own, it can provide more definitive evidence than most cross-sectional designs. The main advantages of these studies are that they employ long-term longitudinal designs and typically examine questions using relatively large numbers of people. For example, the GSOEP has been used in several recent studies that evaluated the effects of various life events on adjustment (e.g., Galatzer-Levy, Bonanno, & Mancini, 2010; Lucas, 2007b; Stutzer & Frey, 2004). This panel study includes a nationally representative sample of more than 40,000 individuals living in Germany who have been assessed at yearly intervals for decades (some since 1984). Because the panel studies used in this research typically follow large cohorts of people over many years, they have offered researchers an economical yet powerful way to evaluate the long-term impact of major life events on SWB. With such large initial sample sizes, researchers using these data have been able to identify relatively large samples of respondents who have experienced even rare life events and have been able to explore the impact of these events over long periods of time.

Another important advantage to using these panel data is that they are prospective and allow researchers to make within-person comparisons of pre-event and post-event levels of SWB over time. Prospective designs are advantageous because they virtually eliminate the possibility that effects of a life event on SWB are due to pre-existing differences among those who experience events and those who do not because the critical test of the effects of experiencing a life event involves comparing average levels of SWB before experiencing an event to average SWB in the years that follow an event within the same person. Of course, these designs are still correlational, so it is not possible to definitively prove the causal association between the event itself and the change that occurred (there could be third variables that caused both the event and the change), but such studies can test whether substantial changes do actually occur when events happen.

Finally, use of panel data to evaluate the association between life events and SWB also minimizes the potential for demand characteristics to bias study findings. As discussed earlier, these panel studies include nationally representative samples numbering in the tens of thousands. These individuals are not recruited for any particular reason or on the basis of any particular individual characteristic. Further, participants in these studies are also asked to respond to a wide range of questions on a variety of topics and characteristics of one's life. Thus, it is unlikely that the variables selected to be included in any one study using these data would be particularly salient to an individual respondent, nor would respondents be influenced by the focus of a particular study incorporating their responses—because they are not recruited with this focus in mind. This is an important advantage because it minimizes the potential for demand characteristics, but in many cases allows researchers to evaluate large enough samples of individuals who experienced a particular life event for tests of how the experiences of these events are associated with SWB.

RESULTS FROM RECENT LONGITUDINAL STUDIES

In contrast to the findings of the initial cross-sectional literature and the adaptation theories that grew from this body of research, longitudinal work that has evaluated the impact of major life events on SWB using panel data like those described earlier indicates that the experience of some major life events is associated with changes—and sometimes even large changes—in individuals' SWB. In some cases, these changes are also long lasting, and some life events affect individuals' SWB many years following an event. However, this research also indicates that the amount of change and the permanence of these changes do vary across event type. For example, studies that have used nationally representative samples of German and British households suggest that, following an initial reaction period, individuals adapt back to pre-event levels of SWB after marriage and childbirth relatively quickly (Clark, Diener, Georgellis, & Lucas, 2008; Dyrdal & Lucas, 2013; Lucas, Clark, Georgellis, & Diener, 2003; Stutzer & Frey, 2006; see also Galatzer-Levy, Mazursky, Mancini, & Bonanno, 2011). However, there is also evidence that the death of one's spouse results in substantial declines in life satisfaction, followed by a gradual adaptation back to baseline levels that can take many years (Clark et al., 2008; Lucas et al., 2003; Specht, Egloff, & Schmukle, 2011). Indeed, other negative life events, such as unemployment, result in lasting declines in life satisfaction that persist even after finding new employment (Clark, 2006; Clark et al., 2008; Lucas, Clark, Georgellis, & Diener, 2004; Powdthavee, 2012). A study by Lucas (2005) that examined reaction and adaptation to divorce in the GSOEP also showed a similar pattern. This study found that the experience of divorce was associated with a decrease in life satisfaction in the time leading up to the year of divorce, and that although SWB began improving in the year of divorce, complete adaptation to premarriage baseline levels did not occur in the years that followed.

Although the advantages of these longitudinal studies make the findings of these studies quite compelling, it is important to note that there is variation in findings from study to study regarding how major life events affect SWB. This is the case even among studies using the same panel dataset to evaluate the impact of the same life event. For instance, Lucas (2007b) used two nationally representative panel studies (the GSOEP and the BHPS) to demonstrate that lasting declines in life satisfaction result from the onset of long-term disability. However, subsequent studies using the same datasets by Oswald and Powdthavee (BHPS; 2008), Powdthavee (BHPS; 2009), and Pagán-Rodriguez (GSOEP; 2012) suggest that individuals' SWB does recover from the losses associated with the onset of disability. Similarly, Lucas (2005) found evidence for incomplete adaption to divorce in the GSOEP, but subsequent analyses by Clark et al. (2008) in the same data show evidence of adaptation to divorce.

As Oswald and Powdthavee (2008) note, the exact reasons for these discrepancies in results are unclear, but given that these studies use the same initial data, it is clear that these discrepancies result from differences in methodology and analytic technique. For example, there are notable differences in Pagán-Rodriguez's (2011) selection criteria for identifying individuals who experienced disability and the selection criteria used by Lucas (2007b). In Lucas's (2007b) study, respondents were included in analyses if they reported experiencing onset of disability during the study and continued to report being disabled for the duration of the study. In contrast, Pagán-Rodriguez's (2012) and Powdthavee's (2009) analyses were limited to respondents who reported experiencing disability during the study—and included both people who remained disabled and those who eventually recovered from their disability. These differences in selection criteria result in important differences in the composition of the sample being evaluated, and it is important to note these differences (among other differences in analytic methods among studies) because they may have implications as to how one should interpret and consolidate findings across studies. It is unclear whether any single technique provides an optimal method for answering the question of how disability affects SWB across time, as this is a relatively new stream of research and the methods for analyzing the major research questions continue to be developed. Indeed, greater consensus regarding the optimal methods for addressing these questions will likely emerge as this research continues to expand.

In light of this variation in findings in this area, there have been recent efforts to synthesize this literature and identify the overall patterns of results across multiple studies. In particular, Luhmann, Hofmann, Eid, and Lucas (2012) conducted a meta-analysis to aggregate the existing life events literature and examine whether life events have differential impact on affect and cognitive aspects of SWB (i.e., life satisfaction) and whether patterns of adaptation differed across various life events. As discussed previously, studies using panel data like the GSOEP and the BHPS indicate that major life events can have strong effects on SWB, and that the strength of these effects and the pattern of adaptation to these events vary from event to event. This meta-analysis offered one of the first empirical evaluations of this observation and extended the test of this notion beyond the commonly used panel studies. SWB is conceptualized as comprising an affective and cognitive component (Diener, 1984), and it is possible that these aspects of SWB are affected differently by the experience of life events (Diener, Lucas, & Scollon, 2006). One of the strengths of this meta-analysis is that it offers a way to evaluate this question in aggregate across multiple studies using multiple measures of these constructs.

The results of this meta-analysis showed that there are differences in how the experience of major life events impacts affective and cognitive components of SWB. Generally speaking, life events appear to have stronger effects on cognitive aspects of SWB, and these effects appear to be more consistent across various samples. The authors reviewed eight distinct life events in their meta-analysis (unemployment, re-employment, retirement, relocation/migration, marriage, divorce, widowhood, and childbirth) and found that patterns of reaction and adaptation differed across life events. This finding is consistent with observations in previous reviews of the literature (Lucas, 2007b) and indicates that the extent to which major life events affect individuals varies depending on the life event.

NEW INNOVATIONS IN RESEARCH ON LIFE EVENTS

As research into the role of life events on changes in SWB matures, studies are continuing to become more sophisticated, and new innovations in analytic techniques used to understand the link between life events and SWB continue to be developed. For example, recent research has recognized that past studies of life events did not account for normative age-related changes in SWB. That is, a study may find that unemployment is related to lasting declines in SWB (e.g., Clark et al., 2008), but it remains possible that these declines would be observed in this sample regardless of whether unemployment occurred. Other research has found evidence that individuals' SWB does change over time due to normative, age-related changes across the life span (Baird, Lucas, & Donnellan, 2010; Blanchflower & Oswald, 2008), and if certain life events tend to occur during these periods of change, observed changes (or lack of changes) following major life events may be conflated with normative changes that are typical for the sample being evaluated.

To separate the influence of normative change from change in SWB due to the experience of an event, recent studies (e.g., Yap, Anusic, & Lucas, 2012; Anusic, Yap, & Lucas, in press a; in press b) have begun to estimate and account for the pattern of normative change that would have been observed if a particular sample did not experience the life event being evaluated. To do this, these studies generate matched comparison samples using propensity score matching (Gelman & Hill, 2009). Each comparison group includes individuals who are similar on various demographic characteristics (e.g., sex, age, income, and education) to the sample experiencing the event, but who have not experienced the event themselves. Normative trends in

Fujita, F., & Diener, E. (2005). Life satisfaction set point: Stability and change. *Journal of Personality and Social Psychology, 88*, 158–164.

Galatzer-Levy, I. R., Bonanno, G. A., & Mancini, A. D. (2010). From Marianthal to latent growth mixture modeling: A return to the exploration of individual differences in response to unemployment. *Journal of Neuroscience, Psychology, and Economics, 3*, 116–125.

Galatzer-Levy, I. R., Mazursky, H., Mancini, A. D., & Bonanno, G. A. (2011). What we don't expect when expecting: Evidence for heterogeneity in subjective well-being in response to parenthood. *Journal of Family Psychology, 25*(3), 384–392.

Gelman, A., & Hill, J. (2009). *Data analysis using regression and multilevel/hierarchical models.* New York: Cambridge University Press.

Headey, B., Muffels, R., & Wagner, G. G. (2010). Long-running German panel survey shows that personal and economic choices, not just genes, matter for happiness. *Proceedings of the National Academy of Sciences, 107*, 17922–17926.

Headey, B., & Wearing, A. (1991). Subjective well-being: A stocks and flows framework. In F. Strack, M. Argyle, & N. Schwarz (Eds.), *Subjective Well-being: An interdisiplinary perspective* (pp. 49–73). Oxford: Pergamon Press.

Kenny, D. A., & Zautra, A. (1995). The trait-state-error model for multiwave data. *Journal of Consulting and Clinical Psychology, 63*(1), 52–59.

Kenny, D. A., & Zautra, A. (2001). Trait-state models for longitudinal data. In L. Collins, & A. Sayer (Eds.), *New methods for the analysis of change* (pp. 243–263). Washington, DC: American Psychological Association.

Lucas, R. E. (2005). Time does not heal all wounds: A longitudinal study of reaction and adaptation to divorce. *Psychological Science, 16*(12), 945–950.

Lucas, R. E. (2007a). Adaptation and the set-point model of subjective well-being: Does happiness change after major life events? *Current Directions in Psychological Science, 16*(2), 75–79.

Lucas, R. E. (2007b). Long-term disability is associated with lasting changes in subjective well-being: Evidence from two nationally representative longitudinal studies. *Journal of Personality and Social Psychology, 92*(4), 717–730.

Lucas, R. E., Clark, A. E., Georgellis, Y., & Diener, E. (2003). Reexamining adaptation and the set point model of happiness: Reactions to changes in marital status. *Journal of Personality and Social Psychology, 84*, 527–539.

Lucas, R. E., Clark, A. E., Georgellis, Y., & Diener, E. (2004). Unemployment alters the set point for life satisfaction. *Psychological Science, 15*, 8–13.

Lucas, R. E., & Donnellan, M. B. (2007). How stable is happiness? Using the STARTS model to estimate the stability of life satisfaction. *Journal of Research in Personality, 41*, 1091–1098.

Lucas, R. E., & Donnellan, M. B. (2012). Estimating the reliability of single-item life satisfaction measures: Results from four national panel studies. *Social Indicators Research, 105*, 323–331.

Luhmann, M., Hofmann, W., Eid, M., & Lucas, R. E. (2012). Subjective well-being and adaptation to life events: A meta-analysis. *Journal of Personality and Social Psychology, 102*, 592–615.

Luhmann, M., Schimmack, U., & Eid, M. (2011). Stability and variability in the relationship between subjective well-being and income. *Journal of Research in Personality, 45*, 186–197.

Lyubomirsky, S., King, L., & Diener, E. (2005). The benefits of frequent positive affect: Does happiness lead to success? *Psychological Bulletin, 131*, 803–855.

Oswald, A. J., & Powdthavee, N. (2008). Does happiness adapt? A longitudinal study of disability with implications for economists and judges. *Journal of Public Economics, 92,* 1061−1077.

Pagán-Rodríguez, R. (2012). Longitudinal analysis of the domains of satisfaction before and after disability: Evidence from the German socio-economic panel. *Social Indicators Research, 108,* 365−385.

Pai, M., & Carr, D. (2010). Do personality traits moderate the effect of late-life spousal loss on psychological distress? *Journal of Health and Social Behavior, 51,* 183−199.

Pavot, W., & Diener, E. (1993). Review of the Satisfaction with Life Scale. *Psychological Assessment, 5*(2), 164−172.

Powdthavee, N. (2009). What happens to people before and after disability? Focusing effects, lead effects, and adaptation in different areas of life. *Social Science & Medicine, 69,* 1834−1844.

Powdthavee, N. (2012). Jobless, friendless and broke: What happens to different areas of life before and after unemployment? *Economica, 79,* 557−575.

Schimmack, U., & Lucas, R. E. (2010). Environmental influences on well-being: A dyadic latent panel analysis of spousal similarity. *Social Indicators Research, 98,* 1−21.

Smith, D. M., Schwarz, N., Roberts, T. R., & Ubel, P. A. (2006). Why are you calling me? How survey introductions change response patterns. *Quality of Life Research, 15,* 621−630.

Specht, J., Egloff, B., & Schmukle, S. C. (2011). The benefits of believing in chance or fate external locus of control as a protective factor for coping with the death of a spouse. *Social Psychological and Personality Science, 2,* 132−137.

Steel, P., Schmidt, J., & Shultz, J. (2008). Refining the relationship between personality and subjective well-being. *Psychological Bulletin, 134,* 138−161.

Steyer, R., Schmitt, M., & Eid, M. (1999). Latent state-trait theory and research in personality and individual differences. *European Journal of Personality, 13*(5), 389−408.

Stutzer, A., & Frey, B. S. (2004). Reported subjective well-being: A challenge for economic theory and economic policy. *Schmollers Jahrbuch, 124,* 191−231.

Stutzer, A., & Frey, B. S. (2006). Does marriage make people happy, or do happy people get married? *Journal of Socio-Economics, 35*(2), 326−347.

Tellegen, A., Lykken, D. T., Bouchard, T. J., Jr., Wilcox, K. J., Segal, N. L., & Rich, S. (1988). Personality similarity in twins reared apart and together. *Journal of Personality Social Psychology, 6,* 1031−1039.

Yap, S. C., Anusic, I., & Lucas, R. E. (2012). Does personality moderate reaction and adaptation to major life events? Evidence from the British household panel survey. *Journal of Research in Personality, 46,* 477−488.

Chapter 8

Increasing Happiness
by Well-Being Therapy

Chiara Ruini and Giovanni A. Fava
University of Bologna, Bologna, Italy

INTRODUCTION

In 1989, in a pioneer work titled "Happiness Is Everything or Is It?" Ryff argued that, when dealing with human existence, the concept of happiness should be better defined and articulated than the simple presence of pleasure and positive affect. Ryff (1989) developed a model of positive human functioning that she called *psychological well-being* (PWB). It could be briefly regarded as the engagement with and participation in the existential challenges and opportunities of life, where human beings enjoy the exercise of their realized capabilities.

Some years later, Ryan and Deci (2001) examined the concept of well-being and described two main approaches: the hedonic and the eudaimonic one. According to the former, well-being consists of subjective happiness, pleasure, and pain avoidance. Thus, the concept of well-being is equated with the experience of positive emotions versus negative emotions and with satisfaction in various domains of one's life. This hedonic point of view concentrated on happiness as the result of experiencing pleasant emotions, low levels of negative moods, and high levels of perceived life satisfaction. It has been identified with the term *subjective well-being* for indicating a person's cognitive (life satisfaction) and affective evaluation (pleasant and unpleasant affect) of her or his life: a subjective evaluation and a condition for a good life.

According to the eudaimonic perspective, happiness consists of fulfilling one's potential in a process of self-realization. Under this umbrella, some researchers describe concepts such as fully functioning person, meaningfulness, self-actualization, and vitality. Importantly, in describing optimal human functioning, Ryff and Singer (2008) emphasize Aristotle's admonishment to seek "that which is intermediate," avoiding excess and extremes. The pursuit of well-being may, in fact, be so solipsistic and individualistic to leave no room for human connection and the social good, or it could be so focused on responsibilities and duties outside the self that personal talents and capacities are neither recognized nor developed (Ryff & Singer, 2008).

These two approaches have led to different areas of research, but they complement each other in defining the construct of well-being (Ryan & Deci, 2001). Some authors have also suggested that they can compensate each other; thus, individuals may have profiles of high eudaimonic well-being and low hedonic well-being, or vice versa. These profiles are also associated with sociodemographic variables, such as age, years of education, and employment (Keyes, Shmotkin, & Ryff, 2002). However, in this investigation, the authors underlined the fact that only a small proportion of individuals present optimal well-being—that is, high hedonic and eudemonic well-being—paving the way for possible psychosocial interventions. The findings that we are going to analyze indicate that the two viewpoints are inextricably linked in clinical situations, and the extent, number, and circumstances of changes in well-being induced by treatments may matter more than *a priori* distinctions.

THE CONCEPTS OF HAPPINESS AND WELL-BEING IN CLINICAL PSYCHOLOGY

In clinical psychology, the eudaimonic view has found much more feasibility, compared to the hedonic approach, because it concerns human potential and personal strength (Ryff & Singer, 1996; 2008). Ryff's model of psychological well-being, encompassing autonomy, personal growth, environmental mastery, purpose in life, positive relations, and self-acceptance, has been found to fit specific impairments of patients with affective disorders (Fava et al., 2001; Rafanelli et al., 2000). Further, the absence of psychological well-being was found to be a risk factor for depression (Wood & Joseph, 2010). Thunedborg, Black, and Bech (1995) observed that quality of life measurement, and not symptomatic ratings, could predict recurrence of depression. An increase in psychological well-being may thus protect against relapse and recurrence (Fava, 1999; Wood & Joseph, 2010). Therefore, an intervention that targets the positive may address an aspect of functioning and health that is typically left unaddressed in conventional treatments.

INCREASING HAPPINESS BY TARGETED INTERVENTIONS: IS "HAPPIER ALWAYS BETTER"?

Ryff and Singer (1996) underlined that interventions that bring a person out of negative functioning are one form of success, but facilitating progression toward the restoration of positive is quite another. Parloff, Kelman, and Frank (1954) suggested that the goals of psychotherapy were increased personal comfort and effectiveness, and humanistic psychology suggested concepts such as self-realization and self-actualization as final therapeutic goals

(Maslow, 1968; Rogers, 1961). For a long time, these latter achievements were viewed only as by-products of the reduction of symptoms or as a luxury that clinical investigators could not afford. This probably is due to the fact that, historically, mental health research was dramatically weighted on the side of psychological dysfunction, and health was equated with the absence of illness, rather than the presence of wellness (Ryff & Singer, 1996). Ryff and Singer (1996) suggested that the absence of well-being creates conditions of vulnerability to possible future adversities and that the route to enduring recovery lies not exclusively in alleviating the negative, but in engendering the positive.

Early pioneer works in this research domain can be considered Ellis and Becker's (1982) guide to personal happiness, Fordyce's (1983) program to increase happiness, Padesky's (1994) work on schema change processes, Frisch's (1998; 2006) quality of life therapy, and Horowitz and Kaltreider's (1979) work on positive states of mind.

More recently, a growing number of investigations on positive emotions (Fredrickson & Joiner, 2002); subjective well-being (Diener, 2000; Diener, Suh, Lucas, & Smith, 1999); human strengths (Peterson & Seligman, 2004); and other positive personality characteristics such as compassion, hope, and altruism (Park, Peterson, & Seligman, 2004) paved the way for developing "positive interventions" (Magayar-Moe, 2009; Seligman, Steen, Park, & Peterson, 2005; Sin & Lyubomirsky, 2009). These interventions include positive psychotherapy (Seligman, Rashid, & Parks, 2006); wisdom psychotherapy (Linden, Baumann, Lieberei, Lorenz, & Rotter, 2011); gratitude interventions (Wood, Maltby, Gillett, Linley, & Joseph, 2008); positive coaching (Biswas-Diener, 2009; 2010); strengths-based approaches (Biswas-Diener, Kashdan, & Minhas, 2011; Govindji & Linley, 2007; Linley & Burns, 2010); hope therapy (Geraghty, Wood, & Hyland, 2010; Snyder, Ilardi, Michael, Yamhure, & Sympson, 2000); and forgiveness therapy (Lamb, 2005).

In a recent meta-analysis, Bolier et al. (2013) showed that these positive psychology interventions significantly enhance subjective and psychological well-being and reduce depressive symptoms, even though effect sizes were in the small to moderate range. Further, the majority of positive psychology interventions considered in this meta-analysis (26 out of 39 studies) were delivered in a self-help format, sometimes in conjunction with face-to-face instruction and support, and on very heterogeneous groups. Even though self-help suits the goals of positive psychology very well, and indeed is highly standardized, it often takes a "one size fits all" approach, which may underestimate the complexity of phenomena in clinical settings and not fully consider the balance between positivity and distress (Rafanelli et al., 2000; Ruini & Fava, 2012).

The main aim of all these positive interventions, in fact, is the promotion of happiness, positive emotions, and positivity in general. This is based on the assumption that the benefits of well-being are now well documented in cross-sectional and longitudinal research and include better physical health (Chida & Steptoe, 2008; Fava & Sonino, 2010; Howell, Kern, & Lyubomirsky, 2007), improved productivity at work, more meaningful relationships, and social functioning (Seeman, Singer, Ryff, Dienberg, Love, & Levy-Storms 2002). In the same line, research has indeed suggested the important role of positive affectivity (Fredrickson & Joiner, 2002) in promoting resilience and growth.

However, specific dimensions of positive functioning, namely, autonomy and independence, have been determined to be related to increased levels of noradrenaline (Seeman et al., 2002) and seem thus to be associated with an increased stress response. Similarly, excessively elevated levels of positive emotions can become detrimental and are more connected with mental disorders and impaired functioning (Fredrickson & Losada, 2005). Larsen and Prizmic (2008) argued that the balance of positive to negative affect (i.e., the positivity ratio) is a key factor in well-being and in defining whether a person flourishes. Several authors (Fredrickson & Losada, 2005; Larsen & Prizmic, 2008; Schwartz, 1997; Schwartz et al., 2002) suggest that, to maintain an optimal level of emotional well-being and positive mental health, individuals need to experience approximately three times more positive than negative affect. Fredrickson and Losada (2005), in fact, have found that above this ratio, there is an excessively high positivity that becomes detrimental to functioning. Excessive positivity in adverse situations, in fact, can signal inappropriate cues to thoughts and action (Fredrickson & Losada, 2005) or may be accompanied by illusions that are easily shattered by the harsh, hostile reality (Shmotkin, 2005). Garamoni et al. (1991) suggested that healthy functioning is characterized by an optimal balance of positive and negative cognitions or affects, and that psychopathology is marked by deviations from the optimal balance.

Positive interventions, thus, should not be simply aimed to increase happiness and well-being, but should consider the complex balance between psychological well-being and distress (MacLeod & Moore, 2000) and be targeted to specific and individualized needs. Wood and Tarrier (2010) emphasized that positive characteristics such as gratitude and autonomy often exist on a continuum. They are neither "negative" or "positive": their impact depends on the specific situation and on the interaction with concurrent distress and other psychological attitudes. For instance, self-efficacy beliefs (Caprara, Alessandri, & Barbaranelli, 2010; Karlsson et al., 2011) and emotional inhibition (Grandi, Sirri, Wise, Tossani, & Fava, 2011) may affect the expression of positive orientation.

All these elements should be taken into account in the psychotherapy process. An example of psychotherapeutic intervention that takes into consideration the preceding concepts for achieving a balanced and individualized path to optimal functioning is well-being therapy (WBT; Fava, 1999; Ruini & Fava, 2012).

THE STRUCTURE OF WELL-BEING THERAPY

Well-being therapy is a short-term psychotherapeutic strategy that extends over 8 to 12 sessions, which may take place every week or every other week (Fava, 1999; Fava & Ruini, 2003; Ruini & Fava, 2012). The duration of each session may range from 30 to 50 minutes. It is a technique that emphasizes self-observation (Emmelkamp, 1974), with the use of a structured diary and interaction between patients and therapists. Well-being therapy is based on Ryff's cognitive model of psychological well-being (Ryff, 1989), encompassing six dimensions of positive functioning and eudaimonic well-being: autonomy, environmental mastery, personal growth, purpose in life, self-acceptance, and positive interpersonal relationships. The development of sessions is as follows.

Initial Sessions

These sessions are simply concerned with identifying episodes of well-being and setting them into a situational context, no matter how short lived they were. Patients are asked to report in a structured diary the circumstances surrounding their episodes of well-being, rated on a 0–100 scale, with 0 being absence of well-being and 100 the most intense well-being that could be experienced.

Patients are particularly encouraged to search for well-being moments, not only in special hedonic-stimulating situations but also during their daily activities. Several studies have shown that individuals preferentially invest their attention and psychic resources in activities associated with rewarding and challenging states of consciousness, in particular with optimal experience (Csikszentmihalyi, 1990). This is characterized by the perception of high environmental challenges and environmental mastery, deep concentration, involvement, enjoyment, control of the situation, clear feedback on the course of activity, and intrinsic motivation (Deci & Ryan, 1985). Cross-sectional studies have demonstrated that optimal experience can occur in any daily context, such as work and leisure (Delle Fave & Massimini, 2003). Patients are thus asked to report when they feel optimal experiences in their daily life and are invited to list the associated activities or situations.

This initial phase generally extends over a couple of sessions. Yet its duration depends on the factors that affect any homework assignment, such as resistance and compliance.

Intermediate Sessions

When the instances of well-being are properly recognized, the patient is encouraged to identify thoughts and beliefs leading to premature interruption of well-being. The similarities with the search for irrational, tension-evoking thoughts in Ellis and Becker's rational-emotive therapy (1982) and automatic thoughts in cognitive therapy (Beck, Rush, Shaw, & Emery, 1979) are obvious. The trigger for self-observation is, however, different, being based on well-being instead of distress.

This phase is crucial because it allows the therapist to identify which areas of psychological well-being are unaffected by irrational or automatic thoughts and which are saturated with them. The therapist may also reinforce and encourage activities that are likely to elicit well-being and optimal experiences (e.g., assigning the task of undertaking particular pleasurable activities for a certain time each day). Such reinforcement may also result in graded task assignments (Beck et al., 1979), with special reference to exposure to feared or challenging situations, which the patient is likely to avoid. Over time patients may develop ambivalent attitudes toward well-being. They complain of having lost it, or they long for it, but at the same time they are scared when positive moments actually happen in their lives. These moments trigger specific negative automatic thoughts, usually concerning the fact that they will not last (i.e., it's too good to be true), that they are not deserved by patients, or that they are attainable only by overcoming difficulties and distress. Encouraging patients in searching and engaging in optimal experiences and pleasant activities is therefore crucial at this stage of WBT.

This intermediate phase may extend over two or three sessions, depending on the patient's motivation and ability, and it paves the way for the specific well-being enhancing strategies.

Final Sessions

The monitoring of the course of episodes of well-being allows the therapist to realize specific impairments in well-being dimensions according to Ryff's conceptual framework. An additional source of information may be provided by Ryff's Scales of Psychological Well-Being (PWB), an 84-item self-rating inventory (Ryff, 1989). Ryff's six dimensions of psychological well-being are progressively introduced to the patients, as long as the material that is recorded lends itself to it. For example, the therapist could explain that autonomy consists of possessing an internal locus of control, independence, and self-determination or that personal growth consists of being open to new experience and considering self as expanding over time, if the patient's attitudes show impairments in these specific areas. Errors in thinking and alternative interpretations are then discussed. At this point in time, the patient is expected to be able to readily identify moments of well-being, be aware of interruptions to well-being feelings (cognitions), utilize cognitive behavioral techniques to address these interruptions, and pursue optimal experiences. Meeting the challenge that optimal experiences may entail is emphasized, because it is through this challenge that growth and improvement of self can take place.

WELL-BEING THERAPY: CLINICAL CONSIDERATIONS

Cognitive restructuring in well-being therapy follows Ryff's conceptual framework (Ryff & Singer, 1996). The goal of the therapist is to lead the patient from an impaired level to an optimal level in the six dimensions of psychological well-being. This means that patients are not simply encouraged to pursue the highest possible levels in psychological well-being, in all dimensions, but to obtain a balanced functioning. This optimal-balanced well-being could be different from patient to patient, according to factors such as personality traits, social roles, and cultural and social contexts (Ruini et al., 2003; Ruini & Fava, 2012).

The various dimensions of positive functioning can compensate each other (some being more interpersonally oriented, some more personal/cognitive) and the aim of WBT, such as other positive interventions, should be the promotion of an optimal-balanced functioning between these dimensions, in order to facilitate individual flourishing (Keyes, 2002). This means that sometimes patients should be encouraged to decrease their level of positive functioning in certain domains. Without this clinical framework, the risk is to lead patients at having too high levels of self-confidence, with unrealistic expectations that may become dysfunctional and/or stressful to individuals.

Environmental mastery. This is the most frequent impairment that emerges, that is felt by patients as a lack of sense of control. This leads the patients to miss surrounding opportunities, with the possibility of subsequent regret over them. On the other hand, sometimes patients may require help because they are unable to enjoy and savor daily life, as they are too engaged in work or family activities. Their abilities to plan and solve problems may lead others to constantly ask for their help, with the resulting feeling of being exploited and overwhelmed by requests. These extremely high levels of environmental mastery thus become a source of stress and allostatic load to the individual. Environmental mastery can be considered a key mediator or moderator of stressful life experiences (Fava, Guidi, Semprini, Tomba, & Sonino, 2010). A positive characterization of protective factors converges with efforts to portray the individual as a psychological activist, capable of proactive and effective problem solving, rather than passively buffeted by external forces (Ryff & Singer, 1998), but also capable of finding time for rest and relaxation in daily life.

Personal growth. Patients often tend to emphasize their distance from expected goals much more than the progress that has been made toward goal achievement. A basic impairment that emerges is the inability to identify the similarities between events and situations that were handled successfully in the past and those that are about to come (transfer of experiences). On the other hand, people with levels of personal growth that are too high tend to forget or do not give enough emphasis to past experiences because they are exclusively future-oriented. Negative or traumatic experiences could particularly be underestimated, as a sort of extreme defense mechanism (denial);

i.e., "I just need to get over this situation and go on with my life" (Held, 2002; Norem & Chang, 2002). Dysfunctional high personal growth is similar to a cognitive benign illusion, or wishful thinking, which hinders the integration of past (negative) experiences and their related learning process.

Purpose in life. Patients may perceive a lack of sense of direction and may devalue their function in life. This particularly occurs when environmental mastery and sense of personal growth are impaired. On the other hand, many other conditions worthy of clinical attention may arise from too high levels of purpose in life. First of all, individuals with a strong determination in realizing one (or more) life goal(s) could dedicate themselves fully to their activity, thereby allowing them to persist, even in the face of obstacles, and to eventually reach excellence. This again could have a cost in terms of allostatic load and stress. Further, Vallerand et al. (2003) proposed the concept of obsessive passion for describing an activity or goal that becomes a central feature of one's identity and serves to define the person. Individuals with an obsessive passion come to develop ego-invested self-structures (Hodgins & Knee, 2002) and eventually display a rigid persistence toward the activity, thereby leading to less than optimal functioning. Such persistence is rigid because it occurs not only in the absence of positive emotions and sometimes of positive feedback, but even in the face of important personal costs such as damaged relationships, failed commitments, and conflicts with other activities in the person's life (Vallerand et al., 2007). The individual engagement for a certain goal could thus become a form of psychological inflexibility (Kashdan & Rottenberg, 2010), which is more connected with psychopathology than well-being. Some individuals, in fact, remain attached to their goals even when they seem to be unattainable, and keep believing that they would be happy pending the achievement of these goals. These mechanisms are associated with hopelessness (Hadley & MacLeod, 2010; MacLeod & Conway, 2007) and parasuicidal behaviors (Vincent, Boddana, & MacLeod, 2004). Further, this confirms the idea that hope, another future-oriented positive emotion, can become paralyzing and hampers facing and accepting negativity and failures (Bohart, 2002; Geraghty et al., 2010).

Autonomy. It is a frequent clinical observation that patients may exhibit a pattern whereby a perceived lack of self-worth leads to unassertive behavior. For instance, patients may hide their opinions or preferences, go along with a situation that is not in their best interests or consistently put their needs behind the needs of others. This pattern undermines environmental mastery and purpose in life, and these, in turn, may affect autonomy because these dimensions are highly correlated in clinical populations. Such attitudes may not be obvious to the patients, who hide their considerable need for social approval. A patient who tries to please everyone is likely to fail to achieve this goal and the unavoidable conflicts that may result in chronic dissatisfaction and frustration. On the other hand, in Western countries particularly, individuals are culturally encouraged to be autonomous and independent.

Certain individuals develop the idea that they should rely only on themselves for solving problems and difficulties, and are thus unable to ask for advice or help. Also in this case, an unbalanced high autonomy can become detrimental for social/interpersonal functioning (Seeman et al., 2002). Some patients complain they are not able to get along with other people, work in teams, or maintain intimate relationships because they are constantly fighting for their opinions and independence.

Self-acceptance. Patients may maintain unrealistically high standards and expectations, driven by perfectionistic attitudes (that reflect lack of self-acceptance) and/or endorsement of external instead of personal standards (that reflect lack of autonomy). As a result, any instance of well-being is neutralized by a chronic dissatisfaction with oneself. A person may set unrealistic standards for his or her performance. On the other hand, an inflated self-esteem may be a source of distress and clash with reality, as was found to be the case in cyclothymia and bipolar disorder (Fava, Rafanelli, Tomba, Guidi, & Grandi, 2011; Garland et al., 2010).

Positive relations with others. Interpersonal relationships may be influenced by strongly held attitudes of perfectionism which the patient may be unaware of and which may be dysfunctional. Impairments in self-acceptance (with the resulting belief of being rejectable and unlovable or others being inferior and unlovable) may also undermine positive relations with others. There is a large body of literature (Uchino, Cacioppo, & Kiecolt-Glaser, 1996) on the buffering effects of social integration, social network properties, and perceived support. On the other hand, little research has been done on the possible negative consequences of an exaggerated social functioning. Characteristics such as empathy, altruism, and generosity are usually considered universally positive. However, in clinical practice, patients often report a sense of guilt for not being able to help someone or forgive an offense. An individual with a strong pro-social attitude can sacrifice his or her needs and well-being for those of others, and this in the long run becomes detrimental and sometimes disappointing. This individual can also become overconcerned and overwhelmed by others' problems and distress and be at risk for burnout syndrome. Finally, a generalized tendency to forgive others and be grateful toward benefactors could mask low self-esteem and low sense of personal worth.

These insights were confirmed by a recent paper (Grant & Schwartz, 2011) suggesting that all positive traits, states, and experiences have costs that, at high levels, may begin to outweigh their benefits, creating the nonmonotonicity of an inverted U. For this reason, traditional clinical psychology has a crucial role in planning and implementing interventions for enhancing positive affect. The important insight that comes from dealing with psychopathology could thus be used in determining the "right" amount of positivity for a certain individual, considering his or her global situation and needs. WBT is an example of this balanced positive clinical approach.

WBT: VALIDATION STUDIES

Well-being therapy has been employed in several clinical studies. Other studies are currently in progress.

Residual Phase of Affective Disorders

The effectiveness of well-being therapy in the residual phase of affective disorders was first tested in a small controlled investigation (Fava, Rafanelli, Cazzaro, Conti, & Grandi, 1998a). Twenty patients with affective disorders who had been successfully treated by behavioral (anxiety disorders) or pharmacological (mood disorders) methods were randomly assigned to either a well-being therapy or cognitive behavioral treatment (CBT) of residual symptoms. Both well-being and cognitive behavioral therapies were associated with a significant reduction of residual symptoms, as measured by the Clinical Interview for Depression (CID; Guidi, Fava, Bech, & Paykel, 2011; Paykel, 1985) and in PWB well-being. However, when the residual symptoms of the two groups were compared after treatment, a significant advantage of well-being therapy over cognitive behavioral strategies was observed with the CID. Well-being therapy also was associated with a significant increase in PWB well-being, particularly in the personal growth scale.

The improvement in residual symptoms was explained on the basis of the balance between positive and negative affect (Fava et al., 1998a). If treatment of psychiatric symptoms induces improvement of well-being, and indeed subscales describing well-being are more sensitive to drug effects than subscales describing symptoms (Kellner, 1987; Rafanelli & Ruini, 2012), it is conceivable that changes in well-being may affect the balance of positive and negative affect. In this sense, the higher degree of symptomatic improvement that was observed with well-being therapy in this study is not surprising: in the acute phase of affective illness, removal of symptoms may yield the most substantial changes, but the reverse may be true in its residual phase.

Prevention of Recurrent Depression

Well-being therapy was a specific and innovative part of a cognitive behavioral package that was applied to recurrent depression (Fava, Rafanelli, Grandi, Conti, & Belluardo, 1998b). This package also included CBT of residual symptoms and lifestyle modification. Forty patients with recurrent major depression, who had been successfully treated with antidepressant drugs, were randomly assigned to either this cognitive behavioral package including well-being therapy or clinical management. In both groups, antidepressant drugs were tapered and discontinued. The group that received cognitive behavioral therapy—WBT had a significantly lower level of residual symptoms after drug discontinuation in comparison with the clinical management group. Cognitive behavioral therapy–WBT also resulted in a significantly lower relapse rate (25%) at a 2-year follow-up than did clinical management (80%). At a 6-year follow-up (Fava et al., 2004), the relapse rate was 40% in the former group and 90% in the latter.

WBT was one of the main ingredients of a randomized controlled trial involving 180 patients with recurrent depression that was performed in Germany (Stangier et al., 2013). Even though follow-up was limited only to 1 year, the findings indicate that psychotherapy had significant effects on the prevention of relapse in patients at high risk of recurrence.

Loss of Clinical Effect During Drug Treatment

The return of depressive symptoms during maintenance of antidepressant treatment is a common and vexing clinical phenomenon (Fava & Offidani, 2011). Ten patients with recurrent depression who relapsed while taking anti-depressant drugs were randomly assigned to dose increase or to a sequential combination of cognitive-behavior and well-being therapy (Fava, Ruini, Rafanelli, & Grandi, 2002). Four out of five patients responded to a larger dose, but all relapsed again on that dose by 1-year follow-up. Four out of the five patients responded to psychotherapy and only one relapsed. The data suggest that application of well-being therapy may counteract loss of clinical effect during long-term antidepressant treatment.

Treatment of Generalized Anxiety Disorder

Well-being therapy has been applied for the treatment of generalized anxiety disorder (Fava et al., 2005; Ruini & Fava, 2009). Twenty patients with DSM-IV GAD were randomly assigned to eight sessions of CBT or the sequential administration of four sessions of CBT followed by the other four sessions of WBT. Both treatments were associated with a significant reduction of anxiety. However, significant advantages of the WBT-CBT sequential combination over CBT were observed, both in terms of symptom reduction and psychological well-being improvement. These preliminary results suggest the feasibility and clinical advantages of adding WBT to the treatment of GAD. A possible explanation to these findings is that self-monitoring of episodes of well-being may lead to a more comprehensive identification of automatic thoughts than that entailed by the customary monitoring of episodes of distress in cognitive therapy (Ruini & Fava, 2009).

Post-traumatic Stress Disorder

The use of WBT for the treatment of traumatized patients has not yet been tested in controlled investigations. However, two cases were reported (Belaise, Fava, & Marks, 2005) in which patients improved with WBT, even though their central trauma was discussed only in the initial history-taking session. The findings from these two cases should, of course, be interpreted with caution (the patients may have remitted spontaneously), but are of interest because they indicate an alternative route to overcoming trauma and developing resilience and warrant further investigation (Fava & Tomba, 2009).

Cyclothymic Disorder

Well-being therapy was recently applied (Fava et al., 2011) in sequential combination with CBT for the treatment of cyclothymic disorder, which involves mild or moderate fluctuations of mood, thought, and behavior without meeting formal diagnostic criteria for either major depressive disorder or mania (Baldessarini, Vazquez, & Tondo, 2011). Sixty-two patients with DSM-IV cyclothymic disorder were randomly assigned to CBT/WBT (n = 31) or clinical management (CM) (n = 31). An independent blind evaluator assessed the patients before treatment, after therapy, and at 1- and 2-year follow-ups. At post treatment, significant differences were found in all outcome measures, with greater improvements after treatment in the CBT/WBT group compared to the CM group. Therapeutic gains were maintained at 1- and 2-year follow-ups. The results of this investigation suggest that a sequential combination of CBT and WBT, which addresses both polarities of mood swings and comorbid anxiety, was found to yield significant and persistent benefits in cyclothymic disorder.

ARE PSYCHOTHERAPY-INDUCED MODIFICATIONS IN WELL-BEING ENDURING?

Well-being therapy's effectiveness may be based on two distinct yet ostensibly related clinical phenomena. The first has to do with the fact that an increase in psychological well-being may have a protective effect in terms of vulnerability to chronic and acute life stresses. The second has to do with the complex balance of positive and negative affects. There is extensive research—reviewed in detail elsewhere (Rafanelli et al., 2000; Ruini et al., 2003)—that indicates a certain degree of inverse correlation between positive and negative affects. As a result, changes in well-being may induce a decrease in distress, and vice versa. In the acute phase of illness, removal of symptoms may yield the most substantial changes, but the reverse may be true in its residual phase. An increase in psychological well-being may decrease residual symptoms that direct strategies (whether cognitive behavioral or pharmacological) would be unlikely to affect. Figures 8.1 and 8.2 illustrate the changes in well-being that were entailed by WBT in two clinical studies (Fava et al., 1998a; Fava et al., 2005). Unfortunately, measurements of

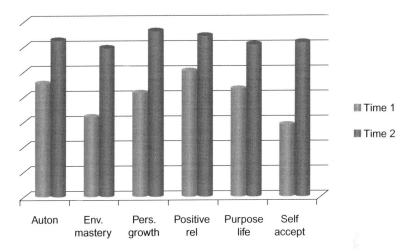

FIGURE 8.1   Modifications of well-being in patients with generalized anxiety disorder (GAD; N = 10) treated with well-being therapy. Auton = Autonomy; Env. mastery = Environmental Mastery; Pers. growth = Personal Growth; Positive rel = Positive Relations with Others; Purpose life = Purpose in Life; Self accept = Self-Acceptance. *(Source: Fava et al., 2005).*

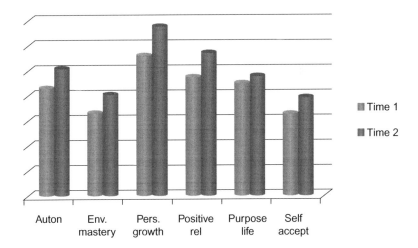

FIGURE 8.2   Modifications of well-being in patients with affective disorders (N = 20) treated with well-being therapy. Auton = Autonomy; Env. mastery = Environmental Mastery; Pers. growth = Personal Growth; Positive rel = Positive Relations with Others; Purpose Life = Purpose in life; Self accept = Self-Acceptance. *(Source: Fava et al., 1998a).*

psychological well-being at follow-up were not available; yet, the stability of clinical gains that was reported may suggest a similar endurance.

Cloninger (2006) attributes the clinical changes related to well-being therapy to three character traits defined as self-directedness (i.e., responsible, purposeful, and resourceful), cooperativeness (i.e., tolerant, helpful, compassionate), and self-transcendence (i.e., intuitive, judicious, spiritual). High scores in all these character traits have frequent positive emotions (i.e., happy, joyful, satisfied, optimistic) and infrequent negative emotions (i.e., anxious, sad, angry, pessimistic). The lack of development in any one of the three factors leaves a person vulnerable to the emergence of conflicts that can lead to anxiety and depression (Cloninger, 2006). These character traits can be exercised and developed by interventions that encourage a sense of hope and mastery for self-directedness. Indeed, in a study performed in the general population (Ruini et al., 2003), several PWB scales displayed significant correlations with Cloninger's Tridimensional Personality Questionnaire (Cloninger, 1987).

Further, it has been suggested that cognitive behavioral psychotherapy may work at the molecular level to alter stress-related gene expression and protein synthesis or influence mechanisms implicated in learning and memory acquisition in neuronal structures (Charney, 2004). Research on the neurobiological correlates of resilience has disclosed how different neural circuits (reward, fear conditioning and extinction, social behavior) may involve the same brain structures, and particularly the amygdala, the nucleus accumbens, and the medial prefrontal cortex (Charney, 2004). Singer, Friedman, Seeman, Fava, and Ryff (2005), on the basis of preclinical evidence, suggested that WBT may stimulate dendrite networks in the hippocampus and induce spine retraction in the basolateral amygdala (a site of storage for memories of fearful or stressful experiences), leading to a weakening of distress and traumatic memories. The pathophysiological substrates of well-being therapy may thus be different compared to symptom-oriented cognitive behavioral strategies, to the same extent that well-being and distress are not merely opposites (Rafanelli et al., 2000).

CONCLUSIONS

The controlled trials of well-being therapy that we have discussed indicate that psychological well-being may be increased by specific psychotherapeutic methods and that these changes are closely related to decrease in distress and improvement in contentment, friendliness, relaxation, and physical well-being. Unlike nonspecific interventions aimed at increasing control or social activity that yield short-lived improvement in subjective well-being (Okun, Olding, & Cohn, 1990), changes induced by WBT tend to persist at follow-up (Fava et al., 2002; Fava et al., 2004; Fava et al., 2005; Fava et al., 2011), underlie increased resilience, and entail less relapse in the face of current events.

WBT was originally developed as a strategy for promoting psychological well-being that was still impaired after standard pharmacological or psychotherapeutic treatments in clinical populations. It was based on the assumption that these impairments may vary from one illness to another, from patient to patient, and even from one episode to another of the same illness in the same patient. These impairments represent a vulnerability factor for adversities and relapses (Fava & Tomba, 2009; Ryff & Singer, 1996; Wood & Joseph, 2010). WBT, thus, can be considered a therapeutic positive intervention developed in clinical psychology, which takes into consideration both well-being and distress in predicting patients' clinical outcomes (Rafanelli & Ruini, 2012). Further, we suggest that the pathway to optimal, balanced well-being can be obtained with highly individualized strategies. In some cases, some psychological dimensions need reinforcement and growth. In other cases, excessive or distorted levels of certain dimensions need to be adjusted because they may become dysfunctional and impede flourishing. Individuals may be helped to move up from impaired low levels to optimal, but also to move down from inappropriately high to optimal-balanced levels. This could be achieved using specific behavioral homework, assignment of pleasurable activities, but also cognitive restructuring aimed at reaching a more balanced positive functioning in these dimensions. Unlike standard cognitive therapy, which is based on rigid specific assumptions (e.g., the cognitive triad in depression), WBT is characterized by flexibility (Kashdan & Rottenberg, 2010) and by an individualized approach for addressing psychological issues that other therapies have left unexplored, such as the promotion of eudaimonic well-being and optimal human functioning. The diverse feasibility and flexibility of WBT are in line with the positive clinical psychology approach, which calls for a number of different interventions to be selected based on individual specific needs (Wood & Tarrier, 2010).

REFERENCES

Baldessarini, R. J., Vázquez, G., & Tondo, L. (2011). Treatment of cyclothymic disorder: Commentary. *Psychotherapy and Psychosomatics, 80*, 131–135.

Beck, A. T., Rush, A. J., Shaw, B. F., & Emery, G. (1979). *Cognitive therapy of depression.* New York: Guilford Press.

Belaise, C., Fava, G. A., & Marks, I. M. (2005). Alternatives to debriefing and modifications to cognitive behavior therapy for posttraumatic stress disorder. *Psychotherapy and Psychosomatics, 74*, 212–217.

Biswas-Diener, R. (2010). A positive way of addressing negatives: Using strengths-based interventions in coaching and therapy. In G. W. Burns (Ed.), *Happiness, healing and enhancement: Your casebook collection for applying positive psychology in therapy* (pp. 291–302). Hoboken, NJ: Wiley.

Biswas-Diener, R., Kashdan, T. B., & Minhas, G. (2011). A dynamic approach to psychological strength development and intervention. *Journal of Positive Psychology, 6*, 106–118.

Biswas-Diener, R (2009). Personal coaching as a positive intervention. *Journal of Clinical Psychology, 65*(5), 544–553.

Bohart, A. C. (2002). Focusing on the positive, focusing on the negative: Implications for psychotherapy. *Journal of Clinical Psychology, 58*, 1037–1043.

Bolier, L., Haverman, M., Westerhof, G. J., Riper, H., Smit, F., & Bohlmeijer, E. (2013). Positive psychology interventions: A meta-analysis of randomized controlled studies. *BMC Public Health, 13*, 119−139.

Caprara, G. V., Alessandri, G., & Barbaranelli, C. (2010). Optimal functioning: Contribution of self-efficacy beliefs to positive orientation. *Psychotherapy and Psychosomatics, 79*, 328−330.

Charney, D. S. (2004). Psychobiological mechanisms of resilience and vulnerability. *American Journal of Psychiatry, 161*, 195−216.

Chida, Y., & Steptoe, A. (2008). Positive psychological well-being and mortality: A quantitative review of prospective observational studies. *Psychosomatic Medicine, 70*, 741−756.

Cloninger, C. R. (1987). A systematic method for clinical description and classification of personality. *Archives of General Psychiatry, 44*, 573−588.

Cloninger, C. R. (2006). The science of well-being. *World Psychiatry, 5*, 71−76.

Csikszentmihalyi, M. (1990). *Flow: The psychology of optimal experience.* New York: Harper and Row.

Deci, E. L., & Ryan, R. M. (1985). *Intrinsic motivation and self-determination in human behavior.* New York: Plenum Press.

Delle Fave, A., & Massimini, F. (2003). Optimal experience in work and leisure among teachers and physicians. *Leisure Studies, 22*, 323−342.

Diener, E. (2000). Subjective well-being: The science of happiness, and a proposal for a national index. *American Psychologist, 55*, 34−43.

Diener, E., Suh, E. M., Lucas, R. E., & Smith, H. L. (1999). Subjective well-being: Three decades of progress. *Psychological Bulletin, 125*, 276−302.

Ellis, A., & Becker, I. (1982). *A guide to personal happiness.* Hollywood, CA: Melvin Powers Wilshire Book Company.

Emmelkamp, P. M. G. (1974). Self-observation versus flooding in the treatment of agoraphobia. *Behaviour Research and Therapy, 12*, 229−237.

Fava, G. A. (1999). Well-being therapy. *Psychotherapy and Psychosomatics, 68*, 171−178.

Fava, G. A., Guidi, J., Semprini, F., Tomba, E., & Sonino, N. (2010). Clinical assessment of allostatic load and clinimetric criteria. *Psychotherapy and Psychosomatics, 79*, 280−284.

Fava, G. A., & Offidani, E. (2011). The mechanisms of tolerance in antidepressant action. *Progress in Neuro-psychopharmacology, & Biological Psychiatry, 35*(7), 1593−1602.

Fava, G. A., Rafanelli, C., Cazzaro, M., Conti, S., & Grandi, S. (1998a). Well-being therapy. A novel psychotherapeutic approach for residual symptoms of affective disorders. *Psychological Medicine, 28*, 475−480.

Fava, G. A., Rafanelli, C., Grandi, S., Conti, S., & Belluardo, P. (1998b). Prevention of recurrent depression with cognitive behavioral therapy. *Archives of General Psychiatry, 55*, 816−820.

Fava, G. A., Rafanelli, C., Ottolini, F., Ruini, C., Cazzaro, M., & Grandi, S. (2001). Psychological well-being and residual symptoms in remitted patients with panic disorder and agoraphobia. *Journal of Affective Disorders, 31*, 899−905.

Fava, G. A., Rafanelli, C., Tomba, E., Guidi, J., & Grandi, S. (2011). The sequential combination of cognitive behavioral treatment and well-being therapy in cyclothymic disorder. *Psychotherapy and Psychosomatics, 80*, 136−143.

Fava, G. A., & Ruini, C. (2003). Development and characteristics of a well-being enhancing psychothcrapeutic strategy: Well-being therapy. *Journal of Behavior Therapy and Experimental Psychiatry, 34*, 45−63.

Fava, G. A., Ruini, C., Rafanelli, C., Finos, L., Conti, S., & Grandi, S. (2004). Six year outcome of cognitive behavior therapy for prevention of recurrent depression. *American Journal of Psychiatry, 161*, 1872−1876.

Fava, G. A., Ruini, C., Rafanelli, C., Finos, L., Salmaso, L., Mangelli, L., & Sirigatti, S. (2005). Well-being therapy of generalized anxiety disorder. *Psychotherapy and Psychosomatics, 74*, 26–30.

Fava, G. A., Ruini, C., Rafanelli, C., & Grandi, S. (2002). Cognitive behavior approach to loss of clinical effect during long-term antidepressant treatment. *American Journal of Psychiatry, 159*, 2094–2095.

Fava, G. A., & Sonino, N. (2010). Psychosomatic medicine. *International Journal of Clinical Practice, 64*, 1155–1161.

Fava, G. A., & Tomba, E. (2009). Increasing psychological well-being and resilience by psychotherapeutic methods. *Journal of Personality, 77*, 1903–1934.

Fordyce, M. W. (1983). A program to increase happiness. *Journal of Counseling Psychology, 30*, 483–498.

Fredrickson, B. L., & Joiner, T. (2002). Positive emotions trigger upward spirals toward emotional well-being. *Psychological Science, 13*, 172–175.

Fredrickson, B. L., & Losada, M. F. (2005). Positive affect and the complex dynamics of human flourishing. *American Psychologist, 60*, 678–686.

Frisch, M. B. (1998). Quality of life therapy and assessment in health care. *Clinical Psychology: Science and Practice, 5*, 19–40.

Frisch, M. B. (2006). *Quality of life therapy: Applying a life satisfaction approach to positive psychology and cognitive therapy.* Hoboken, NJ: John Wiley & Sons, Inc.

Garamoni, G. L., Reynolds, C. F., Thase, M. E., Frank, E., Berman, S-R., & Fasiczska, A. L. (1991). The balance of positive and negative affects in major depression. *Psychiatry Research, 39*, 99–108.

Garland, E. L., Fredrickson, B., Kring, A. M., Johnson, D., Meyer, P. S., & Penn, D. L. (2010). Upward spirals of positive emotions counter downspirals of negativity. Insights from the broaden-and-built theory and affective neuroscience on the treatment of emotion dysfunction and deficits in psychopathology. *Clinical Psychology Review, 30*, 849–864.

Geraghty, A. W. A., Wood, A. M., & Hyland, M. E. (2010). Dissociating the facets of hope: Agency and pathways predict dropout from unguided self-help therapy in opposite directions. *Journal of Research in Personality, 44*, 155–158.

Govindji, R., & Linley, P. A. (2007). Strengths use, self-concordance and well-being: Implications for strengths coaching and coaching psychologists. *International Coaching Psychology Review, 2*, 143–153.

Grandi, S., Sirri, L., Wise, T. N., Tossani, E., & Fava, G. A. (2011). Kellner's Emotional Inhibition Scale: A clinimetric approach to alexithymia research. *Psychotherapy and Psychosomatics, 80*, 335–344.

Grant, A. M., & Schwartz, B. (2011). Too much of a good thing: The challenge and opportunity of the inverted U. *Perspectives on Psychological Science, 6*, 61–76.

Guidi, J., Fava, G. A., Bech, P., & Paykel, E. S. (2011). The clinical interview for depression. *Psychotherapy and Psychosomatics, 80*, 10–27.

Hadley, S., & Macleod, A. K. (2010). Conditional goal-setting, personal goals and hopelessness about the future. *Cognition and Emotion, 24*, 1191–1198.

Held, B. S. (2002). The tyranny of positive attitude in America: Observation and speculation. *Journal of Clinical Psychology, 58*, 965–992.

Hodgins, H. S., & Knee, R. (2002). The integrating self and conscious experience. In E. L. Deci, & R. M. Ryan (Eds.), *Handbook on self-determination research* (pp. 87–100). Rochester, NY: University of Rochester Press.

Horowitz, M. J., & Kaltreider, N. B. (1979). Brief therapy of the stress response syndrome. *Psychiatric Clinics of North America, 2*, 365–377.

Howell, R. T., Kern, M. L., & Lyubomirsky, S. (2007). Health benefits: Meta-analytically deter-mining the impact of well-being on objective health outcomes. *Health Psychological Review, 1*, 83–136.

Karlsson, H., Kronström, K., Nabi, H., Oksanen, T., Salo, P., & Virtanen, M. (2011). Low level of optimism predicts initiation of psychotherapy for depression: Results from the Finnish public sector study. *Psychotherapy and Psychosomatics, 80*, 238–244.

Kashdan, T. B., & Rottenberg, J. (2010). Psychological flexibility as a fundamental aspect of health. *Clinical Psychology Review, 30*, 865–878.

Kellner, R. (1987). A symptom questionnaire. *Journal of Clinical Psychiatry, 48*, 269–274.

Keyes, C. L. (2002). The mental health continuum: From languishing to flourishing in life. *Journal of Health and Social Behavior, 43*, 207–222.

Keyes, C. L. M., Shmotkin, D., & Ryff, C. D. (2002). Optimizing well-being: The empirical encounter of two traditions. *Journal of Personality and Social Psychology, 82*, 1007–1022.

Lamb, S. (2005). Forgiveness therapy: The context and conflict. *Journal of Theoretical and Philosophical Psychology, 25*, 61–80.

Larsen, R. J., & Prizmic, Z. (2008). Regulation of emotional well-being: Overcoming the hedonic treadmill. In M. Eid, & R. J. Larsen (Eds.), *The science of subjective well-being* (pp. 259–289). New York: Guilford.

Linden, M., Baumann, K., Lieberei, B., Lorenz, C., & Rotter, M. (2011). Treatment of posttrau-matic embitterment disorder with cognitive behaviour therapy based on wisdom psychology and hedonia strategies. *Psychotherapy and Psychosomatics, 80*, 199–205.

Linley, P. A., & Burns, G. W. (2010). Strengthspotting: Finding and developing client resources in the management of intense anger. In G. W. Burns (Ed.), *Happiness, healing and enhance-ment: Your casebook collection for applying positive psychology in therapy* (pp. 3–14). Hoboken, NJ: Wiley.

MacLeod, A. K., & Conway, C. (2007). Well-being and the anticipation of future positive experiences: The role of income, social networks and planning ability. *Cognition and Emotion, 18*, 357–374.

MacLeod, A. K., & Moore, R. (2000). Positive thinking revisited: Positive cognitions, well-being and mental health. *Clinical Psychology and Psychotherapy, 7*, 1–10.

Magayar-Moe, J. (2009). *Therapist's guide to positive psychological interventions.* New York: Academic Press, Elsevier.

Maslow, A. H. (1968). *Toward a psychology of being* (2nd ed.). New York: Van Nostrand.

Norem, J. K., & Chang, E. C. (2002). The positive psychology of negative thinking. *Journal of Clinical Psychology, 58*, 993–1001.

Okun, M. A., Olding, R. W., & Cohn, C. M. G. (1990). A meta-analysis of subjective well-being interventions among elders. *Psychological Bulletin, 108*, 257–266.

Padesky, C. A. (1994). Schema change processes in cognitive therapy. *Clinical Psychology and Psychotherapy, 1*, 267–278.

Park, N., Peterson, C., & Seligman, M. E. P. (2004). Strengths of character and well-being. *Journal of Social and Clinical Psychology, 23*, 603–619.

Parloff, M. B., Kelman, H. C., & Frank, J. D. (1954). Comfort, effectiveness, and self-awareness as criteria of improvement in psychotherapy. *American Journal of Psychiatry, 11*, 343–351.

Paykel, E. S. (1985). The clinical interview for depression. *Journal of Affective Disorders, 9*, 85–96.

Rafanelli, C., Park, S. K., Ruini, C., Ottolini, F., Cazzaro, M., & Fava, G. A. (2000). Rating well-being and distress. *Stress Medicine, 16*, 55–61.

Rafanelli, C., & Ruini, C. (2012). The assessment of psychological well-being in psychosomatic medicine. *Advances in Psychosomatic Medicine, 32*, 182–202.

Rogers, C. R. (1961). *On becoming a person*. Boston: Houghton Mifflin.

Ruini, C., & Fava, G. A. (2009). Well-being therapy for generalized anxiety disorder. *Journal of Clinical Psychology*, *65*, 510–519.

Ruini, C., & Fava, G. A. (2012). Role of well-being therapy in achieving a balanced and individualized path to optimal functioning. *Clinical Psychology and Psychotherapy*, *19*, 291–304.

Ruini, C., Ottolini, F., Rafanelli, C., Tossani, E., Ryff, C. D., & Fava, G. A. (2003). The relationship of psychological well-being to distress and personality. *Psychotherapy and Psychosomatics*, *72*, 268–275.

Ryan, R. M., & Deci, E. L. (2001). On happiness and human potential: A review of research on hedonic and eudaimonic well-being. *Annual Review of Psychology*, *52*, 141–166.

Ryff, C. D. (1989). Happiness is everything, or is it? Explorations on the meaning of psychological well-being. *Journal of Personality and Social Psychology*, *6*, 1069–1081.

Ryff, C. D., & Singer, B. H. (1996). Psychological well-being: Meaning, measurement, and implications for psychotherapy research. *Psychotherapy and Psychosomatics*, *65*, 14–23.

Ryff, C. D., & Singer, B. H. (1998). The contours of positive human health. *Psychological Inquiry*, *9*, 1–28.

Ryff, C. D., & Singer, B. H. (2008). Know thyself and become what you are: A eudaimonic approach to psychological well-being. *Journal of Happiness Studies*, *9*, 13–39.

Schwartz, R. M. (1997). Consider the simple screw: Cognitive science, quality improvement, and psychotherapy. *Journal of Consulting and Clinical Psychology*, *65*, 970–983.

Schwartz, R. M., Reynolds, C. F., Thase, M. E., Frank, E., Fasiczka, A. L., & Haaga, D. (2002). Optimal and normal affect balance in psychotherapy of major depression: Evaluation of the balanced states of mind model. *Behavioral and Cognitive Psychotherapy*, *30*, 439–450.

Seeman, T. E., Singer, B. H., Ryff, C. D., Dienberg, Love, G., & Levy-Storms, L. (2002). Social relationships, gender, and allostatic load across two age cohorts. *Psychosomatic Medicine*, *64*, 395–406.

Seligman, M. E., Steen, T. A., Park, N., & Peterson, C. (2005). Positive psychology progress: Empirical validation of interventions. *American Psychologist*, *60*, 410–421.

Seligman, M. E. P., Rashid, T., & Parks, A. C. (2006). Positive psychotherapy. *American Psychologist*, *61*, 774–788.

Shmotkin, D. (2005). Happiness in face of adversity: Reformulating the dynamic and modular bases of subjective well-being. *Review of General Psychology*, *9*, 291–325.

Sin, N. L., & Lyubomirsky, S. (2009). Enhancing well-being and alleviating depressive symptoms with positive psychology interventions: A practice-friendly meta-analysis. *Journal of Clinical Psychology*, *65*, 467–487.

Singer, B., Friedman, E., Seeman, T., Fava, G. A., & Ryff, C. D. (2005). Protective environments and health status: Cross-talk between human and animal studies. *Neurobiology of Aging*, *26s*, s113–s118.

Snyder, C. R., Ilardi, S., Michael, S. T., Yamhure, L., & Sympson, S. (2000). The role of hope in cognitive behavior therapies. *Cognitive Therapy and Research*, *24*, 747–762.

Stangier, U., Hilling, C., Heidenreich, T., Risch, A. K., Barocka, A., Sclosser, R., & Hautzinger, M. (2013). Maintenance cognitive-behavioral therapy and manualized psychoeducation in the treatment of recurrent depression. *American Journal of Psychiatry*, *170*, 624–632.

Thunedborg, K., Black, C. H., & Bech, P. (1995). Beyond the Hamilton depression scores in long-term treatment of manic-melancholic patients: Prediction of recurrence of depression by quality of life measurements. *Psychotherapy and Psychosomatics*, *64*, 131–140.

Uchino, B. N., Cacioppo, J. T., & Kiecolt-Glaser, J. V. (1996). The relationship between social support and physiological processes. *Psychological Bulletin*, *119*, 488–531.

Vallerand, R. J., Blanchard, C. M., Mageau, G. A., Koestner, R., Ratelle, C., Leonard, M., & Marsolais, J. (2003). Les passions de l'ame: On obsessive and harmonious passion. *Journal of Personality and Social Psychology, 85,* 756–767.

Vallerand, R. J., Salvy, S. J., Mageau, G. A., Elliot, A. J., Denis, P. L., Grouzet, F. M. E., & Blanchard, C. (2007). On the role of passion in performance. *Journal of Personality, 75,* 505–534.

Vincent, P. J., Boddana, P., & MacLeod, A. K. (2004). Positive life goals and plans in parasuicide. *Clinical Psychology and Psychotherapy, 11,* 90–99.

Wood, A. M., Maltby, J., Gillett, R., Linley, P. A., & Joseph, S. (2008). The role of gratitude in the development of social support, stress, and depression: Two longitudinal studies. *Journal of Research in Personality, 42,* 854–871.

Wood, A. M., & Joseph, S. (2010). The absence of positive psychological (eudemonic) well-being as a risk factor for depression: A ten year cohort study. *Journal of Affective Disorders, 122,* 213–217.

Wood, A. M., & Tarrier, N. (2010). Positive clinical psychology: A new vision and strategy for integrated research and practice. *Clinical Psychology Review, 30,* 819–829.

Chapter 9

Long-Term Change of Happiness in Nations: Two Times More Rise Than Decline Since the 1970s

Ruut Veenhoven

Erasmus University Rotterdam, The Netherlands; North-West University, Potchefstroom, South Africa

INTRODUCTION

Pursuit of Greater Happiness

Achieving happiness is a major goal in present-day Western society. Individually, people try to shape their lives in such a way that they can enjoy themselves. Politically, there is support for policies that aim at greater happiness for everybody. It is widely believed that we can get happier than we are, and there is also consensus that we should not acquiesce to current unhappiness.

The belief that we *can* get happier is rooted in the Enlightened view of man. Rather than a helpless being expelled from Paradise, man is seen as autonomous and able to improve his condition through the use of reason. This view was at the core of the 19th century Utopian movement and is still at the ideological basis of the 21th century welfare states. Planned social reform guided by scientific research is expected to result in a better society with happier citizens.

The conviction that we *should* try to improve happiness is also rooted in Enlightened thought. The notion that happiness is to be preferred above unhappiness can be found in the ancient Greek moral philosophy, such as in Epicurism. In the 18th century, it crystallized into the Utilitarian doctrine that the moral value of all action depends on the degree to which it contributes to the "greatest happiness for the greatest number" (Bentham, 1789). Although few accept happiness as the only and ultimate goal in life, it is generally agreed that happiness is a worthwhile goal. Happiness ranks high in public opinion surveys on value priorities. See, for example, Harding (1985, p. 231) and Diener and Oishi (2004).

This ideology is not unchallenged, however. It is argued that happiness is not the most valuable goal, and it is claimed that we cannot get happier even if we would want to. In this chapter, I focus on that latter objection.

Claim That Greater Happiness Is Not Attainable

The objection that we cannot raise happiness rests on two lines of thought. The first is that we are unable to create better living conditions. The second denunciation is that even a successful improvement in living conditions would help little because happiness tends to remain at the same level.

Life Not Getting Better

Enlightened progress optimism has been disputed on several grounds. One is the idea of a misfit between recent societal development and human nature. Critics of modernization see growing loneliness and alienation and assume that life was better in the good old days (e.g., Easterbrook, 2003). A related view holds that we are unable to create a more livable society and that attempts at social engineering have brought us out of the frying pan into the fire. In this view, happiness is declining rather than rising, and this is seen to manifest in soaring rates of suicide and depression. The idea that life was better in the past is also rooted in public opinion (Hagerty, 2003).

Happiness Not Responsive

Next, there are psychological theories that hold that an improvement in living conditions will not result in greater satisfaction with life.

Comparison theory One such theory is that our assessment of happiness results from a comparison of life as it is and standards of how life should be, and that happiness is therefore "relative." Any improvement in living conditions would soon result in a rise in our standards of comparison and would therefore leave us as (un)happy as before. In this theory, the pursuit of happiness will lead us on to a *hedonic treadmill* (Brickman & Campbell, 1971).

This theory also predicts that average happiness in nations will tend to the neutral—that is, around 5 on a scale of 0 to 10. Because we compare what we have with what compatriots have, there will always be people who do better or worse, irrespective of the level of living in the country.

Trait theory The other theory is that happiness is a fixed "trait" rather than a variable "state." Improvements of external living conditions will therefore not result in greater happiness, our evaluation of life being largely determined by an internal disposition to enjoy it or not. This theory has several variants.

One is *set point theory*, which holds that humans are hard-wired to maintain a similar degree of happiness—that is, a level 7 or 8 on scale of 0 to 10. In this view, happiness is maintained homeostatically and is, as such, comparable to body temperature. Cummins (1995) is a proponent of this view.

Another variant holds that there are inborn differences in our aptness to be happy or not. In this view, happiness is a *temperamental disposition*, possibly based in the neuro-physiological structure of pleasure centers in the brain. Some people are apt to feel cheerful and hence be positive about their life, even in difficult conditions, whereas others are prone to depression and hence judge their lives negatively even in favorable situations. See, for example, Lykken (1999).

Another variation is that happiness is an *acquired disposition*. Some people will develop a positive attitude toward life, whereas others will become sour. In this vein, Lieberman (1970, p. 74) wrote "... at some point in life, before even the age of 18, an individual becomes geared to a certain stable level of satisfaction, which—within a rather broad range of environmental circumstances—he maintains throughout life."

Sociologists taking this perspective see the happiness of individuals as a reflection of collective *national character*. The outlook on life implied in common values and beliefs is seen to pervade individual perceptions and evaluations. Because collective outlook is largely an invariant matter, individual judgments geared by it are also seen to be rather static.

Easterlin Paradox

All these theories about unresponsive happiness figure in explanations for the Easterlin Paradox, which holds that average happiness in nations has not risen during the past decade in spite of impressive economic growth (Easterlin 1974, 1995, 2005; Easterlin, Aggelescu-McVey, Switek, Sawangfa, & Smith-Zweig, 2010).

Earlier Research

The idea of unresponsive happiness dates from the 1970s, when data about happiness in nations were scarce. Evidence for this theory crumbled when more data became available.

Comparisons of happiness across contemporary nations reveal large differences, such as an average, on a scale of 0 to 10, of 8.3 in Denmark and only 2.7 in Togo. See Veenhoven (2013a) for an overview of average happiness in 146 nations over the years 2000–2009. Most of the averages are far beyond the neutral 5 predicted by comparison theory, and about half of the scores are outside the range of between 7 to 8 predicted by set point theory.

Correlational analysis reveals strong associations between average happiness and several nation characteristics, such as economic development, freedom

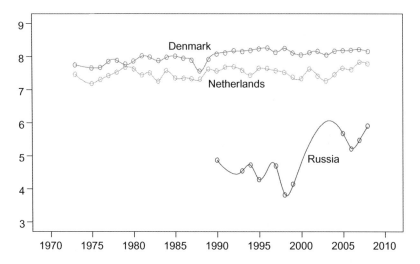

FIGURE 9.1   Change of average happiness in nations over time: Some illustrative cases.

of the press, and rule of law. Abundant data on that topic are gathered in the report "Happiness and Conditions in the Nation" of the World Database of Happiness (Veenhoven, 2013b). This contradicts the idea that happiness is unresponsive to living conditions in the country.

Comparison of happiness over time has further shown that average happiness has risen in some countries and declined in others. An example of gradually rising happiness is Denmark, where the average on a scale 0−10 rose from 7.6 in 1973 to 8.3 in 2012. Examples of declining happiness are found in Russia after the ruble crisis of the late 1990s and in Greece since the economic recession of 2010. These illustrative time trends are presented in Figure 9.1. More such trend data are available in the "Trend Report of Average Happiness" generated from the World Database of Happiness (Veenhoven, 2013c). These data leave no doubt that happiness can change and that happiness is responsive to changes in living conditions within an individual's country.

Research Questions

So the question is not *whether* average happiness in nations can change, but *how often* has it changed and to what *degree?* Answering these questions is a first step to identifying the societal conditions that are most crucial to happiness and to feeding the political process with this information.

Happiness

The answers to the preceding questions depend on the precise concept of happiness used. Some things called happiness are more static than others.

"Eudaimonic" happiness is, for instance, likely to be more stable than "hedonic" happiness, because the former concept denotes a set of personality traits, whereas the latter refers to a variable state of appreciation of life.

Concept

In this chapter, I focus on the latter kind of happiness—hedonic happiness. Happiness is defined *as the degree to which an individual evaluates the overall quality of his or her life as a whole positively*. This definition is delineated in more detail in Veenhoven (1984, ch. 2). This concept is in line with the Utilitarian notion of happiness as the "sum of pleasures and pains." A synonym is "life satisfaction."

Measures

Happiness as defined here can be measured using questions. Various claims to the contrary have been disproven empirically (research reviewed in Veenhoven, 1984, ch. 3). Although happiness is measurable in principle, not all the questions and scales that are used to measure this kind of happiness are valid. Elsewhere, I have reviewed current indicators and distinguished between those that are acceptable and those that are not (Veenhoven, 1984, ch. 4). In this chapter, I consider only data based on indicators that are deemed acceptable. As a consequence, several well-known studies on this matter have been left out. The studies on which this chapter is based were located using the World Database of Happiness (Veenhoven, 2013).

Long-term change

The above-mentioned theories of stable happiness do allow for short-term fluctuations. Comparison theory assumes that meeting aspirations will boost happiness temporarily until this advancement is neutralized by rising aspirations. Likewise, trait theories hold that happiness may vary somewhat with ups and downs in life: a trait happy person will be relatively happy in the year of marriage and unhappy in the year the couple divorces, but in the long run this person will oscillate around the same happiness level. Although such individual variations will balance out in the population of a nation, collective happenings may still affect the average—for instance, an economic recession or threat of war. For this reason, I consider only long-term changes in average happiness in nations, that is, for periods of at least 10 years.

DATA

The data on average happiness in nations were taken from the World Database of Happiness (Veenhoven, 2013). This is a "findings archive" on happiness in the sense of subjective enjoyment of one's life as a whole.

World Database of Happiness

The archive contains research findings yielded with measures that fit this concept of happiness as life satisfaction. All acceptable indicators are included in the collection "Measures of Happiness" (Veenhoven, 2013e).

Most measures are single survey questions, such as the famous item "Taking all together, how happy would you say you are these days; are you very happy, pretty happy, or not too happy?" This is just one of many acceptable measures of happiness. Survey questions have used different keywords, such as "satisfaction with life," and different response options, such as numerical scales. Next to these single questions, there are also multiple questions, some of which constitute a "balance scale."

This diversity of the measures of happiness used in the many surveys makes it difficult to compare scores and, in particular, to assess change in average happiness over time. The different measures of happiness have therefore been sorted into "equivalent" kinds—that is, questions that address happiness using the same keyword and a rating scale of the same length.

Research findings yielded using these acceptable measures of happiness are described in standard excerpts using standard terminology. Two kinds of findings are distinguished: distributional findings and correlational findings. Distributional findings denote how happy people are in a particular population and are often summarized in a measure of central tendency, typically the mean. Correlational findings are about things that go together with more or less happiness and summarized using measures of association, such as Pearson's correlation coefficient.

Distributional findings are sorted into findings among special publics, such as senior citizens, and findings in the general population. The findings on happiness in the general public are further subdivided by the kinds of areas from which samples were drawn, such as regions, cities, and nations. These latter findings are gathered in the collection of "Happiness in Nations" (Veenhoven, 2013d), which we used for this research.

Collection Happiness in Nations

To date (September 2013), the collection "Happiness in Nations" contains 6,539 findings on average happiness in 167 nations over the years 1946–2012. These findings are sorted in three levels: (1) by nation, (2) within nations by kind of measure used, and (3) within measures of the same kind by year.

An example of a "nation page" is presented in Appendix 9.1. This is the case of Argentina for which 35 distributional findings are available. These findings are sorted in blocks of equivalent survey questions. The first block consists of seven findings yielded by a survey question on how "happy" one is, the answers to which are rated on a four-step verbal response scale. The measure codes link to the precise text of that specific question, and detailed information about the investigation can be found behind the "i" icon.

Findings are sorted by year within each block, and this first block consists of the years 1981, 1991, 1995, 1999, 2002, 2005, and 2008. Looking at the blocks in Appendix 9.1, we see no clear trend in the responses to the question on happiness (measure type 111c) between 1981 and 2008, but a gradual change to the better in the responses to questions about life satisfaction (measure type 121C and 122F) and the Cantril ladder (measure type 31D).

Identical Questions

Within these blocks of equivalent questions, there are still small differences in the wording of the lead question and/or response options. These variations are marked by the last symbol in the measure code. There are also variations in the time frame addressed in the question, and these are marked with the third letter code, where "c" stands for "current," "g" stands for in "general," and "u" is used for "unclear." These minor variations in the wording of questions can result in small differences in the mean scores and could, as such, overshadow the small changes in actual happiness over time. Together with Floris Vergunst I selected a set of time series based on identical questions—that is, questions with the same measure code.[1]

In the above-mentioned case of seven questions on how "happy" one is in Argentina, this meant that we considered only the five findings based on the question variant "a." Because the series of answers to question variant "f" covered only 6 years, they were left out.

Transformation to a Common 0–10 Numerical Scale

We used the transformed means, provided in the World Database of Happiness, for reasons of comparability. These transformed means are expressed on a common numerical scale ranging from 0 (low) to 10 (high). Scores on numerical response scales, shorter than this, are linearly stretched to give a range of 0–10. Scores on scales with verbal response options are transformed using a procedure first described by Thurstone (1927), in which experts rate the numerical value of response options. This procedure is described in more detail in Veenhoven (1993, ch. 7).

---

1. We made an exception for the two variants of the question on life satisfaction used in the Latino Barometro—that is, the questions coded O-SLU-g-sq-v-4-b and O-SLu-g-sq-v-4-c, which differ slightly in the wording of the answer options. In this case, we could use the first data yielded by the Happiness Scale Interval Study (Veenhoven, 2009b) in which native speakers rated the degree of happiness denoted by the answer categories in intervals on a scale of 0 to 10. This enabled us to transform the observed frequency distributions to a mean on a common scale.

Series

On this basis, several series of responses to identical questions on happiness in the same nation over time were constructed. We limited our analysis to series that covered a minimum of 10 years. We also limited the analysis to data gathered using probability samples. If the same question was used in several surveys in the same year in the same country, we used the average response to that question. We did not require that a series contain more than two data points, although most series had more. This resulted in 199 time series for average happiness in 67 nations, which together gave 1,531 data points. The data matrix is presented in Appendix 9.2. This work was done in the context of a test of the Easterlin Paradox (Veenhoven & Vergunst, 2014).

From the data discussed above, we selected series that involved at least 30 data points over at least 20 years and that were sufficiently dense for a meaningful test of significance to be performed.

METHOD

The question is whether average happiness has typically remained at the same level in nations, or has it risen in most nations?

One way to answer this question is to consider the effect size and pick a minimum, such as over a 10-year period, a 0.1 point change in happiness. In this case, our conclusions are limited to the series studied here.

Another way is to generalize beyond the observations, and in this context, it is common practice to infer the probability that the change observed in the sample is positive, while there is actually no correlation in the population from which this sample is drawn. In this context, a 95% probability is usually deemed "significant."

Although routinely performed, this test for significance involves making strong assumptions that do not fully apply in this case. One such assumption is that the 199 series provide a random sample of all possible time series in the 67 nations. Another dubious assumption is that the 67 nations provide a random sample of all nations in the world.

Still other points to keep in mind are that significance depends very much on the sample size, small effects are significant in big samples, and big effects are insignificant in small samples. In the time series at hand, the number of data points is typically too small for a meaningful test. Significance also depends on the dispersion in the observations and on choices made by the investigator, with respect to the null hypothesis, one-sided or two-sided testing, and the probability level. All this makes tests for significance precarious.

In my view, the descriptive approach is the most informative in this case. The number of series at hand is large and covers all we will ever be able to obtain for this period. The interpretation is straightforward; we can easily see in Appendix 9.2 where the Easterlin Paradox applies—coefficient 0—and where not—all the positive coefficients.

Still, I realize that many readers are accustomed to significance testing and some are willing to buy into the above-mentioned perils, even when acknowledged. I therefore did some significance tests. I tested whether the observed positive change in happiness was more common than negative change and whether the average change coefficient was significantly different from zero.

I also considered some sufficiently dense time series separately and assessed whether, in each of these cases, the linear change coefficient differed significantly from zero. In this case, the test informs us about the probability that the observed trend in this series mirrors the trend in the general population—in other words, of the probability that another sample of surveys in the same country over the same years would yield the same results.

Change in All 199 Series

I regressed happiness against year in all the 199 time series. The resulting regression coefficients were used to indicate the yearly change in happiness in the period covered by the series. Because happiness is expressed on a scale of 0–10, a regression coefficient of 0.01 means a rise of 0.1 point per year, which amounts to a 1-point gain in happiness over 10 years. These yearly coefficients were used in the following ways.

Ratio of Rise or Decline

We first counted the number of series in which happiness had gone up and the number in which happiness had gone down. On that basis, I assessed the ratio: a ratio greater than 1 indicates that increasing happiness is more common than decline; a ratio of 1, that rising and declining happiness are equally frequent; and a ratio smaller than 1, that a decline in happiness is the most common. The theory of stable happiness predicts a ratio of 1. Deviation from that level was tested for significance.

Average Change Coefficient

The above bipartitions provide a view on the relative frequency of rise and decline in happiness, but do so at the cost of loss of variation. To use the available variance more fully, I computed the average change over all 199 series and assessed whether that average coefficient was positive or negative. I next tested whether the difference from zero was statistically significant.

Grouping by Country

Using the change coefficients in the series, we computed the average change coefficients for each of the 67 nations. Where only one series was available, I took the change coefficient observed in that one, and when more series were available, I computed the average change score.

These change scores in nations were analyzed in the same way as the change scores in the series. First, a ratio of rise or decline in happiness was obtained; then the average change scores were computed and we assessed the statistical significance of these scores.

Significance 18 Dense Series

Following standard practice in the World Database of Happiness, we selected time series of at least 30 data points over a period of at least 20 years. Together, 18 such series are available: one for each of the 10 EU nations where the Eurobarometer surveys started in the 1970s; one for Japan since 1958; and three for the United States, where different series were started in the 1950s. A coefficient of linear change was computed for each of these series, and the statistical significance of that coefficient was tested at the 55 level.

RESULTS: MORE ADVANCE THAN DECLINE IN ALL SERIES

Ratio of Rise and Decline

Of the 199 series, 66% showed a rise in happiness and 34% a decline, which resulted in a ratio of 1.9. Likewise, happiness rose in 64% of the 67 nations and declined in 36%, which is a ratio of 1.6. See Table 9.1. This is clearly more than the ratio of about 1 predicted by the theory of stable happiness.

Average Change Coefficients

The average yearly rise in happiness observed in the 199 series is $+0.016$. The average rise in the 67 nations was $+0.012$.

TABLE 9.1 Change of Average Happiness in 67 Nations[a]
Frequency of rise versus decline over periods of at least 10 years

Pattern of Change	Series		Nations	
	N	%	N	%
Rise	133	66%	42	62%
Decline	66	34%	25	38%
Total	199	100%	67	100%
Ratio rise-decline	**1.94**		**1.64**	

[a]*Source: Veenhoven (2013d).*

These numbers may seem small at first sight but result in a considerable improvement in happiness in the long term. At this growth rate, average happiness will rise 1 point on a 0−10 scale in 70 years. Given that the actual range on this scale is between 2.5 and 8.5 (Veenhoven, 2012a), a 1-point rise equals a gain of 17%.

Similar Across Time Spans

In their latest paper, Veenhoven and Vergunst (2014) argued that happiness rises only in the short term. The data show otherwise. We can see from Table 9.2 that the average change in happiness does not differ very much between the short and the long term and that the rise is slightly stronger in the long term.

Significant in Most of the Dense Series

The changes in happiness observed in series consisting of 30 or more data points over at least 20 years are presented in Table 9.3. The last column presents the change in points on a 0−10 scale. The bold printed changes are significantly different from zero. As one can see, the changes range between a gain of more than half a point in the case of Italy and a similar loss in the case of Portugal. The observed change is significantly different from zero in 11 of these cases and insignificant in 6 cases.

Happiness has remained almost stable in the case of West Germany, which is at least partly due to the influx of many unhappy East Germans after reunification in 1990. In the other cases, statistical insignificance does not denote that happiness has not changed. Happiness has gone up and down in Belgium and Greece, and these bumps are not reflected in the coefficient of linear change. Inspection of trend plots shows greater variation in yearly

TABLE 9.2 Change of Average Happiness in Nations[a]
Average yearly change in points on scale 0−10, split up by length of period

Period	Series		Nations	
	N	b	N	b
Short term	114	+0.017	31	+0.010
Medium term	67	+0.013	27	+0.009
Long term	18	+0.020	9	+0.030
Total	**199**	**+0.016**	**67**	**+0.012**

[a]*Source: Veenhoven and Vergunst (2014).*

TABLE 9.3 Change of Average Happiness in 14 Nations[a]
Time series of at least 30 observations over at least 20 years

Nation	Question	Years	Data Points	Change in Average Happiness on Scale 0–10		
				Average Yearly Change		Total Change in Points
				Change Coefficient	95% Significance Interval	
Belgium	O-SLL-u-sq-v-4-b	1973–2012	70	−.007	−.016 to +.002	−0.27
Denmark	O-SLL-u-sq-v-4-b	1973–2012	69	**+.015**	+.011 to +.018	**+0.59**
France	O-SLL-u-sq-v-4-b	1973–2012	69	**+.016**	+.011 to +.021	**+0.62**
Germany (West)	O-SLL-u-sq-v-4-b	1973–2009	65	+.000	−.007 to +.007	0.00
Greece	O-SLL-u-sq-v-4-b	1981–2012	58	**−.021**	−.036 to −.006	**−0.67**
Ireland	O-SLL-u-sq-v-4-b	1973–2012	69	+.002	−.006 to +.009	+0.08
Italy	O-SLL-u-sq-v-4-b	1973–2012	69	**+.012**	+.004 to +.020	**+0.47**

Japan	O-SLu-c-sq-v-4-e	1964–2013	49	**+.004**	+.000 to +.008	**+.20**
Luxembourg	O-SLL-u-sq-v-4-b	1973–2012	69	**+.009**	+.005 to +.014	**+0.35**
Netherlands	O-SLL-u-sq-v-4-b	1973–2012	69	**+.008**	+.003 to +.012	**+0.31**
	O-HP-u-sq-v-5-a	1977–2011	57	−.001	−.003 to +.000	−0.06
Portugal	O-SLL-u-sq-v-4-b	1985–2012	49	**−.035**	−.048 to −.021	**−0.98**
Spain	O-SLL-u-sq-v-4-b	1985–2012	49	+.011	−.011 to +.016	+0.31
UK	O-SLL-u-sq-v-4-b	1973–2012	68	**+.008**	+.005 to +.012	**+0.31**
USA	O-HL-c-sq-v-3-aa	1974–2008	62	+.009	+.002 to +.016	+0.29
	O-SLP-g-sq-v-2b	1973–2008	45	+.011	+.005 to +.017	+0.35
	O-BW-c-sq-l-11a	1959–2007	60	+.013	+.006 to +.020	+0.62

[a]Source: Veenhoven (2013c).

scores for Japan and the United States, probably due to smaller sample sizes and slight differences in the wording of questions and their place in the questionnaire. As noted previously, significance depends also on the dispersion of observations.

DISCUSSION

The data presented here leave us with no doubt that happiness in nations *can* change; average happiness *has* changed in most countries for which we have data since the 1970s, and typically to the positive. This begs the question of why so many came to believe that happiness is immutable. Another question is how well the observed change in average happiness fits with trends in other aspects of human thriving.

Why the Belief in Stable Happiness in Nations

One answer to this question about change in happiness lies in *data availability*. This theory emerged in the 1970s when the differences across countries were more apparent than the change within countries over time. Time series were scarce in those days and too short to capture the small increments in happiness. The view on change in happiness was also blurred by imperfections in the first available time series. The most prominent series is a series of responses to a question on happiness rated on a three-step scale in the United States, which has shown no rise since the first assessment made in 1945. Yet this series started in the euphoric time of a war won, and the wording of the questions differed slightly until 1972. Identical questions used since 1973 do show a slight rise in average happiness, as shown in Table 9.3. Likewise, changes in the wording of survey questions in Japan have veiled a trend to the positive since 1958, as shown by Suzuki (2009).

Another reason for the belief that happiness is immutable lies in *data analysis* and, in particular, in the interpretation of tests of significance of changes in happiness. Absence of significance is taken as proof of stability, instead of being seen as a lack of statistical power. Remember the earlier "Method" section, in which I argued that most of the time data series on happiness do not meet the requirements for a meaningful significance test.

A third reason lies in the *theory of happiness*. Happiness is commonly seen to result from a cognitive comparison between what one *wants* and what one has, and in that view a hedonic treadmill is plausible. The theory that happiness depends on the gratification of *needs* in the first place has less appeal, in particular among sociologists, although it fits better with the facts (Veenhoven, 2008). Likewise, psychologists tend to focus on stable *traits* rather than on variable *states*, and for this reason the stability of happiness is more prominent in their perspective.

Still another reason lies in *ideology*. The belief that happiness does not rise in spite of economic growth fits well with several strands of social criticism, such as criticism of capitalism, globalization, mass consumption, and environmental degradation. Activists spread this belief to promote their cause, actively using all the media available.

Related Trends in Living Conditions

Material living conditions have improved in most countries since the 1970s, and this gain is reflected in rising GNP per capita. Contrary to the earlier mentioned Easterlin Paradox, there is a clear relation with happiness. The greatest rise in happiness is observed in the countries where the economy has grown the most: $r = +0.22$ (Veenhoven & Vergunst, 2014). The recent economic recession has caused a considerable drop in average happiness in the most affected European countries: Greece, Spain, and Portugal.

There are also strong indications of lessening social inequality in developed nations. Although income differences have grown, differences in happiness have lessened, and inequality in happiness among citizens reflects the total effects of inequalities in all life domains. Inequality of happiness can be measured using the standard deviation. This appears in a comparison of standard deviations of happiness over time (Kalmijn & Veenhoven, 2005). Standard deviations of happiness have shrunk in most nations since the 1970s, partly due to a reduction in the percentage of very unhappy people (Veenhoven, 2005a). So the rise in average happiness is typically accompanied with a reduction in differences among citizens.

Related Trends in Human Flourishing

Human flourishing is reflected in good health and finally in longevity. Life expectancy has also increased in most countries over the period considered here, and together with the observed rise in average happiness, this has resulted in a spectacular rise in "Happy Life Years" (Veenhoven, 2005b), which is paralleled by a similar rise in years lived in good health. Life is getting better, and the rise of average happiness in nations is just one indicator of that development.

CONCLUSION

Average happiness in nations has changed in most nations over the past decade and in most cases for the positive. Stable happiness in nations is the exception rather than the rule.

APPENDIX 9.1. EXAMPLE OF A PRESENTATION OF FINDINGS ON AVERAGE HAPPINESS IN NATIONS[2]

TABLE A9.1 Distributional Findings on Happiness in Argentina (AR)[a]

Measure Type: 111C 4-Step Verbal: Happiness

Taking all things together, would you say you are:
— very happy
— quite happy
— not very happy
— not at all happy
very = 4 ... not at all = 1

Details	Measure Code	Year	On Original Range 1−4		On Range 0−10	
			Mean	SD	Mean	SD
i	O-HL-u-sq-v-4-a	1981	2.95	0.65	6.80	1.88
i	O-HL-u-sq-v-4-a	1991	3.07	0.82	7.00	2.27
i	O-HL-u-sq-v-4-a	1995	3.09	0.73	7.13	2.01
i	O-HL-u-sq-v-4-a	1999	3.13	0.75	7.20	2.08
i	O-HL-g-sq-v-4-f	2002	2.60	0.92	5.11	2.64
i	O-HL-u-sq-v-4-a	2005	3.20	0.67	7.45	1.78
i	O-HL-g-sq-v-4-f	2008	3.03	0.72	6.37	2.03
Average			3.01	0.75	6.72	2.10

Measure Type: 121C 4-Step Verbal: Life Satisfaction

How satisfied are you with the life you lead?
— very satisfied
— fairly satisfied
— not very satisfied
— not at all satisfied
very = 4 ... not at all = 1

(Continued)

---

2. Veenhoven (2013d).

TABLE A9.1 (Continued)

Details	Measure Code	Year	On Original Range 1—4		On Range 0—10	
			Mean	SD	Mean	SD
i	O-SLu-g-sq-v-4-b	1997	2.14	0.96	6.41	2.01
i	O-SLu-g-sq-v-4-b	2000	2.21	1.01	6.52	2.02
i	O-SLu-g-sq-v-4-c	2001	2.81	0.86	5.99	2.34
i	O-SLu-g-sq-v-4-c	2003	2.91	0.77	6.27	2.13
i	O-SLu-g-sq-v-4-c	2004	2.92	0.83	6.30	2.29
i	O-SLu-g-sq-v-4-c	2005	2.92	0.84	6.30	2.31
i	O-SLu-g-sq-v-4-c	2006	3.02	0.74	6.57	2.05
i	O-SLu-g-sq-v-4-c	2007	2.85	0.75	6.11	2.04
i	O-SLu-g-sq-v-4-dc	2008	3.01	0.77	6.82	2.00
i	O-SLu-g-sq-v-4-c	2010				
i	O-SLu-g-sq-v-4-da	2010	2.94	0.89	6.64	2.31
Average			2.77	0.84	6.39	2.15

Measure Type: 122F 10-Step Numeral: Life Satisfaction

All things considered, how satisfied are you with your life as a whole now?
10 satisfied
.
.
1 dissatisfied

(Continued)

TABLE A9.1 (Continued)

Details	Measure Code	Year	On Original Range 1–10		On Range 0–10	
			Mean	SD	Mean	SD
i	O-SLW-c-sq-n-10-aa	1981	6.80	2.10	6.44	2.34
i	O-SLW-c-sq-n-10-aa	1990	7.25	2.03	6.95	2.25
i	O-SLW-c-sq-n-10-aa	1995	6.92	2.32	6.58	2.58
i	O-SLW-c-sq-n-10-a	1999	7.33	2.26	7.03	2.51
i	O-SLW-c-sq-n-10-a	2006	7.79	1.91	7.54	2.12
Average			7.22	2.12	6.91	2.36

Measure Type: 122G 11-Step Numeral: Life Satisfaction

All things considered, how satisfied or dissatisfied are you with your life as a whole these days?
10 very satisfied
.
.
0 not satisfied

Details	Measure Code	Year	On Original Range 0–10		On Range 0–10	
			Mean	SD	Mean	SD
i	O-SLW-c-sq-n-11-a	2007	7.14	1.82	7.14	1.82
Average			7.14	1.82	7.14	1.82

Measure Type: 222 10-Item Affect Balance Scale (Bradburn)

During the past few weeks did you ever feel (yes/no)
— particularly excited or interested in something?
— so restless that you couldn't sit long in a chair?
— proud because someone complimented you on something you had done?
— very lonely or remote from other people?
— pleased about having accomplished something?
— bored?
— on top of the world?
— depressed?
— that things were going your way?
— upset because someone criticized you?

(Continued)

TABLE A9.1 (Continued)

Details	Measure Code	Year	On Original Range 5−5		On Range 0−10	
			Mean	SD	Mean	SD
i	A-BB-cm-mq-v-2-a	1991	1.26	1.93	6.26	1.93
Average			1.26	1.93	6.26	1.93

Measure Type: 235 More Days Like Yesterday

Do you want more days like yesterday?
− yes
− no
% yes

Details	Measure Code	Year	On Original Range 0−100		On Range 0−10	
			Mean	SD	Mean	SD
i	A-AOL-yd-sq-v-2-a	2008	76.00			
Average			76.00			

Measure Type: 236 14-Item Yesterday's Affect Balance

Did you feel yesterday . . . (yes/no)?
− well rested
− worried
− proud
− depressed
. . . etc.
Computation: % positive affect minus % negative affect

Details	Measure Code	Year	On Original Range 100−100		On Range 0−10	
			Mean	SD	Mean	SD
i	A-AB-yd-mq-v-2-b	2008	47.00			
Average			47.00			

(Continued)

TABLE A9.1 (Continued)

Measure Type: 31D 11-Step Numeral: Best-Worst Possible Life

Suppose the top of the ladder represents the best possible life for you and the bottom of the ladder the worst possible life. Where on this ladder do you feel you personally stand at the present time?
10
.
.
0

Details	Measure Code	Year	On Original Range 0−10		On Range 0−10	
			Mean	SD	Mean	SD
i	C-BW-c-sq-l-11-c	2002	5.99	2.40	5.99	2.40
i	C-BW-c-sq-l-11-c	2006	6.27	2.01	6.27	2.01
i	C-BW-c-sq-l-11-c	2007	6.69	1.87	6.69	1.87
i	C-BW-c-sq-l-11-c	2008	6.20	1.80	6.20	1.80
i	C-BW-c-sq-l-11-c	2008	6.00		6.00	
i	C-BW-c-sq-l-11-c	2010	6.30	1.80	6.30	1.80
i	C-BW-c-sq-l-11-c	2011	6.80		6.80	
Average			6.32	1.97	6.32	1.97

Measure Type: 411B 3-Step: Feel Happy

Do you feel … ?
— happy
— fairly happy
— unhappy

Details	Measure Code	Year	On Original Range 1−3		On Range 0−10	
			Mean	SD	Mean	SD
i	M-FH-u-sq-v-3-k	2011	2.61	0.60	6.23	1.22
Average			2.61	0.60	6.23	1.22

[a]Source: Veenhoven (2013d).

APPENDIX 9.2. DATA MATRIX

TABLE A9.2[a]

Period	Country	OHL3	OHL4	OHL5	OSL2	OSL3	OSL4	OSL5	OSL7	OSL10	OSL11	CBW	Term
2002–2011	Argentina											0,078	10–20
1981–2005	Argentina		0,026										21–40
1981–2006	Argentina									0,039			21–40
1975–2008	Australia											0,011	21–40
1981–2005	Australia		−0,005										21–40
1981–2005	Australia										−0,001		21–40
1975–2011	Australia												21–40
1995–2011	Austria						−0,027						10–20
1990–1999	Austria									0,187			10–20
1990–2006	Austria		−0,029										10–20
1990–2000	Belarus		0,072										10–20
1990–2000	Belarus									−0,09			10–20
1981–1999	Belgium									0,011			10–20
1989–2008	Belgium										−0,032		10–20
1975–1986	Belgium	−0,054											10–20
1973–2011	Belgium						−0,008						21–40

(Continued)

TABLE A9.2 (Continued)

Period	Country	OHL3	OHL4	OHL5	OSL2	OSL3	OSL4	OSL5	OSL7	OSL10	OSL11	CBW	Term
1981–2006	Belgium		0,016										21–40
2002–2011	Bolivia											0,046	10–20
1997–2007	Bolivia						−0,05						10–20
1990–2006	Brazil		0,054										10–20
1990–2006	Brazil									0,022			10–20
1960–2011	Brazil											0,046	>40
2001–2011	Bulgaria						0,05						10–20
2002–2011	Bulgaria											0,021	10–20
1990–2006	Bulgaria		0,029										10–20
1990–2006	Bulgaria									0,019			10–20
1968–1977	Canada					−0,009							10–20
1981–2000	Canada		0,01										10–20
1982–2000	Canada									−0,004			10–20
1997–2010	Chile						0,009						10–20
1990–2005	Chile		0,017										10–20
1990–2005	Chile									−0,025			10–20
1990–2007	China		0,002										10–20

1997–2011	China							−0,005	10–20
1990–2009	China					−0,019			10–20
1990–2010	Costa Rica			−0,041					21–40
1995–2007	Croatia					0,019			10–20
1962–2011	Croatia							0,018	>40
2001–2011	Cyprus			0,033					10–20
2001–2011	Czech						0,026		10–20
1990–2006	Czech		0,047						10–20
1981–1999	Denmark					0,003			10–20
1975–1986	Denmark	−0,026							10–20
1972–2006	Denmark		0,019						21–40
1973–2011	Denmark			0,014					21–40
1962–2011	Dom. Republic							0,081	>40
1997–2007	Ecuador			−0,05					10–20
1960–2011	Egypt							−0,012	>40
1991–2010	El Salvador			−0,04					10–20
1997–2006	England				−0,006				10–20
1975–1986	England	0,023							10–20

(Continued)

TABLE A9.2 (Continued)

Period	Country	OHL3	OHL4	OHL5	OSL2	OSL3	OSL4	OSL5	OSL7	OSL10	OSL11	CBW	Term
1973–2011	England						0,008						21–40
1975–2011	England											0,002	21–40
1981–2006	England		−0,002										21–40
1981–2006	England									−0,003			21–40
1990–1999	Estonia									−0,038			10–20
2001–2011	Estonia						0,091						10–20
1990–2006	Estonia		0,051										10–20
1956–2011	Finland						0,01						>40
1972–2005	Finland		0,01										21–40
1981–2005	Finland									0			21–40
1975–1986	France	−0,003											10–20
1973–2011	France						0,016						21–40
1975–2011	France											0,032	21–40
1981–2006	France		0,017										21–40
1981–2006	France									0,011			21–40
1991–2009	Germany	0,009											10–20
1997–2006	Germany		0,001										10–20

1990–2010	Germany			0,001			21–40
1981–2011	Greece			−0,012			21–40
2002–2011	Guatemala					−0,15	10–20
1997–2009	Guatemala			0,05			10–20
1997–2007	Honduras			0,005			10–20
2002–2011	Honduras					−0,12	10–20
1981–1999	Hungary				−0,076		10–20
2001–2011	Hungary			−0,065			10–20
1981–2006	Hungary		−0,006				21–40
1981–1999	Iceland	0,004					10–20
1981–1999	Iceland				−0,003		10–20
1990–2006	India		0,027				10–20
1962–2011	India					0,044	>40
1975–2007	India				0,064		21–40
1981–1999	Ireland				0,028		10–20
1975–1986	Ireland	0,06					10–20
1981–2006	Ireland		−0,006				21–40

(Continued)

TABLE A9.2 (Continued)

Period	Country	OHL3	OHL4	OHL5	OSL2	OSL3	OSL4	OSL5	OSL7	OSL10	OSL11	CBW	Term
1973–2011	Ireland						0,002						21–40
1961–2011	Israel											0,04	>40
1975–1986	Italy	0,053											10–20
1973–2011	Italy						0,019						21–40
1975–2011	Italy											0,027	21–40
1975–2009	Italy										0,011		21–40
1981–2006	Italy		0,024										21–40
1981–2005	Italy									0,008			21–40
1988–2005	Japan							−0,01					10–20
1964–2011	Japan						0,007						>40
1962–2011	Japan											0,023	>40
1978–2002	Japan							−0,021					21–40
1975–2007	Japan										0,022		21–40
1981–2005	Japan		0,026										21–40
1981–2005	Japan									0,013			21–40
1981–2011	Korea											0,072	21–40

Period	Country								Group
1981–2005	Korea							0,081	21–40
1981–2005	Korea			0,035					21–40
1980–2007	Korea		0,028						21–40
1981–2001	Korea				0,017				21–40
2001–2011	Latvia					0,018			10–20
1990–2006	Latvia							0,049	10–20
1990–1999	Latvia			-0,068					10–20
2001–2011	Lithuania					0,04			10–20
1990–2006	Lithuania							0,065	10–20
1990–1999	Lithuania			-0,03					10–20
1975–1986	Luxembourg						0,038		10–20
1975–2004	Luxembourg		0,009						21–40
1973–2011	Luxembourg					0,009			21–40
2001–2011	Malta					-0,011			10–20
1975–2011	Mexico	0,017							21–40
1975–2007	Mexico		0,23						21–40
1981–2005	Mexico							0,045	21–40

(Continued)

TABLE A9.2 (Continued)

Period	Country	OHL3	OHL4	OHL5	OSL2	OSL3	OSL4	OSL5	OSL7	OSL10	OSL11	CBW	Term
1981–2005	Mexico									0,017			21–40
1996–2006	Moldavia		0,023										10–20
1996–2006	Moldavia									0,189			10–20
1975–1986	Netherlands	0,015											10–20
1973–2011	Netherlands						0,007						21–40
1977–2011	Netherlands			−0,005									21–40
1981–2008	Netherlands		0,022										21–40
1981–2008	Netherlands									0,001			21–40
1974–2009	Netherlands							0,012					21–40
1997–2007	Nicaragua						−0,076						10–20
1990–2000	Nigeria		0,16										10–20
1990–2000	Nigeria									0,026			10–20
1962–2011	Nigeria											0,01	>40
1981–1996	Norway									−0,019			10–20
1972–2007	Norway		−0,018										21–40
1962–2011	Panama											0,042	>40

1997–2007	Paraguay		−0,055			10–20
2002–2011	Peru				−0,009	10–20
1997–2007	Peru		−0,013			10–20
1996–2005	Peru	0,015				10–20
1991–2000	Poland	0,028				10–20
1990–2007	Poland	−0,011				10–20
1990–2007	Poland			0,028		10–20
2001–2011	Poland		0,066			10–20
1962–2011	Poland				0,027	>40
1990–1999	Portugal			−0,011		10–20
1990–2006	Portugal	0,036				10–20
1985–2011	Portugal		−0,02			21–40
1990–2006	Romania	−0,003				10–20
1990–2005	Romania			−0,015		10–20
1990–2003	Romania		−0,018			10–20
2002–2011	Russia				0,09	10–20
1990–2005	Russia	0,046				10–20

(Continued)

TABLE A9.2 (Continued)

Period	Country	OHL3	OHL4	OHL5	OSL2	OSL3	OSL4	OSL5	OSL7	OSL10	OSL11	CBW	Term
1990–2005	Russia									0,056			10–20
1992–2005	Russia							0,128					10–20
1996–2006	Serbia						−0,034						10–20
1996–2006	Serbia						0,047						10–20
1990–1999	Slovakia									−0,015			10–20
2001–2011	Slovakia						0,116						10–20
2002–2011	Slovakia											0,061	10–20
1990–2006	Slovakia		0,07										10–20
2001–2011	Slovenia						−0,01						10–20
1990–2007	Slovenia									0,067			10–20
1992–2006	Slovenia		0,111										10–20
1962–2011	Slovenia											0,014	>40
2002–2011	South Africa											−0,038	10–20
1983–2002	South Africa			−0,044									10–20
1981–2007	South Africa		0,03										21–40
1981–2007	South Africa									0,015			21–40

Year	Country					
1983–2004	South Africa		−0,075			21–40
1985–2011	Spain		0,007			21–40
1981–2007	Spain	0,015				21–40
1981–2007	Spain			0,023		21–40
1995–2011	Sweden		0,024			10–20
1972–2006	Sweden	0,001				21–40
1981–2006	Sweden			−0,015		21–40
1990–2007	Switzerland	0,007				10–20
1990–2007	Switzerland			−0,023		10–20
1995–2006	Taiwan	−0,038				10–20
1995–2006	Taiwan			0,002		10–20
2002–2011	Turkey				0,08	10–20
2001–2011	Turkey		0,067			10–20
1990–2007	Turkey			0,061		10–20
1990–2000	Turkey	−0,03				10–20
1996–2006	Ukraine	0,133				10–20
1996–2006	Ukraine			0,188		10–20

(Continued)

TABLE A9.2 (Continued)

Period	Country	OHL3	OHL4	OHL5	OSL2	OSL3	OSL4	OSL5	OSL7	OSL10	OSL11	CBW	Term
1997–2007	Uruguay						−0,092						10–20
1991–2004	USA						0,049						10–20
1991–2008	USA						0,074						10–20
1959–2011	USA											0,009	>40
1957–2010	USA	0,001											>40
1959–2007	USA										0,005		>40
1946–2002	USA		−0,001										>40
1946–1990	USA	−0,002											>40
1981–2006	USA		0,006										21–40
1981–2006	USA									−0,016			21–40
1975–2008	USA	0,008											21–40
1973–2008	USA				0,011								21–40
1968–2000	USA					−0,002							21–40
2002–2011	Venezuela											0,078	10–20
1997–2007	Venezuela						0,046						10–20

Source: Veenhoven and Vergunst, (2014).

Missende data GDP: Egypt 1959, Croatia 1961–1989, Poland 1961–1984, USA 1945–1959, Finland 1955–1959, Estonia 1989–1994, Czech 1989, Lithuania 1989, Moldavia 1989, Serbia 1995–1996, Belarus 1989.

REFERENCES

Bentham, J. (1789). *An introduction to the principles of morals and legislation*. London, UK.

Brickman, P., & Campbell, D. T. (1971). Hedonic relativism and planning the good society. In M. H. Appley (Ed.), *Adaptation level theory* (pp. 287–302). New York: Academic Press.

Cummins, R. J. (1995). On the trait of the gold standard for subjective well-being. *Social Indicators Research, 35*, 179–200.

Diener, E. & Oishi, S. (2004). Are Scandinavians happier than Asians? Issues in comparing nations on subjective well-being. In F. Columbus (Ed.), *Asian Economic and Political Issues, 20*, 1–25.

Easterbrook, G. (2003). *The progress paradox: How life get better while people feel worse*. New York: Random House.

Easterlin, R. A. (1974). Does economic growth improve the human lot? In P. A. David, & W. R. Melvin (Eds.), *Nations and households in economic growth* (pp. 89–125). New York: Academic Press.

Easterlin, R. A. (1995). Will raising the incomes of all increase the happiness of all? *Journal of Economic Behavior and Organization, 27*, 35–47.

Easterlin, R. A. (2005). Feeding the illusion of growth and happiness: A reply to Hagerty and Veenhoven. *Social Indicators Research, 74*, 429–443.

Easterlin, R. A., Aggelescu-McVey, L., Switek, M., Sawangfa, O., & Smith-Zweig, J. (2010). The happiness-income paradox revisited. *Proceedings of the National Academy of Science of the United States of America, 107*(52), 22463–22468.

Hagerty, M. R. (2003). Was life better in the " Good Old Days"? Intertemporal, judgments of life satisfaction. *Journal of Happiness Studies, 4*, 115–139.

Harding, S. D. (1985). Values and the nature of psychological well-being. In M. Abrams, D. Gerard, & N. Timms (Eds.), *Values and social change in Britain* (pp. 227–252). London: Macmillan.

Kalmijn, W. M., & Veenhoven, R. (2005). Measuring inequality of happiness in nations: In search for proper statistics. *Journal of Happiness Studies, 6*, 357–396.

Lieberman, L. R. (1970). Life satisfaction in the young and the old. *Psychological Reports, 27*, 75–79.

Lykken, D. T. (1999). *Happiness: What studies on twins show us about nature. Nurture and the happiness set-point*. New York: Golden Books.

Suzuki, K. (2009). Are they frigid to the economic development? Reconsideration of the economic effect on subjective well-being in Japan. *Social Indicators Research, 92*, 81–89.

Thurstone, L. L. (1927). Psychophysical analysis. *American Journal of Psychology, 38*, 368–389.

Veenhoven, R. (1984). *Conditions of happiness*. Dordrecht, Netherlands: Reidel (now Springer).

Veenhoven, R. (1993). *How the data are homogenized* (Chapter 7). Available at <http://worlddatabase ofhappiness.eur.nl/hap_nat/introtexts/intronat7.pdf>. *Happiness in nations: Subjective appreciation of life in 56 nations 1946–1992*. Netherlands: RISBO, Erasmus University Rotterdam.

Veenhoven, R. (2005a). Return of inequality in modern society? Test by trend in dispersion of life-satisfaction across time and nations. *Journal of Happiness Studies, 6*, 457–487.

Veenhoven, R. (2005b). Apparent quality of life: How long and happy people live. *Social Indicators Research, 71*, 61–86.

Veenhoven, R. (2008). Sociological theories of subjective wellbeing. In M. Eid, & R. J. Larsen (Eds.), *The science of well-being* (pp. 44–61). New York: Guilford Press.

Veenhoven, R. (2009). International scale interval study: Improving the comparability of responses to survey questions about happiness. In V. Moller, & D. Huschka (Eds.), Quality of life and the millennium challenge: Advances in quality-of-life studies, theory and research, *social indicators research series* (Vol. 35, pp. 45−58). Dordrecht, Netherlands: Springer.

Veenhoven, R. (2013). *World database of happiness: Archive of research findings on subjective enjoyment of life*. Netherlands: Erasmus University Rotterdam. Available at <http://worlddatabase ofhappiness.eur.nl>.

Veenhoven, R. (2013a). *Average happiness in 146 nations 2000−2009, World database of happiness*. Erasmus University Rotterdam. Available at <http://worlddatabaseofhappiness .eur.nl/hap_nat/findingreports/RankReport_AverageHappiness.pdf>.

Veenhoven, R. (2013b). *Findings on happiness and conditions in one's nation, world database of happiness*. Netherlands: Erasmus University Rotterdam. Available at <http://worlddatabase ofhappiness.eur.nl/hap_cor/top_sub.php?code = N4>.

Veenhoven, R. (2013c). *Trend average happiness in nations 1946−2010, world database of happiness*. Netherlands: Erasmus University Rotterdam. Available at <http://worlddatabase ofhappiness.eur.nl/hap_nat/findingreports/TrendReport_AverageHappiness.pdf>.

Veenhoven, R. (2013d). Happiness in nations, world database of happiness. Netherlands: Erasmus University Rotterdam. Available at <http://worlddatabaseofhappiness.eur.nl/hap_nat/nat_fp .htm>.

Veenhoven, R. (2013e). Measures of happiness, world database of happiness. Netherlands: Erasmus University Rotterdam. Available at <http://worlddatabaseofhappiness.eur.nl/hap_quer/hqi_fp .php>.

Veenhoven, R., & Hagerty, M. R. (2005). Rising happiness in nations 1946−2004: A reply to Easterlin. *Social Indicators Research*, *79*, 421−436.

Veenhoven, R., & Vergunst, E. F. (2014). The Easterlin illusion: Economic growth does go with greater happiness. *International Journal of Happiness and Development*. In press.

Chapter 10

Set Point Theory
and Public Policy

Richard A. Easterlin and Malgorzata Switek

University of Southern California, Los Angeles, CA, USA

Set point theory is a proposition about the nil effect on happiness of life events in general. The basic idea is that people adjust psychologically to ups and downs in their objective conditions—losing a job, winning the lottery, being involved in a serious accident, being promoted, surviving the death of a loved one, and so on—and that their feelings of well-being return fairly quickly to a personal "set point" established by genes and personality. Richard Kammann, a pioneer of set point theory, states flatly: "[O]bjective life circumstances have a negligible role to play in a theory of happiness" (Kammann, 1983, p. 18). David Myers, writing almost two decades later, enthusiastically echoes this view: "Our human capacity for adaptation ... helps explain a major conclusion of subjective well-being research as expressed by the late Richard Kammann (1983): 'Objective life circumstances have a negligible role to play in a theory of happiness'" (Myers, 2000, p. 60). Csikszentmihalyi and Hunter (2003, pp. 185–186) put it this way: "Chance events like personal tragedies, illness, or sudden strokes of good fortune may drastically affect the level of happiness, but apparently these effects do not last long." According to Kahneman (1999, p. 14), "Each person may be on a personal treadmill that tends to restore well-being to a predetermined set point after each change of circumstances" (cf. also Costa et al., 1987, p. 54; Lykken & Tellegen, 1996, p. 189).

A major implication of set point theory is the futility of public policy. If each individual's happiness reverts to its set point irrespective of the life circumstances experienced, then government attempts to raise subjective well-being (SWB) are useless. This point is made explicitly by Ed Diener and Richard Lucas in the encyclopedic volume *Well-Being: The Foundations of Hedonic Psychology:* "The influence of genetics and personality suggests a limit on the degree to which policy can increase SWB .... Changes in the environment, although important for short-term well-being, lose salience over time through processes of adaptation, and have small effects on long-term well-being"

(Diener & Lucas, 1999, p. 227). Diener and Lucas have since become more open to the possibility of significant policy influences (Diener, Lucas, & Scollen, 2006; Lucas, 2007), but to date there have been few, if any, studies in psychology demonstrating public policy effects.

This chapter argues that government policies can have an important impact on happiness (see also DiTella, MacCulloch, & Oswald, 2003; Easterlin, 2012). The first part of the analysis looks at the point-of-time relation between labor market policies and life satisfaction in 21 European countries. The second considers the trend in China's SWB when, in the transition toward a free market economy, full employment and safety net policies were largely abandoned.

Although there continue to be exponents of set point theory or its equivalent (cf. Cummins, 2010, 2012), there is an emerging literature in psychology that, while not totally abandoning set point theory, seeks to modify it (Diener, Lucas, & Scollon, 2006; Headey, 2010; Headey, Muffles, & Wagner, 2010; Lucas, 2007; Yap, Anusci, & Lucas, 2012). These psychological studies look at happiness over the life course and present evidence that some life events have lasting effects on well-being. Previous work by one of the present authors using cohort analysis yielded similar results (Easterlin, 2006; 2010, chap. 7; see also Plagnol, 2010). The present analysis adds to this work in that it analyzes national rather than life course data and deals explicitly with the effect on happiness of public policies.

POINT-OF-TIME EVIDENCE: 21 EUROPEAN COUNTRIES, 2007

Life satisfaction differs considerably among European countries. The analysis that follows examines to what extent these differences are related to both specific measures of labor market policy and to indicators of macroeconomic conditions. Point-of-time differences among countries in SWB are often interpreted as being due to differences in gross domestic product (GDP) per capita (Diener & Oishi, 2000). An issue of interest in the present analysis is whether differences among countries in SWB largely reflect GDP differences, as is commonly assumed, or labor market policies that may be undertaken independently of GDP. The countries here are selected based on the availability of data for the measures studied.

Data and Methods

The SWB measure is life satisfaction, as reported in the Eurobarometer survey of April−May 2007, a date shortly before the onset of the Great Recession. The individual countries, basic data, and sources are given in Appendix Table 10A.1. Life satisfaction is, specifically, the mean for each country of the responses to the following question: "On the whole, are you very satisfied, fairly satisfied, not very satisfied, or not at all satisfied with the life you lead?" The survey response options are 1 = very satisfied, 2 = fairly satisfied, 3 = not very satisfied, 4 = not at all satisfied (recoded from 4 down to 1) (European

Commission, 2012). Mean life satisfaction here averages 3.04 and ranges from a high of 3.60 in Denmark to a low of 2.44 in Hungary.

Three measures of labor market policy are examined. The net replacement rate (NRR) is the percentage of after-tax household income that is maintained via public income support policies when a worker becomes unemployed. The estimate of NRR is based on legislative provisions and includes unemployment benefits, social assistance, and housing support. For the 21 countries studied here, these benefits, on average, replace 54% of after-tax household earnings and range from a low of 23% in Italy to a high of 77% in Denmark (Table 10A.1). For greater detail on the NRR, see OECD (2013a).

The replacement rate due to unemployment benefits, taken by itself, may be a misleading indicator of differences among countries in maintaining the income of unemployed workers. The replacement rate may be high, but bene-fits are hard to obtain because of stringent eligibility requirements. (Portugal is a case in point.) OECD recently constructed a measure, the benefit strict-ness indicator, based on legislation that defines benefit eligibility. The mea-sure covers entitlement conditions (employment and/or contribution require-ments to gain access to benefits, and sanctions for voluntary unemployment), job search requirements, monitoring of job-search effort, and sanctions for refusing a job offer. The strictness indicator ranges in potential value from 1 to 5 (where 5 = strictest requirements); for the present set of countries, the actual range is 2.44 (Sweden) to 4.44 (Portugal), and the mean is 3.21. For greater detail, see Venn (2012).

Unemployment benefits have typically trended upward over time, and con-cerns have been voiced about undue reliance on benefits by the unemployed and possible reluctance to return to work. Policymakers' attention has turned, therefore, to labor market programs to encourage and facilitate the return to work. The extent of such programs is captured here in the active labor market policies (ALMP) variable, which measures the degree to which each country implements policies to help job seekers to find work and to improve their employment prospects. The summary value published for this measure by OECD includes so-called passive expenditures, those on unemployment bene-fits, which are already captured here in the NRR variable. Hence, in the present analysis, the ALMP variable is confined to the categories designated by OECD as "active" programs—worker training, job rotation, employment incentives, supported employment, and direct job creation (OECD, 2013b). ALMP is measured as the per capita expenditure on these labor market policies, and is obtained by multiplying by GDP per capita by the published percentage of GDP spent on such programs. The mean value is $205 (in dollars of 2005 pur-chasing power), and the range is from $13 in Estonia to $517 in Denmark. For more information on this measure, see OECD (2012).

As mentioned, the SWB data are for April–May 2007, a date prior to the onset of the Great Recession. Public policies for the unemployed may be temporarily expanded in the face of rising unemployment, and such actions may distort basic policy differences among countries due to differences in the severity of a recession and the policy responses thereto. For virtually all of the countries included here, however, unemployment rates were declining prior to the date when SWB was observed; hence, the policy measures should be indicative of fundamental differences in policy. NRR and ALMP measure policies as of the year 2006; the strictness measure is for 2011, the only year for which an estimate has been made.

Three macroeconomic variables that are typically found to be significantly related to SWB are also included in the analysis. The first is GDP per capita in the year 2006, measured in 2005 dollars of purchasing power (Heston, Summers, & Aton, 2012). The second is the inflation rate, the percentage change in the level of prices from 2005 to 2006. The third is the unemployment rate for April–May 2007, the month in which life satisfaction was surveyed.

The unemployment rate for April–May 2007 is more closely related to life satisfaction than rates for alternative dates that were studied. The other dates were for unemployment in periods ranging from one to four quarters prior to the date of the life satisfaction observation. The difference among the dates in the relation to life satisfaction was small, but the April–May rate had the strongest relationship, a result suggesting that life satisfaction is responding most strongly to current, rather than earlier, unemployment conditions. For greater detail on unemployment rate data, see OECD (2013c).

Note that the unemployment rate may itself be viewed as a labor market policy variable. Differences among countries in the unemployment rate may reflect, in part, differences in fiscal and monetary policies aimed at achieving full employment. But unemployment differences may also be due to nonpolicy factors underlying aggregate demand and supply.

The net replacement rate and benefit strictness indicator are measures based on legislation in each country establishing the policies relating to each. The active labor market policies variable, however, is based on spending on such policies, and may not be an accurate indicator of actual policy differences among countries. Two countries may have the same policies, but if one has a higher unemployment rate, this will induce more ALMP expenditure and lead to the impression of a policy difference on ALMP. Hence, in assessing ALMP differences across countries, it is desirable to control for unemployment, as is done in the multivariate regressions described in the following sections.

One would expect that life satisfaction would vary directly with the net replacement rate and active labor market policies, and inversely with the strictness indicator. Higher NRR and ALMP contribute to maintaining one's income, whereas strict eligibility requirements operate in the opposite direction. With respect to the macroeconomic variables, the expectation is that life satisfaction would vary directly with GDP per capita, and inversely with both the unemployment and inflation rates. In what follows, the bivariate OLS regression relationship between life satisfaction and each of the six variables is first examined and then the multivariate relationships.

Results

Two policy variables, the net replacement rate (NRR) and active labor market policies (ALMP), account chiefly for differences among the 21 European countries in subjective well-being, and they are about equally important in explaining these differences. In conjunction with either policy variable, the unemployment rate also makes a significant although smaller contribution. The strictness indicator and the other two indicators of macroeconomic conditions, GDP per capita and the inflation rate, when put up against either or both of the policy variables, NRR and ALMP, add little or nothing to the analysis. These are the principal results of the regression analyses detailed in this chapter.

Taken singly, all six of the explanatory variables considered here are significantly associated with life satisfaction, and the relationship is in the expected direction for each (Table 10.1). Among the policy variables, higher unemployment benefit replacement rates and more spending on labor market policies such as job training contribute to a higher level of life satisfaction. Higher eligibility requirements for unemployment benefits reduce life satisfaction. With regard to the three macroeconomic variables, GDP per capita has the usual positive bivariate association with life satisfaction, whereas the unemployment and inflation rates both have the negative impact on SWB commonly observed (DiTella, MacCulloch, & Oswald, 2001).

In multivariate regressions, three variables are consistently significant: the net replacement rate, active labor market policy, and the unemployment rate (see Table 10.2, columns 2, 3, and 7). Combinations of any two of these three variables explain about two-thirds of the variance among countries in life satisfaction (column 9). The other three variables—GDP per capita, the inflation rate, and the strictness indicator—are never significant when coupled with NRR and ALMP. Regressions with three or more independent variables add nothing to these results and are not presented here.

It is possible to form a rough idea of the relative importance of the three significant independent variables in accounting for life satisfaction differences among countries. The procedure is to estimate the effect on SWB of a difference of two standard deviations in each independent variable's magnitude, two standard deviations being taken as indicative of the comparative variability of the three measures. For example, the standard deviation of NRR is 14% (Table 10A.1). Doubling this and multiplying by the regression coefficient on NRR in Table 10.2, model 1 (.008), one finds that life satisfaction differs by .22 (on a 1–4 scale) for countries differing on NRR by 28 percentage points. If one uses the coefficient on NRR in model 8 (.014), the difference in life satisfaction is .39. A similar estimate for a two-standard deviation difference between countries in ALMP yields an impact on life satisfaction of .29 (model 1) and .41 (model 9). Given that the standard deviation of life satisfaction itself is .29, these results indicate that NRR and ALMP are both important in accounting for country differences in life satisfaction. The

TABLE 10.1 Bivariate OLS Regressions: Life Satisfaction as Dependent Variable (Scale 1–4)

(1)	(2)	(3)	(4)	(5)	(6)	(7)	(8)	(9)
Model	NRR Percent	ALMP $ per Capita	Strictness Scale 1–5 (high)	GDP pc $ 000	IR Percent	UR Percent	Constant	R^2
1	0.016 (5.06)[b]						2.156 (11.5)[b]	0.59
2		0.0016 (6.87)[b]					2.715 (34.7)[b]	0.65
3			−0.237 (2.62)[a]				3.802 (11.8)[b]	0.19
4				0.0220 (3.85)[b]			2.404 (14.5)[b]	0.48
5					−0.144 (2.69)[a]		3.401 (24.5)[b]	0.28
6						−0.070 (3.82)[b]	3.502 (25.67)[b]	0.31

Note: Number of observations = 21 in each model. Absolute values of robust t-stats in parentheses.
[a]*significant at 5%.*
[b]*significant at 1%.*
Legend: NRR = Net replacement rate of unemployment benefits; ALMP = Expenditures per capita on active labor market programs; Strictness = Strictness indicator of eligibility requirements for unemployment benefits; GDP pc = Gross domestic product per capita, in thousands of 2005 international dollars; IR = Inflation rate since previous year; UR = Unemployment rate, percent of labor force.

TABLE 10.2 Multivariate OLS Regressions: Life Satisfaction as Dependent Variable (scale 1–4)[a]

(1) Model	(2) NRR Percent	(3) ALMP $ per Capita	(4) Strictness Scale 1–5 (high)	(5) GDP per Capita $ 000	(6) Inflation Rate Percent	(7) Unemployment Rate Percent	(8) Constant	(9) R^2
1	0.008 (2.28)[b]	0.0010 (2.55)[b]					2.414 (23.10)[c]	0.70
2	0.015 (3.66)[c]		−0.089 (0.75)				2.515 (4.60)[c]	0.61
3		0.0016 (4.78)[c]	0.005 (0.04)				2.697 (6.03)[c]	0.65
4	0.012 (3.23)[c]			0.0100 (1.46)			2.098 (11.98)[c]	0.65
5		0.0013 (3.96)[c]		0.0073 (1.41)			2.567 (18.19)[c]	0.68
6	0.014 (4.82)[c]				−0.069 (1.64)		2.449 (11.34)[c]	0.64
7		0.0015 (5.49)[c]			−0.019 (0.48)		2.780 (18.55)[c]	0.65
8	0.014 (4.38)[c]					−0.032 (1.74) +	2.504 (10.03)[c]	0.64
9		0.0014 (6.08)[c]				−0.038 (2.68)[b]	3.012 (22.16)[c]	0.73

Note: Number of observations = 21 in each model. Absolute values of robust t-stats in parentheses. + significant at 10%.
[a]See also Table 10.1.
[b]significant at 5%.
[c]significant at 1%.

unemployment rate plays a somewhat smaller role. Based on the coefficients in models 8 and 9, the impact on life satisfaction of a two-standard deviation difference between countries in the unemployment rate would be .15 and .18, less than that for equivalent variation in NRR or ALMP.

The variable most commonly viewed as responsible for point-of-time differences in life satisfaction among countries is GDP per capita. The present results point to a different reason: labor market policies. These policies encompass income maintenance programs for those who have lost jobs (NRR), policies aimed at facilitating the movement from unemployment to work (ALMP), and measures to maintain full employment such as fiscal and monetary policy, reflected here in the unemployment rate variable. When life satisfaction is regressed jointly on GDP per capita and either NRR or ALMP, the policy variables remain significant and GDP per capita is no longer significant. In conjunction with either policy variable, the unemployment rate makes a significant, though smaller, contribution to the explanation of happiness differences. These multivariate regression results imply that it is public policies, not income (as reflected in GDP per capita), that are largely responsible for differences among the 21 European countries in life satisfaction, and that job market policies are especially important. It is highly unlikely that causality would run from SWB to policy—that is, that country differences in SWB would be the cause of differences in labor market policy. The net replacement rate and active labor market policy variables appear to be about equally important in accounting for life satisfaction differences among countries.

TIME SERIES EVIDENCE: CHINA SINCE 1990

The recent experience of China provides a second body of evidence on the impact of public policies on subjective well-being. In this case, during the transition toward freer markets, there was a substantial retreat from full employment and safety net policies, with a consequent negative impact on life satisfaction. Although this relationship cannot be demonstrated with the quantitative precision of the preceding analysis, there is considerable qualitative material pointing to this conclusion.

What follows is a summary of a previously published collaborative article. In this study, an attempt was made to assemble all of the time series surveys of China's SWB since 1990, identify the pattern of change in SWB, and explore its causes. The SWB surveys are disproportionately urban, but since around 1990 China's development policy has focused on the urban sector, and urban incomes have risen much more rapidly than rural. (For the full analysis, and details on sources and methods, see Easterlin, Morgan, Switek, & Wang, 2012.)

The surveys indicate that life satisfaction in China declined from 1990 to around 2000−2005 and then turned upward, forming for the period as a whole a U-shaped pattern (Figure 10.1). Because of the limited length of each series, a precise numerical comparison over the entire period is not possible, but there

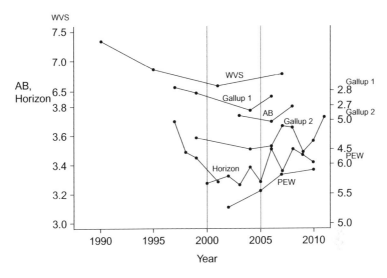

FIGURE 10.1   Mean life satisfaction, six series, China, 1990–2012. *(Source: Easterlin et al., 2012.)*

appears to be no increase and perhaps some overall reduction in life satisfaction. A downward tilt along with the U-shape is evident in the two series with the longest time span (WVS and Horizon).

A set point advocate could conceivably argue that the U-shape movement in China's life satisfaction is consistent with the return to a set point envisaged in the theory. But the theory assumes that adaptation is both quick and complete. In China's case, the decline and recovery of life satisfaction span two decades, and, even then, life satisfaction is arguably not back to where it started.

China's life satisfaction pattern is like that of the central and eastern European transition countries, in that life satisfaction declines early in the transition and then recovers somewhat (Easterlin, 2010, chap. 4). Unlike Europe, however, the real GDP per capita in China rose a staggering four-fold during this two-decade period, whereas in Europe GDP per capita typically declined substantially and then gradually recovered. The apparent lack of significant impact on SWB of GDP per capita in China is consistent with the point-of-time results for European countries reported in the previous section.

It is noteworthy that the 1990 value for life satisfaction in China is high relative to its GDP per capita. Of the 35 countries in the 1990 World Values Survey for which GDP per capita estimates are available, China ranks 18th in terms of life satisfaction, just below most of the developed countries. In terms of GDP per capita, it ranks 33rd out of 35 (Heston, Summers, & Aten, 2012). In 1990, virtually all socioeconomic groups in China—from the lowest to the highest stratum—reported high and fairly similar mean levels of life satisfaction, in excess of 7.0 on a 1–10 scale. These high levels appear throughout the distributions by education, occupation, and income. In 1990, life satisfaction in China was highly egalitarian, as was income.

The high 1990 level of life satisfaction in China was the result of a very low unemployment rate—virtually zero—and the extensive social safety net prevailing at that time. Urban workers were essentially guaranteed lifetime positions and the benefit package associated therewith, including such things as subsidized food, housing, health care, child care, pensions, and jobs for grown children (Cai, Park, & Zhao, 2008; Knight & Song, 2005). They enjoyed what was commonly termed "an iron rice bowl," and their job security was comparable to tenured university faculty in developed countries.

The shift toward a free market economy brought an end to these working conditions. The unemployment rate rose from near zero in 1990 to two-digit levels by 2000–2005 (Figure 10.2). Subsequently, the rate declined moderately but remained well above its initial level. The rise and fall in the unemployment rate corresponds inversely to the U-shaped movement in life satisfaction. The causality suggested by the inverse swings in life satisfaction and the unemployment rate is consistent with the repeated findings in the happiness literature that unemployment reduces life satisfaction (Becchetti, Castriota, & Giuntella, 2006; Blanchflower & Oswald, 2004; Clark, Georgellis, & Sanfey, 2001; Kassenboehmer & Haisken-DeNew, 2009; Lucas, 2007; Winkelmann & Winkelmann, 1998). The evidence is that life satisfaction is reduced not only for those who become unemployed but also for employed persons, due to the anxiety created by a worsening labor market (DiTella et al., 2001; Helliwell & Huang, 2012; Luechinger, Meier, & Stutzer, 2010).

The movement in China's unemployment rate was largely the result of government policy. As was mentioned, in 1990 workers in state-owned enterprises

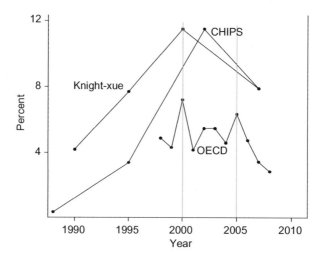

FIGURE 10.2   Urban unemployment rate, 3 series, China, 1988–2008 (percent of labor force). *(Source: Easterlin et al., 2012.)*

(SOEs), the firms that accounted for the bulk of urban employment, had permanent jobs and an extensive employer-provided social safety net. In 1994, in the face of continuing inefficiency and unprofitability of SOEs, the government initiated a restructuring program that shortly evolved into what has been called "a draconian policy of labor shedding" (Knight & Song, 2005). As described in a World Bank Report: "By all measures, SOE restructuring had a profound effect on the functioning of the labor market and the welfare of millions of urban workers. Most urban centers experienced a sharp rise in unemployment and a large reduction in labor force participation as many older and discouraged workers left the workforce" (World Bank, 2007).

Confronted with seriously deteriorating employment conditions, government policy was forced to shift gears. Beginning around 2004, the rate at which SOEs were downsized diminished sharply. Between 1995 and 2003, reduced employment in SOEs far exceeded increased employment elsewhere in the urban sector and unemployment rose markedly; thereafter, the situation was reversed, and the unemployment rate declined moderately, as shown in Figure 10.2.

The rise of the unemployment rate is indicative also of the dissolution of the social safety net. Workers who lost their jobs also lost their benefits, and restructuring of the SOEs meant that even those who kept their jobs experienced a sizeable curtailment of benefits. Workers who shifted from SOE to private employment suffered a similar loss of benefits. Although quantitative measures of safety net coverage are not available, there is qualitative evidence of the substantial decline of the safety net. A World Bank report on China's current unemployment insurance system states that "[t]he level of benefits remains low and provides a much lower income replacement rate than other countries" (Vodopivec & Tong, 2008). Much the same is true of the present pension system, which has been characterized as a "patch work of arrangements" whose "effective replacement rates are fairly low and projected to decline further" (OECD, 2010). As for health care coverage, "[e]conomic restructuring undermined the health care system, which became increasingly privately financed, though remaining largely publicly-provided. While the population's health status was improving, a rising number of people were priced out of treatment or fell into poverty because of health care costs" (OECD, 2010). The initial surge in unemployment and collapse of the social safety net led to a substantial decline in SWB. Subsequently, the government's restructuring policy gradually abated, and SWB recovered somewhat as employment conditions improved and the safety net tended to stabilize at a low level.

China's labor market developments in the transition toward a free market economy are similar to those of the European transition countries in that there is both the emergence of substantial unemployment and the dissolution of the social safety net. Unlike Europe, however, average real wages in China rose markedly in the course of the transition in conjunction with the very high rate of GDP growth. The fact that life satisfaction in China failed to increase noticeably and is similar in its U-shape to that of the European transition countries is indicative of the fundamental importance of employment

TABLE 10A.1 (Continued)

Country	Life Satisfaction (Scale 1–4) Apr–May 2007	NRR (Percent) 2006	ALMP per Capita (2005 PPP Dollars) 2006	GDP per Capita (Thousands of 2005 PPP Dollars) 2006	Inflation Rate (Since Preceding Year) 2006	Strictness Indicator (Scale 1–5) 2011	U.R. (Percent of Labor Force) Apr–May 2007
Czech Rep	2.95	48	64	21.765	2.55	3.25	5.5
Hungary	2.44	44	49	17.135	3.93	2.88	7.2
Mean	3.04	54	205	29.678	2.48	3.21	6.6
Std Dev	0.29	14	147	9.343	1.07	0.54	2.3

Notes:

[a]*The life satisfaction value for Norway is an estimate based on a regression for 14 countries of 2007 Eurobarometer life satisfaction on the ladder of life observation in the Gallup World Poll for the closest date (2007 or 2006) available. Norway's ladder of life value was inserted in the regression equation to obtain an estimated value of life satisfaction.*

[b]*For Germany's life satisfaction, values for West and East Germany were weighted using the approximate population shares in 2007 (from Germany's Federal Statistical Office: 0.8 West, 0.2 East).*

The ALMP per capita measure is obtained by multiplying data from the OECD on ALMP expenditures as percent of GDP and GDP per capita for 2006 (in 2005 purchasing power parity dollars) also from OECD.

Sources:

Life satisfaction. European Commission: Eurobarometer 69.1, February–March 2008. TNS OPINION & SOCIAL, Brussels [Producer]; GESIS Data Archive: ZA4743, dataset version 3.0.0 (2010), doi:10.4232/1.10128.

Net replacement rate. OECD's Directorate's for Employment, Labor and Social Affairs, available at http://www.oecd.org/els/benefitsandwagesstatistics.htm (date of access January 2013).

Active labor market policies. ALMP as percent of GDP obtained from OECD's "Public expenditure and participant stocks on LMP" Dataset, available at stats.oecd.org (date of access April 2013); GDP per capita obtained from OECD's Gross domestic product (GDP) Dataset, available at stats.oecd.org (date of access April 2013). GDP per capita. PWT 7.1, Alan Heston, Robert Summers and Bettina Aten, Penn World Table Version 7.1, Center for International Comparisons of Production, Income and Prices at the University of Pennsylvania, Nov 2012.

Inflation rate. OECD's "Consumer Prices (MEI)" Dataset, available at stats.oecd.org (date of access January 2013).

Benefit strictness indicator, 2011 (the only year available). Venn, D. (2012), "Eligibility Criteria for Unemployment Benefits: Quantitative Indicators for OECD and EU Countries," OECD Social, Employment and Migration Work Papers, No. 131, OECD Publishing. http://dx.dox.org/10.1781/5k9h43kgkv4-en.

Unemployment rate. OECD's "Short-Term Labour Statistics" Dataset, available at stats.oecd.org (date of access January 2013).

REFERENCES

Becchetti, L., Castriota, S., & Giuntella, O. (2006). Unemployment: A source of ECB anti-inflation bias? *CEIS Working Paper #245*, Rome: Tor Vergata Universiti.

Blanchflower, D. G., & Oswald, A. J. (2004). Well-being over time in Britain and the USA. *Journal of Public Economics, 88*(7–8), 1359–1386.

Cai, F., Park, A., & Zhao, Y. H. (2008). The Chinese labor market in the reform era. In L. Brandt, & T. G. Rawki (Eds.), *China's great economic transition* (pp. 167–214). New York: Cambridge University Press.

Clark, A., Georgellis, Y., & Sanfey, P. (2001). Scarring: The psychological impact of past unemployment. *Economica, 68*(270), 221–241.

Costa, P. T., Jr., Zonderman, A. B., McCrae, R. R., Cornoni-Huntley, J., Locke, B. Z., & Barbano, H. E. (1987). Longitudinal analyses of psychological well-being in a national sample: Stability of mean levels. *Journal of Gerontology, 42*(1), 50–55.

Csikszentmihalyi, M., & Hunter, J. (2003). Happiness in everyday life: The uses of experience sampling. *Journal of Happiness Studies, 4*(2), 185–199.

Cummins, R. A. (2010). Subjective wellbeing, homeostatically protected mood and depression: A synthesis. *Journal of Happiness Studies, 11*(1), 1–17.

Cummins, R. A. (2012). The determinants of happiness. *International Journal of Happiness and Development, 1*(1), 86–101.

Diener, E., & Lucas, R. E. (1999). Personality and subjective well-being. In D. Kahneman, E. Diener, & N. Schwarz (Eds.), Well-being: The foundations of hedonic psychology (pp. 229–231). New York: Russell Sage.

Diener, E., Lucas, R. E., & Scollon, C. N. (2006). Beyond the hedonic treadmill: Revising the adaptation theory of well-being. *American Psychologist, 61*(4), 305–314.

Diener, E., & Oishi, S. (2000). Money and happiness: Income and subjective well-being across nations. In E. Diener, & E. M. Suh (Eds.), Culture and subjective well-being (pp. 185–218). Cambridge MA: MIT Press.

DiTella, R., MacCulloch, R. J., & Oswald, A. J. (2001). Preferences over inflation and unemployment: Evidence from surveys of happiness. *American Economic Review, 91*(1), 335–341.

DiTella, R., MacCulloch, R. J., & Oswald, A. J. (2003). The macro-economics of happiness. *Review of Economics and Statistics, 85*(4), 809–827.

Easterlin, R. A. (2006). Life cycle happiness and its sources: Intersections of psychology, economics, and demography. *Journal of Economic Psychology, 27*, 463–482.

Easterlin, R. A. (2010). *Happiness, growth, and the life cycle.* Oxford: Oxford University Press.

Easterlin, R. A. (2012). Happiness, growth, and public policy. *Economic Inquiry, 51*(1), 1–15.

Easterlin, R. A., Morgan, R., Switek, M., & Wang, F. (2012). China's life satisfaction, 1990–2010. *Proceedings of the National Academy of Arts and Science, 109*(25), 9775–9780.

European Commission (2012). Eurobarometer 67.2 (April–May 2007). TNS OPINION & SOCIAL, Brussels [Producer]. GESIS Data Archive, Cologne. ZA4530 Data file Version 2.1.0, Available from http://dx.doi.org/10.4232/1.10984.

Headey, B. (2010). The set point theory of well-being has serious flaws: On the eve of a scientific revolution? *Social Indicators Research, 97*, 7–21.

Headey, B., Muffles, R., & Wagner, G. G. (2010). Long-running German panel survey shows that personal and economic choices, not just genes, matter for happiness. *Proceedings of the National Academy of Science, 107*(42), 17922–17926.

Helliwell, J. F., & Huang, H. (2012). New measures of the costs of unemployment: Evidence from the subjective well-being of 3.3 million Americans. Unpublished paper. *Canadian Institute for Advanced Research.*

Heston, A., Summers, R., & Aten, B. (2012). Penn World Table Version 7.1, Center for International Comparison of Production, Income, and Prices at the University of Pennsylvania.

Kahneman, D. (1999). Objective happiness. In D. Kahneman, E. Diener, & N. Schwarz (Eds.), Well-being: The foundations of hedonic psychology (pp. 3–25). New York: Russell Sage.

Kammann, R. (1983). Objective circumstances, life satisfactions, and sense of well-being: Consistencies across time and place. *New Zealand Journal of Psychology, 12*(1), 14–22.

Kassenboehmer, S. C., & Haisken-DeNew, J. P. (2009). You're fired! The causal negative effect of entry unemployment on life satisfaction. *Economic Journal, 119*(536), 448–462.

Knight, J., & Song, L. (2005). *Towards a labour market in china.* New York: Oxford University Press.

Lucas, R. E. (2007). Adaptation and the set-point model of subjective well-being: Does happiness change after major life events? *Current Directions in Psychological Science, 16*(2), 75–79.

Luechinger, S., Meier, S., & Stutzer, A. (2010). Why does unemployment hurt the employed?: Evidence from the life satisfaction gap between the public and the private sector. *Journal of Human Resources, 45*(4), 998–1045.

Lykken, D., & Tellegen, A. (1996). Happiness is a stochastic phenomenon. *Psychological Science, 7*(3), 180–189.

Myers, D. G. (2000). The funds, friends, and faith of happy people. *American Psychologist, 55*, 56–67.

OECD (2010). *China in the 2010s: Rebalancing growth and strengthening social safety nets.* Beijing: OECD.

OECD (2012). *OECD employment outlook 2012.* OECD Publishing. Available at <http://dx.doi.org/10.1787/empl_outlook-2012–en>.

OECD (2013a). *Directorate for Employment, Labour and Social Affairs, Benefits and Wages: Statistics.* Available at <http://www.oecd.org/els/benefitsandwagesstatistics.htm>.

OECD (2013b). *Dataset: Public Expenditure and Participant Stocks on LMP. Public Expenditure as a Percentage of GDP (Annual).* Available at <stats.oecd.org>.

OECD (2013c). *Dataset: Short-Term Labour Market Statistics. Harmonised Unemployment (monthly), Total, All persons.* Available at <stats.oecd.org>.

Plagnol, A. (2010). Subjective well-being over the life course: Conceptualizations and evaluations. *Social Research: An International Quarterly, 77*(2), 749–768.

Radcliff, B. (2013). *The political economy of happiness: How voters' choices determine the quality of life.* New York: Cambridge University Press.

Venn, D. (2012). Eligibility criteria for unemployment benefits: Quantitative indicators for OECD and EU countries. *OECD social employment and migration working papers, No. 131*, OECD Publishing.

Vodopivec, M., & Tong, M. H. (2008). *China: Improving unemployment insurance.* Washington, DC: World Bank.

Winkelmann, L., & Winkelmann, R. (1998). Why are the unemployed so unhappy? Evidence from panel data. *Economica, 65*(257), 1–15.

World Bank (2007). *China's modernizing labor market: Trends and emerging challenges.* Washington, DC: World Bank.

Yap, S. C. Y., Anusic, I., & Lucas, R. E. (2012). Does personality moderate reaction and adaptation to major life events? Evidence from the British Household Panel Survey. *Journal of Research in Personality, 46,* 477−488.

Chapter 11

Economic Approaches to Understanding Change in Happiness

Nattavudh Powdthavee[1] and Alois Stutzer[2]

[1]*London School of Economics, London, UK*, [2]*University of Basel, Basel, Switzerland*

INTRODUCTION

Is a woman's or a man's happiness her or his fate for life depending on how nature played the wheel of fortune? Is happiness a trait accompanied by some swings of moods and intermezzos of adaptation to life events but generally devoid of change? Economic research on subjective well-being (SWB) suggests the answer is no to the two rhetorical questions motivated by hedonic relativism or the set point theory.[1] This chapter reviews the arguments and the evidence primarily from work by economists that give reason to the assessment that happiness can change.

First of all, there is a tacit understanding in economic research that happiness can change. At the back of many economists' minds, there is the concept of utility as preference satisfaction. Utility and thus also happiness are attained through consumption, whereby a comprehensive concept of consumption is applied that includes the consumption of all sorts of goods and services as well as the experience of activities. The economic approach is flexible enough to include procedures as a source of utility when people live

---

1. The expression "hedonic relativism" was part of the title of the influential book by Brickman and Campbell (1971) proposing the idea of a hedonic (or happiness) set point. Economic research on SWB is surveyed in a number of books (e.g., Bruni & Porta, 2005; Frey, 2008; Frey & Stutzer, 2002a; Layard, 2005; van Praag & Ferrer-i-Carbonell, 2004; and, in prose, Powdthavee, 2010a) and review articles (Di Tella & MacCulloch, 2006; Dolan, Peasgood, & White, 2008; Frey & Stutzer, 2002b; Stutzer & Frey, 2010).

and act under a set of institutional conditions as well as many more aspects of the state of the world or people's minds.[2]

Whether the pleasures and pains from consumption and experience are enduring or only temporary is not conceptually crucial for the economic approach to human well-being. The economic view is thus *prima facie* compatible with adaptation as a phenomenon of reduced well-being gains from some option after some time. It is even compatible with complete adaptation. Temporary changes of happiness are still changes. Suffering low happiness—even for a short time—means lower individual well-being. One might invoke here, "in the long run we are all dead."

However, whether adaptation can actually be fully integrated in the traditional economic approach is questionable, and it would probably not be productive either. Adaptation is often understood as a process or mechanism that reduces the hedonic effects of a constant or repeated stimulus. People get used to a new situation or repeated stimuli, a process that can be recognized as preference change and thus a deviation from the neoclassical economic model of man. Moreover, people might not fully and correctly predict these processes and, in fact, underestimate their capacity to adapt.[3] This aspect of utility misprediction has far-reaching consequences beyond the random mistakes in expected utility theory—the von Neumann–Morgenstern model of expected utility maximization.[4] In this chapter, adaptation is considered as a valuable psychological concept that enriches the economic approach when applied to the study of individual well-being.

As explained, many studies on people's SWB in economics take the possibility of change in happiness for granted. This change in well-being might be a constant shift due to alterations in the environmental conditions or a temporary flow of pleasures and pains. The strong belief in the changeability of happiness motivates the study of its determinants in order to find the drivers of high human well-being (and implicitly this research also tests the underlying hypothesis of change in happiness). The research is supposed to finally lead to policy recommendations regarding environmental conditions that are conducive to SWB. Extending this line of reasoning, the "Life Satisfaction Approach" was developed. It not only tries to identify specific determinants of individual well-being but also aims to value them in monetary terms. By measuring the marginal utility of, say, a public good as well as the marginal utility of income, the trade-off ratio between income and the public good can be

---

2. The differentiation between outcome and process utility is introduced in Frey, Benz, and Stutzer (2004) with the aim to provide a productive concept to think about the sources of individual well-being.

3. A related argument can be phrased that people believe in the possibility to change their happiness and act accordingly (but not always in their best interest).

4. The misprediction of utility and its economic consequences are discussed in Frey and Stutzer (2014); Hsee, Rottenstreich, and Stutzer (2012); Kahneman and Thaler (2006); and Loewenstein, O'Donoghue, and Rabin (2003).

calculated (see more below). This allows taking public good aspects of government projects more easily into account in cost-benefit analyses.

So although economists generally have no qualms about the changeability of individual happiness for the better, there is a fundamental doubt on whether changes in people's well-being can be captured based on the new approach of subjectively reported assessments of one's affective well-being or satisfaction with life. Adaptation is related to false consciousness lurking in the background as a criticism of the whole enterprise of economic SWB research. The criticism points to the potential systematic divergence between true preference (satisfaction) and the satisfaction observed and measured in surveys. People surrender under the impression of an unchangeable "adverse" environment and "falsely" report being happy. This criticism entered the capabilities approach of Sen (1999) as an important argument against utilitarianism (and later against the economics of happiness).[5] In the work on affective well-being by Kahneman, Krueger, and Schkade (2004), the idea of adaptation as distorting the metric of utility (in particular of the disadvantaged) was taken up in the aspiration treadmill hypothesis. It states that people adapt their judgment about life relative to their goals in response to changes in circumstances (while, in fact, still experiencing the same affective well-being). In contrast, the hypothesis of a hedonic treadmill states that people adjust both in response to changes in circumstances: (i) their "objective" happiness and (ii) their assessment of how the new circumstances measure up to their life goals.

The fundamental issue that people are not well equipped to form absolute judgments is a challenge to all research that relies on people's assessment of their own situation as well as needs, whether in empirical happiness or capabilities research. When we think that empirical research on SWB helps as a complementary approach to understand change in happiness and the sources that bring it about, we are probably well advised to approach adaptation head-on as a process of true hedonic habituation, redeployment of attention, or practical adjustment, as well as a process of changing reference standards in people's reporting of their well-being. We try to follow this route in this chapter.

In the following section, we start with how economic research on SWB has taken up the idea of hedonic adaptation from psychology. This approach naturally introduces and emphasizes events in people's lives and thus a time perspective. How do people react to shocks in their life circumstances? Under what conditions is there more or less adaptation to the new situation? What makes people more or less resilient? The section "A Life Course Perspective on SWB" takes up these issues and presents a conceptual view as currently developed in economics. In "(External) Conditions Affecting Subjective Well-Being," we discuss some of the existing work on the

---

5. An analysis of the differences, similarities, and synergies between the SWB approach and the capabilities approach in economics is provided by Comim (2005).

conditions that are supposed to change happiness in the light of research on adaptation and the life course perspective. In particular, we refer to economic conditions, social and political factors, and public goods and bads that are assessed based on the Life Satisfaction Approach. At the end of the chapter, we offer some concluding remarks.

HEDONIC ADAPTATION

Empirical Approaches in Economics

Influenced by the early claims that people have SWB set points (Brickman & Campbell, 1971; Headey & Wearing, 1989), many writings in the psychology literature have worked on the assumption that humans quickly revert back to a relatively stable level of SWB despite major positive or negative shocks in terms of life events. By contrast, traditional economists tend to base their assumption about people's utility function on the idea that there is generically no habituation or adaptation to either good or bad life events. This is the idea that permanent life changes cause permanent changes in SWB.

One reason for such an apparent divide between two social science disciplines is that, until recently, much of the empirical analysis used to support the set point theory of SWB in the psychology literature had been carried out using cross-section—often tiny—datasets. An early (and highly influential) example of such work is the study of happiness of paraplegics and lottery winners by Brickman, Coates, and Janoff-Bulman (1978). In their study, Brickman et al. reported data in which lottery winners were only slightly happier than people in the control group, while the differences in SWB levels between the controls and the paraplegics were not as large as one would expect, thus leading them to conclude that adaptation to both positive and negative life events are generally complete over time.[6] And although Brickman et al.'s findings have found considerable empirical support from subsequent cross-sectional studies in which external conditions have been demonstrated to account for little variance in reports of SWB (Lykken & Tellegen, 1996), it remains inconclusive, at least to economists and some psychologists working in this area, that *all* external conditions do not have a long-lasting impact on people's SWB.

Part of the skepticism revolving around the validity of previous empirical research on adaptation can be attributed to the common perception among economists that causal implications of cross-sectional estimates are hard to interpret. Because cross-sectional studies do not allow for a systematic, within-person comparison between respondents' pre- and post-event levels of SWB to be made, cross-section patterns can only be suggestive. One could

---

6. The sample size in Brickman et al. (1978) was tiny: there were only 22 controls, 22 lottery winners, and 29 paralyzed accident victims.

imagine, for example, that individuals with a spinal-cord injury in Brickman et al.'s study might have been young and athletic before the injury, and, thus, they might have had higher than average SWB. If so, the less than anticipated differences in SWB levels between them and the control groups, which has been referred to by many as the evidence of hedonic adaptation among the paraplegics, might have confounded the fact that spinal-cord injury patients suffered a very large drop in SWB from pre-injury levels, something that they had never adapted to even with time. Hence, in order to make empirical advancement in this area, a test of hedonic adaptation has to have a number of special features:

1. The data must be longitudinal in nature, and individuals in the sample must be followed over a reasonably long period so that information on them is available before and after a good or a bad life event.
2. There needs to be a control group who does not experience the event.
3. The sample should be representative of the population.
4. A set of other variables has to be available in the dataset so that confounding influences can be differenced out.

One of the first studies that made explicit use of a large-scaled longitudinal dataset to estimate the extent of hedonic adaptation to a life event was a study on adaptation to marriage by Lucas, Clark, Georgellis, and Diener (2003). Using a hierarchical linear model, which allows for the mean levels of SWB—which is life satisfaction in their case—to be estimated for different assessment phases (e.g., baseline phase, reaction phase, and adaptation phase), Lucas et al. demonstrated that, on average, people revert back within a few years to their pre-marriage level of SWB. This is interpreted as quick and complete adaptation to marriage.[7] However, there appear to be substantial individual differences in the rate of adaptation, and the extent of adaptation seems to depend critically on the degree to which individuals reacted to the event: people who were strongly affected by marriage tended to adapt more slowly than those who were less affected. The same researchers applied the same empirical strategy to show that there is only partial adaptation to divorce (Lucas, 2005) and unemployment (Lucas, Clark, Georgellis, & Diener, 2004), and essentially no adaptation to severe disability (Lucas, 2007).

The hierarchical linear regression method, which is a special case of random effects models, assumes zero correlations between the individual fixed

---

7. Some psychologists put forward another concept that may explain this pattern, i.e., an event explanation that marital transitions cause short-term changes in SWB (e.g., Johnson & Wu, 2002). There is also a possible selection explanation for the pattern. "Most people only get married if they expect to experience a rewarding relationship in the future. They predict their future well-being as spouses based on their current well-being. Therefore, the last year before marriage becomes the last year, because the couples experience a particularly happy time in their relationship" (Stutzer & Frey, 2006, p. 337).

effects and the life event of interest. However, according to Headey (2007), it is possible that there may be some unobserved fixed personal characteristics that simultaneously determine both SWB and selection into experiencing the life event in question, which, if left unaccounted for, could potentially bias the estimated adaptation effect.[8] One could imagine, for example, that people who were born with predispositions that make them happy might also be risk loving and engage more in risky activities and thus are also more likely than others to get seriously injured. If so, then failure to allow for such heterogeneity will bias the true impact of disability on SWB. As a result, studies in the economic literature tend to prefer fixed effects models, which allow the individual fixed effects to be differenced out from biasing the estimates altogether, to hierarchical linear models when modeling adaptation.

By explicitly controlling for individual fixed effects, Oswald and Powdthavee (2008) reported evidence in which the negative effect of being severely disabled partially dissipates after a few years of disability. Using the same longitudinal datasets as Lucas (2007), which are the British Household Panel Survey (BHPS) and the German Socio-Economic Panel (GSOEP), they estimated the rate of hedonic adaptation to severe disability to be around 30%, while essentially no adaptation to severe disability was found in the estimation of random effects equations. Hence, Oswald and Powdthavee's (2008) results seem to suggest that it is important to take into account unobserved heterogeneity bias in the estimation of adaptation models.

Examples for Evidence from Longitudinal Studies

Controlling for individual fixed effects, a number of other studies in the economic literature have also documented evidence of significant adaptation effects in overall life satisfaction to some but not all external conditions. For instance, in a study of leads and lags in life satisfaction, Clark, Diener, Georgellis, and Lucas (2008a) reported evidence based on 20 waves of the GSOEP in which the rates and the degrees of adaptation appeared to vary significantly across different life events and genders. On the one hand, they found complete adaptation to divorce, widowhood, birth of first child, and layoff for both men and women. On the other hand, they found only partial adaptation to unemployment for women, and essentially zero adaptation to unemployment for men. Frijters, Johnston, and Shields (2011b) reported a similar set of findings in their study of anticipation and adaptation effects to different life events in the Household, Income, and Labour Dynamics in Australia (HILDA) panel dataset. More specifically, they found that people

---

8. For example, based on a panel dataset for Germany over 17 years, Stutzer and Frey (2006) documented substantial differences in reported life satisfaction between singles of a given age who marry later in life in comparison with the well-being of those who stay single, controlling for numerous observable characteristics.

adapt much more slowly to negative life events (e.g., deterioration in financial situation) than positive life events (e.g., marriage). Apart from the death of a close relative and changes in housing, individuals were found to have fully adapted to all life events after 2 years. In another study based on the GSOEP panel data from 1984 to 2005, Frey and Stutzer (2014) explored the adaptation to spending more time commuting to work. They first estimated a panel fixed effect model that integrated current as well as lagged commuting time for 1 to 3 years in the past. Based on the estimations, the pattern of adaptation was simulated. People seem not to adapt but to become even increasingly sensitive toward the burden of commuting (the latter effect not being statistically significant, however).

These longitudinal studies seem to be implying that (i) it would be impossible to use cross-section data to establish the long-term impact of life events because such data cannot identify adaptation effects, and (ii) there is a significant heterogeneity in the rates and the degrees of adaptation across different life events and subgroups of population.

Theoretical Explanations

There is currently little theoretical work in economics to provide a rationale for (differential) adaptation. Previous efforts to delineate economic theories of hedonic adaptation were completed by Rayo and Becker (2007) and Graham and Oswald (2010). Rayo and Becker (2007) linked hedonic adaptation to the ability of the human eye to quickly adjust to changes in the amount of light to optimally perceive contrast. According to their model, nature might have optimally designed human beings' emotional responses to behave in the same way. People evaluate alternatives based on a happiness function with a time-varying reference point. This reference point provides optimal incentives for fitness (i.e., the happiness function is evolutionarily efficient). Graham and Oswald (2010) used the concept of hedonic capital to explain how hedonic adaptation occurs. Adaptation emerges from a model of evolution in which nature "rationally" uses happiness as a motivating device to make agents live their lives efficiently. Happiness in this approach can be thought of as an accumulated stock of psychological resources on which agents can draw to buffer well-being in times of a life shock. In other words, individuals with high levels of hedonic capital will exhibit high psychological resilience, i.e., low volatility of well-being and the ability to adapt to negative shocks faster than people with lower levels of hedonic capital. While useful as a benchmark, these economic models fail at explaining the longitudinal patterns in which adaptation to some life events is quicker and more complete than others.

According to psychologists Schkade and Kahneman (1998) and Wilson and Gilbert (2008), hedonic adaptation cannot be reduced to the type of adaptation found in the sensory systems. Rather, it is a process that occurs due to a reduction of attention from the new circumstance. In the paraplegic case, adaptation occurs when patients' attention is withdrawn from their conditions: spinal cord injury patients are likely to think about their new circumstances many times each day at the beginning, but the allocation of attention eventually changes so that they spend most of their time paying attention to daily experiences such as having breakfast or watching TV (Kahneman, Krueger, Schkade, Schwarze, & Stone, 2006). The extent and speed of withdrawal of attention vary, however, from experience to experience (Dolan & Kahneman, 2008; Wilson & Gilbert, 2008). In the AREA model of Wilson and Gilbert (2008), the process of affective adaptation is determined by people's attempts to understand events that attract their attention. Thereby, people attend and emotionally react to unexplained events that are relevant to themselves. If they are successful and understand the events, they give them less attention, and the affective reactions to them get weaker. Key variables that impede explanation are an event's novelty, unexpectedness, variability, uncertainty, and explanatory incoherence. For example, one reason people adapt to a rise in income much faster than they do with the onset of a severe disability is likely that their paycheck is largely in the background most of the time, whereas being seriously disabled is full-time. We do not spend most of our waking moments thinking about how much money we earn. However, we may still be reminded about our disability from time to time if it incapacitates us from doing day-to-day activities such as climbing stairs or getting dressed by ourselves.

What these so-called attention theories indicate is that the rates and the degrees of adaptation to a life event depend largely on what people are focusing on during the course of their lives. This leads to the idea that a change in the overall SWB is more likely to be permanent if it is caused by a life event that permanently alters the way we evaluate our overall SWB whenever we are prompted to think about it. For example, Powdthavee (2009) used the BHPS to show that people do not fully adapt to severe disability because severe disability permanently lowers respondents' health satisfaction and income satisfaction. Similarly, people do not fully adapt to unemployment because unemployment permanently lowers respondents' income satisfaction and satisfaction with social life (Powdthavee, 2012a).

In recent theoretical and empirical considerations, adaptation is related to people's personality. The focus is thus on identifying groups of individuals who are better (or worse) at adapting to negative life shocks. Using the GSOEP, Boyce and Wood (2011) reported evidence to what extent the "Big Five" personality traits prior to the onset of disability influence how well an individual psychologically adjusts after a disability has occurred. More specifically, they documented evidence that more agreeable individuals adapt significantly more quickly and to a larger extent to disability than their less agreeable counterparts. A recent paper by Powdthavee (2012b) demonstrated using the BHPS that the negative psychological effect of unemployment is significantly larger for workers who had previously reported higher levels of fear of being bullied at school when they were between 11 and 15 years old and that essentially no adaptation to unemployment is found for these individuals over time. Despite the emerging evidence on adaptation in longitudinal data, the findings on systematic heterogeneity are still scarce and imperfectly understood.

A LIFE COURSE PERSPECTIVE ON SWB

A Conceptual Framework

One implication from the recent findings in the area of hedonic adaptation is that the past (including a genetic component) may be an important predictor of how well people habituate and adapt to life shocks in adulthood. More generally, these findings highlight that early life characteristics and circumstances may potentially have significant power in predicting adult SWB in general. This idea is underpinned by substantial findings in the multidisciplinary literature that childhood and parental characteristics strongly predict later life outcomes, including education, employment, income, crime, behaviors, and lifestyles (see, e.g., Blanden, Gregg, & Macmillan, 2007; Case, Fertig, & Paxson, 2005; Conti & Heckman, 2010; Frijters, Hatton, & Shields, 2010; Goodman, Joyce, & Smith, 2011; Headey, Muffels, & Wagner, 2014; Mensah & Hobcraft, 2008).

The conceptual framework of well-being over the life course is embedded in the household production model developed by Becker (1981) and Becker and Tomes (1986). The model essentially argues that children's cognitive and noncognitive abilities are more malleable early on in the life cycle. As children become older, there will be less about them that can be changed through parental and school input. This implies that there is less scope for policy interventions to improve cognitive and noncognitive outcomes later on in a child's life. To the extent that early characteristics of a child—e.g., personality traits, values, cognitive skills—matter for him or her to make successful life choices later, the model also predicts that these early childhood characteristics matter for later life satisfaction.

First Evidence

Focusing on well-being consequences, recent research in economics by Frijters, Johnston, and Shields (2011a) looked at the long-term relationship between childhood characteristics and adult life satisfaction. In their study, they utilized long-term cohort datasets of people in Britain from the National Child Development Study (NCDS), which consists of individuals born in a particular week in 1958. They investigated whether childhood and parental characteristics at ages 0, 7, 11, and 16 strongly predicted adult life satisfaction (or the average life satisfactions observed over the ages of 33, 42, 46, and 50).

It was found that characteristics of the child and family at birth—e.g., birth weight, number of siblings, maternal and paternal education—explain very little variation (approximately 1.2% of variance) in the average adult life satisfaction. Including a comprehensive set of child and parental characteristics at ages 7, 11, and 16 improved the predictive power to only 2.8%, 4.3%, and 6.8%, respectively. Significantly more variance in the average adult life satisfaction could be explained by including contemporaneous adulthood variables, including health and socioeconomic status, in the life satisfaction equation. For example, adding variables such as income, employment status, and health at age 50 increased the model's predictive power to 15.6%. Frijters et al. concluded based on their results that average adult life satisfaction is not strongly predictable from a wide range of early childhood characteristics. They also drew the implication that children from a disadvantaged background are equally likely to lead a satisfied life as adults as are children from a relatively less impoverished background.

Layard, Clark, Cornaglia, Vernoit, and Powdthavee (2013), on the other hand, argued that the past may matter a lot more to adult life satisfaction than what was initially suggested by Frijters et al. Using data from the 1970 British Cohort Study (BCS70), Layard et al. estimated a sequential model in which early childhood and family characteristics were used in the first step to predict different indicators of having a successful life at age 34, including emotional health, income, employment, education qualifications, good conduct, good health, and having a family. The predicted success variables were then used in the second step to predict adult average life satisfaction. What Layard et al. were able to show is that there is a strong link between early childhood characteristics and adult life satisfaction, although the association is mostly indirect and mediated through different indicators of having a successful life. In other words, Layard et al.'s results suggest that early life characteristics matter significantly in determining later outcomes, such as income and employment. It is these outcomes measured contemporaneously with life satisfaction that determine how satisfied we are with our lives as adults.[9]

Of course, many more relationships can and should be modeled theoretically and explored empirically to understand individual time patterns of SWB. A particular challenge will be the systematic integration of external conditions on the life course of happiness.

---

9. Note that the conclusions made by Layard et al. (2013) are similar to the ones made by Headey, Ruud, and Wagner (2010) in which life choices were shown to have a significant impact on a permanent measure of life satisfaction.

(EXTERNAL) CONDITIONS AFFECTING SUBJECTIVE WELL-BEING

People's SWB is better understood if a time dimension is taken into account because dynamics of many sorts play an important role. However, whether specific processes are modeled under a life course perspective or when considering adaptation, external conditions ultimately determine the course of individual well-being. The focus on external (living) conditions fits economists' approach to understanding change in happiness. It extends and complements economic research on the welfare consequences of societal and environmental conditions, economic policies, and alternative sets of institutions.

The Empirical Challenge of Causal Relationships

Research in economics on the determinants of SWB is motivated by the ambition to understand the (external) drivers of individual well-being in order to improve the human lot. In essence, causal relationships and pathways have to be identified to pursue this route. Thus, all the identification issues emerge that are well known in economic evaluation research. Although experiments are attractive to approach identification issues, they are still rare with respect to the conditions of SWB.[10] Accordingly, researchers have to be creative in deriving insights from less than optimal data. In this respect, the study of individual panel data derived from repeated representative surveys of the same persons turned out to be productive. It allows for the control of unobserved individual-specific characteristics that might well be correlated with individual reporting behavior, as well as with the experience of some condition such as unemployment, for example. Similarly, the study of repeated cross-sections at the country level allows for control over factors that generate unobserved heterogeneity among countries. As countries differ in many respects, even with the inclusion of numerous control variables, partial correlations from simple cross-section analyses are at risk of an omitted variable bias. Moreover, as almost any factor can be imagined to have a direct influence on a person's well-being, instrumental variable approaches are oftentimes difficult to be applied with convincing precision.

Despite these inherent difficulties in the study of the determinants of happiness, many valuable insights have been provided. Moreover, economists have started to explore the effect of positive and negative affect as well as life satisfaction on behavior (see, e.g., Goudie, Mukherjee, Neve, Oswald, & Wu, 2014). The better the mutual relationship is understood, the firmer conclusions about the sources of individual well-being are possible. In the

---

10. For an application in development economics, see Cattaneo, Galiani, Gertler, Martinez, and Titiunik (2009).

following, some conditions are briefly discussed emphasizing links to adaptation and the life course perspective.

Economic Condition I: Income

Within the many factors that potentially affect human well-being, income is by far the most prominent in the economics of happiness. This might not come as a surprise because income or a person's material living standard, normally captured by GDP or GNP, is the main empirical indicator of individual welfare in received economics. To put into doubt that income and happiness are close correlates constitutes an important challenge to traditional economics.

Many empirical tests reveal a significant positive correlation between income and SWB. This holds for people living in households with a high income and/or earning a high labor income but also in general for people living in a rich rather than in a poor country. The controversy emerges when it comes to the relationship between income growth and the development of SWB over time. Are the empirical observations consistent with the cross-section correlation between income per capita and average SWB across countries? Does income growth produce higher average SWB? Proponents of the Easterlin Paradox claim that it does not (e.g., Easterlin, 2013). In contrast, critics of the relativist position see the findings compatible with absolute income contributing to higher SWB (e.g., Stevenson & Wolfers, 2013; Veenhoven & Vergunst, 2013). The issue is still debated because of limited long-term data for a large sample of countries. Depending on the set of countries, statistical tests are not powerful enough to reject the hypotheses that there is no correlation between income growth and happiness growth as well as that the correlation between income growth and happiness growth is statistically significantly smaller than the one implied by the cross-section correlation between income per capita and average SWB in a country. Sample selection is important in such tests. Is evidence for the United States—where there seems to be no long-term correlation between income growth and happiness—sufficient to support the claim? Do we interpret the income development in the transition economies as long-term growth or as a recovery from the historic break-up of communism and the command economy?

The latter question hints at an even bigger challenge in the interpretation of the happiness development in countries over time. What are the underlying processes and causal relationships that lead to the observed correlations between income and happiness? To what extent does a happy population indicate conditions that are conducive to a prosperous economy? There might well be factors such as favorable political institutions that promote happiness as well as economic success. Happiness in nations might then well capture the extent to which the institutional structure in a society allows people to benefit from the organizational and technological possibility frontier.

There are, of course, more traditional arguments questioning GDP as an indicator of people's welfare. For example, not all the sources for increases in statistically measured national income are considered welfare enhancing. Public expenditures for reconstruction after a catastrophe are a prominent one. A possible lesson from the debate is that there is more than absolute income. This aspect has been fruitfully explored in the economic analysis of income and happiness (see Clark, Frijters, & Shields, 2008b, for a review). In particular, the notion of relative income has been filled with empirical content. For example, the impact of the relative income position within one's neighborhood is explored in Luttmer (2005), showing a negative effect of local average earnings on self-reported happiness *ceteris paribus*, i.e., controlling for an individual's own income. This empirical finding is consistent with the idea that people form aspirations about their income based on social comparisons and due to processes of adaptation to previous income. Adaptation to previous income is found to be substantial in various studies. For instance, based on the GSOEP panel data for Germany between 1984 and 2000, Di Tella, Haisken-DeNew, and MacCulloch (2010) estimate that 65% of an initial positive effect of higher income on reported satisfaction with life is dissipated over the following 4 years. Income aspirations have been empirically approximated based on people's reports about what they consider a sufficient income for their household. Reported SWB is found to strongly depend on the discrepancy between household income and the reported aspirations (e.g., Knight & Gunatilaka, 2012; Stutzer, 2004). Income aspirations thus seem to be an important mediator variable when we want to understand how income and SWB are related. Income aspirations might also be interesting from a life course perspective as people grow up in households with vastly different consumption standards. Moreover, income aspirations seem to follow a strong, inverted-U age pattern (Stutzer, 2004) echoing the U-shaped statistical relationship between age and SWB.

Many questions have remained open so far in the understanding of income as a condition for high SWB. What are the drivers of income aspirations more generally and—when they are formed by social comparisons—who compares to whom? Interesting first insights are provided based on recent survey evidence (Clark & Senik, 2010). For example, high-income people engage less in income comparisons than low-income people, and colleagues are the most prominent reference group. Another issue concerns the marginal utility of income. Previous research provides evidence that the elasticity with respect to income is smaller than minus one (Layard, Mayraz, & Nickell, 2008). However, partial correlations for the effect of income on SWB are often difficult to interpret. This holds not only in cross-section analyses involving issues of reversed causality and omitted variable bias but also in panel data studies. A specific concern refers to the limited available information about the reasons for the variation in people's or households' income. If people earn more because they put in more effort or time or accept a more stressful job, these income gains are fundamentally different from some vague idea of a windfall income gain. In recent work, new sources for income variation have been exploited to get a better idea of the marginal utility of income, such as, for example, inter-industry wage differentials (Pischke, 2011) and whether a pay slip was shown to the interviewer in order to get a more accurate reading of total income received by the individual (Powdthavee, 2010b).

Economic Condition II: (Un)employment

There is a long tradition of research on the conditions at the workplace that contribute to a satisfying job: either people are directly asked about the importance of various job attributes, or the determinants of reported job satisfaction are explored in multiple regression analyses. This research is meaningfully complemented by recent work on general well-being or life satisfaction in economics. A productive comparison is the one between employees and self-employed people, revealing that autonomy on the job is a valuable source of utility for which self-employed people are willing to accept a lower expected salary (Benz & Frey, 2008). Probably even more is revealed about employment as a source of individual well-being if the phenomenon of unemployment is taken into account.

In many empirical analyses, being unemployed is related to systematically lower scores of evaluative SWB measures than being employed. However, it is also observed that moment-to-moment net affect need not be lower for unemployed people even if they report significantly lower satisfaction with their life (Knabe, Rätzel, Schöb, & Weimann, 2010). This holds even if the loss in income is statistically taken into account. It reflects that individual unemployment involves psychic costs due to a loss of social status, self-esteem, personal relationships, and a disciplining time structure bound to a workplace.

In recent work, this general insight has been refined. For example, company closures are studied as a reason of unemployment revealing large nonpecuniary costs of job loss (Kassenboehmer & Haisken-DeNew, 2009). In other work, the psychic costs of unemployment are related to social work norms (Clark, 2003; Stutzer & Lalive, 2004). Moreover, long-term studies reveal limited adaptation to unemployment (see "Hedonic Adaptation," earlier in this chapter, for references). In a recent analysis, this result is confirmed for panel data from the BHPS on life satisfaction as well as mental stress based on the GHQ12 (Clark & Georgellis, 2013). It has turned out to be difficult to identify conditions that make the lot of unemployed people less burdensome. Studying the interaction with social capital (visiting friends and relatives, engaging in voluntary work, etc.), Winkelmann (2009) did not find that it moderates the effect of unemployment or—in other words—works as a buffer. Informative from a life course perspective are the negative effects of individual unemployment on SWB even after re-employment, so-called scarring effects (Clark, Georgellis, & Sanfey, 2001; Knabe & Rätzel, 2011).

High unemployment rates also have negative effects on people who are not personally affected by unemployment. Based on Eurobarometer data from 12 European countries between 1975 and 1992, Di Tella, MacCulloch, and Oswald (2003) showed that aggregate unemployment decreases average reported life satisfaction beyond changes in aggregate income. The potential reasons include direct effects of unemployment on crime and public finances, but also aspects specific to the workplace like changes in working hours and salaries. Moreover, high unemployment also affects anticipated economic distress. For instance, the probability that a worker may himself experience a spell of unemployment in the future increases. Related literature documents the importance of self-reported job security for individuals' well-being (see, e.g., Green, 2011).

In an empirical study, Luechinger, Meier, and Stutzer (2010) isolated the latter source of reduced individual welfare: the negative anticipatory feelings of angst and stress due to economic insecurity. To distinguish between general negative externalities of unemployment and changes in economic risks to individuals, workers were studied in two sectors of the economy that differ fundamentally in their exposure to economic shocks: people working in the private sector and those working in the public sector. Public sector employees usually enjoy extended protection from dismissal and work in organizations that very rarely go bankrupt. In their study for Germany based on the GSOEP, Luechinger et al. found that people working in the private sector are affected more strongly by general economic shocks than are those working in the public sector. This suggests that a substantial fraction of the psychic costs brought about by general unemployment is due to increased economic insecurity.

Social Factors

To put the economic conditions affecting happiness into perspective, the study of alternative sources of well-being is revealing. It turns out that happiness depends much on personal relationships, i.e., the quantity and quality of social relations that people have with family, friends, work mates, and fellow community members. If these relationships, often referred to as social capital, are good, people experience high SWB (for a review, see Helliwell & Putnam, 2004; Powdthavee, 2008).

Importantly, the benefits of social capital are not confined to outcomes such as informal mutual assistance or access to valuable information due to weak ties. There is rather a strong noninstrumental component of interpersonal relationships that contributes to individual well-being. These so-called relational goods involve socializing as an important aspect. They also have a public good component, as one person's engagement in social relations makes them more rewarding for others (Becchetti, Pelloni, & Rossetti, 2008). In addition to socializing, there is also empirical evidence that performing volunteer work is rewarding in itself (e.g., Meier & Stutzer, 2008).

There are also strong relational aspects to being involved in religious activities. Indeed, many studies document that religious people, on average, report higher SWB (see Steiner, Leinert, & Frey, 2010, for a review). Thereby, two sources are distinguished: internal and external religiosity. Internal religiosity refers to faith, i.e., a belief in God and His will. External religiosity involves observable religious (community) activities such as going to church. Regarding internal religiosity, positive correlations with various measures of SWB have been documented (Pollner, 1989). The same holds for the frequency of church attendance (or external religiosity) being positively correlated with reported happiness (e.g., Greene & Yoon, 2004). An interesting link to research on adaptation emerges because people who report a religious denomination seem to suffer less from adverse life events than people who report they do not belong to a religion. This is found in a cross-section analysis based on the European Social Survey in 2002−2003 (Clark & Lelkes, 2005). The finding holds in particular for individual unemployment as well as for divorce in the case of Protestants but not in the case of Catholics. Surprisingly, there are no such buffering effects over and above someone's denomination, i.e., with religious involvement either in terms of churchgoing or in terms of praying. Based on the Consumer Expenditure Survey and two waves from the National Survey of Families and Households in the United States from 1987−1988 and 1992−1994, Dehejia, DeLeire, Luttmer, and Mitchell (2007) studied the buffering effect of religious involvement in case of income shocks. They found that for people who often attend religious services, consumption expenditures (on nondurables) covary less with changes in household income than for people who report low religious involvement. The implied degree of insurance from religious attendance is even higher for reported happiness. For those who attend service once a week rather than once a year, two-thirds of the reduction in happiness from a negative income shock is buffered. Thereby, the effects are larger for African Americans than for whites. If the large buffering effects were to be explained by transfers within the community, they would have to be large. The results rather suggest that a strong faith and religious involvement are a source of psychological resilience for individuals to cope with stress and adversity.

Political Factors

Living conditions are strongly affected by decisions in the political sphere. Whether the design of policies and institutions makes a difference in people's SWB is thus of utmost relevance when we look for conditions that are conducive to human well-being. As a by-product, we also learn about the possibility to change the SWB in societies counter to the prejudices of hedonic relativism. Two routes for analysis might be meaningfully distinguished. The first route explores how basic institutions of democratic governance *vis-à-vis* autocratic governance or various types of democratic institutions affect SWB. The second route more specifically studies the consequences of single policies on various groups in society. Along both lines, research has only just revealed its potential and waits to be expanded.

Regarding the role of basic political institutions of democracy and federalism, Frey and Stutzer (2000) explored the relationship between direct democracy and local autonomy and people's reported life satisfaction in Switzerland. They found that easier access to direct participation instruments and more autonomy of municipalities *vis-à-vis* the upper level government are correlated with higher SWB. In a large study based on five waves of the World Values Survey and the European Values Survey between 1981 and 2007, Inglehart, Foa, Peterson, and Welzel (2008) analyzed whether the process of democratization observed in many countries led to an increase in SWB. They found that democratization is an important factor over and above economic development and social liberalization. Thereby, all the three main sources seem to work via an increased sense of freedom. This finding on sense of freedom as a mediating variable echoes the analysis and interpretation of Frey and Stutzer (2000) that democracy contributes to people's well-being by generating procedural utility, i.e., well-being people gain from living and acting under institutionalized processes as they contribute to a positive sense of self, addressing innate needs of autonomy, competence, and relatedness. The reference to procedural aspects and the positive sense of self might also explain why the well-being differences turn out sustainable. There is relatively less adaptation to these stimuli than to stimuli that provide less of a feedback of how people see themselves such as with material living conditions per se.

Policy analysis is an important part of applied research in economics. Measures of SWB offer a new dependent variable to generate complementary evidence on the consequences of policy measures. This approach is particularly attractive for policies that have rather unclear net welfare effects on various groups of the population or are per se difficult to evaluate based on observed behavior as a welfare indicator. A question referring to the first case is, for example, how women's rights affect women's well-being. Focusing on birth control rights, Pezzini (2005) studied the relationship between women's rights and women's reported satisfaction with life in 12 European countries. Although the extension of abortion rights and access to the pill may reduce women's bargaining power in the marriage market, evidence indicates that they also lead women to invest more in education and skills valued in the labor market. Moreover, these rights are statistically related to higher life satisfaction of women of childbearing age. Regarding the second case, an area where behavioral reactions are difficult to interpret in terms of welfare consequences is tobacco control policies. Not only many smokers would negate that less smoking due to smoking bans and higher cigarette taxes is per se a welfare improvement. It is rather necessary to explore the net effect of consequences of these policy measures on people's consumption utility as well as possible negative externalities and internalities whereby the latter might emerge due to people's limited willpower. In a longitudinal analysis based on repeated cross-sections from the Eurobarometer, Odermatt and Stutzer (2013) studied how the introduction of smoking bans across European Union member countries and cigarette prices are related to reported life satisfaction. Although they found a generally negative effect of higher prices on smokers' SWB (and no effect on likely nonsmokers), smokers who would like to quit benefit from the introduction of smoking bans and report higher life satisfaction in turn. This finding illustrates the potential of the approach to study the conditions of low and high SWB for specific groups in the population.

There are, of course, many more economic, social, and political factors that affect individuals' well-being and that are of interest to economists. This not only holds for economic variables such as inflation (see, e.g., Wolfers, 2003) or income inequality (see, e.g., Alesina, Di Tella, & MacCulloch, 2004) but also for sociodemographic characteristics that are affected by public policy such as the level of education (see, e.g., Oreopoulos & Salvanes, 2011). Moreover, environmental economists hint of evidence on, for example, the effect of air pollution on people's SWB. Air pollution as a policy outcome can not only be assessed regarding its relevance for people's SWB, but based on the Life Satisfaction Approach also regarding its valuation in monetary terms.

Public Goods and Public Bads

The study of happiness data provides evidence on the extent to which living conditions are adverse or favorable to people. For example, environmental degradation may be reflected in lower SWB. Although this quantification is interesting as such for our understanding of external conditions affecting SWB, it can be extended to a valuation in monetary terms and thus to a new approach for the valuation of public goods.[11] It is called the Life Satisfaction Approach, or LSA (for a review, see Frey, Luechinger, & Stutzer, 2009). It proposes that public goods can be directly evaluated in utility terms when

---

11. The benefits derived from public goods are inherently difficult to measure because they are not directly exchanged on markets. But public agencies in particular have a demand for the measurement of preferences for public goods. Increasingly, they are required by law to provide cost-benefit analyses to evaluate the social desirability of government programs. The economics of happiness provides a promising complementary method that avoids some of the major difficulties inherent in previous approaches to value public goods. The different established stated preference and revealed preference methods for the valuation of public goods are discussed, for example, in Freeman (2003).

reported SWB is used as a proxy measure for individual welfare. The marginal utility of public goods or the disutility of public bads is estimated by correlating the amount of public goods or public bads with individuals' reported SWB. When these marginal utilities and the marginal utility of income are measured, the trade-off ratio between income and the public good can be calculated.[12]

Van Praag and Baarsma (2005) pioneered and successfully applied this approach. They used it to value airport nuisance in Amsterdam. The LSA was further developed by Luechinger (2009) to value the negative consequences of sulfur dioxide in Germany. Using individual level panel data from the GSOEP between 1985 and 2003 and exploiting the variation in SO_2 across 450 German counties, he applied an advanced identification strategy to find that the annual marginal willingness to pay for a one kilogram per capita reduction in SO_2 amounts to US $340 (in 2007 prices).

The LSA has also been used to value other forms of air pollution (MacKerron & Mourato, 2009; Welsch, 2006), terrorism (Frey et al., 2009), droughts (Carroll, Frijters, & Shields, 2009), flood hazards (Luechinger & Raschky, 2009), health problems (Powdthavee & van den Berg, 2011), and scenic amenities (Ambrey & Fleming, 2011). Recent studies applying the LSA have already reached a high standard, and preconditions for its application are better understood and formulated. Because the empirical applications often exploit short-term variation in people's exposure to a public good or a public bad, adaptation issues are so far largely unexplored with the LSA.

CONCLUSIONS

When it comes to people's welfare and statements about some people being happier than others, happier these days than in the past, or happier under some specific circumstances than others, we are reminded of rather absolute claims of truth in particular because many people see happiness as a major goal in life or even as their ultimate one. It might well be a natural protective reaction that we take refuge to some form of relativism in response to such claims.

One line of reasoning questions people's capacity to judge their overall SWB and attributes them a false consciousness in particular when exposed to adverse living conditions. Another line of argument does not question people's judgment of their well-being but sees changes in SWB as only a temporary phenomenon before people revert to their baseline level of SWB.

Both perspectives are exposed to some evidence from research primarily in economics. Empirical findings clearly indicate that people are not indifferent to adverse living conditions when reporting their SWB as observed for

---

12. The LSA is compared to the standard nonmarket valuation techniques in Kahneman and Sugden (2005) and Dolan and Metcalfe (2008).

limited freedom of choice, low levels of democratization, low levels of income, etc. Considering people's adaptation to life events and (external) conditions reveals substantial heterogeneity in the speed as well as the degree of reversion. Together, the evidence suggests that reported SWB is a valuable complementary source of information about human well-being and the phenomenon of adaptation.

Many challenges, of course, remain. First, in our mind, we are only at the beginning of understanding variation in the process of adaptation or what is empirically observed as reversion toward the well-being level experienced prior to some major change in life. In an attempt to provide an economically relevant dimension along which adaptation might systematically differ, Frey and Stutzer (2014) proposed as a criterion the nature of needs—either being intrinsic or extrinsic—that choices are satisfying. The emphasis is thus on the intrinsic and extrinsic attributes of choice options. They hypothesized that people adapt less to intrinsically rewarding activities and goods than to extrinsic satisfiers because the former provide feedback to the self and so attract attention. The positive or negative experiences thus tend to be renewed with every new act of consumption. Beyond these thoughts, economics, with its emphasis on incentives, has a big potential to better understand how people react to life events over and above some narrow hedonic habituation. Related to this, the emerging life course perspective is promising because it invites us to systematically take into account resources of resilience. These resources might turn out as a combination including traditional economic variables such as savings next to psychological resources like willpower.

Second, adaptation might well pose a challenge to individual decision making when people are not good in predicting it. Referring to the differentiation discussed previously, when making a decision and neglecting adaptation, individuals would tend to undervalue the future utility of intrinsic attributes compared to extrinsic attributes. This distortion then leads to a systematic discrepancy between predicted utility and experienced utility and is particularly relevant when people have to make trade-offs between alternatives that satisfy intrinsic needs and ones that serve extrinsic wants (Frey & Stutzer, 2014).

Third, adaptation might have great consequences for public policy and the idea of social welfare maximization, depending on how it is treated. Let us consider the case in which courts have to decide about compensation for losses suffered in a car accident. For the same physical harm, should they award lower damages to people with a strong capacity to adapt and higher damages to others? Or in the area of government taxation, what costs of taxation should be taken into account? Materialists with high income aspirations suffer a great deal from personal income taxes. Should they be exempted from tax and government services and be financed by people who can easily adapt to whatever material living standard they are confronted with? The means for dealing with hedonic adaptation are not part of a simple idea of happiness maximization in public policy. Frey and Stutzer (2012) proposed that a solution can be found at the constitutional level behind the veil of uncertainty in which nobody knows whether he or she will be affected by some life event and whether he or she is a quick or slow adapter. A collective decision-making rule is required to indicate how adaptation and aspiration effects have to be dealt with in public policy. Obviously, such decisions have grave consequences for economic policy, which simple happiness maximization approaches do not address.[13]

In sum, the question about the possibility of change in happiness might generate an easy first affirming response based on economic reasoning. However, the issue of adaptation potentially also poses a serious challenge to our understanding of the optimality of individual decision making. Moreover, welfare implications of happiness changes and policy recommendations are less straightforward when adaptation is taken into account and ask for procedural considerations on how adaptation is taken into account. Ending on the bright side, we are not stuck in a hedonic treadmill and might well be reminded also that the temporary pleasures are pleasures worth cherishing. So we have good reasons to look for the institutional conditions and the personal environment that are most conducive to high individual well-being.

REFERENCES

Alesina, A., Di Tella, R., & MacCulloch, R. (2004). Inequality and happiness: Are Europeans and Americans different? *Journal of Public Economics*, *88*(9–10), 2009–2042.

Ambrey, C. L., & Fleming, C. M. (2011). Valuing scenic amenity using life satisfaction data. *Ecological Economics*, *72*, 106–115.

Becchetti, L., Pelloni, A., & Rossetti, F. (2008). Relational goods, sociability, and happiness. *Kyklos*, *61*(3), 343–363.

Becker, G. S. (1981). *A treatise on the family*. Cambridge, MA: Harvard University Press.

Becker, G. S., & Tomes, N. (1986). Human capital and the rise and fall of families. *Journal of Labor Economics*, *4*, S1–S39.

Benz, M., & Frey, B. S. (2008). Being independent is a great thing: Subjective evaluations of self-employment and hierarchy. *Economica*, *75*(298), 362–383.

Blanden, J., Gregg, P., & Macmillan, L. (2007). Explaining intergenerational income persistence: Non-cognitive skills, ability and education. *Economic Journal*, *117*(519), 43–60.

Boyce, C. J., & Wood, A. M. (2011). Personality prior to disability determines adaptation: Agreeable individuals recover lost life satisfaction faster and more completely. *Psychological Science*, *22*(11), 1397–1402.

---

13. Related work by Loewenstein and Ubel (2008) emphasized the shortcomings of measures of experience utility related to the phenomenon of hedonic adaptation; e.g., due to scale recalibration when assessing subjective health. The authors concluded that methods of deliberative democracy could achieve an approach based on decision utility of people who are informed about research on experience utility. Deliberative democracy could thus be interpreted as their constitutional proposal indicating how to deal with the insights on hedonic adaptation.

Brickman, P., & Campbell, D. T. (1971). Hedonic relativism and planning the good society. In M. H. Appley (Ed.), *Adaptation level theory:* A symposium (pp. 287–302). New York: Academic Press.

Brickman, P., Coates, D., & Janoff-Bulman, R. (1978). Lottery winners and accident victims: Is happiness relative? *Journal of Personality and Social Psychology, 36*(8), 917–927.

Bruni, L., & Porta, P. L. (Eds.), (2005). *Economics and happiness: Framing the analysis.* Oxford: Oxford University Press.

Carroll, N., Frijters, P., & Shields, M. A. (2009). Quantifying the costs of drought: New evidence from life satisfaction data. *Journal of Population Economics, 22*(2), 445–461.

Case, A., Fertig, A., & Paxson, C. (2005). The lasting impact of childhood health and circumstance. *Journal of Health Economics, 24*(2), 365–389.

Cattaneo, M. D., Galiani, S., Gertler, P. J., Martinez, S., & Titiunik, R. (2009). Housing, health, and happiness. *American Economic Journal: Economic Policy, 1*(1), 75–105.

Clark, A. E. (2003). Unemployment as a social norm: Psychological evidence from panel data. *Journal of Labor Economics, 21*(2), 289–322.

Clark, A. E., Diener, E., Georgellis, Y., & Lucas, R. E. (2008a). Lags and leads in life satisfaction: A test of the baseline hypothesis. *Economic Journal, 118*(529), 222–243.

Clark, A. E., Frijters, P., & Shields, M. A. (2008b). Relative income, happiness, and utility: An explanation for the Easterlin paradox and other puzzles. *Journal of Economic Literature, 46*(1), 95–144.

Clark, A. E., & Georgellis, Y. (2013). Back to baseline in Britain: Adaptation in the British household panel survey. *Economica, 80*(319), 496–512.

Clark, A. E., Georgellis, Y., & Sanfey, P. (2001). Scarring: The psychological impact of past unemployment. *Economica, 68*(270), 221–241.

Clark, A. E., & Lelkes, O. (2005). Deliver us from evil: Religion as insurance. Mimeo, Paris School of Economics.

Clark, A. E., & Senik, C. (2010). Who compares to whom? The anatomy of income comparisons in Europe. *Economic Journal, 120*(544), 573–594.

Comim, F. (2005). Capabilities and happiness: Potential synergies. *Review of Social Economy, 63*(2), 161–176.

Conti, G., & Heckman, J. J. (2010). Understanding the early origins of the education-health gradient: A framework that can also be applied to analyze gene-environment interactions. *Perspectives on Psychological Science, 5*(5), 585–605.

Dehejia, R., DeLeire, T., Luttmer, E. F., & Mitchell, J. (2007). The role of religious and social organizations in the lives of disadvantaged youth. In J. Gruber (Ed.), *The problems of disadvantaged youth: An economic perspective* (pp. 237–274). Cambridge, MA: National Bureau of Economic Research.

Di Tella, R., Haisken-DeNew, J., & MacCulloch, R. (2010). Happiness adaptation to income and to status in an individual panel. *Journal of Economic Behavior & Organization, 76*(3), 834–852.

Di Tella, R., & MacCulloch, R. (2006). Some uses of happiness data in economics. *Journal of Economic Perspectives, 20*(1), 25–46.

Di Tella, R., MacCulloch, R. J., & Oswald, A. J. (2003). The macroeconomics of happiness. *Review of Economics and Statistics, 85*(4), 809–827.

Dolan, P., & Kahneman, D. (2008). Interpretations of utility and their implications for the valuation of health. *Economic Journal, 118*(525), 215–234.

Dolan, P., & Metcalfe, R. (2008). *Comparing willingness-to-pay and subjective well-being in the context of non-market goods.* CEP Discussion Paper No. 0890. London: LSE.

Dolan, P., Peasgood, T., & White, M. (2008). Do we really know what makes us happy? A review of the economic literature on the factors associated with subjective well-being. *Journal of Economic Psychology, 29*(1), 94–122.

Easterlin, R. A. (2013). Happiness, growth, and public policy. *Economic Inquiry, 51*(1), 1–15.

Freeman, A. M. (2003). *The measurement of environmental and resource values: Theory and methods.* Washington, DC: Resources for the Future.

Frey, B., Benz, M., & Stutzer, A. (2004). Introducing procedural utility: Not only what, but also how matters. *Journal of Institutional and Theoretical Economics, 160*(3), 377–401.

Frey, B. S. (2008). *Happiness: A revolution in economics.* Cambridge, MA: The MIT Press.

Frey, B. S., Luechinger, S., & Stutzer, A. (2009). The life satisfaction approach to valuing public goods: The case of terrorism. *Public Choice, 138*(3–4), 317–345.

Frey, B. S., & Stutzer, A. (2000). Happiness, economy and institutions. *Economic Journal, 110* (466), 918–938.

Frey, B. S., & Stutzer, A. (2002a). *Happiness and economics.* Princeton, NJ: Princeton University Press.

Frey, B. S., & Stutzer, A. (2002b). What can economists learn from happiness research? *Journal of Economic Literature, 40*(2), 402–435.

Frey, B. S., & Stutzer, A. (2012). The use of happiness research for public policy. *Social Choice and Welfare, 38*(4), 659–674.

Frey, B. S., & Stutzer, A. (2014). Economic consequences of mispredicting utility. Forthcoming in *the Journal of Happiness Studies.*

Frijters, P., Hatton, T., & Shields, M. A. (2010). Childhood economic conditions and length of life: Evidence from the UK Boyd Orr Cohort, 1937–2005. *Journal of Health Economics, 29*(1), 39–47.

Frijters, P., Johnston, D. W., & Shields, M. A. (2011a). Destined for (un)happiness: Does childhood predict adult life satisfaction? Bonn: Institute for the Study of Labor. IZA Discussion Paper No. 5819.

Frijters, P., Johnston, D. W., & Shields, M. A. (2011b). Life satisfaction dynamics with quarterly life event data. *Scand. J. Econ., 113*(1), 190–211.

Goodman, A., Joyce, R., & Smith, J. P. (2011). The long shadow cast by childhood physical and mental problems on adult life. *Proceedings of the National Academy of Sciences, 108*(15), 6032–6037.

Goudie, R. J., Mukherjee, S., Neve, J.-E. D., Oswald, A. J., & Wu, S. (2014). Happiness as a driver of risk-avoiding behavior. Forthcoming in *Economica.*

Graham, L., & Oswald, A. J. (2010). Hedonic capital, resilience and adaptation. *Journal of Economic Behavior, & Organization, 76*(2), 372–384.

Green, F. (2011). Unpacking the misery multiplier: How employability modifies the impacts of unemployment and job insecurity on life satisfaction and mental health. *Journal of Health Economics, 30*(2), 265–276.

Greene, K. V., & Yoon, B. J. (2004). Religiosity, economics and life satisfaction. *Review of Social Economy, 62*(2), 245–261.

Headey, B. (2007). Happiness: Revising set point theory and dynamic equilibrium theory to account for long term change. *Journal of Applied Social Science Studies, 127*(1), 85–94.

Headey, B., Muffels, R., & Wagner, G. G. (2014). Parents transmit happiness along with associated values and behaviors to their children: A lifelong happiness dividend? *Social Indicators Research, 116*(3), 909–933.

Headey, B., Ruud, M., & Wagner, G. G. (2010). Long-running German panel survey shows that personal and economic choices, not just genes, matter for happiness. *Proceeding of National Academy of Science, 107*(42), 17922–17926.

Headey, B., & Wearing, A. (1989). Personality, life events, and subjective well-being: Toward a dynamic equilibrium model. *Journal of Personality and Social Psychology, 57*(4), 731–739.

Helliwell, J. F., & Putnam, R. D. (2004). The social context of well-being. *Philosophical Transactions of the Royal Society of London. Series B: Biological Sciences, 359*(1449), 1435–1446.

Hsee, C. K., Rottenstreich, Y., & Stutzer, A. (2012). Suboptimal choices and the need for experienced individual well-being in economic analysis. *International Journal of Happiness and Development, 1*(1), 63–85.

Inglehart, R., Foa, R., Peterson, C., & Welzel, C. (2008). Development, freedom, and rising happiness: A global perspective (1981–2007). *Perspectives on Psychological Science, 3*(4), 264–285.

Johnson, D. R., & Wu, J. (2002). An empirical test of crisis, social selection, and role explanations of the relationship between marital disruption and psychological distress: A pooled time-series analysis of four-wave panel data. *Journal of Marriage and the Family, 64*(1), 211–224.

Kahneman, D., Krueger, A. B., & Schkade, D. A. (2004). A survey method for characterizing daily life experience: The day reconstruction method. *Science, 306*, 1776–1780.

Kahneman, D., Krueger, A. B., Schkade, D. A., Schwarze, N., & Stone, A. A. (2006). Would you be happier if you were richer? A focusing illusion. *Science, 312*(5782), 1908–1910.

Kahneman, D., & Sugden, R. (2005). Experienced utility as a standard of policy evaluation. *Environmental and Resource Economics, 32*(1), 161–181.

Kahneman, D., & Thaler, R. H. (2006). Anomalies: Utility maximization and experienced utility. *Journal of Economic Perspectives, 20*(1), 221–234.

Kassenboehmer, S. C., & Haisken-DeNew, J. P. (2009). You're fired! The causal negative effect of entry unemployment on life satisfaction. *Economic Journal, 119*(536), 448–462.

Knabe, A., & Rätzel, S. (2011). Scarring or scaring? The psychological impact of past unemployment and future unemployment risk. *Economica, 78*(310), 283–293.

Knabe, A., Rätzel, S., Schöb, R., & Weimann, J. (2010). Dissatisfied with life but having a good day: Time-use and well-being of the unemployed. *Economic Journal, 120*(547), 867–889.

Knight, J., & Gunatilaka, R. (2012). Income, aspirations and the hedonic treadmill in a poor society. *Journal of Economic Behavior & Organization, 82*(1), 67–81.

Layard, R. (2005). *Happiness: Lessons from a new science.* New York: Penguin.

Layard, R., Clark, A. E., Cornaglia, F., Vernoit, J., & Powdthavee, N. (2013). *What predicts a successful life?* A life-course model of well-being. IZA Discussion Paper No. 7682. Bonn: Institute for the Study of Labor.

Layard, R., Mayraz, G., & Nickell, S. (2008). The marginal utility of income. *Journal of Public Economics, 92*(8–9), 1846–1857.

Loewenstein, G., O'Donoghue, T., & Rabin, M. (2003). Projection bias in predicting future utility. *Quarterly Journal of Economics, 118*(4), 1209–1248.

Loewenstein, G., & Ubel, P. A. (2008). Hedonic adaptation and the role of decision and experience utility in public policy. *Journal of Public Economics, 92*(8–9), 1795–1810.

Lucas, R. E. (2005). Time does not heal all wounds. A longitudinal study of reaction and adaptation to divorce. *Psychological Science, 16*(12), 945–950.

Lucas, R. E. (2007). Long-term disability is associated with lasting changes in subjective well-being: Evidence from two nationally representative longitudinal studies. *Journal of Personality and Social Psychology*, *92*(4), 717−731.

Lucas, R. E., Clark, A. E., Georgellis, Y., & Diener, E. (2003). Reexamining adaptation and the set point model of happiness: Reactions to changes in marital status. *Journal of Personality and Social Psychology*, *84*(3), 527−539.

Lucas, R. E., Clark, A. E., Georgellis, Y., & Diener, E. (2004). Unemployment alters the set point for life satisfaction. *Psychological Science*, *15*(1), 8−13.

Luechinger, S. (2009). Valuing air quality using the life satisfaction approach. *Economic Journal*, *119*(536), 482−515.

Luechinger, S., Meier, S., & Stutzer, A. (2010). Why does unemployment hurt the employed? Evidence from the life satisfaction gap between the public and the private sector. *Journal of Human Resources*, *45*(4), 998−1045.

Luechinger, S., & Raschky, P. A. (2009). Valuing flood disasters using the life satisfaction approach. *Journal of Public Economics*, *93*(3−4), 620−633.

Luttmer, E. F. (2005). Neighbors as negatives: Relative earnings and well-being. *Quarterly Journal of Economics*, *120*(3), 963−1002.

Lykken, D., & Tellegen, A. (1996). Happiness is a stochastic phenomenon. *Psychological Science*, *7*(3), 186−189.

MacKerron, G., & Mourato, S. (2009). Life satisfaction and air quality in London. *Ecological Economics*, *68*(5), 1441−1453.

Meier, S., & Stutzer, A. (2008). Is volunteering rewarding in itself? *Economica*, *75*(297), 39−59.

Mensah, F. K., & Hobcraft, J. (2008). Childhood deprivation, health and development: Associations with adult health in the 1958 and 1970 British prospective birth cohort studies. *Journal of Epidemiology and Community Health*, *62*, 599−606.

Odermatt, R., & Stutzer, A. (2013). *Smoking bans, cigarette prices and life satisfaction*. Bonn: Institute for the Study of Labor. IZA Discussion Papers.

Oreopoulos, P., & Salvanes, K. G. (2011). Priceless: The nonpecuniary benefits of schooling. *Journal of Economic Perspectives*, *25*(1), 159−184.

Oswald, A. J., & Powdthavee, N. (2008). Does happiness adapt? A longitudinal study of disability with implications for economists and judges. *Journal of Public Economics*, *92*(5−6), 1061−1077.

Pezzini, S. (2005). The effect of women's rights on women's welfare: Evidence from a natural experiment. *Economic Journal*, *115*(502), 208−227.

Pischke, J.-S. (2011). *Money and happiness: Evidence from the industry wage structure*. NBER Working Papers No. 17056. Cambridge, MA: National Bureau of Economic Research.

Pollner, M. (1989). Divine relations, social relations, and well-being. *Journal of Health and Social Behavior*, *30*(1), 92−104.

Powdthavee, N. (2008). Putting a price tag on friends, relatives, and neighbours: Using surveys of life satisfaction to value social relationships. *Journal of Socio-Economics*, *37*(4), 1459−1480.

Powdthavee, N. (2009). What happens to people before and after disability? Focusing effects, lead effects, and adaptation in different areas of life. *Social Science and Medicine*, *69*(12), 1834−1844.

Powdthavee, N. (2010a). *The happiness equation: The surprising economics of our most valuable asset*. London: Icon Books Ltd.

Powdthavee, N. (2010b). How much does money really matter? Estimating the causal effect of income on happiness. *Empirical Economics, 39*(1), 77–92.

Powdthavee, N. (2012a). Jobless, friendless, and broke: What happens to different areas of life before and after unemployment? *Economica, 79*(315), 557–575.

Powdthavee, N. (2012b). *Psychological resilience and the long reach of childhood bullying.* IZA Discussion Paper No. 6945. Bonn: Institute for the Study of Labor.

Powdthavee, N., & van den Berg, B. (2011). Putting different price tags on the same health condition: Re-evaluating the well-being valuation approach. *Journal of Health Economics, 30*(5), 1032–1043.

Rayo, L., & Becker, G. S. (2007). Evolutionary efficiency and happiness. *Journal of Political Economy, 115*(2), 302–337.

Schkade., D. A., & Kahneman, D. (1998). Does living in California make people happy? A focusing illusion in judgments of life satisfaction. *Psychological Science, 9*(5), 340–346.

Sen, A. (1999). *Development as freedom.* New York: Alfred Knopf.

Steiner, L., Leinert, L., & Frey, B. S. (2010). Economics, religion and happiness. *Journal for Business, Economics & Ethics, 11*(1), 9–24.

Stevenson, B., & Wolfers, J. (2013). Subjective well-being and income: Is there any evidence of satiation? *American Economic Review, 103*(3), 598–604.

Stutzer, A. (2004). The role of income aspirations in individual happiness. *Journal of Economic Behavior & Organization, 54*(1), 89–109.

Stutzer, A., & Frey, B. S. (2006). Does marriage make people happy, or do happy people get married? *Journal of Socio-Economics, 35*(2), 326–347.

Stutzer, A., & Frey, B. S. (2010). Recent advances in the economics of individual subjective well-being. *Social Research: An International Quarterly, 77*(2), 679–714.

Stutzer, A., & Lalive, R. (2004). The role of social work norms in job searching and subjective well-being. *Journal of the European Economic Association, 2*(4), 696–719.

van Praag, B. M., & Baarsma, B. E. (2005). Using happiness surveys to value intangibles: The case of airport noise. *Economic Journal, 115*(500), 224–246.

van Praag, B. M., & Ferrer-i-Carbonell, A. (2004). *Happiness quantified: A satisfaction calculus approach.* Oxford: Oxford University Press.

Veenhoven, R., & Vergunst, F. (2013). *The Easterlin illusion: Economic growth does go with greater happiness.* MPRA Paper No. 43983. University Library of Munich.

Welsch, H. (2006). Environment and happiness: Valuation of air pollution using life satisfaction data. *Ecological Economics, 58*(4), 801–813.

Wilson, T. D., & Gilbert, D. T. (2008). Explaining away: A model of affective adaptation. *Perspectives on Psychological Science, 3*(5), 370–386.

Winkelmann, R. (2009). Unemployment, social capital, and subjective well-being. *Journal of Happiness Studies, 10*(4), 421–430.

Wolfers, J. (2003). Is business cycle volatility costly? Evidence from surveys of subjective well-being. *International Finance, 6*(1), 1–26.

Chapter 12

Personality Traits as Potential Moderators of Well-Being

Setting a Foundation for Future Research

Patrick L. Hill,[1] Daniel K. Mroczek,[2] and Robin K. Young[1]

[1]*Carleton University, Ottawa, ON, Canada,* [2]*Northwestern University, Evanston, IL, USA*

When considering who may become happier or more satisfied over time, laypeople and researchers alike often focus on candidates such as social role changes (including getting married and getting a job), personal wealth, and even physical health and well-being. A less obvious candidate, though, may be one's personality. Although we do not typically think about how traits and dispositions may predict fluctuations in well-being, their potential relevance becomes more apparent with the realization that they tend to predict all the potential catalysts for well-being change discussed above. Indeed, personality traits predict occupational attainment, divorce, income levels, as well as physical health and mortality risk (e.g., Hampson, 2012; Ozer & Benet-Martinez, 2006; Roberts, Kuncel, Shiner, Caspi, & Goldberg, 2007). Therefore, if any of these variables increases or decreases levels of well-being, personality traits may be an underlying catalyst for such changes.

The value of discussing personality traits in the context of changes in well-being is supported by considering four literatures, which serve as the four sections for review in the current chapter. First, personality traits by definition (e.g., Roberts, 2009; Watson, 2000) include affective components, some more so than others, such as extraversion and neuroticism. Therefore, we discuss the evidence for longitudinal changes on these two traits, as these fluctuations provide potential insights into whether subjective well-being also may be capable of changes. Second, we briefly review the wealth of evidence suggesting that personality traits do predict levels of subjective well-being, at least cross-sectionally, demonstrating that certain personality profiles appear more likely to promote well-being. Third, we consider the potential for each of the Big Five traits to moderate trajectories of well-being, noting the extant empirical evidence when relevant. Finally, we discuss the relatively recent work suggesting that "manipulating" personality could lead to changes in well-being, focusing on three specific traits: gratitude, forgivingness, and mindfulness. Our intent is to demonstrate that considering personality traits as moderators of well-being change is an important focus for future research, even though it is one that has been largely neglected to this point. Therefore, we have structured our chapter to guide this work, by producing testable hypotheses for future work using Big Five traits and more specific dispositional characteristics.

PERSONALITY CHANGE AS SUPPORT FOR WELL-BEING CHANGE: THE CASES OF EXTRAVERSION AND NEUROTICISM

We begin by adding another perspective for considering the central question of this volume: namely that evidence for personality change may itself constitute evidence that happiness and well-being can change. Toward this point, we focus solely on the broad dispositions of extraversion and neuroticism. When we consider the lower-order facets that comprise these traits, their relevance becomes immediately clear. Neuroticism has been defined as higher levels of affective traits such as anger, anxiety, and depression (NEO; Costa & McCrae, 1995). Alternatively, extraversion is described with respect to greater positive emotions, warmth, and activity. Although neuroticism and extraversion clearly are not reducible to negative and positive affect, understanding whether these dispositions and their facets change over time provides insight into the broader question of whether well-being itself can change.

Studies have consistently demonstrated that extraversion and neuroticism have the capacity to change across the life course. With regard to mean-level trends, neuroticism tends to decline during young and middle adulthood (Roberts, Walton, & Viechtbauer, 2006), a pattern also mirrored by several of its facets (Soto, John, Gosling, & Potter, 2011). Extraversion often shows a more differentiated age trajectory, depending on the facet of interest (Roberts et al., 2006). However, studies consistently demonstrate that individuals vary in their patterns of change on these traits (e.g., Mroczek & Spiro, 2003; Small, Hertzog, Hultsch, & Dixon, 2003), underscoring the potential for both to fluctuate across time. Perhaps more importantly, these changes do, in fact, matter for aging and life span development. For instance, increases in neuroticism predict greater mortality risk, even when controlling for initial levels (Mroczek & Spiro, 2007).

Similar to the work on well-being, studies have examined the role of life events on the stability of extraversion, neuroticism, and other traits over time (Neyer & Lehnart, 2007). For instance, one study investigated the role of 12 different major life events (e.g., marriage, divorce, unemployment, retirement, etc.) and found some evidence that they may influence trait changes

(Specht, Egloff, & Schmukle, 2011). However, on the whole, relatively few events significantly influenced changes on neuroticism and extraversion, or their patterns of rank-order stability. Such evidence provides another parallel to the well-being literature, which similarly has reported that major life events have less of a long-term influence on well-being than we may expect (see, e.g., Diener & Lucas, 1999). Next, we consider the relationship between personality and well-being more thoroughly, by reviewing the literature linking trait levels to reports of life satisfaction and well-being.

REVISITING THE "HAPPY PERSONALITY": LINKING TRAITS AND SUBJECTIVE WELL-BEING

Our subheading alludes to perhaps the most substantial and well-known examination of personality as a predictor of well-being, namely, the classic meta-analysis conducted by DeNeve and Cooper (1998). Their thorough review of the literature pointed to three particularly important findings. First, all Big Five personality traits were linked to markers of life satisfaction, happiness, positive affect, and negative affect, in the expected ways. Extraverted, agreeable, conscientious, emotionally stable, and open individuals tended to fare better than their peers with respect to reporting greater well-being, with the exception that openness to experience was modestly related to negative affect. Second, although extraversion or neuroticism was the strongest predictor for each well-being outcome, the other three traits were not much weaker in their predictive value. Third, overall, these personality traits were shown to evidence, at best, moderate relationships with the well-being indicators of interest. Indeed, no meta-analytic estimate was greater in magnitude than .27, the effect of extraversion on happiness. As an effect size comparison, this is comparable to the correlation between gender and weight among adults, which is .26 (Meyer et al., 2001), but lower than the association between height and weight, which is .44. However, the extraversion-happiness association is roughly double the size of the association between ibuprofen and pain relief (.14) or college grades on job performance (.16) (Meyer et al., 2001). From this perspective, we may conclude that the effect of traits on happiness is substantial. It also may be the case that individual changes in happiness track, to some extent, individual changes in traits.

However, more recent meta-analytic work (Steel, Schmidt, & Shultz, 2008) suggests that the estimates reported by DeNeve and Cooper (1998) may have underestimated the relationships between personality and well-being, particularly for extraversion and neuroticism. In some cases, these relationships were closer to .4 or .5 in magnitude, although it differed greatly based on the personality measure. If these estimates could be considered more accurate, we might say that the personality-happiness relationship is comparable in size to the association between height and weight—in other words, an effect of considerable magnitude. In addition, this meta-analysis demonstrated the potential for specific traits to evidence stronger relationships with well-being than the broader Big Five composites. For instance, anxiety and depression were stronger (negative) correlates with life satisfaction and positive affect than impulsivity, another facet of neuroticism. Similarly, activity and positive emotions proved stronger correlates of positive affect than other extraversion facets, such as gregariousness and excitement seeking.

While the facet results were based on relatively few studies, they point to the fact that the happy personality lies beyond merely the Big Five traits. For instance, dispositional gratitude has demonstrated consistently moderate-to-strong relations with well-being (see Wood, Froh, & Geraghty, 2010, for a review), even when considering observer-reported personality (McCullough, Emmons, & Tsang, 2002). Although gratitude may appear an obvious correlate, given its natural connection to positive affect in general, this trait provides an interesting discussion point for at least two reasons. First, its influence on subjective well-being appears particularly strong, given that it holds across the adult years (Hill & Allemand, 2011), as well as when controlling for the NEO facets (Wood, Joseph, & Maltby, 2008). Second, the findings for gratitude present an interesting argument for how personality could influence well-being. Namely, when studying how and why well-being changes, researchers may wish to focus less on nominating specific life events that could alter these trajectories, and instead turn to understanding the individual differences that influence our interpretation of these events.

Along this front, another disposition worthy of consideration is forgivingness, defined as a dispositional tendency to forgive across different transgressions and transgressors (Roberts, 1995). As such, forgiving individuals differ in their interpretation and reaction to social stressors and exchanges (e.g., Berry, Worthington, Parrott, O'Connor, & Wade, 2005; Burrow & Hill, 2012). Forgivingness has been consistently connected to subjective well-being, potentially because it may foster relationship success and adaptive self-development (see, for a review, Hill, Heffernan, & Allemand, in press). While it is clearly connected to Big Five traits such as agreeableness and emotional stability (Mullet, Neto, & Rivière, 2005), research has demonstrated that forgivingness cannot be fully characterized by these broader traits (Steiner, Allemand, & McCullough, 2012). In sum, the happy personality appears to comprise both the ability to be thankful for the positive influences that others may bring, as well as to excuse them for the negative ones.

A final trait worth discussing is mindfulness. Mindful individuals are those better capable of observing and describing their internal and external environments, being less judgmental and impulsively reactive to a given event, and acting with awareness of the current and future consequences (Baer, Smith, Hopkins, Krietemeyer, & Toney, 2006; Brown & Ryan, 2003). Therefore, mindfulness reflects a trait similar to gratitude and forgivingness, in its potential for influencing one's daily reactions and social exchanges, which in turn can have cumulative influences on well-being over time. As such, this trait has been nominated by several religious traditions as a catalyst for greater personal well-being (Brown & Ryan, 2003; Kabat-Zinn, 2003), and empirical research has consistently supported this suggestion. Indeed, mindful individuals tend to report greater happiness and positive affect, less negative emotions, and more satisfaction with life (e.g., Brown & Ryan, 2003; Schutte & Malouff, 2011; Weinstein, Brown, & Ryan, 2009). Moreover, a key goal of mindfulness-based stress reduction (MBSR) programs (Kabat-Zinn, 1998; Speca, Carlson, Goodey, & Angen, 2000) is to lessen both the perception and emotional reactivity to stressors as well as increase positive emotion. Indeed, techniques such as MBSR have been linked to improved immune function (Davidson et al., 2003; Witek-Janusek et al., 2008) as well as increased activation in brain regions that promote positive affect (Davidson et al., 2003). Indeed, people with lessened reactivity to stressors have lower mortality risk (Mroczek, Stawski, Turiano, Chan, Almeida, Neupert, & Spiro, 2013). Like gratitude and forgivingness, these effects appear to hold even when controlling for the broader traits like extraversion and neuroticism (Brown & Ryan, 2003; Mroczek et al., in press). Therefore, the happy personality is best described with respect to a collection of both broader and more specific traits.

PERSONALITY AS A PREDICTOR OF WELL-BEING TRAJECTORIES

Given the theoretical, conceptual, and empirical linkages between personality traits and well-being, it appears likely that our dispositions may influence our tendency to become more or less happy over time. Therefore, it is surprising that relatively little research has formally tested whether personality traits can moderate well-being trajectories, although the extant literature does suggest a potential role for personality. To organize this review, and chart the course for future research, we consider the potential for each of the Big Five traits to moderate well-being trajectories, starting again with the two most affective dispositions.

Extraversion and Neuroticism

Given their links to positive and negative affectivity, most extant research has focused on the potential roles for extraversion and neuroticism. For instance, one study examined age and personality traits as predictors of positive and negative affect across a large adult sample (Mroczek & Kolarz, 1998). While cross-sectional in nature, this work provided several important insights regarding the potential for well-being to change over time, as well as predictors of these fluctuations. First, across participants, positive affect tended to increase with age, whereas negative affect tended to decline. However, these trends differed for males and females, insofar that age only seemed to predict negative affect for males. Second, the influence of age on positive affect differed by extraversion level for males. Specifically, highly extraverted males tended to always have high levels of positive affect, regardless of age, whereas age had a stronger influence on development trajectories for highly introverted males. In other words, the aging process appears to only influence positive affect for those men who were not already very extraverted in nature.

Charles, Reynolds, and Gatz (2001) went even further and estimated long-term (23 years) longitudinal positive and negative affect trajectories in more than 2,800 participants in the Longitudinal Study of Generations (LSOG). They used growth modeling to capture intra-individual trajectories of PA and NA. They found that PA trajectories were stable over time for young and midlife adults but declined for older adults. More relevant for the issue of personality moderation of well-being trajectories, higher extraversion was associated with greater stability in PA trajectories among all age cohorts. Consistent with the finding of decreasing NA with age (e.g., Watson & Walker, 1996), Charles et al. found decreasing trajectories of NA for all age cohorts. With respect to personality moderation, higher neuroticism was associated with less decline in NA for all age groups. In essence, Charles et al. (2001) documented that higher extraversion promotes maintenance or stability of PA, and that higher neuroticism attenuates the natural decline in NA seen in most adults. This was the first study using long-term longitudinal data to highlight the crucial role of personality in predicting well-being trajectories.

Building upon Charles et al. (2001), Griffin, Mroczek, and Spiro (2006) estimated decade-long trajectories of PA and NA in more than 1,500 mostly older adults (mean age 69). They found that PA declined, and replicated the finding that NA decreased with age (but increased slightly after age 70). Like Charles et al., they found a critical role of personality as a moderator of NA trajectories, with higher neuroticism associated with fewer declines in NA during midlife and steeper increases in older adulthood. Extraversion was associated with higher levels (intercepts) of PA but not with rate of change.

However, PA and NA are not the only aspects of happiness that personality can modify. Life satisfaction, a more "cognitive" or evaluative indicator of well-being, appears to change systematically over the life course, as documented by Mroczek and Spiro (2005) and Blanchflower and Oswald (2008). The latter found evidence for a U-shaped curve of well-being, with a nadir at around age 40 to 45. Mroczek and Spiro (2005) described the opposite: an inverted U function. However, they used a much older sample: their youngest participants were age 40 to 45. Placing the Blanchflower and Oswald (2008) curve side by side with the Mroczek and Spiro (2005) curve yields a function that has two nadirs. One nadir is at age 40–45 and the other at a much older age, at around 85–90. With respect to personality moderation of these curves, Mroczek and Spiro found that extraversion modified all three aspects of well-being trajectories: level, slope and curvature. In other words, persons higher in extraversion had higher life satisfaction trajectories that were more stable and less peaked than persons who were more introverted.

The aforementioned work presents one of the ways by which personality traits can contour changes in well-being, which is similar to either a "ceiling" or "floor" effect. Namely, individuals initially higher on those dispositions characteristic of the happy personality should be less likely to gain on well-being with time or show less pronounced natural declines in negative indicators of happiness (e.g., NA). Similar examples have been shown by research investigating changes in social well-being over a 9-year span of adulthood (Hill, Turiano, Mroczek, & Roberts, 2012). In that study, initially extraverted adults were less likely to gain on social integration, one aspect of social well-being (Keyes, 1998), and were no more likely to gain on the other facets of social well-being. As would be expected, extraverted individuals were much more likely to report higher social well-being at the start of the study, making it less likely for them to increase on these facets with time.

An alternative moderation effect can occur for individuals initially low on "happy traits." For instance, that same study (Hill et al., 2012) found that initially neurotic individuals were more likely to experience gains in social well-being across three of its four facets. In this respect, personality traits also can act as "floor" effects in their influence on well-being change. Both of these moderation effects reflect ways by which personality traits can identify those individuals most and least likely to become happier with time. However, describing and identifying moderation effects for personality traits becomes more complicated when moving beyond the two Big Five traits most characterized by well-being. Indeed, extraversion and neuroticism accounted for the vast majority of the personality moderation effects shown in that study of social well-being change.

Conscientiousness

When we consider the other Big Five traits, deeper consideration is needed regarding why these dispositions could serve as moderators of well-being trajectories. Although personality traits do not appear to moderate the effect of life events on well-being (Yap, Anusic, & Lucas, 2012), these traits could still serve moderating roles by virtue of motivating the events that influence well-being. For instance, one potential route for personality is through predicting which individuals are more likely to attain those accomplishments that might coincide with greater well-being, such as marital or job success. Or conversely, personality traits may predict an attenuated likelihood to experience the events that can dampen well-being, such as poor health or unemployment.

In both cases, conscientiousness should prove valuable to maintaining or promoting adaptive patterns of well-being over time. Conscientious individuals are likely to achieve higher levels of education (Poropat, 2009), job success (Barrick & Mount, 1991; Judge, Higgins, Thoresen, & Barrick, 2006), and in turn income (e.g., Sutin, Costa, Miech, & Eaton, 2009). In addition, conscientiousness predicts a diminished likelihood of divorce, unemployment, and poor health (Roberts et al., 2007). Given the strong stability of well-being over time (Diener & Lucas, 1999), it is worth noting that none of these effects in and of themselves is likely to change well-being trajectories much. However, it is the cumulative benefit of being conscientious that makes it a likely candidate as a well-being moderator, likely acting more as a stabilizer that allows individuals to immunize themselves against the risks for ill-being that befall others (see also Hill, Nickel, & Roberts, 2013). This largely remains a topic for future inquiry, though, because little research thus far has considered the role of conscientiousness as a well-being moderator.

Openness to Experience

With respect to openness to experience, it is more difficult to make clear and consistent predictions regarding its influence on those events associated with well-being changes. Open individuals may live longer lives than their peers, but this effect appears dependent on which facet is examined (Jonassaint et al., 2007; Turiano, Spiro, & Mroczek, 2012). Mixed results also present with respect to the influence of openness on health (Goodwin & Friedman, 2006) and relationships (e.g., Noftle & Shaver, 2006), with results differing based on the specific outcome of interest. Accordingly, one would likely anticipate the "mixed bag" of results regarding the cross-sectional relations between this trait and well-being.

As such, openness to experience may be less consistent in the direction that it influences well-being change. Instead, one could predict this trait to hold an "opposite" role to conscientiousness. Namely, openness to experience may influence well-being trajectories less in their direction and more by virtue of creating greater fluctuations and variability. Similar to conscientiousness, though, this destabilizing effect may be difficult to identify in typical moderation tests. Therefore, future research needs to examine personality traits as predictors not only of change patterns, but also of well-being stability over time.

Agreeableness also has shown both positive and negative influences on physical health (e.g., Goodwin & Friedman, 2006) and appears to negatively predict income levels (Judge, Livingston, & Hurst, 2012). Moreover, it is less clear whether agreeableness, unlike openness to experience, would play a role on the variance around one's well-being trajectory. One potential reason for this lack of clarity is that the facets of agreeableness are differentially related to life satisfaction (e.g., Wood et al., 2008), which may obscure relationships at the domain level. Indeed, similar claims could be made for most of these larger composite traits. Accordingly, we turn our attention next to how more specific traits can inform us with respect to well-being moderators.

SPECIFIC TRAITS AS POTENTIAL MODERATORS

The study of specific traits is valuable for three primary reasons. First, one often can make clearer predictions regarding the influence of specific traits on well-being, or the potential catalysts thereof, than when discussing the Big Five domains. Second, while initial research focused on the broader Big Five traits, empirical work has accrued to demonstrate consistent relationships between specific traits and well-being (e.g., Wood et al., 2008). Moreover, researchers have suggested the capacity for lower-order, specific trait facets to change over time (e.g., Hill, Payne, Jackson, Stine-Morrow, & Roberts, 2013; Jackson et al., 2009; Soto et al., 2011). Third, building from this work, researchers have demonstrated some efficacy in intervening upon these specific traits, and the outcomes of which are promising for researchers trying to influence well-being. Toward this end, we return to the three case examples we briefly described earlier: gratitude, forgivingness, and mindfulness.

The construct of gratitude provides one of the most frequent candidates for intervention in the field of positive psychology. Such interventions often entail either asking participants to describe something for which they are thankful on each day or sending longer "thank you notes" to individuals who have provided them frequent assistance in their lives. These interventions have shown some potential to increase levels of gratitude in both adolescent and adult samples (see, e.g., Lambert & Veldorale-Brogan, 2013; Wood et al., 2010), although there are still methodological concerns left to be addressed (Froh, Kashdan, Ozimkowski, & Miller, 2009). Perhaps more important to our aims, these interventions often find that participants report greater life satisfaction or positive affect by the end of the study (e.g., Emmons & McCullough, 2003). In other words, it appears that motivating individuals toward greater gratitude may influence changes in well-being. As such, this specific trait may prove an intriguing candidate for influencing long-term trajectories in well-being, because grateful individuals are likely to experience more positive changes over time, as they are oriented toward focusing on the "good" in the world (Wood et al., 2010). In other words, grateful individuals may be more susceptible to increases in well-being over time because they are better at identifying those events and circumstances that have improved their lives.

Another interesting candidate is forgivingness, which reflects a trait that not only changes as we age (Allemand & Steiner, 2012), but also may be susceptible to interventions. Indeed, a wealth of literature has demonstrated that samples ranging from youth to older adults can become more willing to forgive others following interventions (for a review, see, e.g., Baskin & Enright, 2005;

Wade, Worthington, & Meyer, 2005). Moreover, although the literature on forgivingness development is brief, researchers have nominated a number of pathways by which these single sessions of forgiveness are likely to enact broader dispositional changes (Hill, Heffernan, & Allemand, in press). Again, important to our aims, these forgiveness interventions appear also to motivate changes in well-being, particularly with respect to attenuating negative affect (e.g., Allemand, Steiner, & Hill, 2013; Lin, Mack, Enright, Krahn, & Baskin, 2004). As such, forgiving individuals may be less likely to experience upward shifts on this component of well-being over time. Forgivingness may serve as a trait that buffers one against daily increases in hostility or revenge seeking, which in turn has a cumulative effect with respect to influencing longer-term changes in well-being.

A final candidate trait is mindfulness, which also has served as the target for a wide array of intervention studies (Brown, Ryan, & Creswell, 2007; Grossman, Niemann, Schmidt, & Walach, 2004; Shapiro, Carlso, Astin, & Freedman, 2006), mostly given the large interest it has received from the clinical psychology community. These studies consistently demonstrate that mindfulness training can have important effects on well-being over the course of the study (e.g., Grossman et al., 2004). Mindfulness may be a particularly interesting candidate moderator, given its influence on both positive and negative affect. Being aware of the current and future consequences of one's actions could increase positive affect over time, by allowing individuals to recognize and capitalize those experiences that can produce happiness. In addition, increased awareness could reduce negative affect over time, by virtue of responding to daily stressors more flexibly, and in turn reducing allostatic load and the known health issues that it presents (McEwen & Seeman, 1999).

CONCLUSIONS AND FINAL THOUGHTS

The evidence is mixed on whether well-being is stable or changing over the life span. Some studies have indicated stability (Diener & Lucas, 1999), whereas others have documented long-term changes at both the population and individual levels (Blanchflower & Oswald, 2008; Charles et al., 2001; Mroczek & Spiro, 2005). Regardless of the overall trends, personality traits present as excellent candidates for potentially influencing these trajectories over time. First, personality traits include affective components, particularly with respect to extraversion and emotional stability, and thus share conceptual connections with well-being. Second, personality traits, both broad and specific, have demonstrated consistent linkages with happiness and well-being. Third, research has begun to demonstrate long-term effects on this front, with personality traits predicting age trends and longitudinal changes on well-being (Hill et al., 2012; Mroczek & Kolarz, 1998). Fourth, intervening on personality, either in its state or trait form, appears to induce changes in well-being. As such, we encourage future researchers to consider the points made here and begin to examine the potential for traits to moderate changes in well-being, which would point again to the vast predictive power of personality (Roberts et al., 2007).

That said, any well-being changes are likely to be quite modest in magnitude, and may differ for males and females (Mroczek & Kolarz, 1998), which further exacerbates the known power issues with studying moderator effects (e.g., Aguinis, Beaty, Boik, & Pierce, 2005). In addition, as noted earlier, personality traits may moderate not only the direction of well-being changes, but also the variability one has around his or her set point. Therefore, researchers must consider multiple approaches and perspectives regarding what "moderation" means. However, given that other aspects of personality, such as life goals, appear to predict well-being changes (e.g., Headey, 2008; Hill, Burrow, Brandenberger, Lapsley, & Quaranto, 2010), we are encouraged by the ultimate prospects for research with personality traits.

REFERENCES

Aguinis, H., Beaty, J. C., Boik, R. J., & Pierce, C. A. (2005). Effect size and power in assessing moderating effects of categorical variables using multiple regression: A 30-year review. *Journal of Applied Psychology, 90*, 94–107.

Allemand, M., Steiner, A. E., & Hill, P. L. (2013). Effects of a forgiveness intervention for older adults. *Journal of Counseling Psychology, 60*, 279–286.

Allemand, M., & Steiner, M. (2012). Situation-specific forgiveness and dispositional forgiveness: A lifespan development perspective. In E. Kahls, & J. Maes (Eds.), *Justice psychology and conflicts: Theoretical and empirical contributions* (pp. 361–375). New York: Springer.

Baer, R., Smith, G., Hopkins, J., Krietemeyer, J., & Toney, L. (2006). Using self-report assessment methods to explore facets of mindfulness. *Assessment, 13*(1), 27–45.

Barrick, M. R., & Mount, M. K. (1991). The big five personality dimensions and job performance: A meta-analysis. *Personnel Psychology, 44*, 1–26.

Baskin, T. W., & Enright, R. D. (2004). Intervention studies on forgiveness: A meta-analysis. *Journal of Counseling & Development, 82*, 79–90.

Berry, J. W., Worthington, E. L., Jr., Parrott, L., III, O'Connor, L. E., & Wade, N. G. (2005). Forgivingness, vengeful rumination, and affective traits. *Journal of Personality, 73*(1), 183–226.

Blanchflower, D. G., & Oswald, A. J. (2008). Is well-being U-shaped over the life cycle? *Social Science Medicine, 66*, 1733–1749.

Brown, K., & Ryan, R. (2003). The benefits of being present: Mindfulness and its role in psychological well-being. *Journal of Personality and Social Psychology, 84*(4), 822–848.

Brown, K., Ryan, R., & Creswell, J. (2007). Mindfulness: Theoretical foundations and evidence for its salutary effects. *Psychological Inquiry, 18*(4), 211–237.

Burrow, A. L., & Hill, P. L. (2012). Flying the unfriendly skies? The role of forgiveness and race in the experience of racial microaggressions. *Journal of Social Psychology, 152* (639–653).

Charles, S. T., Reynolds, C. A., & Gatz, M. (2001). Age-related differences and change in positive and negative affect over 23 years. *Journal of Personality and Social Psychology, 80*(1), 136−151.

Costa, P. T., & McCrae, R. R. (1995). Domains and facets: Hierarchical personality assessment using the revised NEO personality inventory. *Journal of Personality Assessment, 64*, 21−50.

Davidson, R. J., Kabat-Zinn, J., Schumacher, J., Rosenkranz, M., Muller, D., Santorelli, S., et al. (2003). Alterations in brain and immune function produced by mindfulness meditation. *Psychosomatic Medicine, 65*, 564−570.

DeNeve, K. M., & Cooper, H. (1998). The happy personality: A meta-analysis of 137 personality traits and subjective well-being. *Psychological Bulletin, 124*, 197−229.

Diener, E., & Lucas, R. E. (1999). Personality and subjective well-being. In D. Kahneman, E. Diener, & N. Schwarz (Eds.), *Well-being: The foundations of hedonic psychology.* (pp. 213−229) New York: Russell Sage Foundation.

Emmons, R. A., & McCullough, M. E. (2003). Counting blessings versus burdens: An experimental investigation of gratitude and subjective well-being in daily life. *Journal of Personality and Social Psychology, 84*(2), 377−389.

Froh, J. J., Kashdan, T. B., Ozimkowski, K. M., & Miller, N. (2009). Who benefits the most from a gratitude intervention in children and adolescents? Examining positive affect as a moderator. *Journal of Positive Psychology, 4*, 408−422.

Goodwin, R. G., & Friedman, H. S. (2006). Health status and the Five Factor personality traits in a nationally representative sample. *Journal of Health Psychology, 11*, 643−654.

Griffin, P. W., Mroczek, D. K., & Spiro, A. III. (2006). Variability in affective change among aging men: Findings from the VA Normative Aging Study. *Journal of Research in Personality, 40*, 942−965.

Grossman, P., Niemann, L., Schmidt, S., & Walach, H. (2004). Mindfulness-based stress reduction and health benefits: A meta-analysis. *Journal of Psychosomatic Research, 57*, 35−43.

Hampson, S. E. (2012). Personality processes: Mechanisms by which personality traits get outside the skin. *Annual Review of Psychology, 63*, 315−339.

Headey, B. (2008). Life goals matter to happiness: A revision of set-point theory. *Social Indicators Research, 86*, 213−231.

Hill, P., Burrow, A., Brandenberger, J., Lapsley, D., & Quaranto, J. (2010). Collegiate purpose orientations and well-being in adulthood. *Journal of Applied Developmental Psychology, 31* (2), 173−179.

Hill, P. L., & Allemand, M. (2011). Gratitude, forgivingness, and well-being in adulthood: Tests of moderation and incremental prediction. *Journal of Positive Psychology, 6*, 397−407.

Hill, P. L., Nickel, L. B., & Roberts, B. W. (2013). Are you in a healthy relationship? Linking conscientiousness to health via implementing and immunizing behaviours. *Journal of Personality*. Available from http://dx.doi.org/10.1111/jopy.12051.

Hill, P. L., Payne, B. R., Jackson, J. J., Stine-Morrow, E. A. L., & Roberts, B. W. (2013). Perceived social support predicts increased conscientiousness during older adulthood. *Journal of Gerontology: Psychological Sciences.* [Epub ahead of print].

Hill, P. L., Turiano, N. A., Mroczek, D. K., & Roberts, B. W. (2012). Examining concurrent and longitudinal relations between personality traits and social well-being in adulthood. *Social Psychological and Personality Science, 3*(6), 698−705.

Jackson, J. J., Walton, K. E., Harms, P. D., Bogg, T., Wood, D., Lodi-Smith, J., et al. (2009). Not all conscientiousness scales change alike: A multimethod, multisample study of age differences in the facets of conscientiousness. *Journal of Personality and Social Psychology, 96*(2), 446−459.

Jonassaint, C. R., Boyle, S. H., Williams, R. B., Mark, D. B., Siegler, I. C., & Barefoot, J. C. (2007). Facets of openness predict mortality in patients with cardiac disease. *Psychosomatic Medicine, 69*(4), 319–322.

Judge, T. A., Higgins, C. A., Thoresen, C. J., & Barrick, M. R. (2006). The big five personality traits, general mental ability, and career success across the life span. *Personnel Psychology, 52*(3), 621–652.

Judge, T. A., Livingston, B. L., & Hurst, C. (2012). Do nice guys—and gals—really finish last? The joint effects of sex and agreeableness on income. *Journal of Personality & Social Psychology, 102*, 390–407.

Kabat-Zinn, J. (1998). Meditation. In J. C. Holland (Ed.), *Psycho-oncology* (pp. 767–779). New York: Oxford University Press.

Kabat-Zinn, J. (2003). Mindfulness-based interventions in context: Past, present, and future. *Clinical Psychology: Science and Practice, 10*, 144–156.

Keyes, Corey L. (1998). Social well-being. *Social Psychology Quarterly, 61*, 121–140.

Lambert, N. M., & Veldorale-Brogan, A. (2013). Gratitude intervention in adolescence and young adulthood. In C. Procter, & P. A. Linley (Eds.), *Research, applications, and interventions for children and adolescents* (pp. 117–128). Netherlands: Springer.

Lin, W. F., Mack, D., Enright, R. D., Krahn, D., & Baskin, T. W. (2004). Effects of forgiveness therapy on anger, mood, and vulnerability to substance use among inpatient substance-dependent clients. *Journal of Consulting and Clinical Psychology, 72*, 1114–1121.

McCullough, M. E., Emmons, R. A., & Tsang, J. (2002). The grateful disposition: A conceptual and empirical topography. *Journal of Personality and Social Psychology, 82*, 112–127.

McEwen, B. S., & Seeman, T. (1999). Protective and damaging effects of mediators of stress. Elaborating and testing the concepts of allostasis and allostatic load. *Annals of the New York Academy of Science, 896*, 30–47.

Meyer, G. J., Finn, S. E., Eyde, L., Kay, G. G., Moreland, K. L., Dies, R. R., et al. (2001). Psychological testing and psychological assessment: A review of evidence and issues. *American Psychologist, 56*, 128–165.

Mroczek, D. K., & Kolarz, C. M. (1998). The effect of age on positive and negative affect: A developmental perspective on happiness. *Journal of Personality and Social Psychology, 75*, 1333–1349.

Mroczek, D. K., & Spiro, A., III. (2003). Modeling intraindividual change in personality traits: Findings from the normative aging study. *Journals of Gerontology: Psychological Sciences, 58B*, 153–165.

Mroczek, D. K., & Spiro, A., III. (2005). Change in life satisfaction over 20 years during adulthood: Findings from the VA normative aging study. *Journal of Personality and Social Psychology, 88*, 189–202.

Mroczek, D. K., & Spiro, A. (2007). Personality change influences mortality in older men. *Psychological Science, 18*, 371–376.

Mroczek, D. K., Stawski, R. S., Turiano, N. A., Chan, W., Almeida, D. M., Neupert, S. N., et al. (2013). Emotional reactivity predicts mortality: Longitudinal findings from the VA normative aging study. *Journal of Gerontology: Psychological Sciences*. [Epub ahead of print].

Mullet, E., Neto, F., & Rivière, S. (2005). Personality and its effects on resentment, revenge, forgiveness and on self-forgiveness. In E. L. Worthington, Jr. (Ed.), *Handbook of forgiveness* (pp. 159–182). New York: Brunner-Routledge.

Neyer, F. J., & Lehnart, J. (2007). Relationships matter in personality development: Evidence from an 8-year longitudinal study across young adulthood. *Journal of Personality, 75*, 535–567.

Chapter 13

Statistical Models for Analyzing Stability and Change in Happiness

Michael Eid and Tanja Kutscher
Freie Universität Berlin, Berlin, Germany

Can happiness change? From a statistical point of view, this question can be answered only by measuring happiness repeatedly. When happiness is measured at least twice, it is very likely that the scores do not remain stable. But does the change of a happiness score indicate that happiness has changed? To give an answer to this question, we first introduce a state-trait theory of happiness as a meaningful conceptual framework. In a state-trait theory of happiness, three measures of happiness can be considered:

1. *The momentary measurement of happiness.* This characterizes the happiness state.
2. *The average level of happiness.* This assesses the habitual happiness that is also called the happiness trait or set point.
3. *The deviation of the momentary measurement from the average level.* This deviation represents influences due to the situation and/or the person-situation interaction on an occasion of measurement. If the deviation score is 0, that means that the momentary state does not deviate from the habitual level. If the score is positive, the momentary happiness is higher than a person typically feels. If the score is negative, the individual is unhappier than usual.

In this theoretical framework, two types of change can be distinguished: variability and change (Nesselroade, 1991; Nesselroade & Ram, 2004). *Variability* (also called *state variability*) characterizes the fluctuations of the happiness states around the happiness trait. Beside these short-time, reversible changes, there might be more enduring changes, changes that are more long lasting and that are not due to short-term influences such as having a nice conversation, a great exam, or a wonderful day. These more long-lasting changes are changes on the trait level, the average level. For example, after a critical life event such as the death of a spouse, the average happiness level might change. This type of change is simply called *change* (Nesselroade, 1991). To distinguish this type of change better from variability, which is also a type of change, we could also call it *change in a narrow sense* or *trait change*. For example, the question whether a happiness set point is a fixed constant for each individual or whether it changes over the life course concerns trait change and not state variability. To separate the two types of change, we have to consider different periods of time. Within a period, which is characterized by trait stability, state variability can be analyzed. Between periods, trait change can be scrutinized. There are two problems that have to be solved:

1. What is an appropriate period of time for measuring a habitual happiness level (trait)? Happiness can be repeatedly measured within a workday and within a weekend day, and it is likely that the two mean scores will be different for many individuals. Happiness can be repeatedly measured in a week before an exam and a holiday week at the beach, and it is likely that the average scores will be different. Happiness can be measured in the periods of childhood, adolescence, and adulthood and can be aggregated within each period. The average levels will differ between the different developmental stages. A happiness score could also be measured for the whole life. For analyzing change on the habitual level, we need to define the habitual score in a clear way and to select an appropriate period of time.

2. Is it reasonable to assume that there is a stable trait score within a period of time? Is the aggregation of scores reasonable? Calculating the average score of repeated measures within a period of time makes sense only if the happiness state scores randomly fluctuate around a person-specific level. Statistically speaking, the state scores have to be sampled from the same individual-specific distribution that is characterized by the same expected value. Then it makes sense to aggregate the individual state scores to get an estimate of the happiness trait. However, due to critical life events, the expected value of the individual state distribution could change. In statistical terms, the change of the expected value of the state distribution would indicate trait change. To aggregate state values, we have to test the assumption of the existence of a stable, nonchanging individual trait score (expected value of the state distribution). For testing this assumption, we need statistical models.

Statistical models are also needed for another reason. If we measure happiness with psychometric measures, we have to deal with another source of change: measurement error. Measurement error cannot be avoided in the empirical sciences. In contrast to state change and trait change, it is a form of unsystematic change. If we do not correct for measurement error, systematic change might be overestimated. Moreover, measurement error can produce some statistical artifacts in longitudinal data analysis such as the regression toward the mean and an artificial correlation between change and baseline scores (Rogosa, 1995). Consequently, statistical models are needed that are able to separate three types of change:

1. Unsystematic variability that is due to measurement error
2. Systematic state variability that is due to situational influences and the interaction between the person and the situation
3. Systematic trait change that can be due to events, maturation, and other reasons

DIRECT VERSUS INDIRECT ASSESSMENT

There are two different ways to assess the habitual mood level and the different types of change: the indirect and the direct approach (Eid, Schneider, & Schwenkmezger, 1999; Greenhoot, 2012). The *indirect approach* requires the repeated assessment of the *momentary* happiness of an individual. For example, we have to ask questions like "How happy are you?" or "How happy are you at the moment?" Then we can analyze the different types of change by using psychometric models presented in the following sections. According to the *direct approach*, individuals are asked to assess the different components of a state-trait model and the amount of change directly (see, e.g., Eid et al., 1999). For example, people can be asked to judge their habitual happiness level ("How happy are you in general?"), the momentary deviations of their happiness ("In the moment, are you happier, equally as happy, or less happy than you are in general?"), and change ("Compared to the year of the death of your spouse, how has your happiness been during the past year?"). Often, there are not such pure direct assessments. For example, in many panel studies individuals are asked to rate their happiness during the last 4 weeks, and then change is measured by indirect methods. If the happiness rating covers a longer period, the change measured by the indirect method of change would capture more trait change than state variability.

INDIVIDUAL CHANGE VERSUS MEAN CHANGE

To isolate the three different types of change (measurement error, state variability, trait change), we generally need to have (1) multiple indicators of a construct to separate unsystematic measurement error from the other types of change, (2) a design with multiple short-term measurements within a period of time to assess state variability, and (3) several periods of time with larger time lags between the periods to capture trait change. Usually, longitudinal designs for analyzing change do not follow this type of design. In large-scale panel studies, there are often single-item

measures assessed on equally spaced time lags, usually with a comparatively long time lag such as a year. Often the momentary state, e.g.,
momentary life satisfaction, is assessed (a typical panel item assesses the
"life satisfaction these days"; for an overview, see Fleurbaey & Blanchet,
2013). Therefore, an individual change score can confound all three
different types of change. Nevertheless, these studies have been used to
analyze the amount of trait change, for example, caused by life events
such as unemployment, widowhood, or divorce (e.g., Lucas, 2007;
Luhmann, & Eid, 2009). These studies show that life events can have an
important influence on subjective well-being such as a longer-lasting
decline of life satisfaction after negative events (e.g., widowhood or disability). Do these differences indicate that there is trait change and not
only situational variability or measurement error? Whereas it is harder to
separate the three different sources of change on the level of individual
scores, the conclusions drawn on level of the mean change scores (mean
across all individuals) are more valid. If measurement error and state
variability are fluctuations with random ups and downs, they should be
eliminated by aggregating across individuals. If the mean scores across all
individuals experiencing the same event change over time, this is a strong
hint that there are trait changes on the mean level (not necessarily on all
individual levels). Moreover, if there is a systematic change of the repeatedly measured scores of one individual in one direction over time, it is
also likely that this is not only change caused by measurement error and
occasion-specific variability. Statistical models fitting individual curves to
change like growth curve models might help to see whether there is also a
tendency of trait change underlying the changes of observed individual
scores. Hence, the distinction between intra-individual variability and
change, on the one hand, and mean variability and change, on the other
hand, is important.

OVERVIEW

In the following, we present models that are appropriate to separate the three
sources of change on the basis of repeated state measurements. We start with
basic models for analyzing change such as the latent state model, the latent
change model, and the latent autoregressive model. These models are appropriate to analyze change processes in general, but they do not distinguish
between state variability and trait change. Therefore, we also present latent
state-trait models and latent state-trait change models that allow us to measure the different types of change. For all models, we discuss issues of measurement invariance across time. Finally, we illustrate the application of
these models to panel data modeling the influence of life events on affective
well-being.

PSYCHOMETRIC MODELS FOR ANALYZING VARIABILITY AND CHANGE

Basic Model: Latent State Model

A starting general model for measuring change is the latent state model. In this model, it is assumed that all indicators on an occasion of measurement measure the same common latent state variable. The common state variable represents the true individual differences on an occasion of measurement. If i is an index for an indicator and k for an occasion of measurement, the model can be formulated in the following way:

$$Y_{ik} = \alpha_{ik} + \lambda_{ik}S_k + E_{ik} \tag{13.1}$$

Y_{ik} indicates an observed variable, S_k is a latent state variable, E_{ik} is a measurement error variable, α_{ik} is an intercept, and λ_{ik} is a loading parameter. Moreover, it is assumed that the error variables are all uncorrelated. A model for three indicators and four occasions of measurement is presented in Figure 13.1.

The correlations of the latent state variables are latent stability coefficients. High correlations indicate that there are small inter-individual differences in intra-individual change. Even if the latent retest correlations are perfect, this does not necessarily mean that there is no change. If all individuals change in the same way on the latent level, the latent retest correlation will be perfect. In this case, the change of the latent expected values (mean values) $E(S_k)$ would be equal to the individual change values.

The latent state model often does not fit the data. The major source of misfit is the assumption that all indicators are homogeneous with respect to the latent state variables. Longitudinal data analyses allow identifying the indicator-specific component of an indicator. An indicator-specific component is a part of the true state score of an indicator that is not shared with the other indicators. This indicator-specific component can be represented by an

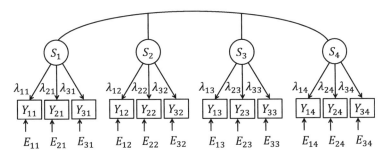

FIGURE 13.1   Latent state model for three indicators and four occasions of measurement.
Y_{ik}: observed variables; S_k: latent state variables; E_{ik}: measurement error variables; λ_{ik}: loadings; i: indicators; k: occasions of measurement.

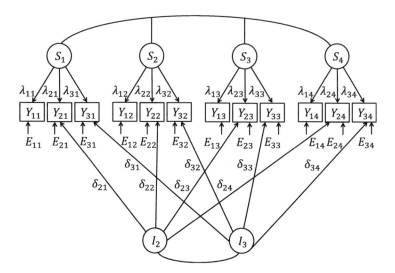

FIGURE 13.2 Latent state model with indicator-specific factors for three indicators and four occasions of measurement. Y_{ik}: observed variables; S_k: latent state variables; E_{ik}: measurement error variables; I_i: indicator-specific factors; λ_{ik}, δ_{ik}: loadings; i: indicators; k: occasions of measurement.

indicator-specific latent variable. Eid et al. (1999) and Geiser and Lockhart (2012) showed that it is sufficient to consider $m-1$ indicator-specific factors I_i, where m is the number of indicators. Figure 13.2 presents such a model. An indicator-specific factor is stable over time. In the model in Figure 13.2, the first indicator does not have an indicator-specific factor. That means that the latent state variable S_k is the true state variable of the first indicator. The indicator-specific factors of the other indicators represent that part of the indicator that cannot be predicted by the reference indicator and is therefore not shared with the reference indicator. The correlations of the indicator-specific factors are allowed so that two indicators can share an indicator-specific part that is not shared with the reference indicator. If the first indicator is taken as reference indicator, the model can be defined by

$$Y_{ik} = \alpha_{ik} + \lambda_{ik}S_k + E_{ik}, \text{ for } i = 1 \tag{13.2}$$

$$Y_{ik} = \alpha_{ik} + \lambda_{ik}S_k + \delta_{ik}I_i + E_{ik}, \text{ for } i \neq 1 \tag{13.3}$$

The expected values (mean values) of all factors I_i and E_{ik} have to be equal to 0, because the variables are residual variables. The proportion of variance of an observed variable that is determined by the common latent variables (S_k, I_i) is the reliability coefficient. The proportion of variance of an observed variable that is explained by an indicator-specific factor I_i alone is the indicator specificity coefficient.

For identification reasons, the following restrictions have to be made:

1. For each latent state variable, one loading parameter λ_{ik} has to be fixed to a value larger than 0 (typically 1), or the variance $Var(S_k)$ of the factor has to be fixed to a value larger than 0 (typically 1).
2. For each latent state variable, one intercept α_{ik} has to be fixed to a value (typically 0), or the expected value of the latent state variable has to be fixed to a value (typically 0).
3. For each indicator-specific factor, one loading parameter δ_{ik} has to be fixed to a value larger than 0 (typically 1). If there are only two occasions of measurement, all factor loadings have to be fixed to a value larger than 0 (typically 1).

Measurement Invariance

In longitudinal data analysis, measurement invariance plays an important role. Measurement invariance means that the same construct is measured over time. This is, for example, a prerequisite for comparing mean values over time. We explain the basic principles of measurement invariance with respect to the latent state model. There are different degrees of measurement invariance (Meredith, 1993; Millsap, 2011):

1. *Configural invariance* means that the number of factors and the general loading structure do not change over time. Configural invariance is assumed in the latent state model because there is only one latent state variable on each occasion of measurement. The assumption of configural invariance will be violated if there is a differentiation on the factorial level. For example, configural invariance will be violated if there is only one latent state variable measuring positive versus negative affect on one occasion of measurement and two latent state variables, one of them measuring positive affect and the other one negative affect on another occasion of measurement.
2. *Weak measurement invariance* requires in addition to configural invariance that the factor loadings belonging to the same observed variable do not change over time, i.e., $\lambda_{ik} = \lambda_i$.
3. According to *strong measurement invariance*, the factor loadings and the intercepts belonging to the same observed variable do not change over time: $\lambda_{ik} = \lambda_i$ and $\alpha_{ik} = \alpha_i$. This type of invariance is also called *scalar invariance*.
4. *Strict measurement variance* assumes that in addition to strong measurement invariance the variance of an error variable does not change over time: $Var(E_{ik}) = Var(E_i)$.

From a psychometric point of view, strong measurement invariance is sufficient for ensuring that the same construct is measured over time. To implement the restrictions of strict measurement variance, we have to consider the following aspects:

1. If, for identification reasons, one intercept and one loading per factor have been fixed, the means and the variances of the latent state variables have to be freely estimated over time. In computer programs for structural equation modeling, the means of the latent variables are fixed to 0 by default. This fixation has to be removed for the latent state variables (but never for the indicator-specific factors).
2. If, for identification reasons, the means and the variances of the latent variables have been fixed, these fixations have to be removed for all latent variables with the exception of one, usually the latent variable on the first occasion of measurement. If these fixations are not removed, we would test not only the assumption of strong measurement invariance but also the assumption that the means and variances of the latent variables do not change over time.

In a latent state model with indicator-specific factors, we would in addition expect that the loadings on the indicator-specific factors do not change over time.

Ordinal Observed Variables

The models described so far are based on a linear decomposition of an observed variable. Such a linear decomposition makes sense for continuous observed variables but is less reasonable for observed variables with ordered response categories such as rating scales. For these types of observed variables, the latent state model can be formulated as a model of confirmatory factor analysis for observed variables with ordered response categories. This model is based on the assumption that there is an underlying continuous variable Y_{ik}^* for each observed categorical variable Y_{ik}. The two variables Y_{ik} and Y_{ik}^* are linked by the following threshold relationship (Eid, 1996; Millsap & Yun-Tein, 2004; Muthén, 1984):

$$Y_{ik} = 0, \text{ if } Y_{ik}^* \leq \kappa_{i1k}$$

$$Y_{ik} = s, \text{ if } \kappa_{isk} < Y_{ik}^* \leq \kappa_{i(s+1)k}, \text{ for } 0 < s < w - 1$$

$$Y_{ik} = w - 1, \text{if } \kappa_{i(w-1)k} < Y_{ik}^*$$

The parameters κ_{isk} are threshold parameters that divide the continuous variable Y_{ik}^* into w categories. For reasons of simplicity of notation, we assume that all items have the same number of categories and that the number of categories does not change over time. However, the model would allow that the number of categories can differ between items. It is usually assumed that the variables Y_{ik}^* are normally distributed. Then their correlations are the polychoric correlations. The variables Y_{ik}^* can be decomposed in the same way as the variables Y_{ik} in the models for continuous observed variables. For example, a latent state model with indicator-specific factors can be defined in the following way:

$$Y_{ik}^* = \alpha_{ik} + \lambda_{ik}S_k + E_{ik}, \quad \text{for } i = 1 \tag{13.4}$$

$$Y_{ik}^* = \alpha_{ik} + \lambda_{ik}S_k + \delta_{ik}I_i + E_{ik}, \quad \text{for } i \neq 1 \tag{13.5}$$

Strong measurement invariance requires that the following assumptions are fulfilled (Millsap & Yun-Tein, 2004):

1. The threshold parameters κ_{isk} do not differ between occasions of measurement.
2. The factor loadings λ_{ik} and δ_{ik} do not differ between occasions of measurement.
3. The variances $Var\ (E_{ik})$ do not differ between occasions of measurement.

For identification reasons, the following restrictions have to be made:

1. All intercepts α_{ik} have to be fixed to 0.
2. For each factor, one loading parameter has to be fixed to a value larger than 0 (usually 1).
3. The variances $Var\ (E_{ik})$ of the error variables have to be fixed to a value larger than 0 (usually 1).
4. On one occasion of measurement (usually the first one), the expected value of the latent state variable has to be fixed to a value (usually 0), whereas on all other occasions of measurement, the expected values of the state variables are not restricted and can be estimated.
5. The expected value of the indicator-specific factor equals 0.

Partial Measurement Invariance and Approximate Measurement Invariance

The assumption of strong measurement invariance might not be fulfilled in all longitudinal studies. This assumption could be relaxed to obtain partial measurement invariance. Partial measurement invariance is given when at least the loadings and intercepts of two indicators for each latent variable do not change over time (Byrne, Shavelson, & Muthén, 1989; Steenkamp & Baumgartner, 1998). If this is the case, the meaning of the latent variables is defined by the invariant indicators. If even partial measurement variance is not fulfilled, the question arises whether the violation of the assumption of measurement invariance is so strong that the comparison of means and the interpretation of latent difference scores would not be reasonable. Van de Schoot et al. (2013) discussed this issue in detail and showed how Bayesian structural equation modeling can be used to test assumptions about

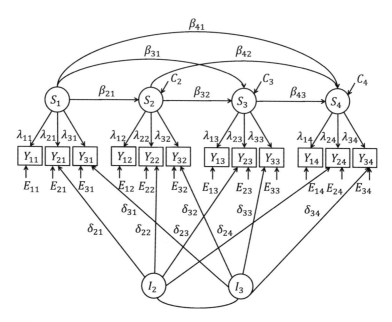

FIGURE 13.4 Latent third-order autoregressive model with indicator-specific factors for three indicators and four occasions of measurement. Y_{ik}: observed variables; S_k: latent state variables; C_k: latent residual variables representing change; E_{ik}: measurement error variables; λ_{ik}: loadings; $\beta_{k(k-1)}$: autoregressive parameters; i: indicators; k: occasions of measurement.

habitual happiness level, or the happiness set point. An extension of the latent state model of Figure 13.2 to a latent state-trait model is shown in Figure 13.5. Formally, this model is defined by the additional equation (Steyer, Schmitt, & Eid, 1999):

$$S_k = \beta_k + \gamma_k T + \zeta_k \qquad (13.8)$$

In this model, a latent state variable is decomposed into a linear function of a latent trait variable T and a latent residual variable ζ_k. The latent trait variable T does not have an index and is time invariant. It does not change over time and characterizes the stable happiness component (disposition, set point, etc.). The residual variable ζ_k represents that part of a latent state variable S_k on occasion k of measurement that is not predictable by the latent trait variable T. This part is due to the influences of the situations that individuals are in and/or the interaction between the situation and the person. The model is based on the idea of *inner* situations that are specific for an occasion of measurement. Although individuals might be in the same outer situation, their inner situation could be quite different depending on what they have experienced before or in the moment of measurement.

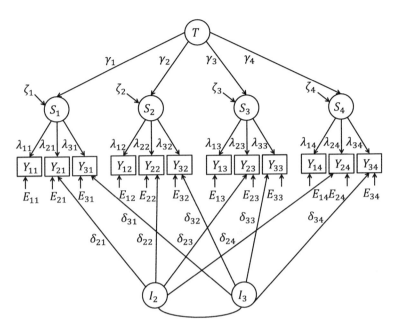

FIGURE 13.5   Latent state-trait model with indicator-specific factors for three indicators and four occasions of measurement. Y_{ik}: observed variables; S_k: latent state variables; T: latent trait variable; ζ_k: latent occasion-specific residuals; E_{ik}: measurement error variables; I_i: indicator-specific factors; λ_{ik}, δ_{ik}, γ_k: loadings; i: indicators; k: occasions of measurement.

Measurement Invariance

Strong measurement invariance requires, in addition to the restriction concerning the latent state variables, that the intercepts and the loadings in Equation 13.8 do not change over time (Geiser et al., in press). For identification reasons, the following restrictions have to be made:

One trait factor loading γ_k has to be fixed to a value larger than 0 (usually 1), or the variance of the trait factor has to be fixed to a value larger than 0 (usually 1).

One intercept β_k has to be fixed (usually to the value 0), or the expected value (mean) of the trait factor has to be fixed (usually to the value 0).

If one assumes strong measurement invariance and fixes the factor loadings to 1 and the intercepts to 0, then Equation 13.8 simplifies to

$$S_k = T + \zeta_k \tag{13.9}$$

In this case, the expected value $E(T)$ of the trait factor can be estimated, whereas the expected values of the residual variables ζ_k always have to be 0 because these are residual factors (Steyer, Ferring, & Schmitt, 1992). Strong measurement invariance is necessary to make sure that the change of the state variables indicates state variability and not trait change (see Geiser et al., in press, for a deeper discussion). As a consequence of strong measurement invariance, the expected values of the state variables do not change over time. Because of Equation 13.9, the expected values of all latent state variables equal the expected value of the latent trait variable: $E(S_k) = E(T)$. If this assumption does not hold in an empirical application, then there will not (only) be a variability process but in addition change due to trait change.

Consistency and Occasion Specificity

According to Equation 13.8, the variance of a latent state variable can be decomposed in the following way: $Var(S_k) = \gamma_k^2 Var(T) + Var(\zeta_k)$. That part of the variance of a latent state variable that is due to the latent trait variable is called the consistency coefficient:

$$Con(S_k) = \frac{\gamma_k^2 Var(T)}{Var(S_k)} \tag{13.10}$$

It indicates the degree of latent stability. Its counterpart, the occasion-specificity coefficient,

$$Spe(S_k) = \frac{Var(\zeta_k)}{Var(S_k)} \tag{13.11}$$

represents that part of the variance of a latent state variable that is due to occasion-specific influences (variability). Both coefficients add up to 1.

Latent State-Trait Autoregressive Model

According to the latent state-trait model, state scores randomly fluctuate around a trait score. There is no carryover effect on the level of the occasion-specific variables ζ_k. Often, however, there is an inertia in the process, and the process is not like a random up and down. Instead, there is a carryover effect between occasions of measurement, particularly if there is a short lag between two adjacent occasions of measurement. If, for example, in one occasion of measurement, the latent happiness state value is higher than the trait value because of a positive event, it is likely that the latent state value will also be higher than the trait value on the next occasion of measurement because the event will still have a positive effect. This inertia is considered by a first-order autoregressive structure on the level of the latent occasion specific residual variables (see Figure 13.6) (Cole, Martin, & Steiger, 2005):

$$\zeta_k = \beta_{k(k-1)}\zeta_{k-1} + \psi_k \tag{13.12}$$

If the autoregressive parameters $\beta_{k(k-1)}$ equal 0, a latent state-trait model (without autoregressive process) holds. The larger the autoregressive parameter $\beta_{k(k-1)}$, the stronger is the inertia. The variables ψ_k are latent residuals representing that part of a latent state variable ζ_k that is unpredictable within

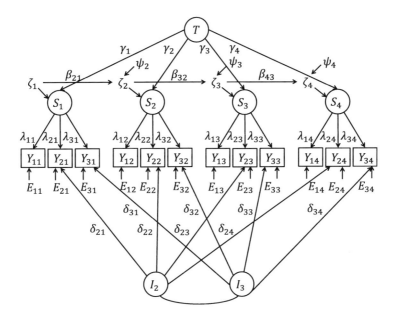

FIGURE 13.6 Latent autoregressive state-trait model with indicator-specific factors for three indicators and four occasions of measurement. Y_{ik}: observed variables; S_k: latent state variables; T: latent trait variable; ζ_k: latent occasion-specific residuals; ψ_k: latent residuals; E_{ik}: measurement error variables; I_i: indicator-specific factors; λ_{ik}, δ_{ik}, γ_k: loadings; $\beta_{k(k-1)}$: autoregressive parameters; i: indicators; k: occasions of measurement.

the model. Usually, it is assumed that the autoregressive process is time invariant, and the autoregressive parameters do not change over time.

Latent State-Trait Change Models

The latent state-trait models presented so far assume that there is no change on the level of the trait variables. To consider trait change in addition to state variability, we can extend the models. Two types of trait change can be distinguished: continuous and discontinuous. Continuous trait change can be characterized as a change process that follows a specific function of time—for example, a linear or curvilinear growth or decline over time. Developmental processes are typically characterized by such a process. In discontinuous change models, trait change does not follow a continuous function. For example, trait scores could be different in different periods of one's life due to life events or interventions. Happiness could suddenly decrease after an accident, and trait happiness could be on different levels in time periods before and after the accident. Both types of change could also be combined—for example, in models with continuous change within time periods but stepwise trait change between periods of time.

Latent State-Trait Change Models: Continuous Trait Change

An example of a latent state-trait continuous trait change model with indicator-specific factors is the latent autoregressive state-trait growth curve model (Eid, Courvoisier, & Lischetzke, 2012). Such a model with linear growth is depicted in Figure 13.7. In this model, a common latent state variable is decomposed in the following way:

$$S_k = I + \gamma_k G + \zeta_k \tag{13.13}$$

with $\gamma_k = k - 1$. The common factor I is the intercept factor. The values of the intercept factor are the latent individual trait values on the first occasion of measurement. The values of the common G factor are the individual slopes. These individual slopes represent the individual growth rates. The loadings on the growth factor have fixed values. The loading on the first occasion of measurement is $\gamma_1 = 0$, the loading on the second occasion of measurement is $\gamma_2 = 1$, etc. The values of the occasion-specific residual variables ζ_k are the deviations of the individual state scores from the growth line indicating trait change (see Eid et al., 2012). This model allows the

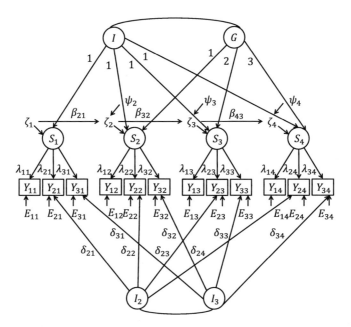

FIGURE 13.7   Latent autoregressive state-trait continuous trait change model with indicator-specific factors for three indicators and four occasions of measurement. Y_{ik}: observed variables; S_k: latent state variables; I: latent intercept variable; G: latent growth variable; ζ_k: latent occasion-specific residuals; ψ_k: latent residual; E_{ik}: measurement error variables; I_i: indicator-specific factors; λ_{ik}, δ_{ik}: loadings; $\beta_{k(k-1)}$: autoregressive parameters; i: indicators; k: occasions of measurement.

measurement of four types of change: (1) trait change characterized by the growth line, (2) state variability represented by the fluctuations of the occasion-specific residuals around the growth line, (3) inertia indicated by the autoregressive parameters on the level of the occasion-specific residuals, and (4) unsystematic variability due to measurement error. This model can easily be extended to a model with curvilinear change by adding further latent variables.

Latent State-Trait Change Models: Discontinuous Trait Change

A latent state-trait model with a discontinuous change process is depicted in Figure 13.8 for two time periods. It is a combination of two different latent state-trait models, one for each time period. Within each period of time, a latent state-trait model is defined, and the two latent trait variables are allowed to be correlated as well as the different indicator-specific factors. The correlation of the latent trait variables could also be represented by an autoregressive process. It is also possible to define a latent trait change variable as the difference between two adjacent trait variables. In this latent state-trait discontinuous trait change model, measurement invariance can be assumed by fixing the intercepts and loadings over the whole study period as explained for the latent state-trait model previously. It can easily be extended to more than two periods of time.

Latent State-Trait Change Models: Continuous and Discontinuous Trait Change

A latent state-trait model with continuous and discontinuous change can be defined by combining different latent state-trait continuous trait change models. It looks like the model in Figure 13.8 but with additional growth factors within each period of time. The intercept and growth factors are allowed to be correlated over the periods of time.

LST Mixture Models

The models presented so far assume that the model parameters are the same for all individuals of the population. However, this is a strong assumption. The degree of stability and variability might be different between subpopulations, and there might be individuals being more or less stable. Moreover, the influence of situational covariates on happiness might be different for different individuals because not all individuals might react to events in the same way. That means that individuals might differ in the link between happiness and events that is represented by differences in the regression parameters. To consider heterogeneity of the population with respect to the parameters of change models, we can extend the models to mixture

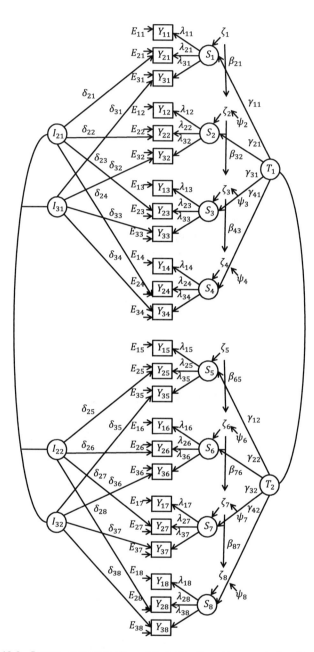

FIGURE 13.8 Latent autoregressive state-trait discontinuous trait change model with indicator-specific factors for three indicators and four occasions of measurement. Y_{ik}: observed variables; S_k: latent state variables; T_1, T_2: latent trait variables; ζ_k: latent occasion-specific residuals; ψ_k: latent residuals; E_{ik}: measurement error variables; I_i: indicator-specific factors; λ_{ik}, δ_{ik}, γ_{kl}: loadings; $\beta_{k(k-1)}$: autoregressive parameters; i: indicators; k: occasions of measurement; l: period of time.

distribution models. For example, Courvoisier, Eid, and Nussbeck (2007) showed how the latent state-trait model can be extended to a mixture distribution model. Using this model, they detected two subgroups differing in the variability and stability and differing in the influence that daily events have on momentary mood. All other models presented so far can be extended to mixture distribution models.

Choice of a Model

The latent state, change, and autoregressive models are general models that can be applied in all longitudinal studies. The choice of one of the three models depends on the research question. If the research interest is in estimating the degree of stability of happiness, the latent state model will be appropriate. If one is interested in analyzing change, the latent change and the latent autoregressive model can be chosen. If one wants to consider a change variable that is the difference between two states and that is, therefore, not independent from the baseline state measurement, the latent change model is appropriate. If one wants to measure influences on a latent state variable by correcting for all influences of previous states, the autoregressive models are appropriate.

The latent state-trait models are more restrictive than the latent state, change, and autoregressive models because the latent trait and growth factors restrict the covariances of the latent state variables. The latent state-trait (change) models assume that there is either a stable trait variable or a systematic change on the latent trait level. To separate the different types of change, we need specific research designs. For example, there should be periods with small time lags in order to estimate the degree of state variability and the influence of situational factors causing state variability. On the other hand, there should be time lags between the time periods that are large enough that trait change can happen. However, these research designs are seldom realized, and we do not know any application of the general model in long-term studies on subjective well-being. There are many applications of the latent state-trait model (for an overview, see Geiser & Lockhart, 2012), but only very few applications of latent state-trait change models. For example, Eid and Hoffmann (1998) applied this model in educational psychology in order to see in which way the Chernobyl disaster might have caused trait change in interests in physics. Eid et al. (2012) applied latent state-trait change models to ambulatory assessment data analyzing the change of day-specific levels in mood between days. Long-term studies on SWB, however, often have a different design.

Application of the Models in Long-Term Panel Studies

In panel studies, individuals are often assessed over many years but with a rather long time lag of one year between the repeated measurements. The application of the models presented so far in these contexts might cause some conceptual problems:

1. It is unlikely that there is no trait change because over many years many events happen and developmental processes occur that would cause trait change. Hence, it is questionable whether the assumption of a stable trait variable over the whole time period is reasonable. If one assumes a time-stable latent variable in this research context, the meaning of such a time-stable variable should be clarified. One might interpret this time-invariant latent variable as a variable representing the influences of factors that do not change over time (e.g., genetic influences).

2. Because it is reasonable that trait change occurs, the modeling of trait change in this research context might not be an easy task. One problem is that the timing of trait change is individual specific. Because life events occur at different time points for different individuals, there can not be a general trait change model for all participants, but also mixture distribution models might not be able to handle this problem because they require that the different change processes that are assumed for different subgroups have to be specified, and there might be too many individual patterns of trait change.

3. To analyze trait change due to a specific event, one can select participants experiencing this event somewhere along their path of life and can structure the data by centering the time points around this event. This way of analyzing the data is reasonable for learning more about the specific effects of an event, and special models of multilevel data can be applied (see, e.g., Lucas, 2007; Luhmann & Eid, 2012). One might also think about the application of latent state-trait change models with continuous and discontinuous trait change to analyze the effect of life events. There could be one period before and one period after the event happened. However, for understanding the stability and change of happiness in individual lives in general, this approach is restricted in two ways. First, it does not consider that there are usually multiple events happening in one's life (e.g., marriage, birth of a child, unemployment). Second, participants not experiencing an event are excluded from the analyses.

How can these problems be solved in long-term studies with almost equally spaced time points? One solution could be not to assume a time-invariant latent trait variable and just define a model with specific latent state variables for each occasion of measurement or consider latent change or latent autoregressive models. Moreover, the occurrence of multiple events can be represented by dummy variables, and they can be included with other covariates of change in the model. We illustrate such an approach in the next section.

Predicting and Explaining Change

To predict change, one can include covariates in the different models. The covariates can be observed or latent variables. Moreover, the same covariate can have an influence on several dependent variables, and the covariates can be correlated. We illustrate models with life events as covariates.

Application

We illustrate the models with an application to two items selected from the Household, Income, and Labour Dynamics in Australia (HILDA) Survey, a representative Australian panel study that started in 2001 (http://www.mel-bourneinstitute.com/hilda/). We use data from the first four waves (2001, 2002, 2003, 2004). Because the application of the models requires at least two indicators measuring the same construct, we selected the two items of an affective well-being scale that seemed to fulfill this requirement. The items were

1. Have you felt down? (Item 1 in the analyses)
2. Have you felt so down in the dumps that nothing could cheer you up? (Item 2 in the analyses)

The participants answered these questions on a six-point rating scale (response categories: 1-all of the time, 2-most of the time, 3-a good bit of the time, 4-some of the time, 5-a little of the time, 6-none of the time). The data were analyzed with the computer program Mplus version 7.11 (Muthén & Muthén, 1998–2013). The items were considered as categorical, and all applications presented refer to factor models for observed variables with ordered response categories. To analyze the data appropriately, we used the estimator WLSMV and the THETA parameterization. In addition, two life events were included as covariates: (1) death of a close relative/family member during the past year and (2) serious personal injury/illness during the past year. Data from the second to fourth waves were included in order to analyze change in negative affect. The total sample size was $N = 15,838$.

Results

The results of the different analyses are reported in Table 13.1. The first model is a latent state model for the two indicators measured on the four occasions of measurement. The fit coefficients indicate that the hypotheses of perfect fit (χ^2-test) and approximate fit (RMSEA) have to be rejected, although the CFI shows that the comparative fit of the model is very good. To test the assumption that the misfit is due to the heterogeneity of the items, we specified an indicator-specific factor for the second indicator. This model (Model 2) fits the data very well and has not been rejected ($\chi^2 = 15.525$,

TABLE 13.1 Goodness-of-Fit Coefficients for the Different Models Analyzing Change

	Model	χ^2-Value (df)	p-Value	RMSEA	p-Value	CFI	χ^2-Difference Test (df) p-Value
1	Latent state model	737.965 (14)	<0.001	0.057	<0.001	0.994	
2	Latent state model with indicator-specific factor	15.525 (10)	0.114	0.006	1.000	1.000	
3	Latent state model with indicator-specific factor (strong measurement invariance)	79.010 (43)	0.001	0.007	1.000	1.000	Model 3 vs. Model 2: 63.790 (33) 0.001
4	Latent state model with indicator-specific factor (strong measurement invariance with the exception of the first loading on the indicator-specific factor)	60.738 (42)	0.031	0.005	1.000	1.000	Model 4 vs. Model 2: 46.468 (32) 0.047
5	Model 4 with measurement invariant latent trait variable (latent state-trait model)	234.154 (50)	<0.001	0.015	1.000	0.998	

6	Model 4 with measurement invariant latent trait variable and time-invariant autoregressive effects (time-invariant autoregressive latent state-trait model)	121.178 (49)	<0.001	0.010	1.000	0.999
7	Model 6 with measurement invariant latent linear growth curve structure (time-invariant autoregressive latent state-trait growth model)	81.034 (46)	0.001	0.007	1.000	1.000
8	Model 4 with event dummy variables	60.578 (60)	0.455	0.001	1.000	1.000

Note: df: degrees of freedom; RMSEA: Root mean square error of approximation; CFI: Comparative fit index.

TABLE 13.2 (Continued)

Variances (Diagonal), Covariances (Lower Triangle), and Correlations (Upper Triangle) and Means of the Latent Variables

	S_1	S_2	S_3	S_4	I	Means (unstandardized)	Means (standardized)
S_1	4.274	0.635	0.602	0.574	0	0	0
S_2	2.648	4.065	0.685	0.631	0	0.067	0.033
S_3	2.539	2.819	4.163	0.682	0	0.110	0.054
S_4	2.408	2.580	2.821	4.111	0	0.108	0.053
I	0	0	0	0	0.767	0	0

Note: All estimated parameters are significantly different from 0 ($p < 0.01$).

present their fit coefficients in Table 13.1. The application of the autoregressive model showed that all regression coefficients are significantly different from 0, meaning that we need an autoregressive model of the highest order.

In the next step, we tested the assumption that the stability of the latent states can be explained by the existence of a time-invariant latent trait variable. Although the approximate fit of this latent state-trait model is quite good (Model 5), the model shows a significant misfit according to the χ^2-test. Moreover, the χ^2-value is much higher than the χ^2-value of the less restrictive Model 4. The fit of both models, however, cannot be compared by an χ^2-difference test because Model 4 is a special case of Model 5 in which the variance of the trait factor is fixed to 0. A value of 0, however, is a boundary value for a variance, and in such a case, the χ^2-difference test is not admissible (Stoel, Galindo-Garre, Dolan, & van den Wittenboer, 2006). One reason for the misfit of Model 5 is that the mean values of the latent state variables differ between the occasions of measurement, showing that change cannot be explained by a pure variability process. Adding a time-homogeneous first-order autoregressive structure on the occasion-specific residuals does not result in a fitting model (Model 6), which is also the case for a model allowing the autoregressive process to be time homogeneous. Adding a growth factor (Model 7) results in an improvement of fit and a generally well-fitting model. If one compares the fit of Model 4 with Model 7, the fit of Model 4 still seems to be superior. Moreover, the variance of the growth factor is not significantly different from 0, indicating that individuals do not differ in the growth curve. The mean value of the growth factor is positive (0.036) and significantly different from 0, showing that the misfit of the latent state-trait model is mainly due to the change of the means of the latent state variables. Because of the better fit of Model 4 and the nonsignificant variance of the growth factor, we chose Model 4 for including event variables.

MODELS WITH LIFE EVENTS

In Model 8, the event dummy variables were included into Model 4. The following dummy variables were included:

1. Death (t_2): Death event occurring between the first and second occasions of measurement
2. Death (t_3): Death event occurring between the second and third occasions of measurement
3. Death (t_4): Death event occurring between the third and fourth occasions of measurement
4. Illness (t_2): Illness event occurring between the first and second occasions of measurement

5. **Illness** (t_3): Illness event occurring between the second and third occasions of measurement
6. **Illness** (t_4): Illness event occurring between the third and fourth occasions of measurement

The four latent state variables and the indicator-specific factor were regressed on all dummy variables. Therefore, there are $5 \times 6 = 30$ regression slopes. This model fits the data very well. Because event information was available only for $N = 8{,}732$ participants, the sample size is reduced in this analysis. The estimated regression coefficients are presented in Table 13.3. The regression coefficients of the event occurring between the first and second occasion of measurement are presented in the column t_2. The columns t_3 and t_4 contain the coefficients for the other occasions of measurement. The standardized regression parameters of the life events refer to the standardization of the latent variables only, not to the dummy variables that remain unstandardized. Therefore, a standardized regression parameter indicates the expected change in terms of standard deviations of the latent dependent variables for the event occurring. In the model, all dummy variables are allowed to have an influence on all latent variables. For example, the event *death of a close friend/relative* occurring between occasion 1 and occasion 2 has a significant effect on the latent state measured before the event. These coefficients are backward prediction coefficients. There are at least two explanations for such an effect (Luhmann, Lucas, Eid, & Diener, 2013). First, it could be an effect due to the coming event. For example, a relative or good friend might be seriously ill, and it is likely that she or he will die. This situation could influence subjective well-being. Hence, the effect of the later event would be an anticipatory effect. This explanation is reasonable for the event *death*. It might be reasonable for the event *serious illness* if a serious illness is anteceded by a less serious illness affecting well-being. Second, the event might be due to the subjective well-being of the individuals because the events people experience in their lives are not independent from their well-being (Luhmann et al., 2013). That means that negative affect might be a cause of illness. There are several studies showing that negative affect might have a negative effect on health (for an overview, see Lyubomirsky, King, & Diener, 2005). The second explanation might be at least partially reasonable for the event *serious illness* but less reasonable for the event *death*. The effects of an event on subsequent occasions of measurement (forward prediction) represent the long-term influence of an event.

The results reveal several interesting findings (see Table 13.3):

1. The event occurring during the year before the state measurement always has a significant negative effect. This means that the occurrence of the event goes along with higher negative affect.
2. The effects are stronger for illness than for death. Considering the standardized effects, the effect of the event *death* during the year before is

TABLE 13.3 Model 8: Estimated Regression Parameters for the Daily Event Variables in the Extended Latent State Model

	Death						Illness					
	t_2		t_3		t_4		t_2		t_3		t_4	
	Unstand	Stand	Unstand	Stand	Unstand	Stand	Unstand	Stand	Unstand	Stand	Unstand	Stand
S_1	**−0.184**[a]	**−0.088**	−0.049	−0.024	**−0.292**[b]	**−0.140**	**−0.572**[b]	**−0.273**	**−0.325**[b]	**−0.155**	**−0.504**[b]	**−0.241**
S_2	**−0.249**[b]	**−0.118**	−0.134	−0.064	**−0.217**[b]	**−0.103**	**−0.809**[b]	**−0.385**	**−0.391**[b]	**−0.186**	**−0.465**[b]	**−0.221**
S_3	−0.090	−0.042	**−0.253**[b]	**−0.119**	**−0.351**[b]	**−0.165**	**−0.478**[b]	**−0.224**	**−0.784**[b]	**−0.368**	**−0.632**[b]	**−0.297**
S_4	0.014	0.007	−0.093	−0.044	**−0.386**[b]	**−0.185**	**−0.599**[b]	**−0.287**	**−0.529**[b]	**−0.254**	**−0.813**[b]	**−0.390**
I	−0.018	−0.022	**−0.119**[a]	**−0.143**	0.034	0.041	−0.037	−0.045	−0.062	−0.075	−0.017	−0.021

Note: Unstand: unstandardized regression parameter; Stand: standardized regression parameter. Significant estimated parameters are printed in bold (two-sided tests).
[a]$p < 0.05$.
[b]$p < 0.01$.

between -0.12 and -0.19 and comparably small. The event *illness* in the year before the measurement has a stronger effect (-0.37 to -0.39), which is relatively high.

3. For the event *illness*, there are relatively strong long-lasting effects but also backward prediction effects. This is amazing because the occurrence of illnesses on the other occasions of measurement is controlled for.

4. There are only a few unsystematic anticipatory and long-lasting effects of the event *death of a close friend/relative*.

Table 13.4 presents the correlations between the event dummy variables showing that there is comparatively high stability in the event *illness*. Because the events have backward-prediction and long-lasting effects, the stability of affective well-being is partly due to the stability of situations in one's life. Therefore, the partial correlations of the latent state variables (after correcting for the events in Model 8) are smaller than the zero-order correlations (Table 13.5). Given that we have analyzed only two events, it is

TABLE 13.4 Correlations (phi coefficients) and Means of the Event Dummy Variables

	Death (t_2)	Illness (t_2)	Death (t_3)	Illness (t_3)	Death (t_4)	Illness (t_4)
Illness (t_2)	0.029					
Death (t_3)	0.151	0.038				
Illness (t_3)	0.010	0.212	0.030			
Death (t_4)	0.054	0.022	0.135	0.011		
Illness (t_4)	0.029	0.139	0.026	0.213	0.023	
Means	0.111	0.082	0.104	0.085	0.110	0.087

TABLE 13.5 Partial Correlations (lower triangle) and Zero-Order Correlations (upper triangle) of the Latent State Variables

	S_1	S_2	S_3	S_4
S_1		0.635	0.602	0.574
S_2	0.607		0.685	0.631
S_3	0.580	0.662		0.682
S_4	0.553	0.602	0.663	

likely that the stability of subjective well-being might, to a large degree, be due to the stability of situations in one's life.

The advantage of the latent state model is that the influence of events on the latent states can be analyzed and that it can be scrutinized to which degree the stability of happiness is due to the stability of situations. In this model, however, there are no variables representing individual change. The influence of life events on individual change variables can be analyzed in the latent change model. The estimated regression coefficients of the life events in this model are given in Table 13.6. These results show that the life event *death* during the year before the measurement cannot explain individual differences in the change scores. There is only one long-lasting effect of the event occurring before the second occasion of measurement on the change between the second and third occasion of measurement. This effect is positive, meaning that the individuals who have experienced the death of a close friend/relative will have a larger decline of their negative affect. This could be explained by adaptation processes. The second event (illness), however, also has a systematic influence on the change variables for the periods in which the event occurred. Individuals experiencing this event show an increase of their negative affect. Also, the backward predictions are negative, showing that an increase of negative affect is related to the occurrence of the later event. The long-lasting effects are positive, which can also be explained by adaptation processes. These adaption processes might also be the reason for the negative correlations of the residuals of the latent change variables: $Cor(S_4 - S_3, S_3 - S_2) = -0.418$, $Cor(S_4 - S_3, S_2 - S_1) = -0.049$, $Cor(S_3 - S_2, S_2 - S_1) = -0.424$. The residuals of the latent change variables are also negatively correlated with the baseline measurement on the first occasion of measurement: $Cor(S_2 - S_1, S_1) = -0.443$, $Cor(S_3 - S_2, S_1) = -0.027$, $Cor(S_4 - S_3, S_1) = -0.046$.

In the latent change model, the change variables can be correlated with the baseline measurements. Therefore, change is not independent from the baseline. In the latent autoregressive models, the influence of the preceding states is controlled for. The estimated regression coefficients of the events for this model are presented in Table 13.7. The results show that the events occurring during the year before a measurement have—with one exception—a significantly negative influence on the following state. For the event *death*, there is one long-lasting positive and one anticipatory negative effect. The positive effect might indicate an adaptation process. The event *illness* shows a clear pattern: all later events have a significant backward prediction regression coefficient. The significant backward-prediction effects of the events can be explained in the same way as in the latent state model. If, for example, the hypothesis is true, that negative affect is one cause of illnesses, the associations between well-being and illness could be modeled in a crossed-lagged panel study in which the antecedent affective states have an influence on events that have an influence on the subsequent states. In such a model,

TABLE 13.6 Estimated Regression Parameters for the Daily Event Variables in the Extended Latent Change Model

	Death						Illness					
	t_2		t_3		t_4		t_2		t_3		t_4	
	Unstand	Stand	Unstand	Stand	Unstand	Stand	Unstand	Stand	Unstand	Stand	Unstand	Stand
$S_2 - S_1$	−0.065	−0.036	−0.084	−0.046	0.076	0.041	−0.238[a]	−0.129	−0.065	−0.035	0.039	0.021
$S_3 - S_2$	0.158[a]	0.092	−0.119	−0.069	−0.134	−0.078	0.333[b]	0.194	−0.393[b]	−0.229	−0.167[a]	−0.098
$S_4 - S_3$	0.104	0.061	0.161	0.094	−0.036	−0.021	−0.123	−0.072	0.254[b]	0.149	−0.181[a]	−0.106

Note: Unstand: unstandardized regression parameter; Stand: standardized regression parameter. Significant estimated parameters are printed in bold (two-sided tests).
[a] $p < 0.05$.
[b] $p < 0.01$.

TABLE 13.7 Estimated Regression Parameters for the Daily Event Variables in the Extended Latent Autoregressive Model

	Death						Illness					
	t_2		t_3		t_4		t_2		t_3		t_4	
	Unstand	Stand	Unstand	Stand	Unstand	Stand	Unstand	Stand	Unstand	Stand	Unstand	Stand
S_1	**−0.183**[a]	**−0.088**	−0.049	−0.023	**−0.292**[b]	**−0.140**	**−0.570**[b]	**−0.273**	**−0.325**[b]	**−0.155**	**−0.502**[b]	**−0.240**
S_2	−0.137	−0.065	−0.103	−0.049	−0.039	−0.018	**−0.463**[b]	**−0.220**	**−0.195**[b]	**−0.093**	**−0.160**[a]	**−0.076**
S_3	0.086	0.040	**−0.172**[a]	**−0.081**	**−0.160**[a]	**−0.075**	0.087	0.041	**−0.497**[b]	**−0.234**	**−0.257**[b]	**−0.121**
S_4	**0.137**[a]	**0.066**	0.047	0.023	**−0.145**[a]	**−0.070**	−0.129	−0.062	−0.069	−0.033	**−0.366**[b]	**−0.175**

Note: Unstand: unstandardized regression parameter; Stand: standardized regression parameter. Significant estimated parameters are printed in bold (two-sided tests).
[a] $p < 0.05$.
[b] $p < 0.01$.

there would be no backward-prediction regression coefficients but only forward-prediction effects. Such a crossed-lagged study might be less reasonable if the backward-prediction effects are due to anticipatory effects. In general, the pattern is the same as for the latent state model, but the effects are weaker for the second to third occasion of measurement because of the autoregressive effects. Most interestingly, the long-term effects of the events on the states that were found in the latent state model vanish. The events do not have a direct effect going beyond the previously measured affective states.

DISCUSSION

The analysis of change requires different psychometric models that allow us to specify the variability and change process in such a way that specific substantive hypotheses can be tested. Several models have been presented, and some rules for choosing an appropriate model have been described. The chapter focused on latent variable models in which the latent variables are continuous. The basic ideas of these models can be transferred to models with latent categorical variables (latent classes). Eid (2007) as well as Eid and Langeheine (1999, 2007) described latent class models for measuring change and how they can be applied to analyze variability and change in happiness. There are many more methodological approaches for analyzing change that have not been considered (for an overview, see, e.g., Laursen, Little, & Card, 2012; Singer & Willet, 2003). For example, multilevel models are often applied in longitudinal research, and there are also multilevel models with latent variables that allow us to separate measurement error from variability and change (Little, 2013). Multilevel and structural equation models can often be transferred into each other (Mehta & Neale, 2005) and have different advantages and limitations. If there are many occasions of measurement, multilevel models are easier to apply, and the results are less complex to present. On the other hand, the application of multilevel models is more complex if specific assumptions with respect to the error structure and the homogeneity of the change process are violated and have to be considered. Classical structural equation models are more flexible in this regard. For example, if the error variances, the loading structure, and the influence of time-varying covariates change over time, this can easily be modeled with classical structural equation modeling. Moreover, it can easily be tested whether the assumption of time-homogeneity holds, which is not always possible with multilevel models. Therefore, for analyzing data from large panel studies, classical structural equation models might have some advantages if the change process is influenced by historical influences. The models presented in this chapter have been extended to multimethod longitudinal studies in which a construct is measured by multiple methods (e.g., self-ratings, peer ratings, physiological methods). These models are described in detail by Geiser (2009); Geiser, Eid, Nussbeck, Courvoisier, and Cole (2010a, 2010b); and Koch (2013).

Note: This paper uses unit record data from the Household, Income, and Labour Dynamics in Australia (HILDA) Survey. The HILDA Project was initiated and is funded by the Australian Government Department of Social Services (DSS) and is managed by the Melbourne Institute of Applied Economic and Social Research (Melbourne Institute). The findings and views reported in this paper, however, are those of the authors and should not be attributed to either DSS or the Melbourne Institute.

REFERENCES

Byrne, B. M., Shavelson, R. J., & Muthén, B. O. (1989). Testing for equivalence of factor covariance and mean structures: The issue of partial measurement invariance. *Psychological Bulletin, 105*, 456–466.

Cole, D. A., Martin, N. M., & Steiger, J. H. (2005). Empirical and conceptual problems with longitudinal trait-state models: Support for a Trait-State-Occasion model. *Psychological Methods, 10*, 3–20.

Courvoisier, D., Eid, M., & Nussbeck, F. W. (2007). Mixture distribution state-trait models. *Psychological Methods, 12*, 80–104.

Eid, M. (1996). Longitudinal confirmatory factor analysis for polytomous item responses: Model definition and model selection on the basis of stochastic measurement theory. *Methods of Psychological Research—Online, 1*, 65–85.

Eid, M. (2007). Latent class models for analyzing variability and change. In A. Ong, & M. van Dulmen (Eds.), *Handbook of methods in positive psychology* (pp. 591–607). Oxford: Oxford University Press.

Eid, M., Courvoisier, D. S., & Lischetzke, T. (2012). Structural equation modeling of ambulatory assessment data. In M. R. Mehl, & T. S. Connor (Eds.), *Handbook of research methods for studying daily life* (pp. 384–406). New York: Guilford.

Eid, M., & Hoffmann, L. (1998). Measuring variability and change with an item response model for polytomous variables. *Journal of Educational and Behavioral Statistics, 23*, 193–215.

Eid, M., & Langeheine, R. (1999). Measuring consistency and occasion specificity with latent class models: A new model and its application to the measurement of affect. *Psychological Methods, 4*, 100–116.

Eid, M., & Langeheine, R. (2007). Detecting population heterogeneity in stability and change of subjective well-being by mixture distribution models. In A. Ong, & M. van Dulmen (Eds.), *Handbook of methods in positive psychology* (pp. 608–632). Oxford: Oxford University Press.

Eid, M., Schneider, C., & Schwenkmezger, P. (1999). Do you feel better or worse? The validity of perceived deviations of mood states from mood traits. *European Journal of Personality, 13*, 283–306.

Fleurbaey, M., & Blanchet, D. (2013). *Beyond GDP: Measuring welfare and assessing sustainability*. Oxford: Oxford University Press.

Geiser, C. (2009). *Multitrait-multimethod-multioccasion modeling*. München: Martin Meidenbauer.

Geiser, C., Eid, M., Nussbeck, F., Courvoisier, D., & Cole, D. (2010a). Analyzing true change in longitudinal multitrait-multimethod studies: Application of a multimethod change model to depression and anxiety in children. *Developmental Psychology, 46*, 29–45.

Geiser, C., Eid, M., Nussbeck, F., Courvoisier, D., & Cole, D. (2010b). Multitrait-multimethod change modeling. *Advances in Statistical Analysis, 94*, 185–201.

Geiser, C., Keller, B. T., Lockhart, G., Eid, M., Cole, D. A., & Koch, T. (in press). Distinguishing state variability from trait change in longitudinal data: The role of measurement (non)invariance in latent state-trait analyses. *Behavior Research Methods*.

Geiser, C., & Lockhart, G. (2012). A comparison of four approaches to account for method effects in latent state trait analysis. *Psychological Methods, 17*, 255–283.

Greenhoot, A. F. (2012). Retrospective methods in developmental science. In B. Laursen, T. D. Little, & N. A. Card (Eds.), *Handbook of developmental research methods* (pp. 196–210). New York: Guilford.

Jöreskog, K. J. (1979). Statistical estimation of structural models in longitudinal investigations. In J. R. Nesselroade, & P. B. Baltes (Eds.), *Longitudinal research in the study of behaviour and development* (pp. 303–351). New York: Academic Press.

Koch, T. (2013). *Multilevel structural equation modeling of multitrait-multimethod-multioccasion data*. Free University Berlin: Unpublished dissertation.

Laursen, B., Little, T. D., & Card, N. A. (Eds.), (2012). *Handbook of developmental research methods*. New York: Guilford.

Little, T. D. (2013). *Longitudinal structural equation modelling*. New York: Sage.

Lucas, R. E. (2007). Adaptation and the set-point model of subjective well-being: Does happiness change after major life events? *Current Directions in Psychological Science, 16*, 75–79.

Luhmann, M., & Eid, M. (2009). Does it really feel the same? Changes in life satisfaction following repeated life events. *Journal of Personality and Social Psychology, 97*(2), 363–381.

Luhmann, M., & Eid, M. (2012). Studying reaction to repeated life events with discontinuous change models using HLM. In G. D. Grason (Ed.), *Hierarchical linear modeling: Guide and applications* (pp. 273–289). Newbury Park, CA: Sage.

Luhmann, M., Lucas, R. E., Eid, M., & Diener, E. (2013). The prospective effects of life satisfaction on life events. *Social Psychological and Personality Science, 4*, 39–45.

Lyubomirsky, S., King, L., & Diener, E. (2005). The benefits of frequent positive affect: Does happiness lead to success? *Psychological Bulletin, 131*, 803–855.

Mehta, P. D., & Neale, M. C. (2005). People are variables too: Multilevel structural equations modeling. *Psychological Methods, 10*, 259–284.

Meredith, W. (1993). Measurement invariance, factor analysis and factorial invariance. *Psychometrika, 58*, 525–543.

Millsap, R. E. (2011). *Statistical approaches to measurement invariance*. New York: Routledge.

Millsap, R. E., & Yun-Tein, J. (2004). Assessing factorial invariance in ordered-categorical measures. *Multivariate Behavioral Research, 39*, 479–515.

Muthén, B. O. (1984). A general structural equation model with dichotomous, ordered categorical and continuous latent variable indicators. *Psychometrika, 49*, 115–132.

Muthén, L. K., & Muthén, B. O. (1998–2013). *Mplus user's guide* (7th ed.). Los Angeles, CA: Muthén & Muthén.

Nesselroade, J. R. (1991). Interindividual differences in intraindividual changes. In L. M. Collins, & J. L. Horn (Eds.), *Best methods for the analysis of change: Recent advances, unanswered questions, future directions* (pp. 92–105). Washington, DC: American Psychological Association.

Nesselroade, J. R., & Ram, N. (2004). Studying intraindividual variability: What we have learned that will help us understand lives in context. *Research in Human Development, 1*, 9–29.

Rogosa, D. R. (1995). Myths and methods: "Myths about longitudinal research," plus supplemental questions. In J. M. Gottman (Ed.), *The analysis of change* (pp. 3–65). Hillsdale, NJ: Lawrence Erlbaum Associates.

Singer, J. D., & Willet, J. B. (2003). *Applied longitudinal data analysis.* London: Oxford University Press.

Steenkamp, J. B., & Baumgartner, H. (1998). Assessing measurement invariance in cross-national research. *Journal of Consumer Research, 25,* 78−90.

Steyer, R., Eid, M., & Schwenkmezger, P. (1997). Modeling true intraindividual change: True change as a latent variable. *Methods of Psychological Research Online, 2,* 21−33.

Steyer, R., Ferring, D., & Schmitt, M. J. (1992). States and traits in psychological assessment. *European Journal of Psychological Assessment, 8,* 79−98.

Steyer, R., Partchev, I., & Shanahan, M. J. (2000). Modeling true intraindividual change in structural equation models: The case of poverty and children's psychosocial adjustment. In T. D. Little, K. U. Schnabel, & J. Baumert (Eds.), *Modeling longitudinal and multilevel data: Practical issues, applied approaches, and specific examples* (pp. 109−126). Mahwah, NJ: Lawrence Erlbaum.

Steyer, R., Schmitt, M., & Eid, M. (1999). Latent state-trait theory and research in personality and individual differences. *European Journal of Personality, 13,* 389−408.

Stoel, R. D., Galindo-Garre, F., Dolan, C., & Van den Wittenboer, G. (2006). On the likelihood ratio test in structural equation modeling when parameters are subject to boundary constraints. *Psychological Methods, 4,* 439−455.

Van de Schoot, R., Kluytmans, A., Tummers, L., Lugtig, P., Hox, J., & Muthén, B. (2013). Facing off with Scylla and Charybdis: A comparison of scalar, partial, and the novel possibility of approximate measurement invariance. *Frontier in Psychology, 4,* 770.

Chapter 14

Stable Happiness Dies in Middle-Age: A Guide to Future Research

Ed Diener

University of Illinois, Champaign-Urbana, IL, USA; The Gallup Organization

This volume is a must-read for anyone involved in research on well-being. A stunning array of data is presented that demonstrates that subjective well-being can and does change. From nation changes over time to panel studies that follow individuals to experimental interventions, all the data converge on the fact that people are not locked to a concrete set point or baseline level. Furthermore, deviations from the set point need not be temporary, but can last for years or more. Even a set point range is thrown into question by the data presented in this volume. Although people inherit some propensity to certain moods and emotions, the range over which their subjective well-being can vary is quite large. Nonetheless, there are a set of processes that do tend to stabilize subjective well-being and reduce the likelihood that it will permanently take on an extremely positive or negative level.

In terms of data on change, Veenhoven (Chapter 9) shows that nations can change in average levels of well-being, and in the past decades, the majority of societies have been improving. Easterlin and Switek (Chapter 10) review evidence indicating that circumstances and public policies can influence average subjective well-being in societies. For example, they show that the safety net provided by active labor policies (e.g., job training programs) can increase citizens' subjective well-being. Powdthavee and Stutzer (Chapter 11) review evidence showing that unemployment hurts subject well-being beyond the effects of lost income, in that it produces psychic costs due to insecurity. The fact that all these societal factors can move levels of subjective well-being indicates that there is not an absolute set point for subjective well-being. Hill, Mroczek, and Young (Chapter 12) show how affect can change across the adult life span. Ruini and Fava (Chapter 8) show that interventions can raise the subjective well-being from those suffering from low levels of it.

Frank Fujita and I (2005) showed that life satisfaction changed substantially for some individuals over a period of years. Importantly, even the average life satisfaction averaged over 5-year periods changed significantly for some respondents, suggesting that the instability was not simply due to event-related short-term spikes. For two 5-year periods separated by 7 years, life satisfaction correlated .51, indicating substantial instability. Headey, Muffels, and Wagner (Chapter 6) follow our lead in showing that people in the GSOEP can change in life satisfaction over the years. They then extend our work in pinpointing several of the factors that lead to change. Thus, multiple types of data all point to the fact that subjective well-being can change, and is not always firmly rooted at a homeostatic set point.

Armenta, Bao, Lyubomirsky, and Sheldon (Chapter 4) take the important next step of specifying several of the factors that can move people up or down in subjective well-being. Like Cummins, they specify a set point—not an absolute fixed point for each person but a range in which that person can take on various levels. For people to move upward within their set point range, Armenta et al.'s HAP (Happiness Adaptation Prevention) model points toward certain factors that help people resist adaptation to good events—surprise and variety, appreciation, and not allowing one's aspirations to continually rise. They also make the important observation that we do not adapt to every circumstance; occasionally, we become more sensitized to them over time.

DeHaan and Ryan (Chapter 3) add an important new element to subjective well-being research, in suggesting that the fulfillment of psychological needs leads to positive feelings. Therefore, their theory suggests the kinds of events, leading to need fulfillment versus deprivation, that are mostly likely to alter people's levels of subjective well-being. If people change significantly in fulfilling their universal psychological needs, their levels of subjective well-being should follow. Thus, DeHaan and Ryan offer a strong theory on what might produce long-term changes in subjective well-being.

Other valuable contributions to this volume are the chapters on methodology and statistics. Røysamb, Nes, and Vittersø (Chapter 2) thoroughly present what heritability and genetics have to do with happiness and dispel many of the misunderstandings that have arisen. Anyone who plans to discuss genetics in a paper on subjective well-being should read this chapter first. For one thing, the chapter explains why the genetic effects do not mean that subjective well-being is fixed. Eid and Kutscher (Chapter 13) explain the sophisticated statistics of analyzing change over time. Their thorough chapter will help readers decide among various analytic approaches to change data. Yap, Anusic, and Lucas (Chapter 7) describe the methodological and analytic issues in collecting and analyzing panel data. They also review the recent findings from longitudinal studies using sophisticated analytic techniques. In terms of analyses and methods, these chapters, which describe the most advanced approaches to assessing change, are a must-read for researchers. Nobody should do longitudinal studies in this field without reading these two chapters.

The book contains a number of approaches to what may cause change in long-term subjective well-being:

1. Armenta and colleagues' (Chapter 4) description of factors such as novelty and surprise that influence adaptation.
2. Ruini and Fava's (Chapter 8) intervention, which is based in part on cognitive approaches but also on Self-Determination Theory principles.
3. DeHaan and Ryan's (Chapter 3) description of how self-determination explains happiness, and the psychological needs on which it is based. If fulfillment of basic psychological needs changes, then changes in levels of subjective well-being should follow.
4. Easterlin and Switek's (Chapter 10) suggestion that public policies can influence citizens' well-being, as well as the economic and noneconomic factors reviewed by Powdthavee and Stutzer (Chapter 11).
5. Headey and colleagues' (Chapter 6) suggestion that life choices such as exercising and volunteering can increase subjective well-being. Importantly, Headey et al. review evidence that the values parents transmit to their children can influence the offsprings' subjective well-being even in adulthood. Furthermore, the personality of one's marital partner can raise or lower a person's well-being over time.

What these approaches together reveal is that there are many and diverse factors that appear to change the levels of people's subjective well-being. How these various factors relate to one another is a topic for future scholarship.

Another fact that stands out to me in suggesting that subjective well-being can be quite different depending on circumstances is the enormous differences in well-being between nations. Table 14.1 shows life satisfaction, positive affect, and negative affect levels for a number of nations. As can be seen, the differences are extremely large. Because of the very large numbers of respondents in the Gallup World Poll on which Table 14.1 is based, most of the country differences are statistically significant. But most surpass this statistical threshold and represent very large absolute differences in subjective well-being. Life satisfaction scores are based on Cantril's self-anchoring ladder scale. Positive affect in the table is the percent in a nation who report two positive emotions: (a) enjoying most of yesterday and (b) smiling and laughing yesterday. Negative affect is the percent in the nation who report several negative emotions: anger, fear, depression, and sadness. The percentages are the number of people on average who reported each of the emotions in that category.

TABLE 14.1 Subjective Well-Being in Nations

Nations	Life Satisfaction (0–10 Scale)	Positive Feelings (0–100 Scale)	Negative Feelings (0–100 Scale)	Affect Balance (Positive Minus Negative)
Denmark	7.8	83	15	68
Canada	7.5	86	24	62
United States	7.3	83	27	56
Costa Rica	7.2	88	22	62
Mexico	6.9	82	21	61
Brazil	6.7	80	23	57
China	5.0	82	19	63
Iraq	4.9	51	46	5
Syria	4.5	60	41	19
Armenia	4.4	49	33	16
Zimbabwe	4.1	72	19	53
Togo	3.1	54	27	27

The differences we see in Table 14.1 map onto what we know about circumstances in these nations. Toward the top are economically prosperous nations that are high in social capital, have a respect for human rights, and are not mired in conflict. Toward the bottom are poor nations with tumultuous politics, where day-to-day life is insecure. In some nations, almost as many people feel negative emotions as frequently as the number who experience positive emotions, with conflict being a prime suspect of producing the low scores. The distribution of life satisfaction scores for Togo and Denmark overlap almost not at all, indicating that extreme conditions can make most everyone in a society satisfied or dissatisfied. If people were returning to a set point, the societal differences should not be so large. If there is a set point range, it too must be large.

One might argue that the national differences do not contradict set points. However, because the conditions in many of these nations have persisted over decades or more, there has been time for adaptation to baseline, if it were to occur. The other alternative explanation of the huge differences among nations in subjective well-being is in terms of heredity and genetics. This seems implausible for several reasons. First, the differences are sometimes very large, and it seems unlikely that two groups of humans could differ genetically that much. Furthermore, migration patterns suggest that the changes are largely due to differences in the circumstances in nations, not differences in genes. The ancestors of African Americans came largely from West Africa, where the slave trade was intense. Yet African Americans show much higher levels of life satisfaction than do people in nations of West Africa such as Togo. Furthermore, it is unlikely that happier people were those taken as slaves to the new world. Thus, neither genetics nor selective immigration seems able to explain the differences among nations in subjective well-being. One last piece of evidence supporting the explanation that the differences are due to long-term differences in circumstances is that the variations are predictable from measures of circumstances, such as income, longevity, lack of corruption, and level of strife. It seems almost a certainty that the differences are due to the felicitous versus unfortunate circumstances existing in different societies.

One chapter stands out in contrast to the rest. Robert Cummins (Chapter 5) argues for a set point, or at least set point range, for positive affect. Armenta et al. (Chapter 4) propose a related idea—a set point range, but with fairly stable values often occurring over time within that range. I would like to note several things in defense of Cummins. First, most of the chapters in this volume examine life satisfaction, whereas Cummins is focused on a set point for positive affect. Life satisfaction might be more subject to changeable aspiration levels, whereas affect might be more subject to homeostatic forces because people's nervous systems have control mechanisms for the intensity of emotions and moods. The distinction that Kahneman, Krueger, Schkade, Schwarz, and Stone (2004) draw between experienced and judged well-being is important here.

Another fact to be noted in support of Cummins is that there certainly must be some homeostatic mechanisms in the affect system. People rarely stay elated for long after some wonderful event, and in fact, they usually do not stay permanently depressed after some bad event. People's emotions do drop quickly in intensity after the initial response to the event. Furthermore, even in terms of life satisfaction people's aspirations sometimes rise so that new and better circumstances do not lead to a permanent increase in subjective well-being. Thus, Cummins must be correct in pointing to some adaptation and homeostatic processes that influence subjective well-being. What the other chapters show is that these mechanisms are not absolute, and a new average baseline can sometimes be achieved. The data I present in Table 14.1 suggest that homeostasis does not completely bring emotions or life satisfaction back to some predetermined set point. Nonetheless, we need an integrated model that explains when levels of subjective well-being will move to a new level and what the limits to this are due to homeostatic forces.

Figure 14.1 shows the moods of one of our research participants, "Harry," who was undergoing chemotherapy for cancer. Harry completed two moods forms at random times each day for 6 weeks. As can be seen,

Randy Larsen and I (1984) examined the consistency of moods, and found that although it was substantial, it was far from 1.0. Since that time there has been comparison of people's moods at work versus home, in terms of a discussion spillover versus compensation, and so forth. Nonetheless, much more research is needed. Are people happier in the situations that match their personality? Do people make comparisons of situations in their lives to one another?

3. One important methodological advance we need is to use more methods to assess subjective well-being. Although self-reports of well-being might be the best single measure, other types of measures such as reports by informants, biological measures, and experience-sampling measures can be used to complement scores from the self-report surveys. Experience sampling in particular is a method that might be used more frequently in adaptation research, as it is less likely to be affected by memory biases than are global measures, and the method could potentially shed light on the details of how adaptation occurs. To the extent that the different methods yield the same adaptation curves, we gain confidence in our conclusions. To the extent that the methods yield different conclusions about adaptation, an opportunity arises for deeper understanding of the underlying psychological processes.

4. Adaptation is a generic name that points to a variety of different stabilizing processes that are quite distinct from each other. An important development in research on adaptation and change will be to measure the processes over time. One factor that can lead to adaptation is new behaviors. For example, one might adapt to the loss of a spouse by going out with friends more or visiting family more. One might adapt to a spinal cord injury by learning how to operate an electric wheelchair and other behaviors that make life easier. The person is not necessarily habituating to the new circumstances but is changing the quality of those circumstances. Another factor that leads to adaptation is attention, or lack of attention in this case. As pointed out in this volume, novelty draws attention, but over time novelty decreases and so new circumstances become commonplace and are noticed less. A third factor that might lead to adaptation is that one comes to develop a reasonable understanding or explanation of an event or new circumstance (Wilson & Gilbert, 2008), and it thereafter comes to evoke less of an emotional response. Finally, adaptation may come about because one develops a new set of goals and comparison standards. The paraplegic may change goals from becoming a fast runner to becoming a wheelchair athlete. A person who cannot walk might develop the goal of being adept at manipulating her or his wheelchair. These and other explanations have been discussed in the literature, but we need more measures over time of them, and in finer temporal detail. Each explanation might be most relevant to adaptation to circumstances with specific types of characteristics.

5. We need much more research on intervention studies designed at reducing the long-term impact of negative events and increasing the long-term response to positive events. Certainly, these questions have been addressed in past research, but we need studies of more types of interventions, increasingly long timespans covered, and increasingly stronger methodologies. For instance, multimethod measurement of well-being will help eliminate the possibility of response biases in the measures after the interventions, and more control groups with alternate treatments will help better eliminate potential explanations in terms of placebo effects. The chapters in this book focus on the influence on subjective well-being of changes of external events and circumstances. However, we need more intensive studies of a variety of interventions designed to change cognitive factors that could influence well-being, such as presented in Chapter 8 by Ruini and Fava. Meditation, mindfulness, positive thinking, exercise, and other interventions have received some scientific attention, but more and better studies are needed. Just because happiness can change, often in response to lifelong choices people make or to substantial alterations in their circumstances, does not mean that it is easy to purposefully change levels of subjective well-being with interventions. Changing it is challenging.

CONCLUSIONS

The field has come a long way since Brickman et al. (1978) claimed that we are on a hedonic treadmill and adapt to all circumstances. We now know that we do adapt to some circumstances, not to others, and partially adapt to yet others. We know that affective and cognitive measures of well-being may show different patterns of adaptation, and we have clues about what causes adaptation. We know that adaptation is an umbrella name that covers a whole set of somewhat independent psychological processes. The next wave of research will be to use strong methodologies to study how and why people do or do not adapt to events, in which researchers separately track different types of adaptations.

The homeostatic processes that prevent intense emotions from being long term must be identified and tracked. However, what we see as a stable set point might often be due to the fact that many circumstances in people's lives remain fairly stable, as do their relationships and personality, even after some significant event that alters their lives in certain ways. Furthermore, the habitual cognitive habits people have developed over many years of appraising life and situations are ingrained and likely to remain relatively stable. Thus, resistance to changes in subjective well-being must be analyzed in terms of specific factors that inhibit change rather than attributing them to an unseen "set point." By examining stabilizing variables, researchers will be more likely to determine the factors that promote as well as interfere with change. We must parse "adaptation" into the factors influencing subjective well-being that, in fact, remain stable over time and therefore create what appears to be a set point from the psychological processes that tend to bring people back to an original state after a true change occurs. We have come a long way, but there is exciting territory yet to explore.

REFERENCES

Brickman, P., Coates, D., & Janoff-Bulman, R. (1978). Lottery winners and accident victims: Is happiness relative? *Journal of Personality and Social Psychology, 36*, 917–927.

Diener, E., & Larsen, R. J. (1984). Temporal stability and cross-situational consistency of affective, behavioral, and cognitive responses. *Journal of Personality and Social Psychology, 47*, 871–883.

Diener, E., Larsen, R. J., & Emmons, R. A. (1984). Person X situation interactions: Choice of situations and congruence response models. *Journal of Personality and Social Psychology, 47*, 580–592.

Fujita, F., & Diener, E. (2005). Life satisfaction set point: Stability and change. *Journal of Personality and Social Psychology, 88*, 158–164.

Kahneman, D., Krueger, A. B., Schkade, D., Schwarz, N., & Stone, A. A. (2004). A survey method for characterizing daily life experience: The day reconstruction method (DRM). *Science, 306*, 1776–1780.

Luhmann, M. M., Hofmann, W., Eid, M., & Lucas, R. E. (2012). Subjective well-being and adaptation to life events: A meta-analysis. *Journal of Personality and Social Psychology, 102*, 592–615.

Wilson, T. D., & Gilbert, D. T. (2008). Explaining away: A model of affective adaptation. *Perspectives on Psychological Science, 3*, 370–386.

Index

Note: Page numbers followed by "*f*", and "*t*" refers to figures and tables respectively.

CPI Antony Rowe
Eastbourne, UK
November 25, 2014